CHRISTINE MATHIEU

VOYAGES SYNTASTIQUES

a comparative-narrative method
for teaching
French grammar to English speakers

Littlefox Press

VOYAGES SYNTASTIQUES
Christine Mathieu

Littlefox Press
PO Box 816
Kyneton VIC 3444
christine@lechido.com

Copyright©2019 Christine Mathieu
ISBN - 978-0-6480838-5-6
[Second printing]

Cover design Cassis Lumb
Compass image courtesy of Max Pixel
https://www.maxpixel.net/Compass-Vintage-Nautical-Sign-Ship-Old-Sea-1064142
Creative Commons Zero CC0

Note: Names have been changed to preserve the privacy of the persons concerned.

No part of this publication may be re-sold, hired out, reproduced, stored in a retrieval system or transmitted in any form or by any means without the prior written consent of the author.

To my parents

Foreword

'Doing grammar' in the French language classroom often consists of exercises whereby students write out sentences following a model, with minimal explicit explanation. Why indeed waste time on unaccountable complications or unanswerable questions in the vein of: How come a shirt is female and a blouse is male? Isn't it crazy how French people say that the weather does hot? Why are French verbs *so* complicated? Why, in other words, can't French be like English? To which the sensible and patient teacher must reply, year after year, that this is just the way things are: different languages are different.

But what if it is *not* the way things are? What if different languages are not *just* different? And what if the French classroom were about learning about language, learning about French and learning about English *as well as* learning French? What if our students were to learn that English once upon a time not only had gender like French, but three of them? What if students learned that when they say that *they have been learning French for two years*, they are using the present perfect continuous of the verb to learn, one of several present tenses used in English in contrast to the single French present – would they still think that French verbs are *so* complicated? What if students could reflect on the fact that when they conjugate verbs in French, the passage of Time may not feel as it does in English? And what if we could show students how to experience this subtle existential difference? What if students learned that learning another language is not only about saying things differently but also about 'being' in a different way? What if they learned that language is a key to the mysteries of human cognition? And what if they learned what the word cognition means? What if students learned from speaking about French and speaking about English, from speaking French and speaking English, that grammar turns words into thoughts? What if they were to discover that grammar is at once the heartbeat and the soul of a language?

Would it be so bad? Would it be boring?

CONTENTS

BOOK ONE

SPEAKING OF LANGUAGE TEACHING AND LANGUAGE ACQUISITION

1. Introduction   p. 11
2. The Backstory
   The Wonderlands of French Language Instruction
3. A Discussion of the Communicative Method   p. 35
   And Other Ideas about Second-language Teaching
4. Thinking about Language and Second-language Acquisition
   Part One: The Mystery of Language   p. 68
   Part Two: Language, Thought and Why Syntax Rules.   p. 89

BOOK TWO

FRENCH GRAMMAR: HOW TO ORGANISE IT AND HOW TO TEACH IT

5. Mapping the French Language and Essentials of French Grammar
   La grammaire étant l'art de parler et d'écrire
6. Phonology, Pronunciation and Grammatical Acquisition   p. 165
   With a focus on gender and number
7. Teaching techniques: The Comparative-cognitive Approach   p. 206
   With a focus on pronouns
8. Teaching Techniques: The Comparative-Experiential approach   p. 229
9. Verbs and their Conjugations   p. 242
   Conclusion   p. 278

   References   p. 285
   Detailed Table of Contents   p. 293
   Index   p. 304
   Acknowledgements   p. 308
   Previous works by the author   p. 309

BOOK ONE

SPEAKING OF LANGUAGE TEACHING

AND LANGUAGE ACQUISITION

I

Introduction

Only forty years or so ago, Australian high-school students in their final year of French studies read Maupassant and studied Albert Camus's *L'Etranger* in French. These students were also expected to produce short essays in grammatically accurate French, which, for the most part, they could do. Yet most had never had the luxury of spending time in a language exchange program. Moreover, all knew what 'perfect', 'person', and 'object complement' meant, all could identify the infinitive of a verb and enunciate the various rules of agreement. Today, we may ask: how did they do it? But how they did it was simple, they studied French grammar. Furthermore, they not only studied French grammar, they studied English grammar, and many studied Latin. French was also taught like Latin, a dead language, and so we now have an idea that having suffered through the drudgery of interminable rote, these students might have excelled at reading and writing while being perfectly useless at conversation. Well, there may have been little in the way of oral skills and general enthusiasm, but surely the criticism overshoots the mark. These students did reap some rewards for their efforts – they could read French literature in the original. And, surely, they could not speak, not because they had learned grammar, but because they had not learned to speak.

Although the text-based translation method was still widely used in the instruction of French as late as the 1970s, the 'natural' methods of language instruction we now take for granted have relatively deep historical roots. We owe to nineteenth century educators the Direct Method, the Natural Method, the New Method, and the Phonetic Method, which all emphasised oral practice in lieu of the centuries-old grammatical rote of Latin and Greek studies. Since the mid-twentieth century, the psychological sciences (behavioural psychology, cognitive psychology) and linguistics have also had some influence on the teaching of languages in the classroom, inspiring various approaches – such as the Text-Based Method, the Aural-Oral and Audio-Lingual Method, the Code-Cognitive method, and the Communicative approach, which comprises many methods such as, for example, the Functional-Notional Method, the Immersion Method, the Whole Language Approach, the Natural Method, the Acquisition-Learning Theory.

Today, we continue to set our goals on cultural skills and communicative purpose rather than grammatical competence. We take it for granted that learning a language through grammatical rote is not conducive to speaking a language, and we have excellent reasons for being suspicious of grammatically based language instruction – after all, no one learns to speak a maternal language by learning about grammar. In fact, the rejection of grammatically oriented pedagogies has been with us for so long that the idea of *prioritising* grammar in the teaching of French may appear retrograde. And yet, this is what this book is proposing. Grammar is at the core of the comparative-narrative method because, as I will explain in the following chapters, we do not learn a second language as we acquired our mother tongue(s), and because learning grammar with the comparative-narrative method has nothing to do with rote learning and everything to do with experiencing the life pulsing in *la langue vivante*.

Boredom and the art of language learning
How well students can learn a language in the classroom does indeed depend on the number of students in a given class, on students' own commitment to shared learning, and on teachers' enthusiasm and skills. Students' success, however, also depends on the methods used to teach, which is to say on our teaching techniques and on the ideas we hold about what language is and how we can best acquire it. Teaching and learning a language are difficult tasks. Language is vast, subtle and complex, and acquiring a second language takes years. Given this, how should we or could we go about teaching French or any other language in school?

Since the 1980s, we have certainly purged the language classroom of grammatical grind, but we have replaced it with another kind of tedium: we have traded the sequential drudgery of the translation and the Audio-Lingual methods for the chaotic drudgery of the communicative methods – and we have little to show for it. The number of Australian students graduating with a second language has declined steadily and dramatically since the 1960s, from forty per cent of all graduating students to now only thirteen per cent.[1] There are many reasons and issues at stake here, from teacher training to educational planning and classroom size, to name only the usual suspects, and while I am not about to argue that our methods of teaching are actually responsible for this crisis, I have no doubt that they play some part in our shrinking student numbers.

Unlike other subjects, like maths, science or history, language learning, especially in the lower school, offers little in the way of objective knowledge and

---

[1] See *Language in Crisis*, at https://gov.edu.au/files/agreements/go8-languages-in-crisis-discussion-paper.pdf

transferable skills and a great deal in the way of procedure and indeterminate attainment. Many of our students fail to see the value in the current fare; students want to speak French, but the bits of language they acquire in the classroom do not take them there. In fact, the more pieces they learn, the more complicated things seem to get, with the result that in Year 10, students may be no more able to speak French than they were in Year 9, in Year 8, and or in Year 7, although they are likely to be more aware of the fact. Notwithstanding teachers' efforts to liven up classes with cultural activities, only the most dedicated learners are prepared to sit through hours and years of instruction to see such a process to the end. And even so, aside from the extraordinarily gifted and those who have spent time in immersion or in language exchange programs, very few Year 12 students are able to hold a truly natural, unrehearsed conversation or write in French with grammatical accuracy.

All of this has immediate consequences for student retention because students who are bored and feel that they are not learning have no reason to stay in an elective subject. It also has implications for the status of language learning in our schools, and the learning of French in particular, and this too feeds back into the educational loop and retention rates. Language classes, being elective, have relative value in the Australian school programme. They also have relative and inconsistent value for the Australian public at large. On the one hand, there is a general idea that multilingualism is a good thing and that children who are raised bilingual or multilingual have a certain life advantage. There is also genuine admiration for multilingualism of the learned variety because acquiring languages is a difficult and clever thing to do. Not least, there is a near universal agreement that it must be a wonderful thing to be able to speak other languages. But on the other hand, there is the question of how necessary language studies are, given that English has become a global language and that our own national linguistic interests are well served by a large pool of multilingual immigrants and second-generation multilingual speakers. One relatively common view on the matter is that language learning in the classroom should be 'useful', which is to say that learning a language should help students get jobs.

Beyond this, there exists a dual perception of the value of learning French specifically. While students and parents may have a genuine interest in the French language and French-speaking cultures, there is also a view that the French themselves should get better at speaking English as everyone else in the world does, and that the teaching of French in our school is a manifestation of somewhat *passé* notions about cultural refinement. Learning French is at times perceived as something schools do for traditional reasons, a strange indulgence which translates into weekly hours that students would perhaps be better off spending learning 'something'. To this, educators reply that French is an international language (the sixth or tenth or so most spoken language in the world, according to different sources), that France is the third largest economy in the E.U. with important trade relations and other ties to Australia, and that learning a language (any language) is good for developing the essential knowledge and skills needed in a multicultural society and in a global world. To cite from Australian minister Julie Bishop: 'For our nation to continue to prosper we must enhance our links with the world – we do that by improving our cultural understanding, our language skills'.[2]

The method outlined in the pages of this book may ease concerns about the usefulness of learning languages generally and of learning French in particular. I am certainly hoping that it will inspire fellow teachers, and that it may confirm for the colleagues who never gave up on teaching grammar that learning grammar is not only the most effective but also the most rewarding and the most interesting way to learn a language.

English and reflection in the task-based learning classroom

Successive approaches to second-language teaching have been in large part reactive, since every new method will necessarily attempt to remedy the weaknesses of its predecessor. Reaction, naturally enough, tends to become over-reaction. The textual-grammatical method had little to show in the realm of oral skills but it had the merit of building students' analytical skills and of developing their literary and cultural sensitivities. The Audio-Lingual method that supplanted it focussed on listening and speaking skills, and on building language competence and reflexivity though oral and written grammatical drills. The Audio-Lingual method, like its predecessor, was relatively effective and no doubt boring in equal amounts, and it eventually fell out of favour along with other behaviourist educational inclinations. In the late 1980s, language studies switched to the communicative approach, which includes many methods, among them our contemporary task-based and content-based methods.

Like its predecessor, the communicative approach took for its premise that students learn by 'doing the language' rather than by 'knowing about the language', but it had a broader (and I think better) understanding of what linguistic competence might include besides the formulation of accurate grammatical sentences. Trusting that additional languages are acquired through the same natural process as first languages, however, the communicative methods adopted motivation and immersion as core pedagogical concerns, and thus invested in the power of natural communication. Its methods eschewed students' own language and explicit grammatical instruction, and consigned explanation to the list of things to be avoided while teaching languages, along with translation, oral drills, and correction. And in this way, the proverbial baby followed after the bath water... until, inevitably, new ideas began to offer degrees of correction, and 'mother tongue' reclaimed a place in the teaching of additional languages..

---

[2] Ibid.

Today, the use of English has returned to the language classroom. The Victorian Curriculum and Assessment Authority recommends the following:

> Students are encouraged to use French as much as possible for classroom routines, social interactions, structured learning tasks, and language experimentation and practice. English is used for discussion, explanation and reflection, enabling students to develop a language for sharing ideas about language and culture.[3]

On the issue of grammar, however, our educational guidelines remain cautious and we are inclined to speak about 'texts', 'patterns', 'forms', 'culture' rather than grammar and grammatical rules. Furthermore, curriculum materials focus on the itemisation of learning tasks, activities and outcomes rather than on cognitive strategies: 'students create bilingual texts'; 'students access information from different sources', 'students use regular verbs in the *passé composé*', and so forth. Hence, even though English has a legitimate place in the second-language classroom, we are nevertheless working from the premise that our students will learn to speak French by doing French. Therefore, we focus on activities that motivate students and maximise their practice of French, which minimises the use of English, and consequently, reduces the time spent in explanation and reflection.

Evidently, many teachers of French have the knowledge to teach French grammar explicitly in English, and some teachers do just this, according to their own methods and the wisdom they have gained from years of experience. However, for decades, language teachers have been trained in pedagogies that forcefully maintain that learning *about* the language takes away from learning the language itself and that the key to successful acquisition is practice and more practice. Understandingly, teachers may be lacking the confidence as well as the enthusiasm to spend time speaking about French in English, if they believe that their students should be spending the precious time available to them speaking in French. In addition, French teachers are often at a loss as to where to start teaching grammar because they are all too aware that their students lack the most basic knowledge of formal English grammar to be able to learn French grammar explicitly. Language teachers may feel that it is not their place to teach English grammar, nor the aim of the French class. Others feel that they lack the knowledge of English to teach English grammar. And, last but not least, teachers are dependent on textbooks and other resources that are embedded in communicative and immersive principles and thus offer little in the way of explicit grammatical instruction. In sum, the use of English for reflection about language and for teaching grammar is constrained by powerful circumstances.

---

[3] Cited from the Victorian Curriculum and Assessment Authority website: http://victoriancurriculum.vcaa.vic.edu.au/languages/french/introduction/learning-in-french

Grammar is not simply speaking 'form'

Rather than torturing students with endless irregular conjugations and abstract rules devoid of obvious linguistic purpose, communicative pedagogies engage learners in situational learning, which is to say in language activities that have immediate communicative purpose. Students learn the formulaic language needed to communicate when they are 'shopping' or 'speaking about their hobbies' or 'having a party' and so forth. The assumption is that, in due course, they will be able to transfer the patterns they encountered in these communicative contexts to novel semantic contexts requiring similar grammatical constructions. This is a bold assumption. Indeed, how can students who learn with this approach know that, in French, a common syntactic feature underpins 'I have a headache' and 'I am at the train-station'?

There is a missing step in our teaching of grammar, and this step *is* reflection. Whether we expect students to learn grammar through drills or language exposure, we are attempting to teach students 'to do' grammar reflexively, while what they need to do is to learn grammar consciously, by reflecting on what grammar is and what grammar does. And we have not thought of applying reflection to the learning of grammar because, from the translation method to the task-based communicative methods, we have thought of grammar as mere form, as a set of patterns, external features, arbitrary rules, artificial norms and conventions. But grammar is not simply speaking 'form'. Let me show you what I mean.

Let's take two truly, purely and undeniably *grammatical* features: the future and the conditional in English and in French. Let's begin with the future. In English, in the indicative mood, the future is expressed by the auxiliary 'will', which in Old English meant 'to want', 'to wish', 'to desire'. Although syntactic intention (the desire to express something that is to come) obscures this semantic foundation, the latter is still accessible since the word will, whether it is used as a noun or a lexical verb, does express volition in Modern English. In English, therefore, we can marvel at the fact that 'will do' conforms to a natural truth since any future action is necessarily 'intentional'. We *will* do something if conditions remain as they are – or we won't if something gets in the way. And then, we can also marvel at the fact that the future acquires a different quality when it is used in the second and third persons. Stripped to the following minimal forms: 'I will come' expresses an intention or an assurance, 'you will come' may see us commanding or beseeching and 'they will come' may well imply a certainty and a confidence that is not so decisively expressed in 'I will come'.

In modern French, the *futur simple* is formed with the infinitive form of the verb to which is attached the auxiliary *avoir* freed from the stem *av*. The *futur simple* is not a direct descendant of the Latin future tense. Simply speaking, its origins lie in the construction: *infinitive* + *habere*, which meant 'destined to'.[4] Hence, in French, the future finds its genesis in notions of fate rather than in will and intention as it does in English. This dimension of the *futur* is evidently truly opaque, mostly of interest to historical linguists and philologists, and the verbal construction appears to us today as pure formality, and yet there is something of undeniable cultural interest in this grammatical difference between English and French. Funnily enough, there is also something worth noticing about the grammatical formality.

Cross-culturally speaking, the passing of time finds a sympathetic expression in a spatial perspective; we stand in the present, and the future and the past are either before or behind us. In Western thought, when time is linear, the past lies behind and the future lies ahead. And interestingly, past and future conjugations in French reflect this outlook since we form the *passé composé* by placing the auxiliary *before* the verb and we form the *futur simple* by placing the auxiliary endings *after* the verb. Of course, the evolution of the *passé composé* into the aoristic-perfective tense which we use today is too complex to even suggest purpose,[5] and the fact is that in Latin, auxiliaries followed the verb, but the fortuitous position of the auxiliary and endings in the *passé composé* and the *futur simple* provides students with a playful and rather neat mnemonic device.

The conditional mood too lends itself to reflection. In French as in English, so-called conditional tenses actually belong to two moods: the indicative and the conditional. In the indicative, the 'conditional' expresses the future in the past or more precisely, the future envisioned in the past: 'he said that he would come and see me yesterday' (and he did come) or 'he said that he would come and see me tomorrow' (and I expect that I will see him) – *il m'a dit qu'il viendrait me voir plus tard ou qu'il viendrait demain*. The *conditionnel* thus expresses the future in the past somewhat as the *plus-que-parfait* expresses the past before the past, and the *futur antérieur* the future before the future or the past in the future. And in English as in French the 'future in the past' is quite logically formed by joining the future stem to a past ending 'I would do' and *je ferais*.[6]

---

[4] See Jean-Marie Merle, Les origines du conditionnel français et de ses traductions en anglais, *Linguistique contrastive et traduction*, 2–7080-0983-4, Ophrys, 2001; pp. 24-29.

[5] See Denis Apothéloz, 'Sémantique du passé composé en français moderne et exploration des rapports passé composé / passé simple dans un corpus de moyen français', in Cahiers Chrono, *Aoristes et parfaits*, Vol 28, 2016; pp. 199-246.
https://apps.atilf.fr/homepages/apotheloz/wpcontent/uploads/sites/59/2015/06/Cahiers_Chron_28.pdf

[6] Merle (op. cit., pp. 28-29) argues that the equation: conditionnel = futur + imparfait, is invalid because it would signify: conditionnel = [V infinitif + avoir présent] + imparfait. Merle concludes that the correct equations are:
- Futur = V infinitif + avoir présent
- Conditionnel = V infinitif + avoir imparfait

On this basis, Merle refutes the terms 'futur imparfait', 'imparfait futur', 'futur du passé' and 'futur dans le passé'. I do not quite agree with this perspective. The *conditionnel* seems to me more V futur

In the conditional mood, these verbal formations are no less exemplary of grammatical intelligence. In a sentence such as 'I would read if I had a book' – *je lirais si j'avais un livre*, the conditional expresses an unfulfillable opportunity; an impossible outcome founded on an absent condition. Interestingly, English and French grammars express this impossibility by fusing 'the future *and* the past', in other words, by fusing what cannot be fused. The conditional, however, does not only express the corollary of a non-existent hypothesis in the present (*Si j'avais un livre, je lirais*) or in the past (*Si je l'avais vu, je lui aurais parlé*), it is also the mood of speculation mixed with incredulity (*Pourquoi donc ferait-il ça?* 'Why would he do that?'); of intent or supposition modulated by indecision (*Tiens, j'aimerais bien revoir ce film;* 'I would quite like to see this movie again'); of demand tempered with suggestion (*Pourriez-vous m'indiquer où est la banque?* 'Would you show me where I might find the bank?'). Thus, the conditional is the mood of unfulfillable possibility, the mood of open-ended prospect, and the mood of politeness. It is, in other words, the mood of imaginable temporality. Truly, there is food for wonder in grammar.

The comparative-narrative approach is a multi-modal approach

The fact is we have never done a lot of reflection about grammar in second-language teaching even when language education was rooted in grammatical instruction. There is an idea of what it means to teach and learn a language grammatically that has escaped the reforming spirit, and runs through the translation, the drill, the communicative and even the more recent bilingual methods. This idea is that the study of grammar necessarily engages students in boring, mechanical and repetitive learning. The translation and drill methods

---

+ imparfait than V infinitif + avoir imparfait since we say *je serais* and *j'irais* and not *j'étrerais* or *j'allerais*. The equation: future in the past = the thing was destined to happen (= future stem) and had not yet happened and therefore was incomplete (= imperfect ending) is both formally logical and logically consistent. The indicative mood is the mood of actualised and realisable eventualities, and the 'future in the past' fits this modality. By contrast, constructions such as *Si j'avais un livre, je lirais* and *Et bien, tu pourrais le faire* express unrealised and/or unrealisable open-ended possibilities in the present. These conjugations are thus not indicative and it is reasonable to class them in another mood: the conditional mood (*le mode conditionnel*). Nonetheless, I agree with Merle that 'the *imparfait* and the *conditionnel* must share certain fundamental values'. One value shared by the *imparfait* and the *conditionnel* is the incomplete or open-ended aspect of the *imparfait*, as distinct from the habitual and progressive aspects. In French, the *imparfait* helps form the *conditionnel* endings but it also drives the *si* clause, whereas the 'if clause' in English is quite logically expressed in the subjunctive (the mood of supposition): 'If I were more talented, I would be happier'. In French, the open-ended value of the *imparfait* conveys the open-endedness of the imagined condition in the *si* clause (*si j'avais du talent*), while the two parts of the *conditionnel* (the *futur* and the *imparfait*) are vectors for expressing the unlikelihood of what comes next. Thus, the *imparfait* combined with the *futur* expresses an imaginable rather than a predestined eventuality (*je te l'aur**ais** dit*).

were resigned to it, the communicative methods rejected it. The comparative-narrative method also rejects it, because it has a very different idea of what grammar is and what learning grammar is about.

Reflecting, noticing patterns, asking why, making connections, reasoning, intuiting, and putting connections to the test, in short seeking to understand, is the key to learning anything. We can take for granted that understanding French means understanding the things we say in French but for language students understanding French gets a lot more interesting when it involves understanding what French does and what French is, when it involves learning about French and learning about English, when it entails not only discovering the new in what is novel but the new in what we take for granted. Indeed, meaning arises from a language's grammatical depths as well as from its metaphors and kaleidoscopic real-life contexts. Grammar *is* of the essence because grammar not only informs the conventions that turn speech into a language that we may call French or English, it is the very thing that enables our faculties of speech and thought (see Chapter IV). And since understanding begins with reflecting and reflecting goes with comparing and contrasting, there is no better place to start to learn the grammar of French than in the comparative study of English and French grammars. The good news is that grammatical differences between French and English are not only substantial but in such plentiful supply that language learning and language teaching may never be boring again.

At the heart of the comparative-narrative method is the idea that language is more than communication and grammar more than a machine. A language is a grammar; an organised expression of cognition, affect, culture, history, personhood and social membership. In subsequent chapters, I will attempt to show how the comparative-narrative approach 'grows' rather than builds students' knowledge of French by taking a cognitive, constructivist, anthropological, philosophical, philological, multisensory and multidimensional approach to language learning. In fact, the comparative-narrative method is a cross-linguistic rather than a bilingual approach to language learning. I have called this approach comparative because it teaches French by leveraging and translating what students can already do – which is to speak, think, feel and intuit in English. I have also called it comparative because it infuses the language class with all sorts of comparative reflections about English and French. And I have called it narrative because it engages students in stories about language, about French and about English, and not least because it engages students in learning to speak French through stories as well as through conversation.

In part, the teaching of languages requires a multi-modal approach because there is no single way to teach a second language any more than there is a single way to learn a second language. Different learners have different intellectual and psychological dispositions; different interests and linguistic backgrounds. A multi-modal approach increases our chances of reaching out to more students –

although some learners may well fare better in language immersion, left to their own social instincts and unfettered by even the best classroom practices, exigencies and restrictions; although some learners may lack enthusiasm for French because they would ideally prefer to learn another language. The comparative-narrative approach cannot and does not presume to suit all language students. However, it does propose that it is neither unrealistic nor over-ambitious to expect that every student enrolled in a French class, no matter what their ultimate degree of success, their immediate or lasting interest in the language, will have gained *something significant* from having learned French at school.

Anthropology, language teaching and the comparative-narrative method

Voyages Syntastiques is a reflection on language and language acquisition (Book One), and an outline of a comparative grammatical method of instruction (Book Two). *Voyages Syntastiques* is not a language course, for this project is in the making, and it is not, properly speaking, a scholarly thesis, for the comparative-narrative method is not proposing a theory of language teaching so much as a practice. Indeed, in this book, rather than trying to prove an idea, I have attempted to make sense of the real-world effectiveness of the comparative-narrative method in the context of some of the ideas presently informing second-language instruction. I should add that I have discussed only the ideas that I find most challenging and fascinating. I should also inform the reader that my own interests and academic fields are in anthropology, history, and traditional language studies (literature, grammar and translation), and not in applied linguistics or educational theory. I must therefore leave to colleagues in these fields the possibility of discovering whatever else may be of theoretical value in the following chapters, as well as the theoretical constructs I may have left un-named because they lie outside my purpose, outside my academic and professional experience, or outside my personal competences.[7]

In the next chapter, I will provide more information on the development of the comparative-narrative method. For the moment, it is enough to say that the method proposed in this book draws on several streams of experience: my experience as a teacher of English, and languages (French, English, Chinese, and Spanish); my experience of learning these languages and forgetting a few more (Latin, Greek, Russian, American Sign Language); my experience as a

---

[7] In personal communication, Janine Oldfield brought to my attention that the comparative-narrative method uses 'translanguaging techniques'. But the comparative-narrative method is doing translanguaging as Monsieur Jourdain did prose – *sans le savoir*. I discuss aspects of Translanguaging theory in Chapter III (pp. 55-58).

multilingual speaker and occasionally published translator; and not least my academic and professional experience in anthropology. Anthropology has given me the opportunity to learn about languages which I am not able to speak: the Sino-Tibetan languages of the Naxi and Mosuo people whose history and customs were the subject of my doctoral work, as well as Western Australian Aboriginal languages which I have studied in the course of my professional work in Native Title research. Reading about languages is less work than learning to speak languages, but it is almost as interesting because languages are meaningful systems, energised by relational logic, metaphor, collective and individual experience, accident, history and culture. Teaching languages is also more work than learning about languages but it is equally fascinating because speech and the processes by which we acquire it are both observable and deeply mysterious, at once science and alchemy. Anthropology is a comparative discipline. Its practice has taught me ways of perceiving the world and methods of enquiry, ways to observe over time, ways of thinking, questioning, seeing from others' perspectives, making connections and constructing systems of interpretation. It is through the lens of anthropology that I began to pay close attention to what my language students heard and understood, as well as to what they did not hear that I heard, what they did not understand that I understood, and why.

What grew out of this experience is a fascinating approach to language teaching and learning. Just as anthropology is an all-inclusive discipline, engaged in all aspects of culture and society, in ways of seeing and being, in geography and history, the comparative-narrative approach is concerned with *all aspects* of language and *all aspects* of language learning. And just as the goal of anthropology is 'to make the strange familiar and the familiar strange', the comparative-narrative approach encourages inter-linguistic inquiry as well as reciprocal and self-understanding. Learning a new language is a cultural adventure. It is a journey into a world of unknown sounds and unfamiliar meanings where we encounter the world as we already know it and the world we thought we knew, where we discover other sensibilities, other experiences, other persons and other versions of ourselves, and out of which we may one day conjure another 'us'.

II

The Backstory

The Wonderlands of French Language Instruction

In the late 1980s, when the Communicative approach was introduced in the Australian classroom and the Audio-Lingual method went out of the door, I was enrolled at the University of Western Australia, in a post-graduate Diploma of Education, majoring in what was then called Languages Other Than English (LOTE) with a minor in English and Drama. Our lecturers were practitioners of the Audio-Lingual method, and they were more than a little sceptical about the new fashion. Their students, who had successfully slogged through the translation and drill methods, were equally suspicious.

All the same, our principal instructor, Brian Willis, taught us invaluable classroom techniques and dispensed a few pearls of wisdom – don't ask students if they have understood, make sure they have; and don't waste students' time trying to answer their *why questions*: there is no why, French is not English, end of story. I still abide by the first principle, but I now answer the *why* questions, and I encourage them. Yet, on this count too, I owe a debt to Brian Willis, who instilled in us the notion that good teaching means thinking about how students think, and it is never about sticking to a method or a book. A good teacher, Brian Willis told us, can teach out of the phone directory.

Over a decade ago, when I began working as a professional anthropologist, I opened a private practice to provide tuition for secondary and university students and independent learners. The students who came knocking were ambitious highflyers, determined strugglers and others who wished to enhance their learning, to pursue a professional or educational interest or to realise a life-long dream. My students were of all ages and from diverse linguistic and cultural backgrounds – Thai, Chinese, Iranian, Russian, French, Spanish,

Lebanese, Indian, Sri Lankan, native Australians and second-generation Australians of Vietnamese, Greek, Italian, Indian, and other heritage. I soon found myself tutoring a broad range of subjects from academic writing to anthropology, sociology, psychology, English, French, Chinese, and Spanish. Perhaps because I was doing something right or maybe because they were desperate, my French language students grew more numerous, and I became particularly invested in the teaching and the learning of French.

The private tutor has no captive audience, and she has no other purpose than to teach all students according to their individual needs. Individual tuition puts a teacher under equal pressure to find effective means of enriching a learner's experience and to remedy problems, but it also provides a teacher with a uniquely privileged space in which to identify students' needs as well as to exercise the pedagogical and academic freedom to question, adapt, experiment, and try out alternative courses of action. In the teaching of languages especially, individual tuition required me to pay close attention to how each of my students learned. As I tried to respond to their needs, to accelerate or facilitate their learning, I began to notice common misunderstandings and to recognise the systemic dimension of apparently individual problems. I then reviewed my methods and I adjusted my teaching accordingly. Eventually, I found solutions in places I might never have reached for, had I not been able to observe *individual* learning processes over a long period of time.

The method I outline in this book prioritises grammatical instruction and grammatical accuracy over language 'fluency'. It organises knowledge and skills on the basis of a formal and sequential learning of grammar, and it makes communication the end-point, the goal and the reward of language instruction rather than the starting point or the means of instruction. Yet this approach addresses and meets all of the Victorian Curriculum Assessment Authority's guidelines, teaching all listed skills and knowledge, including the fundamental grammar upper-school students are required to learn, if not to master. I now hope to share some of these ideas with fellow teachers who may discover in the following pages new horizons and renewed inspiration, and perhaps a confirmation of their own methods and techniques.

Developing a grammatically-based, comparative pedagogy

All my secondary school and university students struggled with French grammar to some degree. At first, I simply assumed that they had trouble learning because they found French grammar too complicated. It took me some time to realise (because it seemed inconceivable) that they had never actually been taught grammar. What students called grammar and what they understood by 'doing grammar', was little more than the repetitive oral and written practice of model sentences. Students believed they were doing grammar because their exercises were accompanied by words like prepositions, object pronouns or the passive voice. But none could explain what a preposition, an object pronoun or a passive voice was or did – and none could use prepositions or place object complements with entire confidence or accuracy. None of the secondary students who sought my help had ever heard of 'word order' or 'inflection'. Most felt funny speaking about 'accents' because the things seemed so strange and quite useless to them, placed on the planet to make their lives more complicated; and quite a few referred to the feminine and masculine genders as male and female. In other words, my students had no explicit knowledge of grammar or phonology and no understanding of the most fundamental linguistic principles. What they called grammar was not the logical analysis I had learned and practised as a French school student, it was blind rote.

When I set out to fill the gaps in my students' knowledge, to teach about word order and object pronouns, it became obvious that I needed to teach general grammatical principles to contextualise what I was trying to convey. Then, it became obvious that I had to find means of relating students' learning of French grammar to their native English grammar. And then it became obvious that I had to teach students about English grammar. At this point, I began to question a central tenet of my pedagogical approach: that in order to learn a second language, we have to set aside our own language. Rather than forgetting about English, we (because the language class is a joint enterprise) began exploring the fascinating syntactic and stylistic differences between French and English along with the poetics, the metaphors and the respective histories of both languages. I became so interested in the differences between English and French that I joined medieval scholar Robert DiNapoli's Old English seminars in Melbourne.[8] Although the limited time at my disposal guaranteed that my progress in Old English would be dismal, 'reading *Beowulf* and the *Maxims* in the original texts helped me develop a qualitatively different sensibility for the English language and English grammar, and I now teach gender and verbal inflection in French by way of Old English and Latin comparisons.

The bilingual approach I adopted to the teaching of French grammar worked well. Students mastered articles and prepositional and pronominal usage. However, verbs remained problematic, and although there were quantitative differences in the problems individual students experienced, the problems occurred along the same fault-lines. The very gifted students got most conjugations right but they did not get them right all of the time – for no good reason that I could see. Other students simply struggled. Evidently, there were degrees of difficulty in French verbal usage that I had not identified and which my teaching was not addressing. Peeling the layers of assumptions in my approach, I

---

[8] Robert DiNapoli's latest book is *Far Light, A reading of Beowulf*, Cambridge Scholars Publishing, 2016.

became aware of other types of systemic transferences from English into French, which originate less in structural or mechanical differences between the two languages than in the cognitive and affective habits generated by their respective phonologies and productive syntactic rules. At this point, I understood the deep and unconscious reach of native grammar. I became aware of how English speakers experience their natural language, and how French must necessarily pull them into another realm of 'being'. In short, I understood that acquiring another language requires us to bridge *many* differences (more on this in Chapter IV).

Of course, as a language learner, I had long been conscious of the fact that different grammars order distinct logical systems. And as a multilingual speaker and occasionally serious translator, I had long been aware of the subtle and not so subtle experiential shifts we operate in different languages by way of phonology, stylistics, metaphors, clichés, and registers, which at once reflect and express culture. I had read and appreciated Vinay and Darbelney's classic *Stylistique comparée du français et de l'anglais*[9] and more recently Michael Edwards' wonderfully perceptive *Dialogues singuliers sur la langue française*.[10] But it is in exploring the *whys* and the *hows* of comparative grammar along with the *whys* and the *hows* of the stumbling blocks my students experienced that I encountered the *intelligence* of syntax – the fact that language does not only make meaning in what Saussure calls *parole* and what Chomskyan linguistics may relegate to the semantic field, but creates 'meaning' and 'being' in its grammatical depths, indeed, as cognitive linguists argue. I was compelled to develop new teaching techniques, to address content and to re-organise the sequence and the categories of learning.

Teaching French and French grammar with the comparative-narrative approach

Today, I teach French grammar and French language via a sequential approach guided by the internal properties of both English and French, taking into account the phonology, syntax, stylistics, metaphorical and cultural outlooks of both languages. My concerns, however, are not focused only on communication but on cognition as well, and my language classes go far beyond the dialogical tasks that were once the common fare of my classroom teaching. For my students as well as for myself, the French class is a journey of discovery into the nature of language, into the fascinating mental processes involved in language learning, the connections of language to thought and knowledge, the connections of language to emotions and to lived experience: personhood, culture, history and the social world.

---

[9] J.P. Vinay and J. Darbelnet, *Stylistique comparée du français et de l'anglais*, Didier, Paris, 1958
[10] Michael Edwards, *Dialogues singuliers sur la langue française*, Presses universitaires de France, 2016.

The comparative-narrative method does not attempt to teach language through conditioning as the Audio-Lingual and the communicative methods do, although it does not minimise or neglect the power or the value of conditioning in learning and training. The comparative-narrative method, however, is foremost a cognitive and experiential method. To learn French, students need to know what they want to say, what they are saying and how and why what they are saying works. Students need to understand how languages are constructed, and how French and English differ and resemble each other. Finally, they have to inhabit the language. They have to make it real and make it their own.

To enable students to build and retain the range of skills and knowledge they need to acquire, the comparative-cognitive method focuses on the comparative and contrastive study of French and English. It also utilises comparative and experiential techniques to bridge students' linguistic experience from English into French. These techniques include 1) grammatical and linguistic reasoning as opposed to grammatical rote; 2) the comparative study of grammar and stylistics; 3) oral and written translation, both of which enable students to become aware of the differences between French and English and to develop skills in valid transposition; 4) textual analysis which reinforces students' understanding of the grammatical codes; 5) mental imaging and sensory reflection, which enables students to perceive the effects of language on their internal landscapes; 6) bridging grammars, which allows students to internalise syntactic structures as semantic procedures;[11] 7) creative imitation, which teaches learners to hear their interlocutors' language and to respond accurately while by-passing reflexive translation; 8) conscious repetition through creative and reflexive drilling which builds pronunciation, promotes memory and language reflexivity; and 10) active listening, and listening and reading. These cognitive and experiential techniques help students to internalise French syntactic structures in real time in the classroom, as well as to learn how to learn. In addition, in every unit of study, students engage in immersive activities where they converse, read, write and address problems directly in French. However, with the comparative-narrative method, immersion is much more an end goal than a means of instruction. To sum up, with the comparative-narrative method there is little 'passive learning': students learn to listen by speaking as much as they learn to speak by listening. I explain these dynamics and techniques in Book Two.

To illustrate the comparative-narrative approach: teaching the weather

Let's consider teaching language that speaks about the weather: *il fait froid*, *il fait chaud* and so forth. Grammatically, this language introduces the impersonal pronoun *il*. Stylistically, French uses the verb *faire* where English uses 'to be', and *il*

---

[11] Note that aspects of what I call the Bridging Grammar may be considered 'translanguaging'.

y a where English may use adjectival forms: 'it's icy', 'snowy', etc. Hence, speaking about the weather involves several grammatical, syntactic, and stylistic shifts from English to French and extends well beyond the assimilation of vocabulary – so much so that that even in Year 12, students can still say *il est chaud* or *c'est chaud* when asked *Quel temps fait-il?*

When we first inform students that in direct translation *Il fait froid* means it makes cold, we may hear a little scoffing: 'What! It makes cold! That doesn't make sense! You just don't say: It makes cold!'

Now, we can teach that 'it makes cold' or 'it does cold' is just the way the French say it and leave our students to deal with their bamboozlement, but there are good reasons for not doing this. First, when students add 'it makes cold' to all the other weird things the French say, like 'it makes sun,' 'I have heat', 'the male blouse', 'the female shirt', 'the trouser,' 'you me it give', 'you not it him give not' and 'four-twenty-twelve', to say nothing of the profusion of never-ending verbal endings, we are providing them with one more reason for wanting to run out of the madhouse.

Secondly, by allowing students to memorise *il fait froid* by way of the nonsensical 'it makes cold' or 'it does cold', we miss a good opportunity to introduce them to the idiomatic, structural, contextual, and semantic uses of the verb 'to be' in contrast to the verbs *être* and *faire* – because *il fait froid* is only one of several instances in which French uses 'to do' where English uses 'to be', and there is a reason why French does this.[12]

So, instead of providing a simple translation or an approximation, and shutting down rebellion along with potential curiosity by telling students that it's just the way things are, we can go about things in this way...

To begin

Let's think about this: When we say, 'it's cold' or 'it's hot' in English, what might we be referring to? The cup is hot or the weather is hot? Hey, we even say, 'it's hot' when we mean 'it's cool', and what does 'cool' mean, incidentally? Oh, and we say 'it's hot' to mean 'it's spicy'.

Students notice something about English they had not thought of before.

Can you see that in English we actually make sense of 'it's hot' or 'it's cold' because of context? In English, 'it's hot' and 'it's cold' can give us information about

---

[12] For more on this, see: *To be and ne pas être*, in Chapter IX, p. 248.

completely different situations which may only have one point in common: temperature or not even that. French is at times less contextual than English, more declarative. Let me show you something else.

The teacher writes sentence examples in French and their English counter-parts on the board: il fait froid, *it's cold, and so forth. She explains*:

➢ In French, we say: *il fait froid* (it's cold), when we refer to the weather; we say *c'est froid*, when we are pointing to something that is cold ('Wow, that's cold!'). We might say, *il est froid*, when we are actually referring to something that is cold to touch or taste, as for example the coffee you don't want to drink anymore. Now, the French way might sound fussy, but you have to admit that there's a precision to it. In French, you would never mistake your cup of coffee for the weather.

At this point, it is not unusual for students to reach the conclusion that French is not so stupid after all. The teacher continues or a student comes up with something like:

➢ As an English speaker, I can talk to someone on the phone, in my living room with my cup of tea in my hand, and say: 'Oh, it's cold, and unless I add something like *yuk* or *brrrr*, the person at the other end may well wonder what I am actually speaking about.

It is also usual at this point for students to voice a little surprise at how funny English is beginning to look. The teacher resumes:

➢ And now think about this… it is quite difficult to say what the weather actually is. Would we say: What's the weather today? Or are we more likely to say: What's the weather *like*? And we can certainly speak about what *the weather is doing*, as for example when we say: 'it's raining, 'it's snowing'. In fact, in English we can say: 'What's the weather *doing*?' without sounding weird, because when we say 'it's snowing', something is happening, 'something' outside is actually doing something. If we can inquire about what the weather is doing, then why not answer, as French does, that 'it' is doing something. And then again, let's think of that other meaning of *faire*: 'to make'. What is 'to make'? Isn't it to produce something? So, we can see that *il fait chaud* can also be understood as 'something out there' is producing the weather, 'something' is producing heat or cold or wind.

<u>The impersonal *il*</u>
Students have already learned that *il* and *elle* are third-person personal pronouns and that they replace a noun-phrase or a noun which is called the antecedent. The

word for 'weather' in French is *le temps*. It is masculine, and since students know that in French everything is a 'he' or a 'she', they naturally assume that the *il* in *il fait froid* is a 'he' that replaces the word weather. We must explain that *il* is in actual fact an impersonal pronoun. Formally speaking, an impersonal pronoun has no antecedent: the pronoun is empty; it represents nothing. But this formal explanation will probably raise some suspicion since it is counter to what students have learned so far. Therefore, we need to make students aware of the impersonal pronoun in English before they are able to grasp it in French. This is the technique I call the bridging grammar.

Bridging the impersonal 'it' and *il*
The 'it' in 'it's raining' is impersonal, but this is not something our students can understand without explanation. In the English-thinking mind, all that is not human or biologically sexed is an 'it', hence the world at large is an 'it'. Since the weather is a thing and we are speaking about the weather, how can the 'it' in 'it's cold' not be about the weather? And, in fact, when we answer the question 'What's the weather like today?' with 'It's hot', it is not clear that 'it' is not actually replacing the word weather. The impersonal pronoun is more obvious when we think about things in this way: If I say: 'it is on the table' or 'it is blue', do you know what I am saying? No, why not? Because I have not named the thing I am speaking about in the first place; more formally, I have not named the antecedent: the book, the pen. 'Have you seen my book? Oh, it's on the table'. Now you know what 'it' stands for. And notice that if I look out of the window and I say: 'it is raining; it is cold', you will know straightaway what I am saying, and you will know what I am saying precisely because 'it' is not referring to anything. We do not usually say, 'I need to take my umbrella because the weather is raining' but 'I need to take my umbrella because it is raining'. But what is actually raining or freezing or snowing? Notice how we might say: 'It is sunny and warm' and therefore 'the weather is beautiful' or conversely 'it is cold and pouring rain and windy' and therefore 'the weather is awful'.[13] We can say this because it is not the weather that is raining or snowing. *Something* is making snow or rain – as to what that something is, we do not know.

    Now, we also say 'it is raining' for the simple reason that in English, we do not say 'is raining today'. See how funny that sounds? Is raining, is hot, is snowing. The 'it' in these constructions is an impersonal subject. It is also called the dummy subject, which stands for a subject we cannot name. In French, *il* likewise

---

[13] Students may pursue this topic further. There is an interesting discussion on the impersonal it in context of weather expressions with excellent extracts from the works of 15th century English grammarians at:
https://english.stackexchange.com/questions/286789/when-was-it-first-used-in-weather-sentences

represents nothing. It only helps conjugate the verb *faire*. In fact, in casual or playful speech, French people often say *fait froid aujourd'hui*, as it is normal for people to say in Italian – *fa freddo, fa caldo*, and in Spanish – *hace frio, hace calor*.

Once students understand this principle, they are ready to learn to speak about the weather because they now understand what they will be saying semantically, stylistically and grammatically. At this point, the method of teaching is communicative and conventional.

The teacher uses visual aids, showing examples of different weather conditions, sunny days with sun, sky and clouds, rainy days, snowy days. She asks:

➢ So, what's the weather doing here? *Il neige.*[14] What's the weather doing there? It's raining: *Il pleut* [students repeat the French words] – how would you say *il pleut* in English? How do you say 'it is snowing' in French? What does: *Il neige* mean? What is happening here? *Il fait chaud ou il fait froid? Il fait froid, il fait chaud, il fait soleil, il fait du vent...* And so forth

➢ Now, let's ask about the weather in French. Could anyone tell me how we ask about the weather in French? Did you notice how I said this? Do you remember?

Students may be able to produce the sentence Quel temps fait-il? *But they may not, because understanding and imitating language are not the same thing (see Chapter IV).*

➢ *Quel temps fait-il?* The teacher can explain in passing that in this context *quel* actually means 'which' or 'what kind' rather than 'what?' (*qu'est-ce que*). *Regardez, quel temps fait-il aujourd'hui? Il fait beau?*

➢ Teacher and students practise asking: *Quel temps fait-il?* Then, the teacher writes the name of a month on the board and asks students to tell her what the weather is like at this time of the year. At this point, she can also add a location, Melbourne or Paris. *C'est dans l'hémisphère sud? C'est en Australie? C'est au nord de l'Australie? C'est au sud? C'est en janvier: Il pleut? Il neige?*

---

[14] Students will have already learned that the present tense in French may be expressed by the present continuous in English. Nevertheless, it is worth pointing out the progressive aspect in this novel context.

➢ What else can we say when speaking about the weather in English? We can describe weather conditions rather than what the weather is actually doing, as for example, 'it's icy', 'it's cloudy', 'there's a frost', etc. In French, we use *il y a*. The idea, in other words, is to describe what *there is* out there: there's snow, ice, clouds (on the ground or on the road or in the sky) – *il y a de la neige, il y a du verglas, il y a des nuages*. We can also say, *il y a du soleil, il y a du brouillard*.

Grammar points to do with the weather

The expressions above are two instances in which English uses the verb 'to be', and French uses *il fait* and *il y a*, both of which are impersonal constructions. Can students think of other instances when English uses the verb 'to be' and French uses another verb? How about *j'ai froid, j'ai chaud*?

When teaching the weather, visual aids are a must: viewing a landscape with snow falling, students can say: *il neige*, and then looking at a landscape covered with snow, they may say: *il ne neige pas mais il y a de la neige*. In addition, it is helpful to write the ways in which we speak about the weather on the board, using two columns, one for English and one for French.

What's the weather doing?	*Quel temps fait-il?*
It is raining	Il pleut
It is snowing	Il neige
It is freezing	Il gèle
What's the weather like?	*Quel temps fait-il?*
It is hot	Il fait chaud
It is cold	Il fait froid
It is sunny	Il fait soleil/ il y a du soleil
It is windy	Il fait du vent/il y a du vent
It is cloudy	Il y a des nuages
There is snow	Il y a de la neige
There is black ice (on the road)	Il y a du verglas

After this, students are ready to hear or read a story that will include climate and weather conditions within a broader narrative; they may write a translation from English into French and then from French into English; they may also write a little story or a poem and read out their composition to their peers.

And then, for something not entirely different…

Students will have noticed that the word for weather is also the word for time in French. They may already have learned that French uses different words where English uses the word 'time' as for example in: *Quelle heure est-il?* and *une ou deux fois*.

When I ask students to think of why the word for time and the word for weather might be the same, to think of what weather and time might have in common, they usually answer that weather and time are connected on account of the sky and the seasons – the sky brings on the seasons and seasons bring on the weather, the sky also brings in the wind and the clouds. We may just leave it at this but what if we looked up where the word 'weather' comes from in English? We find out that it comes from Old English *weder*, meaning air, sky, wind, storm, tempest. French also has the word *tempête*, which comes from *tempesta* in the Latin vulgate, which meant a strong wind. *Tempesta* is evidently related to the word *tempus* from where *temps* is derived. When we write these words on the board, we can see the common threads between them: wind/weather/time. In fact in most European languages, the more ancient words for weather and time are the same. In modern English, the word time may refer to a period of history, to time passing and also to clock time but how do we measure clock time? By the hour, that's right. And how do we ask for the time in French? *Quelle heure est-il?* In French, clock time is *l'heure*.

We can think of French time like this: *l'heure* is clock time and therefore human time, but human time merges into universal time, *le temps*, as the natural passage of day following night brings about the seasons and with them, the cold, the clouds, rain, snow, and sun – all that in English we call the weather.

In addition, there are other interesting comparisons to be made between English and French. English has two words for sky – sky and heaven. What is the difference between them? Does anyone know where these two words originate? French has only one word for sky *le ciel* but *ciel* has two plurals – *les ciels* and *les cieux*. *Cieux* is a religious reference and *ciels* is a secular reference. We may then discuss the importance that time and sky have held for humanity beginning a very, very, long time ago; how time and weather are still so vitally important to us today; we may discuss climate change, but also the solstice festivals, Stonehenge and the menhirs of Brittany; we should certainly mention that according to legend, the Gauls, like many ancient people, feared that the sky might fall on their heads (and why not bring Asterix into the discussion?).

At the end of this lesson, students know how to speak about the weather in French using *il fait* and *il y a*, and they are able to differentiate between the two expressions; they have internalised the legitimate place of the verb *faire* and of the expression *il y a* in constructions where English uses 'to be'. Students have revisited other places where English uses the verb 'to be' and French uses other verbs like *avoir (j'ai faim)* and *aller (je vais bien)*. They have also acquired some knowledge of ancient mythological sensibilities. In turn, all this will help them to remember the words and the grammar as well as to appreciate and understand what linguistic differences imply for cultural and individual experience. And, of course, the grammar that students have encountered in learning the impersonal *il* will help them make sense of the difference between saying *c'est* and *il est*.

A MAGICAL MYSTERY TOUR OF OUR COMMON AND UNCOMMON HUMANITY

Evidently, I am not suggesting that every French class should be about the origins of English words or turn into an anthropological reflection on the meaning of life: if we were to do this, students may not have much time left to learn French. However, I know that to take the time to reflect on language, on what language does for us that we are not aware of, and on what language may teach us of our own histories and cultures creates an enthusiasm for learning that beats talking about *le shopping*.

With the comparative-narrative approach, we can do something far more interesting than simply teach students to replace the things they say in English with the things they might say in French. At the very least, we can make French appear a little less nonsensical and English a little less transparently sensible and intuitive, which rights the scales and helps learners accept the differences between the two languages. As all language teachers know, accepting differences is a first step in learning a language. But at its best, this comparative-narrative experience can be revelatory because it injects meaning and therefore life into the new words and structures. It unveils mysteries, divergence as well as common cultural grounds. In short, it introduces students to the enigma and the miracle of human language and human memory, how we communicate not only in different languages but in our own language even when we don't entirely understand how the latter works or what it is actually saying.

Students who learn with this approach improve their competence and performance in French, but, just as significantly, they acquire a sense of wonder about the workings of language, communication, knowledge and the mind. They acquire a sense of wonder about their own language as well as about French. This approach is linguistically effective because it helps students internalise the rules; it is intellectually satisfying because it helps students understand what they are doing; and it is ontologically convincing because it allows students to experience the rules. Finally, this approach is highly motivational because it can provide every class with an opportunity to learn and do something new, and to think about things, even very ordinary things, in a very different way. When students encounter the tangible and intangible dimensions of human cognition and communication, they encounter *homo sapiens symbolicus*. They are ready to embark on a magical tour of our common and uncommon humanity, a voyage into Frenchness *and* Englishness. And we will give them new stories they can take home and recount because we are taking them travelling.

III

A Discussion of the Communicative Method

And Other Ideas about Second-language Teaching

Current pedagogies hold dear the idea that second-language learning should emulate a natural process of language acquisition and 'real-life language'. Since we all learn to speak by speaking and by being spoken to, second-language learning should privilege 'natural communication'. Thus, at beginner and intermediate levels, French language instruction is largely based in situational learning where students engage in a range of fun and friendly activities covering topics like the self, family, friends, going shopping, hobbies and so forth. Ideally, students begin by learning simple formulaic language and then progress to more complex and grammatically conscious exchanges. In advanced classes, students engage with a variety of authentic texts and complex spoken and written tasks, as they explore topics ranging from the environment, history, literature, the arts, politics, society, technology and more. With this approach, from beginner to advanced level, students learn grammar 'as needed'. In practical terms, this means that students learn grammar when prompted by the contents of their textbooks and other course materials, and, not least, by the formal requirements of the educational authorities – for our curriculum guidelines prescribe a sequence of learning outcomes appropriate at each year level leading up to Year 12 and the final examination. This program, if students master it, provides secondary school graduates with serious foundations in French. Indeed, the problem for teachers is not the program but with how to teach it effectively, and not least, with how to keep students in it. From the perspective of the comparative-narrative method, the obstacles teachers and students encounter keeping up with curriculum requirements are in large part due to the way we think and go about teaching grammar. This is to say: the ideas and theories that have led us to approach grammatical instruction in second-language learning as a 'subject within a subject'. I discuss these ideas in this chapter.

UNCONSCIOUS LANGUAGE ACQUISITION OR CONSCIOUS LEARNING?

Immersion, language learning and language retention

The communicative approach holds that we can learn languages naturally, by communicating, because we speak in order to communicate. And this, of course, is correct because all humans learn to speak by being spoken to and by hearing people speak. And the communicative approach is correct on another fundamental level – a second language can be acquired without any formal grammatical knowledge or, indeed, any classroom instruction. The communicative approach is also correct that a second language, like a first language, may be at least partially acquired through 'unconscious' processes. The proof lies in the fact that after six months or a year spent in exchange language programs, most language students return to Australia speaking French fluently, even if with varying degrees of grammatical accuracy. Realistically speaking, learners are highly unlikely to develop second-language fluency in the classroom. Language immersion is where we expect students to become fluent and to discover the 'truer' dimension of language. Hearing and speaking French in a country where French is spoken acquires a tangibility that cannot be experienced in the classroom in Australia. In France, in Senegal, in Canada, in Belgium, in Switzerland, and other places where French is a common language, French is used to communicate about the full spectrum of human interest, from the most inconsequential to the most vital. Given this, one could be forgiven for concluding that, where language acquisition is concerned, classroom learning can only teach so much, if anything at all. Still, none of our students goes on language exchange without some prior knowledge of French, and while I am tempted to believe that even the poorest instruction must give at least some comfort to learners in immersion, I am convinced that effective classroom learning can provide an invaluable foundation for successful and *lasting* language acquisition.

As we all know, language learning is a nebulous concept, as nebulous as the idea of speaking a language. What do I mean when I say: I speak English, I speak Chinese, I speak French? What does it mean 'to know' a language? Not all native speakers of English or French are Jane Austen or Marcel Proust. Knowing a language implies degrees of competency and knowledge that may or may not have anything to do with schooling: How well do we understand the subtleties of humour, what do we know of the ambiguities of poorly formed sentences, of the misuse of vocabulary in our first as well as in our other languages? Where does language competency end and cultural competency begin or the other way around? Where do social, political and cultural expectations and educational needs meet?[15] It is certainly true that we do not learn our first language by going

---

[15] See Dell Hymes' linguistic-anthropological approach in answer to Chomsky's linguistics, 'On communicative competence', in J. B. Pride & J. Holmes (Eds.), *Sociolinguistics: Selected readings*,

to school and by learning about subjects and direct objects, but it is equally true that all English and French speaking children must study their own language as a core subject for the duration of their primary and secondary schooling with a view to improving and developing their competence with it and in it, in writing and in speech, and it is true too that we continue to learn our own language well beyond our school years and for the rest of our lives. Steven Pinker argues that language acquisition is an instinct and a property of the brain. For Pinker, a three-year-old child is a natural grammatical genius and the living proof that language is a birthright that grows spontaneously out of communicative need and requires no schooling. Pinker is only partially correct. The three-year-old *is* a grammatical genius but it is also a safe bet that few adults would pride themselves on speaking like they did at age three.

To gain natural fluency in a second language is one thing, to have oratory and literary skills in it is quite another, to appreciate its humour is something else again, and to get its variations of dialects, social registers, transnational and historical expressions something else still. And then there is the problem of retaining and remembering the languages that we have learned. And I will pause here, because the way in which students who have learned French in immersion retain their language offers a window on the long-term effectiveness of natural language acquisition, and on why learning languages in the classroom may be valid and worthwhile so long as we don't expect the classroom to do what is best left to nature.

As I wrote earlier, from the perspective of our students, a great deal of French appears nonsensical. Interestingly, the idiosyncrasies of the French language do not make much more sense to students who have become fluent in it than to the lower-school students who are counting the minutes before they are allowed to drop out of the French program. A few years ago, young persons who had spent several months in France were expressing their frustrations to me about the craziness of the French language. In jovial indignation, they asked: 'But why is the weather a *he*?' As it turned out, they had never heard of the impersonal pronoun *il*.

These young people speak French fluently; they have acquired a natural ease with the language, their speech is idiomatic and it is produced spontaneously. Yet, they do not speak with perfect native grammar, their writing is in part phonetic, and they still find much of French incomprehensible. Tellingly, they don't expect French to make sense because they have internalised, either by learning this objectively or by default, that different languages are necessarily different. There has been no 'why' and no 'because' in their learning experience,

---

Penguin, 1972. And for the theoretical range of what communicative competence can mean in applied linguistics, see Vesna Bagarić and Jelena Mihaljević Djigunović, 'Defining Communicative Competence' in *Metodika*, Vol. 8, br. 1, 2007; pp. 94-103.

and they have no idea that there could be. In large part, they owe their success to their graceful acceptance of the unreasonable demands the French language has placed on their native speaking instincts and their credulity.

A couple of years down the track, these students are dismayed and bothered at the speed at which they are beginning to forget the French they could speak so easily when they were in France. Their disquiet is understandable. Their French is much less easy and much less secure. Frustratingly, they know that they are making mistakes even when they don't know what these mistakes are. I can hear the approximate use of tense, gender, prepositions and articles. It occurs to me that the students are not so much forgetting French as falling back onto English at the weakest points of their French competency. English syntax, the thing they are unconscious of, is filling the cracks in their French syntax, the thing they are equally unconscious of. The students believe that they need more practice to retain their language skills, and they are largely correct. We cannot learn or retain a language without practice, and we will forget (to varying degrees) the languages we have learned if we do not speak them. However, there is more to it.

The students believe that they acquired French in immersion, and that they had learned very little of value before going to France. And whatever part may be fairly attributed to their classroom learning and to their stay in France, it remains a fact of their experience that they have learned French successfully without having acquired formal metalinguistic knowledge. They have learned by listening, observing, imitating and repeating. Naturally, they cannot think of other strategies to hold onto their French than to revisit their learning experience – which is to say, to 'practise more'. Indeed, they have no other strategy. They do not have other means to decelerate the erosion of the language they worked so hard to acquire. They do not have the explicit knowledge of either French or English that would allow them to form correct sentences in French consciously or to check and edit the incursions of English into their French, all of which could rescue them when automatic recall fails them.

Thinking of the Natural Method
The communicative approach comprises several schools of thought that have deep historical roots, and its practices are not monolithic. However, if its methods are varied, they have this in common: they place high value on language exposure and are inclined to value language fluency over grammatical accuracy. In the following pages, I have chosen to focus on Stephen Krashen's Natural Method for two reasons: First, because the Natural Method goes further than most in rejecting explicit grammatical instruction, and, second, because Krashen's ideas have been especially influential. I should stress that teaching with a communicative approach does not imply the total rejection of explicit grammatical instruction. However, it

does mean working from the premise that communication should drive grammatical instruction rather than the other way around. In actual fact, taken on principle, the proposition is not unreasonable. The devil, as always, is in the details, for what do we mean when we speak about communication, language acquisition and grammar?

Krashen distinguishes two pathways to second-language acquisition: a natural innate process, which he calls Acquisition, and an explicit formal process, which he calls Learning. Together, they make up the Acquisition-Learning Theory. Krashen's approach advocates for Acquisition over Learning on the grounds that we acquire additional languages via a universal process of natural sequencing (the Natural Order Hypothesis) *when* and *if* we are able to engage in meaningful language exchanges. In the right circumstances, learners may spend weeks or months listening before they begin to utter single words. Later, they will put a few words together and eventually they will be able to form sentences much like toddlers do when they learn to speak. Krashen believes that the differences in learners' rate of acquisition are in the larger part dependent on motivation and individual psychological dispositions. Low self-esteem, anxiety and stress are the true obstacles to second-language acquisition. These emotions act as a 'screen' that prevents the language input from reaching the part of the brain where Chomsky's Language Acquisition Device (LAD) is purportedly located. Krashen calls this proposition, the Affective Filter Hypothesis.

Krashen's theory resonates with nativist linguistics, which claims that we have an innate, brain-based capacity for language – what Chomsky has called the Universal Grammar (UG). In the simplest terms, we may understand the Universal Grammar as a 'device' for the acquisition and the making of language, hence also Krashen's use of the term Language Acquisition Device. The UG or LAD is transformative. It is capable of 'rewriting the rules' and thus of generating all the grammars produced by all and any human language. Chomsky's theory has certainly generated a lot of ink from both its supporters and its critics, and I will return to it in the next chapter. For the moment, it is enough to keep in mind the few basic principles I have just enunciated because they are relevant to Krashen's approach, and perhaps, more to the point, to how Krashen's approach has been understood and how it has influenced language teaching.

The most crucial aspect of Krashen's theory lies with his Input Hypothesis, and the key here is that we learn to speak by 'going for meaning first', and we acquire structure later.[16] To be acquired, language must be meaningful, and it must be understood. Hence, vocabulary comes first. In the Krashen-inspired classroom, learners learn by listening and by making associations. They are encouraged to make sense of the language they are hearing by way of visual clues and Comprehensible Input. Comprehensible Input holds that students acquire

---

[16] Stephen Krashen, *Principles and Practices in Second-Language Acquisition*, University of California, 1983.

more language as they are exposed to language just beyond their current level of comprehension (1+1 principle). In short, the Natural Method favours immersive techniques and shuns correction along with the learning of explicit grammatical rules, especially if, and when, grammatical instruction is in the learners' own language.

Today, we may question the wisdom of 'target-language-only instruction', but we do not question the wisdom of natural language acquisition. If we learned our first language by listening and speaking with others, why would we learn a second language in any other way? Thus, communicative principles continue to guide second-language instruction. We favour maximising language exposure over providing explanations because we presume that we can learn to speak so long as we want to speak, and not least because we think that a language acquired naturally is more authentic than a language learned grammatically. As Olenkah Bilash (University of Alberta) puts it: 'natural communication helps students acquire language rather than just learn it.'[17]

While I have no doubt that the natural acquisition of a second language may proceed as Krashen claims, I cannot help thinking that proponents of the natural methods are missing the elephant in the room. Indeed, there is a very obvious difference between first and additional language acquisition. While small children can be expected to acquire any language according to the rules and standards of the linguistic environment they happen to live in, we have no such expectations of older second-language learners. As we all know, it is possible to learn to speak a second language fluently and accurately just as it is possible to learn to speak a second language very imperfectly. It is possible to pick up little more than essential survival sentences after months and years of 'language exposure'. And this surely implies that second-language acquisition does not involve the same natural processes as first language acquisition.

Acquiring is also learning

Watching a video of Krashen demonstrating Comprehensible Input in German,[18] I see that he makes his language lesson explicit by drawing images, by using prosodic techniques (accenting certain words) and through repetition. Krashen is a gifted teacher and there is efficacy in his method. But Krashen is indeed teaching and his students are Learning. To begin with, Krashen is not speaking as an average native speaker might when addressing another native speaker. He is speaking carefully and purposefully, conscious of his audience, providing visual

---

[17] Olenkah Bilash, *Best of Bilash*, *'Krashen's 6 hypothesis'* at:
'https://sites.educ.ualberta.ca/staff/olenka.bilash/Best%20of%20Bilash/krashen.html
[18] See Stephen Krashen's demonstration of Comprehensible Input on YouTube:
https://www.youtube.com/watch?v=NiTsduRreug

and aural clues. Krashen's students are not Acquiring language unconsciously; they are Learning by paying attention to what Krashen is saying and doing. They are learning by *noticing* salient words and connecting what they are hearing to the images their teacher is drawing or pointing to on the board. What I understand from this demonstration is that Acquisition means learning by association. Robert Schmidt who argues that awareness plays a decisive role in second-language learning comes to a similar conclusion. Krashen's method requires conscious attention and 'Meaning-focused instruction' is about learning a language by associating words to various clues without metalinguistic awareness.[19]

Evidently, Krashen does not claim that we acquire language by just hearing it, quite the opposite. However, his understanding of what conscious attention means is unnecessarily narrow. There is no doubt that students can get the meaning of a word by associating what they hear with pictures or real objects or by deducing meaning from context – although there is a significant difference between understanding what a word means and actually remembering it. On this count, Laufer and Girsai have found that learners *retain* vocabulary learned through translation better than vocabulary learned through 'meaning-focused instruction'.[20] From the perspective of my own experience as a language teacher and a language student, we learn and retain words when we engage in *a number* of activities – paying attention to what we are doing, translating a word back and forth, writing the word down, then trying to visualise it without translating it, and then using the new word in various sentences both orally and in writing. We learn vocabulary by being hyperconscious and by using new words in grammatical context.

Indeed, I have no disagreement with Krashen regarding the value of engaging students in genuine, meaningful and conscious communication. However, I am also convinced that teaching a language implicitly, which is to say teaching grammar implicitly, is one of the least effective ways of making a second language meaningful for learners. I will explain my reasons for thinking so in the remainder of this chapter.

The Monitoring Hypothesis and the teaching of grammar
Krashen argues that language learners cannot acquire a second language by learning grammatical rules. He acknowledges that there is a limited place for explicit grammatical instruction insofar as learning rules can help learner-speakers

---

[19] R. Schmidt, 'The Role of Consciousness in Second-Language Learning', *Applied Linguistics*, 11 (2) 1990. Also cited in Giulia Borelli, 2018, p. 9
https://www.academia.edu
[20] Cited from Graham Hall and Guy Cook, 'Own language use in language teaching and learning, state of the art', in *Language Teaching*, 45 (3) 2012, pp. 271-308; p. 289.

who have already acquired a language to monitor their output. In other words, Krashen argues that knowing the rules is helpful because it can help learner-speakers to self-correct. Krashen, however, differentiates between anxious Monitor over-users who are overly conscious of the rules, and Monitor under-users who self-correct by feel and make little use of explicit rules, mostly because they do not know them. For Krashen, sound language education aims to produce optimal Monitor users whom he describes as 'the performers who use the Monitor when it is appropriate and when it does not interfere with communication'.[21] Monitoring can be problematic because it is dependent on three conditions: time, form and knowledge of the rules. Learners need to have sufficient time to respond in the new language without feeling pressured. Then, learners need to focus on form, so that they can think about the rule and the correctness of the form at the point of speaking.[22] Monitoring is therefore more useful for writing than speaking, since it is likely to interfere with the flow of communication. Regarding the third condition, however, Krashen believes that knowing the rules of any given language is 'a formidable requirement'. Language is too vast and complex for students to be exposed to anything but a small part of the total grammar of any language. Hence, monitoring necessarily involves simple language rules.[23]

When all is said, Krashen contends that outside of the limited use of monitoring, formal grammatical study is really about language appreciation and not about language acquisition. Grammar *may* contribute positively to language acquisition if it is taught in the target language, and only because students happen to think of grammar as an interesting topic.[24] But then again, Krashen has expressed serious doubts that students can truly enjoy learning grammar.[25] And since Krashen's approach is also very much concerned with *motivation*, it is clear that explicit grammatical instruction presents a conundrum for language teachers convinced of the validity of the Acquisition-Learning Theory, and those convinced of the idea that we necessarily acquire a language by communicating in it rather than with it.

Evidently, language and communication go together. However, there is more to communication than language, and there is more to language than communication. As we all know, we communicate with language and beyond it, through complex neuro-linguistic processes, and an array of social and emotional signals. Yet language is sufficiently resonant in and of itself to allow us to converse and thrive in abstractions. Language is vast and complex, as Krashen sees it – but

---

[21] Krashen, 1983, p. 19.
[22] *Steven Krashen's Theory of Second-Language Acquisition*, p. 3; at http://www.sk.com.br/sk-krash-english.html
[23] Ibid.
[24] Krashen, *Theory of Second Language Acquisition*, pp. 5-6; and Krashen, 'Why not give Immersion a try?', at http://www.sdkrashen.com/content/articles/1995_immersion
_try_fvr.pdf
[25] Ibid.

this is less the result of its syntactic rules, which are relatively few, than that of its creative powers. Language is complex because it is metonymic, polysemic, homonymic, contronymic, metaphoric. It is vast because it is protean – because it materialises in a cultural flux where the phonological and syntactic rules that add up to the commons we may call French or English are distilled, twisted, broken and remade. Language is a plasma of shared expectations. To speak French or English means to be in the know. But if language commands more than syntactic obedience, all *parole* necessarily flows from *langue* as Saussure saw it, and in second-language teaching, there cannot be a lot of sense in 'going for meaning-focused instruction' at the expense of 'form-focused instruction' or the other way around. 'John loves Mary' does not mean that 'Mary loves John' because words and form are more than interdependent, they are synergistic.

Krashen is right that 'going for meaning first' means 'going for vocabulary'. But this is not because vocabulary is inherently more meaningful than grammar, but because the words that carry meaning overtly are more salient than the words that make up grammar (more on this in Chapter IV). Indeed, once second-language students can get their mouths around a few alien phonemes, they can learn to name *concreta* by watching their teachers point to pictures. And my point is this: if 'vocabulary' is what language learners can pretty much learn on their own, should we not entertain the thought that our students need more help learning grammar than they do learning words? Krashen cites a number of studies that show the marginal effect of learning grammatical rules on second-language acquisition. I do not dispute these results, but I should question the way we go about teaching grammar before concluding on the futility of doing so.

Are there multiple paths to learning a second or additional language?

Krashen makes no claim that we learn a second language spontaneously or by mere contact. Rather, he argues that we begin to speak another language when we are able to make *meaningful* connections *in* the new language. I fully agree with this. However, from personal and professional experience, I am quite certain that learners who are past the formative childhood years do not make such connections directly in the language they are learning. In second-language learning, making meaningful connections, which is to say connecting words to their signification, is less an act of cognition than an act of *recognition*. The light-bulb moment when we think 'Oh, it means...' happens when we connect new words to something equivalent in our own language, when we think 'I get it. *Pomme* means apple!' At the same time, as I will explain in some detail in Chapter IV, this act of recognition partly explains what gets in the way of students learning the grammar of the target language, for without further instruction and in the absence of conscious intent, new words can only be absorbed in a learner's existing syntax.

Beyond this, Krashen claims, on the basis of various researches and statistical analysis, that we all learn languages in a particular order, which he calls the Natural Order Hypothesis. We learn this way because we are 'wired' this way, and not because we are taught this way or that. What I have observed teaching and learning languages does not tally with this claim.

When I was a doctoral student, I was employed by my university to tutor two international Ph.D. students to help improve their English competence and assist with academic reading in the biological sciences. Abyasa was Indonesian and Chanchai was Thai. When we began our tutoring sessions, both had been living in Australia for six months, during which time they had learned English in the intensive ESL program, and at the end of which, they could perform survival communicative tasks – greeting people, ordering food, asking for directions, etc. These two remarkable students had very clear priorities. There was an expiry date on their scholarships and they could not 'waste more time learning to speak English'. So we read molecular biology out loud, with me pointing out sentence structure and word order, and we used the dictionary together. The result was that Abyasa and Chanchai learned to read fluently in their discipline through translation, and thus could read and write biology in English before they were able to engage in casual conversation. Evidently, there was nothing natural in this process, if by natural we understand toddler modes of language acquisition.

Looking at my own learning experience, I am fluent in four languages including my native French, and I have studied several others, some of which I have almost completely forgotten. I did not acquire fluency in English, Chinese and Spanish at the same rate, in the same circumstances, or in the same manner.

After learning English at school for five years at the rate of three hours a week, I spent a short time in London before moving to the north of England. I did not speak French to anyone during this entire time, which amounted to a full three months, after which I returned home entirely fluent in English and somewhat hesitant in French. When I first arrived in London, I really could not do much more than engage in the most basic communication. In Yorkshire, however, I encountered a language so different from the Standard English I had been exposed to at school that I could barely make out even familiar words. Indeed, a lasting result of this experience was that I would have no troubles understanding any of the English accents I encountered later in life when I moved to Australia and then to the US.

During these three months of language immersion, I learned to understand by asking people to repeat or write what they said and by comparing what I'd heard with what I had learned at school. After six weeks, I could hear every single English word spoken in any sentence even if I did not understand the words. Within two months, I was expressing myself spontaneously and fluently. When I could not make out the meaning of a word through context, I asked for an explanation in English, and then, I would think of what the word meant *in French*.

After this, I would write down the word in English, making sure to spell it correctly. As soon as I had translated a new word into French and spelt it in English, I knew it and I remembered it. The new word was *definitively* acquired. At this point of fluency, I acquired dozens of words daily and very easily. I also extended my grammar by listening to conversations, imitating and copying, and by benchmarking novel ways of turning a sentence against what I had learned so far. I am still grateful to all the people who were patient enough to correct me, to think of examples and to allow me to rephrase my words. Once I resided permanently in the United Kingdom, and then in Australia, I learned new words just as native speakers do, by learning new things. Like native speakers, I have continued to expand and improve my English, through reading, studying, and writing.

Acquiring Chinese followed a different process. After one year of intensive university level study in second-language classes in Australia, and another year spent at Hangzhou University in content-based learning, I was able to communicate relatively fluidly in a range of situations. When I learned a new word or a new grammatical structure in class, I would hear it everywhere for a week or two until it became part of my acquired language.[26] I also wrote myself a comparative Chinese-English-French grammar to complement our lessons, and I devised additional exercises that enabled me to acquire grammatical patterns without forgetting them. Unlike how I progressed with English, remembering vocabulary proved at least as arduous as learning grammar, for obvious reasons. Commonalities between French, English and Chinese are found in phonology (French and Chinese) and syntax (for example, English and Chinese word order), but not in the vocabulary. Thus, in the first two years, I acquired few words through context and relied almost exclusively on my class readings and the dictionary. Once I was fluent in Chinese, however, I was able to acquire new words easily.

Short of living in Beijing, Mandarin Chinese is not a language in which one is immersed as one might be in French or English. Everywhere in Mainland China people speak local dialects and local languages. Nevertheless, Mandarin is usually spoken on university campuses, by *waidi* (people who have come from other parts of China), on the television, radio, and so forth, and there are plenty of opportunities to hear the language. Since Chinese and my other languages had *very* little in common, acquiring Chinese *may* have resembled aspects of first-language acquisition in a way that learning English did not. In the initial stages, imitation played a larger role in my learning of Chinese than in my learning of

---

[26] For similar experiences see: 'The Role of Consciousness in Second-Language Learning', in which Schmidt systematically documents the part that *noticing* played in his learning of Portuguese. The study was published in Schmidt, R. and S. Frota, 'Developing basic conversational ability in a second language: a case study of an adult learner of Portuguese' in R. Day, *Talking to Learn: Conversation in Second-language Acquisition*, Newbury House, Rowley, 1986.

English. I copied the language spoken to me or that I overheard other people speak. I also have a very clear memory of imitating prosodic patterns to acquire tones. This was a good thing at the time, but it resulted in my acquiring tonal patterns in sentences rather than with individual words, so that with distance from China, my memory of tones eroded. And while I did not forget the syllables making up a word, I forgot the tones that went with the syllables, or at the very least I doubted them. During my second year in China (my third year as a learner of Chinese), I became entirely fluent in Mandarin and I acquired a very large vocabulary. I was then working on my doctoral research in close collaboration with Mosuo poet and academician Lamu Gatusa, and we spoke only in Chinese. With Gatusa's insightful help, I translated into English hundreds of pages of ritual texts, mythology and songs which Gatusa had translated from his native Mosuo into Mandarin poetic form. In addition, I read in Chinese anthropology and history, often with the help of Chinese friends who read out loud with me, very much as I had read biology with Abyasa and Chanchai. Hearing the phrasing helped me hear the grammar and therefore helped me make sense of the words. I made ample use of the dictionary but as time went on, I was able to elucidate the meaning of a new word from explanations given in Chinese. As I did when I learned English, I translated new words in either English or French. Thus, friendship, imitation, translation, and poetry all played a part in my internalising Chinese. Unlike in my experience of learning English, however, the written word, being a character, added both clarity and a level of difficulty. On the other hand, I acquired hearing competency in the local Yunnanese dialect in the same way as I had acquired Yorkshire-accented English and I would Basque-accented Spanish, by translating what I heard into the standard language. Eventually, I was able to hear the regional language in its own right. Still, I always felt much more at ease in Mandarin, and I was never able to speak the local dialect except for a few idioms. Indeed, I never had to, since almost everyone around me understood standard Mandarin even if they did not speak it.

 Where Spanish is concerned, I cannot remember how or when exactly I started to understand. I studied Spanish at school a long time ago and forgot almost everything I had ever learned except for a few conjugations. Since I cannot remember how I came to understand Spanish, I am happy to say that I 'picked it up' around Spanish speaking in-laws and friends while living in California and visiting Mexico (my husband is Mexican). At some point, although I had attended only one semester of evening classes at beginner level, I understood enough Spanish to enrol in a Spanish literature class and the third-year language program at San Francisco Community College. I learned the grammar and the vocabulary needed to sit tests and exams and retained most of it just long enough to sit the tests and the exams. We then lived in Spain for close to a year, which helped me understand Spanish better but still I did not learn to speak it. Since all our Spanish friends spoke either English or French or both, they had little patience with my hesitant Spanish. The result of this combined experience was that I could understand Spanish very well long before I was able to speak it. I finally learned to speak fluently in just a few weeks and at the rate of a few hours a day, when our friend Eduardo came to live with us in San Francisco from Argentina. My tentative Spanish being more functional than Eduardo's not-as-yet-existent English, Spanish became the home language. I improved my grammar by noticing differences and similarities between Spanish, French and English, by imitating and through correction.

From this experience, which is more than likely not universal, it seems to me that I acquired additional languages through a range of formal and informal learning, conscious and parallel processes, through speaking and reading, dedication, motivation, interest, and necessity. There is no denying that the relative difficulty and time involved in these processes had to do with the distance between my native language and my acquired languages. I picked up Spanish, I did not pick up Chinese. There is also no denying the role played by the combined powers of education and immersion in my becoming fluent in English and Chinese. However, in the *process* of learning all three languages, I never entirely set aside my native and other languages, because I always made conscious connections in the new language by reference to my existing languages. I stopped comparing and translating into my other languages only after I was entirely fluent and after I had acquired a substantial vocabulary. What is more, in the three additional languages I have acquired, I was able to learn vocabulary far more easily once I had acquired syntactic fluency, which is to say, once I was able to say anything I wished to say effortlessly.

CAN THE CLASSROOM SIMULATE A NATURAL LANGUAGE ENVIRONMENT?

No doubt there are parallel or unconscious processes at work in the acquisition of additional languages. Many learners confirm experiencing something 'kicking in' at a certain point of their learning experience, when they find themselves producing meaningful language spontaneously. But no one acquires a second language by osmosis, and least of all *in the initial stages* of learning. Learners who have acquired a language in immersion may well be unconscious of how they learned. They may have forgotten what they actually did and simply recall their experience as *I just learned it* or *I just picked it up*, but almost all the second-language speakers I know remember the initial psychological disorientation, the isolation and the frustration, and how hard they listened, before they broke through the fog around them.

Krashen's Comprehensible Input is very possibly the best way to teach a second language to very young learners. It is also an essential tool for teaching English as a Second or Additional Language in initial stages when teachers cannot speak the language(s) of their students. Of course, this does not mean that students should not formalise their knowledge of English or make use of their own languages to process what they are learning *of* English as well as what they are learning *in* English. When teaching English, I have encouraged students whose language I do not know to compare English with their own languages. However, I have also taught English successfully with the Direct Method in quasi-immersive conditions. My collaborator in this experiment was my very first private student Farsheed, who was then fifteen years old, and who had just arrived in Australia from Iran, with a little school English and a genuine desire to learn a lot more. I taught Farsheed six hours a day for two weeks, and then three hours a day for a few months. He then went to language school for a term but continued to take classes with me after school for an hour a day which we spent going over the things he was learning in class and working on the inaccuracies which inevitably slipped into his language from using English as a *lingua franca* in the school environment. The following year, he enrolled in mainstream education and a few years later, he graduated from engineering school.

During the entire time we learned together, we used *Tintin, Destination Moon*, no textbooks and no grammar books. And we squeezed so much out of this *Tintin* that Farsheed used to joke that he would be speaking English like a native before we would finish it. He was quite right, and we never did finish the book. Farsheed learned by speaking, pointing, describing, reading, explaining and questioning. However, we built his grammar sequentially and systematically, from simpler to more complex structures, and by paying *very* close attention to grammatical accuracy. Grammatical consciousness and accuracy were both the goal and the means of instruction. Within three months, Farsheed was hearing and speaking English fluently. After we ended our classes, he continued to learn English, and over the following years, to bridge, and eventually to close unconscious differences between his English and Standard English.

When language is taught intensively through content-based learning and at the rate of several hours a day, several days a week, the classroom can provide something akin to language immersion albeit with some limitations. In immersion, we are individuals among many native speakers who engage with us socially, respond to us directly and provide us with reliable modelling. In the classroom, unless students are sitting in laboratory cubicles, a learner is one among other speakers whose second-language skills exemplify degrees of unreliability. Realistically, the collective language classroom cannot possibly provide students with unlimited access to natural, native conversation.

The second-language classroom has all the disadvantages of the EAL (ESL) classroom and more. At the rate of three fifty-minute periods of study per week, lower-school language students have little time to learn, let alone process new words and new forms in class. Thus, we must ask students to memorise vocabulary and grammar by doing homework, which runs the risk of their learning something incorrectly or, should they not do their homework, of not learning a lot. Above all, classroom instruction cannot provide the linguistic authenticity that learner-speakers encounter in natural language environments. Language teachers may engage their students in exercises inspired by real-life situations but simulation is not real life. The language classroom cannot provide the social and existential imperatives that drive us to learn in language immersion. In a natural language environment, *we have to learn* because we have to engage with real people about real things that really matter. Learning a language at school, especially as an elective subject, only obligates us to sit out each learning period until such time as we may exit the classroom – or such time as we may opt out of the language program.

Somewhat paradoxically, one of the least authentic language exercises, role-play, is also a favourite of the communicative classroom. When students engage in role-play, they know that they are playing, that they are pretending. Role-play is a valid and valuable activity insofar as it allows students to practise and have fun with language, but it does not engage the socio-psychological conditions inherent in natural language acquisition. Furthermore, role-play does little to prepare learners for the disorientation they are bound to experience when they encounter language that does not match the formulaic exchanges they have practised and internalised. Role-play has a legitimate place in the language classroom, but to pretend that one is lost and ask for the post-office is not a true act of communication. On the other hand, to describe what is going on in a picture is, and so is reading a story, and so is answering questions about it, and relating the content of this story to personal experience.

Motivation, authentic language and language resources
Babies do not need to be motivated to learn to speak any more than they need to be motivated to learn to walk. But our school students do. All teachers of French know that motivation is key to student retention, and that student retention is key to maintaining a French program in their schools. Teachers find it hard to juggle the double task of teaching something worthwhile and keeping students motivated, which is to say, motivated to remain in the language class. By default, motivating students turns to 'culture' and perhaps more to the point, to entertainment – outings, food, music and movies. The assumption is that very few students actually enjoy *the learning* of French; and these are the few who may just stay in the language class in the upper-school. It could be objected of course that equally few

students enjoy learning maths but that they have no choice in the matter, and there is certainly some truth in this.

Meanwhile, current pedagogical wisdom holds that language students will be motivated to learn French if we engage them in interesting topics. Hence, lower-school textbooks are replete with items about teenage life, home, food, school, fashion, movies, music, and new technologies, all of it supplied with more than a dash of informal adolescent language, and sprinklings of grammatical teaching delivered in short bursts of colourful fonts and lots of images. And there is a problem with this approach and with our resources. Firstly, of course, we might ask how students can possibly go about making interesting conversation in French when they cannot speak French. A second problem lies with the layout of teaching resources which, in the hope of making language learning palatable, turn out multi-coloured, disjointed and rather distracting presentations. Then, there is the issue that we go over the same topics year after year: hobbies, family, shopping, school life, food, which gives students the impression that they are never learning anything new, an impression that is reinforced when grammar, which involves learning new concepts, is not taught explicitly. And then, there is the problem that fashions, music, clothes and technologies go out of date very quickly, so that what was cool before the textbook was actually printed is fated to look *ringard* only five years down the track. Five years is a long time in an adolescent's life.

Web-based programs and, in general, the Internet play a crucial role in keeping language and culture current and lively. However, screen-based programs are no substitute for curriculum planning or real-life interaction. Students interact with software but software does not speak with students. Just as importantly, Web-based publications aimed at native French speakers cannot provide the basis for instructing learners of French. Authentic native language is by definition accidental. Since there is always another way of saying the same thing and there are always exceptions, authentic language is too random to provide learners with the syntactic and lexical constancy needed to develop a knowledge of, and a feel for, vocabulary and language rules. Evidently, advanced language studies are all about working with authentic materials, but at the beginner and intermediate levels, authentic texts, unless they are very carefully selected and partially edited, are almost guaranteed to expose students to language that is too difficult and too peripheral to our pedagogical objectives. Instruction based in authentic texts will keep the language opaque, and while opacity is a fact of life in language immersion, it is highly demotivating in the language classroom.

Educational resources that attempt to teach languages through situational learning run into the same problem. Situational learning presents students and teachers with serious obstacles because the most banal everyday action is likely to require a range of speech acts which, although logically connected in real life, have little to offer in the way of grammatical connection. Take our first lessons, Introductions – *Je m'appelle Christine, je suis australienne, j'ai douze ans, j'habite à*

Melbourne, j'aime les animaux, il y a quatre personnes dans ma famille, j'ai un chien mais je n'ai pas de chat—a reflexive verb, an adjectival agreement, no capitalisation on the adjective, the use of a global definite article that inflects in the plural form, the verb 'to have' to express age, two negative locutions, and the use of a preposition to signify 'any'...

I am not suggesting that we should avoid teaching idiomatic or authentic French. I am not suggesting that we should refrain from teaching *je m'appelle* to beginning students, but I am making the point that a language pedagogy that adopts authentic language and situational learning at the expense of rational grammatical planning and sequenced instruction is bound to submerge students in ever thickening incomprehension.

Whose French are we teaching?

The Victorian Curriculum and Assessment Authority requires language students to learn standard French. This is a sensible policy. It is true, of course, that standard French is not the only or even the most widely spoken form of the language. French exists in the personal languages of individual speakers, in ethnolects, sociolects, regional dialects and national variations. It is important that students be aware of these differences and know that a standard language is never the sum total of any language. It is important for students to know this, even if we cannot expect them to do much more than be conscious of the fact. Indeed, there are good reasons to teach 'standard French'. Where French is a national or an official language, standard French is the language that is taught at school, the language of examinations, administration and media outlets. In other words, it is the French that most French speakers can understand because most of them have learned it. Not least, standard French is the language of a significant and universally recognised literature, and a language that many treasure.[27] Thus, the

---

[27] In France, the standard language is 'defined' by the Académie française. The very idea that an 'official' body should decide on 'correct language' raises incredulous Anglo-Saxon eyebrows (see Pinker, op. cit., p. 385). In fact, the Académie is an independent body, and it does not decide on the standards of speech used by the *Français moyen ou autre*, which is accomplished through formal education, etiquette, fashion, and other cultural forces. The Académie does not enact laws to force French people to use correct language, contrary to what even serious linguists have construed (see Fromkin-Rodman, *An Introduction to Language*, Holt, Rinehart and Winston, 1974, p. 259). And it does not decide on the standards of language learned at school, which is in the domain of the ministry of education. The Académie makes recommendations on 'good usage', and provides the standard reference along with a dictionary of the standard language, which is not the only dictionary used in France (Robert, Larousse), just as *The Oxford English Dictionary* is not the only dictionary available in England, *The Merriam-Webster Dictionary* in the United States, and *The Macquarie Dictionary* in Australia. Furthermore, the standards of the French language are also checked by the citizenry at large, which might be adept at Franglish, drop half of its negative

standard language is key to communication, culture, and to the other forms of French which learners will come across when they have the opportunity to spend time in a French speaking community.

Learning about language registers is also important. It is legitimate to teach students casual language – *boulot, marre, engueuler* – and vital to inform them of the difference between casual and vulgar registers. Awareness of register is as integral to our students' cultural and social education as it is to their language education. I have met students who had no idea that *un froc* is not just 'a pair of pants' and *dégueulasse* is not just 'dirty' or even 'very disgusting', and indeed, students who had no idea of the shock value of certain words (even if relatively infrequent by contemporary French standards) until their horrified host families set them straight.

This said, much of the casual register can simply be construed as 'authentic' French – a French that is widely spoken, and the French our language exchange students are most likely to be exposed to, and therefore most likely to learn. We should not underestimate the need that students who learned French in immersion may have of learning to speak and write the standard language – or the work involved in this. Spoken casual French not only uses its own vocabulary, it is ruled quite differently from standard French. When speaking casually, French speakers use *c'est* instead of *ce sont* and *on* rather than *nous*; they drop the impersonal pronoun *il (yaka, yapadquoi, faut)* as well as the negative *ne*; they say *en vélo* rather than *à vélo*; use *à* instead of *de* or the other way around in various prepositional phrases; and they frequently defer to contradictory syntactic impulses that manage to combine redundancy, contraction *and* extension in a single sentence –*Et ben, moi, j' l'ai pas eu c' boulot*. The grammar of informal French is based on usage, creative hybridization, fashion, analogy and so forth rather than on academic reasoning. We certainly cannot expect spoken French to morph into standard French by telling students to mind their registers – for even native speakers must learn this standard language at school.

Still, it could be objected that there is a broader and legitimate issue at stake in all of this. Given that most native speakers do not, may not, or even wish to meet and abide by all the academic standards of their own language, what should we expect from learners of French? Should we not simply accept that

---

locutions and double its subjects and direct objects for effect, but is prepared to rise like sans-culottes at the Bastille in the defence of its *accents circonflexes* should the Académie find itself inclined to indulge in a little reformist fancy. The 2016 outrage over the *accents circonflexes* was particularly intriguing given that the Académie had recommended the controversial reform in 1990. The Académie's website is at http://www.academie-francaise.fr. On the circumflexes, see the articles in Le Monde, 'Non, l'accent circonflexe ne va pas disparaître' at http://www.lemonde.fr/les-decodeurs/article/2016/02/04/non-l-accent-circonflexe-ne-va-pas-disparaitre_4859439_4355770.html; and the BBC, 'The Circumflex: A battle over an accent mark' at http://www.bbc.co/culture/story/20160215-the-circumflex-a-battle-over-an-accent-mark.

second-language learners and second-language speakers make mistakes, and let our students get on with communicating the best way they can? This is one of the ideas underpinning the principle of valuing 'fluency over accuracy' in current language pedagogies. I will now examine the thorny issues this proposition raises.

ON VALUING LANGUAGE 'FLUENCY OVER ACCURACY' AND WHY IT IS NOT AN ENTIRELY GOOD IDEA

Acknowledging that psychological well-being plays a central part in language learning, current pedagogies claim that students will be happier and acquire better language skills if they are given the opportunity to learn without feeling stressed. Learners should therefore be encouraged to communicate in French without worrying about making grammatical errors. Yet, in every other subject, in maths, science or sports, we do not assume that making mistakes is fine because it makes students feel good, nor do we assume that making mistakes makes anyone learn better. Rather, we give students the means to learn to do things right, as for example by organising learning tasks in such a manner as to allow gradual mastery. We do this because we assume that practising errors inevitably leads to learning errors. What could be so different about language learning that teachers should be encouraged to value language fluency over language accuracy?

In actual fact, language learning differs from the learning of maths and other subjects in at least one significant aspect. Unlike maths or science, learning a new language is not so much about learning something new as it is about learning to do something that we can already do (speak) in a different and, in the shorter term at least, much less efficient manner. This has some implications for the relative value of 'practising errors' but, as I will now explain, none of them can provide a truly good reason for encouraging students not to worry about grammatical accuracy.

From what I have observed, students who have been taught French in the grammar-less communicative classroom operate on a combination of three modes: toddler speak, formulaic language, and varying degrees of hybridized English. Learning with a natural or communicative approach, beginning students will attempt to 'give it a go' and speak in French as we all learn to speak our first language. For example, they may answer the question: *Tu aimes le poisson?* with: *Pas poisson*. With the same method, a couple of years down the track, in fact, even in Year 12, learners may come up with statements in this vein: *je suis manger oon grosse poisson*. Now, Interlanguage theorists explain that second-language learners construct 'an overlapping grammar' which they revise gradually and improve upon as they move through various stages of learning.[28] According to Guy Cook,

---

[28] Giulia Borelli, op. cit., p. 3

for example, learners have their own language system at each stage of this development that is 'independent of both their L1 and the target language'.[29] While it may be valid to think of utterances like *je suis manger oon grosse poisson* as interlanguage (also called compound language by some linguists) or as translanguaging (drawing from one's linguistic repertoire without concerns for grammatical rules), such productions are evidently not independent from English syntax. Surely, this sentence is nothing less than a case of learners embedding French words into their native English grammar.[30]

In the short-term, embedding French vocabulary into English grammar is not a pressing issue. Since the patterns are produced by the language rules which students already know (English), this sort of practice is less likely to teach students something wrong than to teach them nothing much: students are not actually learning their errors because they are not as yet learning to speak French, they are practising English with French sounding words. However, in the long-term, it can become a problem. All practice eventually makes perfect enough, and if language learners have no opportunity to reflect upon and correct their use of the language, they run the risk of consolidating their own version of French into the hybridized mode of communication which Interlanguage theory calls fossilization.

This said, the idea that language fluency is more valuable than language accuracy is not the preserve of the communicative approaches. Translanguaging theory may also be invoked in support of fluency over accuracy. For unlike Interlanguage theorists, Translanguaging theorists regard language hybridization as an authentic and idealised state of multilingualism.

Translanguaging: hybridization, communication and cognition

Translanguaging theorists, among them, García, Wei, and Lin, take as a premise that 'language purity is a myth'; all languages are hybrids and all languages are

---

[29] Borelli, op. cit., p. 2.

[30] A sentence such as 'I was in Australia since three years', which I recently heard a native French speaker say, may fit the concept of interlanguage better than the example cited in the text. Strictly speaking, the grammar of this sentence is neither English, which would require either the present perfect or the present perfect progressive, nor French, which would require the *présent de l'indicatif*. But this utterance is also not independent from either French or English grammar, nor can we ascertain that it is at a halfway mark between English and French, or that it is a creative synthesis since it is an unconscious one. The speaker has evidently *noticed* that English does not make use of the present tense to express *Je vis en Australie depuis trois ans*, but she has not actually *heard* the English past tense, because this aspect of time that has one foot in the past and the other in the present has no place in her native French grammar. She has neither *learned* nor *acquired* this conjugation, and so she has converted what she has heard (at times the present perfect, at other times the present perfect progressive) into the next best thing that makes sense from the perspective of her own native syntax: the simple past progressive, which is to say, an imperfect English form and a version of her own *imparfait* (the open-ended tense).

idiolects since, beyond class, gender and regional differences, every speaker of any language necessarily speaks a little differently from other speakers of the same language. Translanguaging theory thus promotes bilingualism and multilingualism in the classroom as a 'Thirdspace', a personal language in which bilingual and multilingual speakers think and process 'without regard for socially and politically defined language names and labels' and where they are able to deploy 'the full powers of creativity of their linguistic repertoire'.[31] 'True' multilingual speakers not only speak and think beyond the 'artificial conventions' of standard languages, they think beyond 'mere' language hybridity, and better yet – as Wei puts it, 'multilinguals do not think unilingually in a politically named linguistic entity ... they think beyond language'.[32]

Translanguaging theorists are no doubt correct to argue that no individual speaker ever owns every word, convention and possible permutation of his or her native language. No single individual could possibly own the totality of their language because that would not only mean owning the totality of its structural, lexical, etymological, metaphorical, social and political possibilities, but also the totality of its knowledge, past and present. However, the Translanguaging position overlooks a couple of significant points. Firstly, it dismisses rather off-handedly the fact that a 'politically named' language which may be spoken by a few hundred or millions of people cannot be justly or fairly reduced to a collection of arbitrary and artificial features sustained by mere social convention. This, indeed, is making too little of both language *and* social convention. And secondly, it makes light of the fact that, in any language community, speakers own far more than a share of the collective linguistic space because they also own the *possibility* of accessing any part of this space. Unlike second-language speakers, native speakers need only degrees of exposure and degrees of education to access the regional dialects, class registers, professional, literary and academic manifestations of their own languages. A living language, in each and all of its variegated forms, is at once a collective granary and the key that opens its coffers.

In fact, for García and Wei, Translanguaging is more than a pedagogy, it is a political and, not least, an ideological project. And like all ideological projects, Translanguaging promotes its own essentialised constructs. Wei lauds Translanguaging as a place of 'extraordinary openness' where speakers have the possibility of 'accessing multiple resources' and 'multiple perspectives', where they do 'languaging' rather than speak differentiated languages, and where the 'dominant ideologies of monoglot standards'[33] and the 'artificial boundaries of politically named languages' are broken down. Translanguaging 'decolonizes' the

---

[31] Li Wei, 'Translanguaging as a Practical Theory of Language', *Applied Linguistics*, Vol. 39, 1, 2018; pp. 9–30. https://doi.org/10.1093/applin/amx039
[32] Ibid.
[33] Ophelia García and Li Wei, *Translanguaging, Language, Bilingualism and Education*, Palgrave Macmillan, Basingstokem, 2014; p. 105.

'cultural dominance' of monolinguistic mode.[34] Clearly, beyond passion and enthusiasm, Translanguaging theorists have their own idea of what 'true' if not 'good' multilingualism is about.[35] But are they turning the tables on conventional ideas about monolingualism, multilingualism, language hybridization and language proficiency or are they throwing their own undesirables on the scrapheap of inclusive politics?

Monolingualism may well be a 'dominant ideological construct' but it is also a pragmatic comparative reference that is as fluid and slippery as anything else to do with language. We describe people as monolingual because we differentiate them from the people we call multilingual, and whom we can define in a general manner as relatively proficient speakers of two or more mutually unintelligible languages. Most people, however, are 'multilingual' insofar as they are able to understand shifts in language registers as well as the various dialects of their national and community languages. From an anthropological perspective, monolingualism and multilingualism are not necessarily mutually exclusive. People can be monolingual by virtue of speaking the sole language of their community and at the same time be multilingual on account of the overlaps between theirs and the languages of their neighbours. All over the world, there are languages that are sufficiently differentiated to confirm socio-political boundaries and in-group identities and yet possess sufficient overlap for neighbours to be able to converse with one another, each speaking in their own language.

The politics of language inclusivity are as complex as the political and social relations that produce and reproduce them, and they have only so much to do with how many languages or versions of a language are spoken in a community. All human relations are political relations, and in-group/out-group linguistic regimes are found *across* and *within* societies: standard national languages coexist with other national languages, with community languages, regional languages, official languages, secret languages, gendered languages, urban languages, the languages of thieves, trades, professions, law, commercial and political propaganda, ideologies, religions and academia, not to forget the registers of caste and social class. Indeed, multilingualism is the destiny of the migrants and the exiles but it has long been *de rigueur* among the aristocratic classes, and it is a prestige marker of the cosmopolitan elites for whom 'translanguaging' offers privileged means of citing from this language and that other, and of showing off experiences of travel and fabulous friends around the world. Until relatively recently, rather than being the preferred marker of a 'monolithic dominant cultural ideology', monolingualism was the lot of the educationally marginalised, a default condition that denied the lower classes not only the opportunity to learn

---

[34] Wei, op. cit.
[35] For a critique of the ideological and political positioning of Translanguaging, see Jürgen Jaspers, 'The transformative limits of Translanguaging', *Language & Communication* 58 (2018); pp. 1–10.

additional languages but their fair share of the standard 'politically named' language.

But do Translanguaging theorists really mean to take down the edifice of 'monolingualism' in all of its manifold variations? It seems not entirely: García, Wei and Lin acknowledge that bilingual students not only need to translanguage but to engage in the standard language of academic learning and examinations: 'students need practice and engagement in translanguaging, as much as they need practice of standard features used for academic purposes';[36] and 'bilingual education must develop bilingual students' ability to use language according to the rules and regulations that have been socially constructed for that particular language'.[37] Jürgen Jaspers notes the contradictions in these writers' position which he sees as 'diametrically opposed to their political agenda (interrupting monolingualism)' and concludes that Translanguaging theorists 'risk suggesting that while translanguaging practices are valuable and pupil-friendly, they are in the end less important than pupils' ability in socially valued or academic registers.'[38] Jaspers also notes the ethical paradox: how do we value linguistic diversity and yet enable students to partake in the linguistic commons required in academic learning and other spheres of life? Jaspers answers the question he raises in a sensible academic manner, which, for consistency of style, I may boil down thus: life is full of contradictions that we resolve by finding the best compromise under the circumstances.

Translanguaging theory is primarily concerned with bilingual education, but it does have some implications for second-language learning. Where second-language education is concerned, Wei says this: 'The actual purpose of learning new languages—to become bilingual and multilingual, rather than to replace the learner's L1 to become another monolingual—often gets forgotten or neglected, and the bilingual, rather than monolingual, speaker is rarely used as the model for teaching and learning.'[39] What Wei means by 'replacing' a learner's first language or 'becoming another monolingual' is not entirely clear. Evidently, no additional language class on offer in Australia intends to replace learners' own languages. However, it is true that the goal of our language classes is to teach students to speak *differentiated* languages, and that we often teach a second language by treating learners' own language as a hindrance rather than an asset in this process.

In actual fact, the comparative-narrative method and Translanguaging theory share an understanding about cognition and language: students can best process and learn in the languages and linguistic forms they can best think in and with. However, there is a significant difference between what 'using own language'

---

[36] García and Li Wei, op. cit., p. 71–72; cited in Jaspers, op. cit., p. 7.
[37] García O. and A Lin 'Translanguaging and bilingual education' in García, O., Lin, A., May, S. (Eds.), *Bilingual and Multilingual Education*, Springer, Dordrecht, 2016, also cited in Jaspers (2018).
[38] Jaspers, op. cit.
[39] Wei, op. cit.

might imply in bilingual education and in the second-language classroom. In bilingual education, learning-content (mathematics, biology, history) may be taught in one language (say English), while the language in which students may do their best processing is another (their own language), hence it may be crucial for students to process new information and concepts in their own language(s) as well as to learn to process and think in their additional language. Likewise, in the second-language classroom, students can best process in their own language (i.e. English), but the learning-content is no less than the target language (i.e. French). In the bilingual classroom, valuing language fluency over language accuracy can free students to process information the best way they can, whereas in the second-language classroom, valuing language fluency over language accuracy in the target language might amount to simply avoiding learning the target language.

The comparative-narrative method does 'translanguaging' insofar as it uses first language and code-switching (mixing languages) to enable students to process the rules of French. However, with the comparative-narrative method, students do not mix their languages without regard for the rules of 'named languages', conventions and norms, but (preferably) in full awareness of the rules. Code-switching is not 'free languaging': it is a technique for *bridging* students' English into a new and differentiated language named French.

To correct errors or not, and how?

In a real-life situation, as Krashen argues, it is often necessary to let go of overly self-conscious language. Grammatical accuracy in a second language is never as important as keeping one's interlocutor awake and *in situ*. We also need to transcend grammatical self-consciousness, because we can become so afraid of making mistakes that we will be too afraid to speak and thus learn nothing. Furthermore, some inaccuracies are truly inconsequential while others are highly entertaining. In my own language-learning career, I have brought a few smiles to people's faces and, at times, provoked outright hysterics. I did not usually find it quite as funny as the native speakers did, but none spelt 'the end of the beans', as a French friend once said to the delight of our university classmates, who wasted no time turning this homely French cliché into a meme. Evidently, grammatical accuracy is not so important that we cannot trust our shared communicative instincts to make up for the gaps in our language skills. However, all of this is a matter of degree, because unintelligible pronunciation, inappropriate vocabulary, erroneous inflection, the absence of functional words and garbled word order will not achieve a lot more for real-life communication than the interminable silences of the over-anxious speaker searching for the right word and the right turn of every phrase. Grammatical mistakes and misplaced metaphors might turn out to be the life of the party, but incomprehensible language is sure to kill the conversation. For our own sake, as well as that of the people with whom we interact, giving it our best shot may begin with maintaining a positive attitude, but this is not where it needs to end.

In the classroom, common sense should prevail. We need to consider the context: students' personalities, their abilities, their levels of enthusiasm and not least the point of the exercise. If students are attempting to master the position of the object pronouns, it is a good idea to let them concentrate on this and not to worry about an erroneous gender agreement. In addition, learners need to be given time to speak the best way they can, unhindered by corrections, because this provides an opportunity for teachers to take note of what their students have and have not learned. Finally, communicative skills are important, and it is part of language learning to learn not to become flustered and over-anxious about making errors, as well as to guess and deduce meaning from the context when we do not quite understand what is being said. Therefore, in an oral examination, we should not expect students to speak perfectly grammatical or perfectly idiomatic French, and we should appreciate and acknowledge learners' communicative skills, their ability to repair, to try and get a meaning across the best possible way – as recommended by our current curriculum guidelines. Of course, we can and should also appreciate students' ability to produce clear and accurate language, and idiomatic language.

This said, if we learn best what we practise most, speaking without awareness of grammatical rules cannot be a goal or a means of second-language learning, because language hybridity is not what students are hoping to achieve, even if it is the best they can achieve in some circumstances. Evidently, we should not make students' lives miserable. Some students are afraid of making mistakes, and we should do our best to alleviate their anxiety, but there is no reason to do this at the cost of their learning. There are many ways to correct errors, such as providing clearer models, explaining things and simplifying the task at hand. We should also be aware that anxiety in second-language learning more often than not stems from a deeper place than the fear of making errors. We take our faculty of speech for granted, just as we take breathing for granted, until we run out of air and begin to panic. Finding ourselves incapable of speech or not understanding what is being said to us can be profoundly unsettling. The best antidote to momentary panic lies in explaining these psychological vulnerabilities to students, and in reminding them that they are *learning*, that incomprehension, unlike the lack of air, is not life-threatening. It is also worth informing students that learning a language takes time and that it is not easy.

We should, of course, dispel unrealistic expectations. Recently, a student who had been learning French for two semesters complained to me that his teacher had taught him nothing because if he went to France tomorrow, he would not be able to say anything of interest. Finally, we should remember that anxiety and demotivation do not always spring from the desire to over-achieve or the fear of failure, and that boredom is more often than not the result of disengagement than the result of hard work. Students will be reluctant to listen, let alone speak, and they will be bored if we convince them that they can't understand and can't do by correcting them without explanations; if we let them say whatever they can when they are aware that they don't know what they are doing, or if we do not give them any means of gauging their own progress and of having some control over their learning. In the classroom, students must be given every opportunity to learn, and therefore they must have every opportunity to learn and to practise grammatically accurate French.

To conclude, I am not suggesting that we should expect nothing but grammatical perfection from our students. What I *am* arguing is that we need to differentiate between real-life conversation, examination performance, and classroom learning. Given the vastness and the complexity of language, it is inevitable that language learners will make mistakes and that they will often find themselves at a loss for what to say next, but learning a language is precisely about learning to figure out what to say next and how to go about doing this most effectively, and students cannot learn to do this in French when they are placed in a position of *practising* errors, which is to say, when they are placed in a position of practising their English grammar.

On the difficulties of correcting grammatically inaccurate language
Not all advocates of the communicative and natural methods believe that second-language learners should not be corrected. Claude Germain, like Krashen, believes that the desire to communicate is key to learning a language and that the acquisition of language is of a neurological rather than a pedagogical order. According to Germain, the implicit or the 'natural' grammar of a language is a matter of statistical regularity and frequency rather than rules, and therefore effective language learning needs to focus on authentic communication, oral language and *'utilisation et re-utilisation'*, which is to say practice or repetition. In Germain's perspective, explicit grammatical instruction is counter-productive because it tries to achieve the impossible: there can be no crossover between the conscious and the unconscious, and therefore the implicit grammar of natural speech cannot possibly turn into the explicit grammar of the educated, school produced language or the other way around. Nevertheless, Germain argues that learners' errors must be corrected by way of reasonable pedagogical practice so as to ensure language precision and accuracy. '*Sans la correction des erreurs, il y a grand*

risque de fossilisation de celles-ci.' In Germain's scheme, correction should replace the conscious and explicit learning of grammar.[40]

    Although I agree with Germain that a language that goes uncorrected is at risk of fossilisation, I also think that his theoretical position is paradoxical. Correcting students' errors means making students aware of what they are doing wrong and supplying them with an alternative. In other words, correcting is about making students conscious of the new rules operating in the new language in contrast to the unconscious 'natural' rules of their own language. And whether or not the new rules are brought to consciousness by way of formal grammatical instruction or by other methods, correcting grammatical errors contributes to the acquisition of language by doing what Germain argues cannot be done, which is bringing conscious input to bear upon unconscious processes.

    From experience, correcting errors without recourse to explicit grammatical reasoning is not only taking the opportunity to waste our best intellectual tools, it usually means one of two things: either the error is corrected as Germain recommends, through unexplained examples and repetition, or students are corrected incidentally. In the first instance, correction may help students remember a particular sentence or a set of sentences, but it will not teach them to apply the rule to grammatically similar language in semantically novel circumstances. In the second instance, correction engages students' short-term memory and is therefore entirely ineffective. So-called conversation classes, where errors are corrected by the bye or not at all, do not improve learners' language. Free conversation may lead to more fluency and better aural comprehension, but it does not improve grammatical accuracy in any noticeable manner.

    We can gauge just how unproductive incidental correction is by considering how long it can take second-language speakers who are living, studying or working in language immersion to match their language to the standards expected of native speakers. From years of coaching and teaching non-native English speaking students in a range of academic disciplines, I know that it is very difficult to correct a well-functioning second language in which speakers are unconscious of their mistakes, whether that language is laden with grammatical inaccuracies or, indeed, the mistakes amount to a few speech habits. Certainly, there is endurance as well as creative power in the hybridized idiolect. Improving the grammar of a second language requires speakers to notice the differences between their own language and the language of native speakers, and then to understand the systemic nature of their mistakes and the need to remedy errors systematically. It also requires speakers to care about this enough to want to

---

[40] Claude Germain, 'Acquisition ou apprentissage de la grammaire?' in Melba Libia Cárdenas y Nora M. Basurto Santos (eds), *Investigación-Research-Recherche En Lenguas Extranjeras y Linguisticas Aplicada*, primera edición, Bogóta, Universidad National de Colombia; Faculdad de Ciencias Humanas, Departamento de Lenguas Extranjeras, 2017; pp. 149-169. The citation is on page 159.

change their habits and to be willing to persist, and, not least, it requires that they have access to effective strategies with which to build new speech habits.

Non-native speakers who are fluent in their version of a language may know that they make mistakes, they may know that they have troubles with aspects of the language, or they may not know how and where their speech differs from native speakers' speech and to what extent. Some of the students I taught at university were surprised to discover how many errors they made in written tasks, while others were surprised to discover how few mistakes they made. In fact, I am always a little surprised myself when I look back at the French infused English I wrote as an undergraduate student enrolled at the University of Western Australia, a long time ago now. It surprises me somewhat because I never had a sense that I could not express what I wanted or needed to express. I wrote fluently, and I thought deeply and effectively in my own version of academic English. From the point of view of cognition, a second language can be highly efficient even when it is not entirely accurate by native language standards. Second-language speakers may not be especially adept at evaluating their own linguistic competence because they can have a perfect understanding of their second language, while their own 'imperfect' idiolect makes perfect sense to them. The problem for second-language speakers may be less a matter of understanding others than of being understood. More often than not, it is a problem of convincing native speakers that there is no need to turn up the volume.

Does grammatical accuracy matter, ever?

My approach to grammatical accuracy has to do with several things: what we learn languages for, what language accuracy does for second-language acquisition (what we practise tends to stick), and what a teacher owes her students. Fundamentally, learning a language is about human connection and it is plain that, on this count, grammatical accuracy comes a distant second to a lot of things. It is also plain that degrees of language competency can serve different linguistic purposes. There is a legitimate and important place for phrase-book language, for basic and communicative language, for computer and phone applications that help us make contact with people where we travel, live or work. And then there are circumstances when we may have to learn a language in greater depth. I am a multilingual speaker, and I have lived my adult life as an immigrant and a linguistic alien among native speakers and other linguistic aliens, and this on three continents. I know first-hand that linguistic competency is about personal, social, economic and cultural empowerment. There is great joy in acquiring a language that allows us to engage and share in a different community of meaning and culture, and there is real suffering in the isolation, in the smaller and the greater moments of disconnection, humiliation and helplessness which linguistic limitations impose on us when we cannot speak with others or as others do. Indeed, multicultural societies have a responsibility to help their citizens master the national language as well as to foster acceptance and appreciation of linguistic diversity. And, if nothing else, learning a second language at school may help monolingual learners appreciate just how difficult it can be to learn, let alone to master, an additional language.

But where does all of this leave the issue of grammatical accuracy in second-language instruction? The following anecdote seems an appropriate way to close the discussion. A few years ago, Laura, one of my adult students, became impatient with the switching of auxiliaries from *avoir* to *être* in the *passé composé*. Her impatience was justified – she only wished to brush up on her school French before going to France for a few weeks of travelling, and she had little desire to master the subtleties of *la langue de Molière*. Finding the whole thing too fussy, she objected: 'But surely if I said *j'ai allé*, people would understand me?'

I answered: 'Of course, they would. And no one is going to expect you to speak like a native. Besides, when I was a kid, people in the country said exactly that: *j'ai allé* and *j'm'ai lavé les mains*.'

'Then, what's the point of me learning all that?'

'In absolute terms, none. But what if my English teacher had taught me that if I said, I goed to the station and I falled down the stairs, it would be neither here nor there because English speakers would understand me? Would that have been a reasonable approach for her to take?'

Looking at it this way, Laura had a bit of a chuckle and agreed that this would not have done.

WHY THE ACQUISITION OF FRENCH GRAMMAR CANNOT BE ENTRUSTED TO NATURE

The French language presents many difficulties for English-speaking learners. The Victorian Curriculum and Assessment Authority highlights some of these, along with salient differences between French and English:

> French uses the same Roman alphabet as English, although its pronunciation of the letters differs significantly and the use of accents on some letters is an additional complexity for English-speaking learners. There are many similarities between the two grammatical systems, such as the same basic subject-verb-object order, but also differences, such as in the use of tenses, the gendering of nouns and adjectives, the marking of plural forms

of nouns and adjectives, and the use of articles and capital letters. The sound system is usually the main challenge for English-speaking learners, including as it does some novel sounds (such as the pronunciation of the letters *r* and *u*), letters which are silent, and unfamiliar liaisons and intonation and rhythm patterns.

As every teacher knows, these differences account for quite a lot. From experience, however, the challenge for English-speaking learners lies not only in the sound system but also in French grammar, especially when the latter is in written form. To the differences listed above, we may add that French observes a subject-verb-object order, as English does, when it is using nouns, but a subject-object-verb order when it is using pronouns. French may also opt for an object-verb-subject order for literary effect, and especially where relative clauses are involved. And then, French differentiates between definite direct object and indefinite direct object pronouns, it differentiates between the infinitive object of a modal verb and the infinitive object of an action verb, and between the placement of the pronominal direct objects of an infinitive that follows a modal verb and of an infinitive that follows a catenative verb. French differentiates between the animate and inanimate subject and direct object cases when using interrogative pronouns but not when using relative pronouns, and it differentiates between animate and inanimate personal pronouns of the oblique variety, but not so when dealing with subject and direct object personal pronouns, except when the latter are used with verbs expressing likes and dislikes. Not surprisingly there are more pronominal cases in French than in English. Besides those already alluded to, there are the dative and directional cases, to which we might add the possessive and demonstrative pronouns, which are not only numbered but gendered and among which is found a unique example of gender neutrality which even French speakers commonly mistake for the third person impersonal pronoun that does not make the weather a 'he'. And then French, unlike English, uses a selection of prepositions with syntactic rather than lexical value to form verbal complements, as well as compound nouns and complements of adjectives. And this is before we begin speaking of the many stylistic differences between French and English and about the agreements of past participles.

    There are good reasons to doubt the pedagogical soundness of approaching the teaching of French grammar by stealth (besides those already discussed) because there is another, very obvious and major problem. The grammar of standard French is not simply a manifestation of natural linguistic usage and evolution. It is also the product of the minds of generations of literati and poets. As Alain Ray put it, the French language is a product of conscious codification, of an aesthetic quest, cultural aspiration, refinement, Latinisation and formal rationalisation.[41] French orthography, which under the original influence of Bossuet and other luminaries, hoped to sort 'the people of letters from the ignoramuses and mere women', has undergone several reforms over the past three centuries, but it is still a highly refined and rather treacherous artefact.[42] We can be quite sure that our secondary school students will never see their way through the complexities of this grammatical system, which owes only so much to nature, by leaving their learning to nature. Native French speakers themselves cannot do this. When native French speakers speak formally and when they write, they have to remain alert to all the rules governing grammatical agreements, together with the placement of accents and letters which are either not sounded in speech (*e/s/ent/t/x*) or sounded in exactly the same way (*er/ez/é/és/ée/ées*).

However, there is an up side. Like all languages, French does appear incoherent in parts but the conventions of standard French shape what is in many respects a beautifully organised structure that can be explained to students by way of its own rationale and history, and through fascinating comparisons with English. The French and the English languages are like French and English gardens. The genius of English lies with flexibility, creativity, and apparent naturalness, the genius of standard French lies in formality, symmetry, and apparent orderliness.

Written French and its many complications

French orthography is grammatically conscious in a way that English orthography is not, and this by orders of magnitude. For the greater part, the difficulties of English orthography lie with the *seemingly* erratic spelling of words, and not, as it happens in French, with the addition or substitution of silent and other letters to mark not only real or presumed etymologies but to identify the syntactic relationships between words. As we know, the cases where English spelling is dependent on grammatical function produce confusion for native English speakers who have not been taught principles of formal grammar: my friend's dog, my friends' dog, there, their, they're, could have, who's, whose... Native English speakers are also confused by the inflection of the relative pronoun who-whom, by the singular agreement of the indefinite pronoun none, and they are not bothered by a sentence such as: a spouse must support their partner, which would very much bother a French speaker. In fact, the *Chicago Manual of Style* rejects this usage in standard American English, but to English speakers who are lexically oriented

---

[41] See the lecture by Alain Ray, 'Le Français, une langue à l'épreuve des siècles' at https://www.youtube.com/watch?v=qrza2HMjsSw

[42] Cited from Danielle Béchennec and Liliane Sprenger-Charolles, *Guide Pratique de l'orthographe rectifiée*, CNRS et Université Paris-Descartes; p. 3. http://www.cahiers pedagogiques.com/IMG/pdf/GuidePratiqueOrthographeRectifie_c-2-09-2011.pdf

rather than syntactically conscious, the singular-plural disagreement makes perfect sense: the speaker intends to produce a gender-neutral statement and the third person plural, being gender neutral, does just this.[43] Of course, French does something similar when it uses the singular indefinite pronoun *on* in place of the first person plural *nous*.

Whatever the relative differences between English and French, the fact is that English and French children need to spend many years at school developing their native language skills. Without *some* explicit instruction, no native English or French speaker can be expected to read or to write according to academic standards. Given this, and the particular difficulties involved in the writing of French, it seems self-evident that our second-language students need to learn about grammar to be able to learn to write in French.

CONCLUSION: Why learning grammar can be more fun than talking about *la fête et les copains*

The reader may wonder how learning about subjects and object complements could possibly prove more stimulating than grammatically unhindered speech and cultural entertainment, but the fact is that it does – because learning something new and acquiring the means of doing something the right way is intrinsically more motivating than not knowing what one is doing and losing one's purpose.

The plainest grammatical explanation I offer to new students invariably elicits this response: 'Oh, so that's how it works!' and invariably it is followed by: 'I never knew this. Sorry, I should know that.' There are layers of meaning in these responses. Firstly, the grammatical explanation comes as a relief because it dispels anxiety. Then, because students do not know the difference between grammatical explanation and grammatical rote, they assume that they should have learned what I have just taught them by doing the written exercises they practised in class. Furthermore, the explanation I have given them makes the solution to the problem look so obvious and simple that they feel somewhat embarrassed that they did not come to it on their own. This gives an idea of how much unnecessary anxiety is created by not explaining things.

Grammatical explanations bring relief because grammar provides students with answers and strategies as well as with objective criteria to learn and measure their learning by, to know what they get right, to know what they get wrong and

---

[43] Note the plurality implied in 'every' in a sentence like 'every child must bring their umbrella' although this sentence also breaks the formal number agreement. Every child of course means all the children, and it translates as *tous les enfants* in French.

why. Just as importantly, grammatical knowledge gives students the possibility of mastering one thing at a time and seeing their results as the just rewards of their efforts, as in other learning areas like mathematics and science. And this has the added bonus of raising the status of language learning to a 'real' school subject. In a nutshell, grammatical instruction offers practical and pragmatic solutions to a number of pedagogical problems because learning grammar gives students the means to apply rules to the construction of correct and brand-new sentences, in the same way that rules allow us to resolve mathematical equations or, as Saussure saw it, to play a game of chess.

Learning a new language means entering a new and unknown landscape. We can set students free to roam at will and hope that they will find their way, and indeed, some will. Or we can give them the means to orient themselves and more. As I will explain in the next chapter, learning grammar takes language students on a voyage of discovery into communication and culture, and into the very making – the *becoming* of cognition.

IV

Thinking about Language and Second-language Acquisition

Part One: The Mystery of Language.

Our language pedagogies are anchored in the belief that we acquire additional languages as we did our first, a belief largely legitimated by nativist theories of language acquisition and very much opposed by cognitive linguistics. But whichever side of the argument one may find more convincing, the debate between nativist and cognitive linguistics confirms one thing: that we do not acquire a second language in quite the same way as we acquire our mother tongue.

THE NATIVIST-COGNITIVIST DEBATE

We can take for granted that we do not simply learn to speak on account of having ears and a voice box, thanks to the nineteenth-century physician Paul Broca, who discovered that we speak with our brain.[44] In large part, we also owe this knowledge to Noam Chomsky. Chomsky's theoretical outlook on language acquisition has evolved and changed over time, but what has remained constant and how it is generally understood, at least as far as applied linguistics is concerned, goes as follows: As small children we are exposed to largely fragmented, imperfect and incomplete language which is made meaningful and limited by the pragmatic context and out of which we are able to accomplish this feat – in a short time (three years or so), we are able to internalise the grammar of our language in a manner that 'cannot be derived by induction or abstraction from what is given in experience.' Hence, Chomsky concludes that 'the

---

[44] Fromkin-Rodman, op. cit., p.31.

internalized knowledge must be limited very narrowly by some biological property.'[45] Using plain English, Steven Pinker explains Chomsky's concept of the Universal Grammar as a 'recipe or a program' common to all human brains that allows children to acquire any language by 'distilling the syntactic patterns out of their parents' speech'.[46] This program can build an unlimited set of sentences out of a limited number of rules. Pinker also proposes that language acquisition should be understood as an instinct, as a biological adaptation to communicate information.[47]

As might be expected, not all linguists agree with the finer points of Chomsky's proposition, or even with the whole idea. In fact, there exists no consensus among linguists regarding the mysteries of language acquisition or the nature of language, and while some scholars are prepared to seek multi-causal explanations, theoretical positions can span the full spectrum of acrimonious exchanges and radically opposing views.[48] In the 1980s, cognitive linguists Ronald Langacker and George Lakoff challenged Chomsky's nativist position, arguing that language is not distinct from other areas of cognition, and that there is no specialised brain function dedicated to language.[49] And whereas a central principle of Chomsky's theory holds that syntax is independent from semantics, cognitive linguistics argues that syntax, morphology, lexicon and grammar form a continuum rather than distinct domains.[50] More recently, Geoffrey Sampson and Vyvyan Evans have objected to Chomsky and Pinker's nativism that insists we learn language as we learn anything else, largely through trial and error.[51] Sampson also takes Pinker's 'language instinct' to task: If by 'instinct' is meant a type of behaviour which is produced without any learning at all, Sampson writes, the range of behaviours that are encoded in our DNA can be surprising, but while it will include such things as unconscious hand gestures, it will not include language, for the simple reason that no child grows English spontaneously out of his head.[52]

Sampson objects (and it is difficult not to agree with him) that little children do not acquire language spontaneously or rapidly or perfectly, despite what Chomsky and Pinker argue, and that both Chomsky and Pinker

---

[45] Noam Chomsky, *On Language*, The New Press, New York, 2007; p. 63
[46] Steven Pinker, *The Language Instinct*, Harper, Modern Classic editions, 2007; quoted and slightly rephrased from Chapter One; p. 9.
[47] Ibid.
[48] See Farrell Ackerman and Robert Malouf, 'Beyond Caricatures, Commentary on Evans 2014' in *Language*, 92 (1), 2016.
[49] Ronald Langacker, *Concept, Image, and Symbol: the cognitive basis of grammar*, Berlin, New York, Mouton de Gruyten, 2002; George Lakoff, *Women, Fire and Dangerous Things: what categories reveal about the mind*, Chicago University Press, 1987.
[50] Mikolaj Domaradzki, 'Cognitive Critique of Generative Grammar', available at: http://lingua.amu.edu.pl/Lingua_17/lin-4.pdf; p. 41.
[51] Geoffrey Sampson, *The Language Instinct Debate*, London, New York, Continuum.
[52] Sampson, op. cit., p. 9.

underestimate the role which imitation plays in language acquisition. Indeed, it is a universally observable truth that children are expert imitators. Children imitate everyone and everything: adults, other children, pets, cars, trucks and airplanes. All pretending games are imitating games, and most are also learning games. This is confirmed by research into human cognition, which has shown that children imitate even when there is no cause for them to do so. Unlike apes, who imitate with purpose in order to achieve a specific result and who will stop imitating when they find a more direct way to obtain what they want, small children imitate *on principle*, presumably because they are motivated by the social pleasure of doing as others do.[53] Where language acquisition is concerned, small children respond to the faces around them and to being spoken to. Very small children are also keen to listen to adult conversations in a way that older children no longer are. They try to understand and look for material to imitate. They are highly sensitive to the reactions they produce when they speak, and they will say and repeat things they do not understand for the pure joy of speaking or eliciting a reaction. Of course, not all children are fond of amusing people, some delight in the exercise and others shy from it, but few are indifferent.

Whatever nativists have to say about it, cognitive linguists are undeniably correct to argue that children copy their parents and other adults, and that parents and familiars correct children's speech. Parents point to things and name them, they repeat words, they show approval, admiration and appreciation at what their children say, they sing and teach their children the words of songs and so forth. Furthermore, children speak and play with other children who also provide modelling and offer corrections, sometimes more brutally than parents might. In sum, rather than being exposed to limited and imperfect language as Chomsky and Pinker maintain, children are exposed to a great deal of language, much of which is in complete and varied sentences, and some of which they are eager to imitate, whether or not they actually understand what they are saying.

Cognitive linguists not only object to the idea that children acquire language reflexively, they also object to the idea that children acquire language rapidly. And again, it is difficult not to agree with them. After all, children have little else to do but to learn to speak twenty-four seven in the school of life. And while some children are already beginning to form sentences at about fourteen months of age, many will take three years or so to master a functional grammar. Quite a few English-speaking children will have learned to run, skip, throw a ball, and tie their shoelaces before they are able to use the simple past of the verb to

---

[53] See Zanna Clay and Claude Tennier, 'Is over-imitation a uniquely human trait: insights from human children as opposed to bonobos', *Child Development*, September-October 2018, Vol. 89, Number 5; pp. 1535-1544.

fall, and to articulate their language well enough to be understood by people other than their parents and familiars.[54]

Nevertheless, not all the arguments put forward by cognitivists are entirely convincing. Take Evans' criticism of Chomsky's Universal Grammar:

> When a child equipped with an inborn Universal Grammar acquires her first language, spotting a grammatical rule in her mother-tongue should lead her to apply the rule across the board, to all comparable situations. Take the noun *cat*. Hearing a parent refer to *the cat* – using the definite article, *the* – should alert the infant to the fact that the definite article can apply to all nouns… Just a few instances of hearing *the* followed by a noun should be sufficient; any infant acquiring English should immediately grasp the rule and apply it freely to the entire class of nouns. In short, we would expect to see discontinuous jumps in how children acquire language…

But what actually happens (still according to Evans) is the following:

> It's a striking prediction. Sadly, it doesn't stand up to findings in the field of developmental psycholinguistics. On the contrary, children appear to pick up their grammar in quite a piecemeal way. For instance, focusing on the use of the English article system, for a long time they will apply a particular article (e.g., *the*) only to those nouns to which they have heard it applied before. It is only later that children expand upon what they've heard, gradually applying articles to a wider set of nouns. This finding seems to hold for all our grammatical categories. 'Rules' don't get applied in indiscriminate jumps, as we would expect if there really was an innate blueprint for grammar. [55]

Evans' example somewhat stretches the imagination. While psychologists are able to make statistical observations of how children speak and progress through various stages of phonological, lexical and syntactic performance, we would be hard pressed *in real life* to account for all the nouns which a sufficiently representative sample of children might hear in a single day (not to say over weeks and months) that may or may not be accompanied by the definite article, all the while keeping a true and reliable record of which noun-phrases these same

---

[54] Note that although I am making this argument in support of cognitive linguistics, Evans is of the opinion that children will have mastered the past tense of the verb to fall before they do all of the above.

[55] Cited from Vyvyan Evans, 'Real Talk' Eon, 4 December 2014, at https://aeon.co/essays/the-evidence-is-in-there-is-no-language-instinct. See also V. Evans, *The language myth, why language is not an instinct*, Cambridge University Press, 2014.

children might have heard prior to using them. What Evans writes next is theoretically problematic: '[according to Chomsky's theory] just a few instances of hearing *the* followed by a noun should be sufficient; any infant acquiring English should immediately grasp the rule and apply it freely to the entire class of nouns'. Here, Evans ignores that the Universal Grammar could not account for the rule governing the English definite article because the latter is obviously a product of history. The definite article being derived from the Old English demonstrative articles belongs to what Chomsky calls the external rules of language.

Actually, we should think it equally miraculous if children were to master the use of the definite article in English through observation alone as if they were to do so on the basis of a spontaneous brain reflex. 'The' is a determiner but it does not modify the noun as determining adjectives do. Demonstratives and possessives have an obvious referential and lexical dimension (this book is not that one; my mummy is not your mummy), which is lacking from the definite article. The definite article is formal and somewhat redundant since it is used in English not to complement or modify a noun (usually of the concrete variety) but to reference what could be considered obvious: that the noun we have uttered has already been mentioned. What is more, American and Australian English do not agree on its usage, and 'the' is in appearance such an unnecessary item of speech that some languages, as for example Chinese and Russian, don't bother with it. Not surprisingly, the definite article presents great difficulties for second-language learners of English. Based on the aforementioned propositions, however, Evans argues that:

> We seem to construct our language by spotting patterns in the linguistic behaviour we encounter, not by applying built-in rules. Over time, children slowly figure out how to apply the various categories they encounter. So while language acquisition might be uncannily quick, there isn't much that's automatic about it: it arises from a painstaking process of trial and error.

Language acquisition is certainly a mystery, and while I agree with Evans that the nativist position raises questions nativists do not answer, the proposition that little children learn language by figuring out how to apply patterns rather than on account of built-in rules is not entirely convincing. Many Russian, French and Chinese immigrants who live, work and study in English-speaking countries do not acquire the use of 'the' after years of exposure to English and quite in spite of the fact that the frequency of this article is indisputable. If language acquisition is about spotting patterns, could we not expect highly motivated second-language speakers of English who can play chess and solve algebraic equations and who have mastered thousands of lexical English items to spot and 'figure out' the use of the definite article at least as easily as five-year-old English native speakers do?

Evidently, the difference between a five-year-old native speaker of English and an adult second-language speaker of English is that the five-year-old native has a referential need for the article that the second-language speaker does not have. However, this does not explain why a five-year-old should be able to spot and figure out a grammatical pattern better than an adult, whether the latter is a native speaker or not.

Significantly, native English speakers who have had no schooling in formal grammar in their own language are entirely unconscious of their speech patterns until or unless they hear someone utter what they identify as erroneous usage. Native speakers correct second-language speakers by pointing out that something is not English or not 'proper' English, but unless they have studied grammar formally, they cannot explain *why* what was said was incorrect, and more importantly, they are rarely able to think of valid like-examples to make their point clearer. Small children are surely as unconscious of their speech patterns as 'grammatically unschooled' adults. This is not to say that children do not learn by trial and error or that they do not apply themselves to language learning, but surely children are far more likely to imitate whole language items than they are to spot and apply a syntactic principle running through semantically divergent statements. Cognitive linguists may also not make enough of the fact that even if children do not acquire aspects of grammar in indiscriminate leaps, they seem to acquire language at a *statistically* predictable rate and in a *statistically* predictable order, with most children eliminating similar grammatical errors by the time they are four or five years old.[56]

Richard Schmidt, who argues that learning a second language requires conscious input, says something very interesting regarding the different ways in which children and adults may acquire first and second languages. He writes:

> It is commonly observed that children learn the rules of grammar as a by-product of trying to communicate (McLaughlin et al. 1983), and just as commonly noted that adults may fail to learn grammar through communicative interaction (Schmidt 1983)… Ceci and Howe (1982) report a number of other experiments in support of the hypothesis that the major change from child to adult consciousness is a shift from a passive mode that includes an open awareness of the environment, to a more controlled mode that includes the strategic allocation of attention. It is intriguing to note that the age range during which this shift takes place approximates to the sensitive period for language acquisition. If developmental cognitive changes of this sort are irreversible, we would predict incomplete acquisition of form by adults to the extent that they do not deliberately attend to form, especially for redundant and

---

[56] Madorah E. Smith, 'Grammatical errors in the speech of pre-school children', in *Child Development*, Vol. 4 No 2, June 1933; pp. 183-190.

communicatively less important grammatical features. Because children have less control over the spotlight of attention, they may not be able to avoid noticing these communicatively less important grammatical features, and in that sense may acquire grammar unconsciously.[57]

Schmidt tells us as much about the way in which children acquire their native grammar as why adult learners find it difficult to acquire the grammar of a second language, and I shall return to the latter issue in due course. Meanwhile, what Schmidt has to say about the imitative powers of children speaks to both cognitivist and nativist theories: children learn by imitation but they acquire grammar unconsciously as a by-product of imitation. Indeed, the acquisition of a grammar cannot depend solely on imitation for, as Chomsky and Pinker argue, children who have learned to speak do not regurgitate whole sentences but generate semantically novel language according to 'constant' rules of grammar. Returning to Evans' example, we can surmise that English-speaking children learn to use the definite article, not because they understand a rule, nor because they actually spot a pattern, but because at some point in their intellectual development, the word 'the' conveys what they intend to say about the world they are observing. It is likely that English speakers learn to say 'the' dog when they have learned to differentiate 'the dog' from 'a dog' and it is equally evident that they have learned this without being conscious of the fact. Acquiring this grammar is an expression of *cognition* but it is also the manifestation of a procedural event that no native speaker of English is conscious of having learned or is able to define or explain unless he or she has been schooled in formal grammar.

The language children speak and the language children invent

Just as fascinating are the things children get wrong. Little children speak spontaneously and grammatically, but their grammar is not entirely like the grammar of their parents – which confirms that although imitation is an essential factor in language acquisition, there is more to the acquisition of speech than imitation. While chunking ('my thecat', *le nélephant*) is a factor of imitation, children's use of certain verbal forms and plural nouns is not. How can we explain that children, who are so good at imitating, say things like 'mices' and 'I falled'? 'Falled' is especially interesting because it is something a child undoubtedly experiences on a regular basis, and it is a word that he is not likely to have ever heard from the adults or the older children around him. 'Falled' is not a word that a child utters on the basis of observation. Evidently little children say 'I falled' because they are overgeneralising what linguists call the productive rule of modern English, a rule which applies to the 'regular' verbs. And this too is intriguing

---

[57] Schmidt, op. cit., p. 145.

because the English verbs most frequently used in everyday tasks, and therefore the verbs children are most likely to hear on a frequent and regular basis and those we could expect them to imitate and 'figure out' relatively quickly are of the irregular type such as: speak, go, eat, drink come, hear, read, break, find, stand, sit, throw, bring.

Just as significantly, many children not only speak their own version of their parents' grammar, they also *invent* words. Adults who have had limited education as well as creative types (Chaucer, Shakespeare, Proust) and professionals in positions of linguistic authority likewise invent words as well as idiosyncratic syntactic expressions – with entirely different social consequences: the former are considered ignoramuses, the others geniuses and experts. But do words and syntax become language when they are socially sanctioned, or is it not the case that the language of thought is not exactly alike the language of communication? Are word invention and syntactic creativity about 'doing language' or 'languaging' as Languaging theorists may propose,[58] or are they simply speaking a manifestation of 'cognition'?

I was very intrigued when I overheard my then three-year-old grandson, explaining to his teddy bear that I was his grandfather. To get to the bottom of it, I asked him to tell me who he thought his Nanny (his maternal grandmother) might be, to which he answered without hesitation that she was his grandmother. And I? He confirmed what he had told his teddy: You're my grandfather. Well, I asked, what about Poppy and Pop, to which he answered: They are Poppy and Pop. A few weeks later, my grandson came home from kindergarten announcing that there was to be a special afternoon tea at school for grandparents. 'Do I have grandparents?' he asked. When I confirmed that he did have quite a nice collection of them and explained what grandparents were, he found the idea very amusing and a little hard to take. How could it be that his parents were once upon a time as little as he and his sister?

How did my grandson deduce that his paternal grandmother was his grandfather and his maternal grandmother was his grandmother, when he did not know the word 'grandparent'? My grandson of course had *heard* his parents speak of their own mothers and fathers. Evidently, he had also *noticed* the words 'grandfather', 'grandmother', 'grandson' and so forth. Thus, he had deduced that I was his *grand* [what-ever-that-meant] to do with his *father* whilst his Nanny was his *grand* [what-ever-that-meant] to do with his *mother*. In other words, although he had no real understanding that his parents had parents, he had nevertheless understood that both his parents' mothers belonged to a category of persons who stood in a specific and unique generational relationship and gender category *vis à vis* his own mother and father.

---

[58] Hadrian Lankiewicz, 'From the Concept of Languaging to L2 Pedagogy', in Hadrian Lankiewicz and Emilia Wasikiewics-Firlej, *Languaging Experiences, Learning and Teaching Revisited*, Cambridge Scholars Publishing, 2014.

Should I conclude from this anecdote that anthropology is wired in our grey matter? Possibly not, but as an anthropologist aware of structuralist theory, I cannot miss the fact that my grandson's terminology involved the organizational dynamics which Lévi-Strauss identified in human mental processes, from languages to mythology, ritual and kinship rules: the pairing of opposite elements.[59] There is little doubt in my mind that trial and error did not inform my grandson's initial take on kinship terminology and that here was an instance of a particular process of cognition, a window into an innate capacity for classification, systemisation, social identification and word production. Evidently, as Sampson argues, the structures of English grammar are not innate, and in fact, they have changed and will keep changing over time but this does not cancel out the proposition that we have an innate ability to perceive and to think along structural lines, and that speech is at once the product of our interaction with the physical and social world and the product of an innate brain capacity to generate a dialectic of signing, parsing, inflecting and ordering. And it seems to me that we may call this capacity a grammar or that we may call it cognition. [60]

Neuroscience and the nativist-cognitivist debate

Neuroscience may well decide on the nativist-cognitivist debate in the near future. For the moment, however, the state of knowledge appears inconclusive. Both Pinker and Chomsky cite certain speech-brain disorders to support the claim that language not only begins in our brain but that it is a distinct element of brain function, as well as distinct from thought. It has long been established that damage to specific areas of the cerebral cortex causes speech disabilities. Damage to Broca's area, which is located in the inferior frontal gyrus, results in non-fluent agrammatic aphasia or telegraphic speech (speech that leaves out functional words), and damage to Wernicke's area which is located in the dominant cerebral hemisphere, results in fluent aphasia (fluent speech that is empty of meaning).[61] Fluent aphasia points to a differentiation of language and cognition, which Chomsky's theory advances, whilst non-fluent aphasia supports Chomsky's take on the differentiation of syntax and lexicon.

---

[59] Claude Lévi-Strauss, *La pensée sauvage*, Plon 1962, among other works, and no doubt one of the most insightful and readable introduction to his works Octavio Paz, *Claude Lévi-Strauss: An Introduction*, Cape Editions, London, 1971, which incidentally had a much more beautiful title in Spanish, *Claude Lévi-Strauss o el nuevo festin de Esope* (published by Joaqim Mortíz in 1967).

[60] See also Jenny R. Saffran, Ann Senghas, and John C. Treswell, 'The acquisition of language by children', *Proceedings of the National Academy of Sciences of the United States of America*, PNAS November 6, 2001. 98 (23) 12874-12875.
https://doi.org/10.1073/pnas.231498898

[61] See Pinker, op. cit.

According to its current Wikipedial status, however, imaging technology is now allowing scientists to study the connections between brain and language beyond observing the results of injuries to the cerebral cortex, confirming that large areas of the brain are actually involved in language processing. Notably, there is a consensus that the superior temporal gyrus plays a role in syntactic and semantic information processing, that the inferior frontal gyrus is involved in syntactic processing and working memory and the middle temporal gyrus in lexical and semantic memory. Most speech processing takes place in the dominant brain hemisphere, which corresponds to the opposite dominant hand and therefore the left hemisphere since most people are right-handed. Meanwhile, prosody, which among other things allows us to connect language to emotions, involves the right brain hemisphere. What is more, as Claude Germain notes, different areas of the brain are activated in connection to different types of language productions: when a person is saying the word 'table', listening to the word 'table', reading the word 'table', and thinking up the word 'table', blood flows to distinct parts of the brain.[62] Recent research in neuroscience has also confirmed that we perceive language by way of neuronal hierarchical structuring in which abstract categories (syntax) provide the scaffolding for the production of meaning. Chomsky believes that such findings support his theory.[63] But then again, neuroscience also supports the position of cognitive linguists since it is able to locate language memory in parts of the brain where other aspects of cognition and skills are likewise located.[64]

Where language acquisition (as distinct from language processing) is concerned, neuroscientist Patricia Kuhl concludes that

> it does not resemble Skinner's operant conditioning and reinforcement model of learning, nor Chomsky's detailed view of parameter setting. The learning processes that infants employ when learning from exposure to language are complex and multi-modal, but also child's play in that it grows out of infants' heightened attention to items and events in the natural world: the faces, actions, and voices of other people.[65]

---

[62] Germain, op. cit., p. 152. Note that Germain draws from neuroscience to construct a highly nativistic approach to second-language acquisition.
[63] Joel Shurkin, 'Colourless green ideas sleep furiously. Or maybe not', in *Inside Science*, December 10, 2015. https://www.insidescience.org/news/colorless-green-ideas-sleep-furiously-or-maybe-not.
[64] Michael T. Ullman, 'The Declarative/Procedural Model of Lexicon and Grammar', in *Journal of Psycholinguistics*, Vo. 30. No 1, 2001
[65] Patricia Kuhl, 'Brain Mechanisms in Early Language Acquisition', *Neuron*, Vol. 67, Issue 5, 9 September 2010; pp. 713-727. https://www.sciencedirect.com/science/article/pii/S0896627310006811

This, however, resonates with the passage which I cited from Schmidt (1990), regarding children's powers of observation and imitation.

In short, neuroscience confirms that small children are primed to acquire language and that the social and affective environment plays a decisive role in this process. It also confirms a distinction between syntax and lexicon, but it has not located a Universal Grammar or Language Acquisition Device in any particular part of the brain. Neuroscience has also established that different language functions light up different parts of the brain and that brain plasticity allows us to learn, in other words, to operate brain and mind changes as a result of environmental input. In fact, brain plasticity also allows us to *rebuild* brain functions, including the ability to speak, following brain injuries in the places where language memory is stored. And since Chomsky does not argue anything so crude as the idea that there is a 'language box in the brain' [66] and cognitive linguists do not deny that we are neurologically primed for the acquisition of language,[67] the findings discussed above may support the position of both nativists and cognitivists.

LANGUAGE ACQUISITION AND SOCIAL INTERACTION

Discussing Chomsky's theories of language acquisition, Mitsou Ronat in conversation with Chomsky drew attention to the so-called 'wolf children', the feral children abandoned in the woods and left to survive by their own devices. Making the point that past a certain age, we cannot acquire a second language to the same degree of proficiency as we acquired in our native language, she says: '[past adolescence], it is no longer possible to learn a language; the wolf children never learned to speak, and we speak a foreign language we have learned late in life with an accent. Without these biological constraints, foreign accent would be inexplicable'. Chomsky replies: 'Yes there seems to be a critical age for learning a language'.[68]

Indeed, there is general agreement in the psychological sciences that early childhood is a critical period at which to acquire language.[69] But Mitsou Ronat

---

[66] See Chomsky's lecture at University of Cologne: Noam Chomsky: 1. Lecture; https://www.youtube.com/watch?v=2v6XFkSwVys

[67] See Vyvyan Evans's article, 'Is Language an instinct?' *Psychology Today*, December 19 2014, at: https://www.psychologytoday.com/au/blog/language-in-the-mind/201412/is-language-instinct

[68] Chomsky, *On Language*, p. 98.

[69] See, for example, 'The critical period for language acquisition and the deaf child's language comprehension: a psycholinguistic approach,' a report supported by Rachel I Mayberry, University of McGill (undated)
http://www.acfos.org/publication/ourarticles/pdf/acfos1/mayberry.pdf

was making a sweeping statement about second-language acquisition. Many people learn languages as adults and become highly proficient. John De Francis, co-author of famous Chinese textbooks and Frederick Bodmer, philologist and Chomsky's predecessor at MIT, were of the opinion that adults make better language learners than children, in large part, because they are better at putting up with tedium and have clearer ideas of their goals and motivations.[70] For Bodmer, 'to be able to speak more than two new languages without any trace of a foreign accent or idiom is a life-work'. Acquiring such a skill is not, however, a product of biology but of social privilege and wealth, the benefit of travel and childhood experiences with foreign speaking nannies.[71]

In actual fact, grammatical accuracy and accents are tricky criteria for gauging linguistic competence because speakers can have perfect command of the syntax and lexicon of a second language while speaking with an accent, while speakers who learned a language as young children can forget a great deal of it in later life but nevertheless maintain perfect pronunciation. Conversely, second-language speakers may make grammatical errors which sound undeniably foreign to a native speaker, but then again, as Bodmer points out: 'very few adolescents can speak and write the home language with fluency and grammatical precision before eighteen years of age.'[72] And of course language plasticity ensures that not all grammatical errors, be they native or non-native, impede either cognition or communication. There is also more to say about the 'wolf children' cited by Mitsou Ronat and about the critical age for learning a language.

The wolf child, Victor de l'Aveyron

Victor de l'Aveyron (1788-1828) is among the most famous feral children. Victor was found in the woods, aged about twelve. His case aroused a great deal of public interest and in particular Jean-Marc-Gaspard Itard's, who took the boy in his care and proceeded to try and rehabilitate him to a social and intellectual existence. Itard taught Victor for five years during which time he designed many experiments to develop his sensory, intellectual and moral self, all of which he documented and later compiled into two detailed reports. In spite of Itard's dedication, however, Victor never learned to speak. Was Victor incapable of learning to speak because the Language Acquisition Device has an expiry date, as Ronat suggested? Had he learned to speak and then forgotten how? Had he been

---

Oliver Sacks, *Seeing Voices*, Vintage, 2000; and Kuhl, op. cit.
[70] J. De Francis with Yung Teng Chia-yee, Beginning Chinese, Yale University Press, New Haven and London, 1963; p. xx. See also F. Bodmer, *The Loom of Language*, Tingling and Co, Liverpool, London and Prescot, 8th printing, 1968; p. 19.
[71] Bodmer, op. cit., p. 20.
[72] Ibid.

abandoned because he had shown signs of an intellectual or speech disability?[73] Was Victor autistic, as Bruno Bettelheim has argued?[74]

A striking aspect of Victor's condition concerned his sensory perceptions. Victor was first believed to be deaf, as he would not react even to the sound of a gun fired next to him. But Victor was not deaf: he could hear a walnut falling in the orchard. Remarkably, he was equally insensitive to burning heat and extreme cold until Itard taught him to appreciate the comfort of mid-temperatures. While we may conclude today that Victor's sensory perceptions confirm the likelihood of his having been deeply autistic, Itard believed that Victor's sensory capacities had been dulled by the years of isolation, and honed by and for individual survival rather than by and for social interaction. Itard was convinced that isolation had played a decisive role in Victor's inability to develop speech and he compared his experience to those of other feral children abandoned at a very early age, among them a little girl who was able to learn to speak and then to recount her language-less experiences. Itard noted the remarkable fact that the girl's memory was intact and accessible through her newly acquired language, and he attributed both her learning to speak and her faculty of recall to a fundamental difference between hers and Victor's experience. The girl had been abandoned with another child, unlike Victor who had survived in total isolation. Itard surmised that 'having lived in the woods with a companion, [the little girl] already owed to that simple association a certain development of her intellectual faculties'.[75]

The story of Helen Keller may support Itard's hypothesis. At seven, Helen Keller who was deaf and blind burst into tactile language as infants burst into speech at around eighteen months of age. With the help of her teacher Anne Sullivan, she went on to learn to read with the Braille method, to study Latin, French and German, and to graduate from University. She also learned to 'hear'

---

[73] Jean-Marc-Gaspard Itard, *The Wild Boy of Aveyron*, Appleton-Century-Crofts, Meridith Corporation, New York, 1962. See the discussion by George Humphrey who provides an introduction to the same work.

[74] Bettelheim argues that 'feral children' were profoundly autistic. He contends that we are likely to favour the idea that these children were raised by animals because we consider their behaviour animalistic. See Bruno Bettelheim, 'Feral Children and Autistic Children', *The American Journal of Sociology*, Vol. 64, No 5 (March 1959); pp. 455-467.

[75] Itard, op. cit. p. xxii, xxiii and footnote 3, p xxiii. After she learned to speak the little girl recounted how she had accidentally killed her companion during a fight over a rosary they had found. Itard remarked on the fact that the little girl's memory was intact and accessible through language. The story of Ildefonso told by Susan Schaller in *A Man Without Words* tells a similar experience. After Ildefonso had learned to sign as an adult (he had no language before then), he was able to tell his story. Pinker argues that Ildefonso's story shows that thought and language are independent (Pinker, op. cit., p. 58). In fact, I do know persons who are able to recall and describe events that occurred in their early pre-verbal years – but it seems to me that any memory that is accessible to consciousness is by definition accessible to thought and therefore to language. We can all find the words to recount physical sensations and wordless events such as accidents, after the fact.

by feeling people's lips, nose and throat, and she learned to speak successfully enough for friends and family to understand her, although she relied on an interpreter for public speaking.[76] Thus, Helen Keller acquired speech and went on to have a full and extraordinary intellectual life in spite of having spent the 'critical childhood period' in a language-less world, in darkness and silence. It may be profoundly significant that Helen Keller, unlike Victor de l'Aveyron, was a well-loved child who was never deprived of human contact, affection and attention.

IS LANGUAGE AN INSTINCT?

Pinker proposes that language acquisition is part biology and a sort of instinct. He also argues that cognition must be differentiated from language: Language is a unique and complex human biological adaptation to communicate information and not 'an insidious shaper of thought'.[77] Pinker argues that the 'complexity of language, from the scientist's point of view, is part of our birth-right; it is not something that parents teach their children or something that must be elaborated in school.' [78] He writes:

> language is not a cultural artifact that we learn the way we learn to tell the time (...). It is a distinct piece of the biological makeup of our brain. Language is a complex, specialised skill, which develops in the child spontaneously, without conscious effort or formal instruction, is deployed without awareness of its underlying logic, is qualitatively the same in every individual. (...) Cognitive scientists have described language as a psychological faculty, a mental organ, a neural system, and a computational module. But I prefer the admittedly quaint term "instinct".[79]

Pinker recognises that 'a language instinct may seem jarring to those who think of language as the zenith of human intellect and who think of instinct as brute impulses', but for Pinker human intelligence itself is none less than a manifestation of a unique human instinct and human biology.[80]
    Pinker attributes the genesis of his idea to Darwin, who explained human language as 'an instinctive tendency to acquire an art' and 'a design that is not peculiar to humans but seen in other species such as song-learning birds'.[81]

---

[76] Helen Keller, *The Story of My Life*, Hodder and Stoughton, 1904.
[77] Pinker, op. cit., p. 6.
[78] Ibid.
[79] Pinker, op. cit., p. 7.
[80] Ibid.
[81] Ibid.

However, the language instinct is not easily reconciled with what Darwin had to say about the songbirds since the latter cannot sing unless they are taught by other birds. Little Helen Keller's hunger for words also struck Anne Sullivan as instinct: 'She learns because she can't help it, just as the birds learn to fly.'[82] But Anne Sullivan never doubted that Helen needed *to learn*. Language did not grow out of Helen Keller's brain spontaneously. However, the *desire* to speak did.

This said, Pinker is correct up to a point: speaking must be somehow innate since *all* human beings have language. Nevertheless, if language is not learned the way we learn to tell the time, it is also not innate in the way that breathing is innate, because no human being develops language outside of human society, and no human being acquires language extemporaneously. Hence, Pinker's take on the language instinct makes too little of the *social* dimension of language acquisition. As cognitive linguists rightly object, all children learn to speak the language that is spoken to them and which surrounds them, and not another language they have never heard. Evidently, Pinker's language instinct also dismisses the role that *imitation* and the desire to be with and to be like others, and therefore to do as others do, might play in early language acquisition. Controlled experiments in neuroscience have shown that nine-month old babies exposed to language via artificial informational devices like recordings and television showed poor results compared to infants engaged in the same language activities with human persons. Human presence and interaction appear to be critical conditions for infants to acquire language.[83] These findings are profoundly interesting because they suggest that language learning is not only socially and affectively dependent but also *species-sensitive*. A baby may not acquire language from exposure to a machine for the same reason that he will acquire speaking from other humans rather than learn barking from the family dog. The latter would support the Nativist position regarding the innate human capacity for language learning. However, the research also supports Vytgotsky's Interactionist theory, which places socialisation and the desire to communicate at the core of language development, and Itard's take on Victor's condition. Taken together, the data suggest that learning to speak should be understood as a socio-biological drive, in other words, *a social instinct*. However, for Pinker:

> Thinking of language as an instinct inverts the popular wisdom, especially as it has been passed down the canon of the humanities and social sciences. Language is no more of a cultural invention than is upright posture. It is not a general capacity to use symbols: a three year old ... is a grammatical

---

[82] Keller, op. cit., p. 318.
[83] Kuhl, op. cit.; see also Maxine Sheets-Johnstone,'Kinetic Tactile-Kinesthetic Bodies: Ontogenetical Foundations of Apprenticeship Learning', *Human Studies*, 2000.

genius, but is quite incompetent in the visual arts, religious iconography, traffic signs, and the other staples of the semiotic curriculum.[84]

Pinker is right to remind us that culture does not make us bipedal but culture nonetheless shapes upright posture and bipedalism just as it shapes other human behaviours, perhaps all the more so in that, as a species intent on asserting our unique position in the universe, we cannot fail to notice that standing, walking and speaking distinguishes us from the other animals who walk on four legs and do not speak, or at least do not utter the sorts of noises we recognise as speech. Putting this in anthropological terms, the cultivation of obviously natural behaviours 'humanises' us. Thus, in all societies people cultivate posture and gait as well as opinions on what posture and gait say about the individuals who abide by the cultural standards and those who don't.[85] It is also why in some societies, babies are not allowed to crawl and will learn to walk after they have learned to sit.[86]

Above all Pinker doth protest too much when he argues that language does not derive from a general capacity for using symbols. Whether speech, gestural or tactile, language is a system of signs, which is to say, a system of 'things' that stand for other things, in other words, a system of symbols. From an anthropological perspective, humans are animals whose social instincts are mediated and extended through symbolic production, and all human instincts, including the instinct to communicate, to name things, and to think about things (language), are ultimately shaped by social experience, collective meaning and learning. No socialised person in any human society eats directly from a kill and none mates as the urge takes them. In the same vein, no human speaks 'naturally' because all languages, like all societies and all cultures, are ruled by conventions that exceed basic biological survival.

While we are conscious that some of our behaviours and values, as for example our appreciation of the visual arts, music or religious iconography, are the products of our education rather than products of nature, we take a great deal of culture for granted because culture becomes 'naturalised' through habit and in the absence of alternative models. So much so that we become aware of our own cultural values and idiosyncrasies when we experience other cultural modes, when we encounter those in real life or when we read about them (in the present and in

---

[84] Pinker, op. cit., p.5.
[85] See the works of anthropologist Edward T. Hall, *The Hidden Dimension*, *The Silent Language*, and so forth, in which Hall shows that the way we sit, we walk, we position ourselves in others' physical space, the way we make eye contact, the way we modulate our voices, and communicative gestures are culturally learned.
[86] See Bateson, G and M. Mead, *Balinese Character: A photographic Analysis*, New York Academy of Science, 1942 and 1962. Cross-cultural studies are leading psychologists to question whether crawling is necessary to children's healthy development. See Kate Wong 'Crawling May Not Be Necessary For Normal Child Development; in some tribes, babies skip the crawl', *Scientific American*, July 1, 2009.

history). In the same way, we may become aware of the particularities of our mother tongue when we learn another language. And of course, we are far more likely to become aware of the particularities of other languages than of the particularities of our own language. We are likely to find other languages, like other cultures, strange – which is to say somewhat 'unnatural'.

Does language make us human?

Pinker concludes that thinking of language as having a biological basis necessarily cancels out thinking of language as a manifestation of the human capacity for making and using symbols. But, again, if all human beings speak, all human beings also draw, paint, decorate, and make music and dance – all of these are symbolic behaviours, and all are universal human behaviours. Why not, then, think of our capacity for making symbols as being integral to our biological make-up? At this particular juncture, the nature-culture dichotomy is surely something of a false problem. If all human behaviour is mediated by symbolic behaviour, then symbolic behaviour is natural for humans. We may, in this manner, conclude that culture, the social production of symbolic behaviour, and language, the socio-cognitive production of symbolic behaviour, derive from human 'instincts', and that our language faculty is dependent on our biology *and* our social nature *and* our cognitive capacities, which is none less than the nature of our species taken as a whole.

In some respects, human symbol making can be understood as an *augmented* capacity for categorisation and generalisation which all animals otherwise possess. Thanks in part to Descartes, we have had too many centuries of thinking of non-human animals as nature's automata but the mental capacity to generalise and create order is the baseline of all animal survival and perhaps of all living organisms.[87] At the most fundamental level, in the animal world predators know how to identify 'prey' and prey animals know how to recognise 'predators'. But this behaviour is at once instinctual, learned and conscious. Dogs who have been raised among chickens and ducks learn to eat what is in their plates and not their feathered cousins. They learn to differentiate insiders from outsiders as well as visitors from intruders by modelling on the territorial behaviours of their humans. Lambs raised among cats and dogs need to learn to eat grass when the time comes to supplement their feeding bottles, and although they will become mothers without explicit instruction, they may show no sign of the so-called flight instinct as adults. It seems that sheep learn to run away from danger like humans learn to speak – by doing what others do. In other words, it is not because behaviour manifests reflexively that it is not learned or that it cannot be improved upon.

We may find it as difficult to think of mind operations as being at once biologically based and learned, as to think of animals as thinking beings but both

---

[87] See Peter Wohlleben (Jane Billinghurst transl.), *The Hidden Life of Trees*, Greystone Books, 2016.

non-human and human animals are capable of both generalising and learning, and both need to generalise and learn in order to survive and thrive. Human languages come in speech, whistling, gesture, touch and a great variety of writing systems, and we believe that language makes us human. Genetic research has shown that FOXP2, the so-called language gene (and actually one of several genes associated with language), is uniquely human, while other versions of FOXP2 contribute to brain plasticity and communication in non-human animals. But how can we be certain that language is a uniquely human trait? That a kangaroo who has never met me knows to run from me and not to run from cows grazing in a paddock, surely demonstrates a *socialised* capacity for mental categorisation.

We have long been fascinated by the possibilities of animal-human communication. The shaman who mediates between the visible world of the living and the invisible world of the spirits speaks the language of the birds and engages with animal powers. In the twenty-first century, animal intelligence goes viral on the Internet. Millions of users are familiar with Koko, the gorilla who was raised by Penny Patterson and learned English and American Sign Language, and with Kanzi, the bonobo raised by Susan Savage-Rumbaugh who taught him, among other transgressions into what we believe to be uniquely human behaviours, to start a camp-fire with a lighter. Remarkably, Kanzi has learned to communicate with humans by using graphic *symbols* on a portable board.[88] In other language experiments, chimpanzees have learned to sign and read a range of English words and scientists have detected chimpanzee words in chimpanzee barks.[89]

Perhaps, indeed, we should curb our enthusiasm or sense of wonder, for experiments with apes and human language have been met with serious criticism on ethical grounds, and they have also been met with serious scepticism.[90] Robert Trustwell, who has analysed Kanzi's language tests, argues that his grasp of human grammar is limited. Kanzi becomes confused when processing verbal

---

[88] See Paul Raffaele, 'Speaking Bonobo', *Smithsonian Magazine*, November 2006.
https://www.smithsonianmag.com/science-nature/speaking-bonobo-134931541/
Refer to the numerous YouTube videos featuring Kanzi.
[89] For a fascinating view into animal language, see the documentary co-authored by Bertrand Loyer and Keebe Kennedy, directed by Keebe Kennedy, *Animal Language*, for the award winning series *Animals like us*, 2004-2006.
[90] On an overview of the ethical issues raised by animal language research see:
Jane C. Hu, 'What do talking apes really tell us?' *Slate Magazine*, August 20, 2017.
https://slate.com/technology/2014/08/koko-kanzi-and-ape-language-research-criticism-of-working-conditions-and-animal-care.html.
For a linguistic appraisal of Kanzi's skills, see Catherine Matacic 'Ape ""language ace"" gets tripped by simple grammar', in *Science Magazine*, March 25, 2016.
http://www.sciencemag.org/news/2016/03/ape-language-ace-gets-tripped-simple-grammar, and Robert Truswell, 'Dentrophobia in bonobo comprehension of spoken English', Edinburgh University, linguistics and English language, paper given at the *Evolution of Language Conference*, Louisiana, 2016.
http://evolang.org/neworleans/pdf/EVOLANG_11_paper_87.pdf

phrases requiring the decoding of two object complements. He understands linear grammar well enough but when asked: 'Show me the milk and the doggie' he shows only the dog, and when told 'Give the lighter and the shoe to Rose', he will give only the lighter.[91] For his part, Pinker argues that Kanzi's language is not grammatical at all and little more than fixed formulas. Pinker sees this as no shame on the apes and points out quite rightly that 'a human would surely do no better if trained to hoot and shriek like a chimp'.[92] And surely, in the light of our own limited ability to swing from trees, it seems a strange idea to evaluate animal cognitive and communicative powers on their ability to learn English and behave like humans. But when Pinker objects that people who spend a lot of time with animals 'are prone to developing indulgent attitudes about their powers of communication' and when he cites his great-aunt Bella who 'insisted in all sincerity that her Siamese cat Rusty understood English,'[93] I do find myself obliged to side with Aunt Bella and Rusty the cat. For there is also Chaser the dog, who was taught over a thousand English words by psychologist John Pilley, and I know for a fact that my dogs and cats and no doubt the reader's are able to understand at least aspects of human speech – not only prosody, facial expressions, tone and gestures, but actual words. This was also the conclusion reached by Neil deGrasse Tyson when Chaser demonstrated that she was able to acquire new words, not only by association but also through deduction.[94] It is certainly intriguing that animals are able to acquire *any* degree of competency in human languages, for how can we reconcile this with the idea that language is uniquely human, that it is not learned, and more importantly, that it is independent from cognition?

How the language instinct partially explains the limitations of the communicative language classroom

Thinking of language as a 'social instinct' certainly helps shed some light on the gap between first language and second-language acquisition. The fact that language acquisition is propelled by a socio-biological drive as fundamental as the drive to eat, to stand up and to be counted among the living, explains in part the difficulties we experience learning additional languages later in life. Rather than assuming that our language-making device atrophies beyond a relatively narrow window of opportunity in childhood, it may be that the drive to learn to speak, which is none other than the drive *to speak*, is resolved and put to rest once we are actually able to speak. As mentioned above, we take for granted that infants and

---

[91] Trustwell, op. cit.
[92] Pinker, op. cit., p. 351.
[93] Pinker, op. cit., p. 344.
[94] See NOVA PBS short video 'Chaser the Dog Shows Off Her Smarts to Neil deGrasse Tyson'. at: https://www.youtube.com/watch?v=omaHv5sxiFI

young children learn additional languages with greater ease than older children and adults do (hence the idea that additional languages should be taught at primary school if not kindergarten). However, in language immersion, teenagers and adult learners can acquire a second language much faster and far more completely than infants and toddlers acquire their mother tongue. Depending on the degree of relatedness of the new language to their own, and depending on the schooling they have received, many adult learners can become fluent in a new language within three to six months. Of course, five-year-old children will acquire a new language without a trace of accent, but they will also take between six months to a year to become fluent (as Krashen has noted), and we should not forget that six months in the life of a five-year-old child is far longer than six months in the life of a teenager.

If the language instinct partially explains why language immersion works miracles for second-language learners, it also explains why it is so hard to learn another language in the classroom. Immersion recalls the environment we were born into. In immersion, we are once again speechless in a world of incomprehensible noise and we are desperate for understanding and human connection. Anyone who has experienced spending hours, days or weeks as an alien speaker among speaking Others will understand that the word 'desperation' is not an exaggeration. There is no such motivation at work in the language classroom, and we may give serious thought to the proposition that the absence of communicative and cognitive necessity plays a vital role in *demotivating* language learners. To put it simply, students don't learn very well in the language classroom because they don't have to, and not (only) because the language class is an elective subject and their exposure to the language is limited, but because they can already do what we are attempting to teach them to do – they can already communicate about anything they need or want to talk about. This is why hoping that students will be motivated to learn French by speaking about themselves or other interesting topics is not enough, because learners can do this so much better and with no effort at all in their own language.

In fact, it is sometimes counter-productive to set students up to speak about interesting things. The more we want to speak about something, the more we are compelled to use our best means of communication. As all bilingual and multilingual speakers know, it is extremely frustrating to try and say something we really want to say in a language that resists our desire to express ourselves, and we will naturally switch to the language that requires the least effort if our interlocutor can understand it. Bilingual and multilingual speakers who share languages shift in and out of their native and learned languages to suit their immediate linguistic and cultural purposes, because natural communication demands that we speak in the language in which we are most at ease.

If speaking about interesting things cannot stimulate the natural drive to speak in a language we cannot speak, are there other means of motivation? Yes, of course. If we take a broad look at any other type of learning, we find motivation in the desire to learn something we want to achieve (goal oriented) and in the enjoyment of learning (process oriented). Our current methods at best are goal oriented: the goal is to speak French. This may be enough for students who are truly motivated but at the rate of three or four classes per week, the goal is too remote to maintain most learners' interest. Conversely, our processes, the idea that motivation happens naturally when students speak about interesting topics, are faulty for the simple reason that we can't make interesting conversation when we can't talk. I am not saying that we should not bother to provide students with interesting narrative content or information – in fact we have every reason to develop classroom materials with interesting narrative and informational content, for curiosity is a great motivator and the birthright of every student. Rather, I am making the point that while it might be fun for a while to try to speak in funny noises to say something one can already say and much better in normal life, after several weeks, months and years, that is bound to wear thin. To compound the problem, older children and adolescents live in another time dimension to adults who have a long view of things, and in another time dimension to little children who live in the moment. Adolescents are able to project themselves into the future and reflect on the past, but a year, let alone five or six, is a long time – a third or half of their lives. If trying to speak about interesting things does not work, teachers are likely to generate moderate levels of motivation by making the French class enjoyable through activities that are not language-related. The problem is that baking *une tarte aux pommes* might make the French class fun but it does not necessarily make learning French fun. Ultimately, or ideally, the way to make learning French fun is to have fun learning French. And how do we do this?

Part Two: Language, Thought and Why Syntax Rules.

It may take an adult in immersion several months to a couple of years to learn a new language. It takes a baby two to three years to learn to speak. That, actually, is a long time. It seems that even babies do not find language learning so easy, which should give us reason to think that when it comes to second-language learning, there is more to demotivation than lack of motivation, there is a very real difficulty inherent in the language learning process. And this must have to do with the nature of language, with the things that language does for us and the thing that language is.

LANGUAGE AND THE MIND

According to Chomsky, language is the external manifestation of the Universal Grammar, which is to say the external manifestation of deeper and deeply unconscious and as yet inexplicable brain processes. The phonological and syntactic systems that make up human speech are the result of a surface process of 'rewriting the rules' of the Universal Grammar. This surface grammar we can understand as scaffolding made of a limited number of organisational principles and restrictions from which speakers can generate a potentially infinite number of sentences. Hence, modern languages like English and French are the products of the mind as much as they are the product of the brain. And the advantage of looking at language as a mind rather than a brain process is obvious – the mind lends itself to direct and practicable observation.

Is syntax truly autonomous from semantics?

One of the most fascinating aspects of language is that we tend to be conscious of the meaning of the things we say rather than to be conscious of the language which allows us to say things. While we are sensitive to prosody, we are entirely unconscious on the phonological level. We do not hear what our own language sounds like because we hear what it means. According to Chomsky, however, we are especially unconscious of syntax. In other words, we are conscious of language only on the semantic level because we are conscious of words but not of the sounds of which they are made, and not of the grammar that organises them.

There is no doubt that when we are speaking, it *feels* like we are producing syntax unconsciously and notional words consciously. And when we are looking for 'our words' we are usually looking for just that: words, by which we mean units of language that carry meaning overtly; signs that represent the things we are talking about – a noun, an adjective, a verb, or an adverb. If we ask students who have not studied grammar formally to identify the important words they hear in a sentence such as: 'I went to the shop and bought some eggs', they will identify 'shop' and 'eggs', some may select 'I went', but they will not select 'to, 'the', 'and', and they may or may not notice 'some'. And in fact, we can remove the articles, the conjunction, the quantifying adjective, and the preposition and end up with: 'I went shop bought eggs' and still make perfect sense, which shows that the functional words we have removed are, at least in this case, unnecessary for effective communication and thus superfluous. There is no argument that we can make sense of the grammatically incomplete English sentence 'I went shop bought eggs' because the word order alone makes sense. On the other hand, should we keep all the words in this sentence but jumble them up, 'Bought shop and to the eggs went I', we would end up with a nonsensical statement. We may well convert this jumble of words to suit what is generally known of reality – that one is more likely to go to the shop than to go to the eggs – but we could not possibly hold a conversation along such a disordered line. In English, word order rules signification.

So, are we unconscious of syntax generally or are we unconscious of *correct* syntax? Are we unconscious of the mechanics of language or of the mechanics that produce *meaningful* language? Are we, in other words, unconscious of language so long as language is making sense?

If we think about this a little more, the idea that we are conscious of lexical production and unconscious of syntax starts to appear somewhat blurry. When we are speaking, so long as we are making sense to ourselves, we are actually unconscious of both syntax and lexicon. In fact, we can be so unconscious of language that, as Pinker writes, 'our thoughts come out of our mouths so effortlessly that they often embarrass us'.[95] But even when our language is purposeful, we are usually thinking as we are speaking and we are speaking as we are thinking, so that whether we are aware of it or not, meaning rather than words comes out of our mouths. Importantly, we can go on speaking spontaneously right up until something untoward happens to our thinking process. At which point, we will stop and we will begin searching for a word or, as the case might be, the means of phrasing the thought, which is to say, searching for the syntax.

That words are not always produced purposefully and that syntax is not always produced automatically becomes very obvious when we engage in higher-

---

[95] Pinker, op. cit., pp. 8-9.

level thinking and in serious writing tasks. When we need to clarify our thoughts, we search for both the best words and the best way of arranging the words, in sum we search for both lexical and syntactic meaning. The more complex the language task and the more evident this becomes, which is why we have to learn to write syntactically correct English through practice, through editing, modelling, noticing and replicating patterns and by studying and understanding the rules of prescriptive grammar and style. We cannot produce the lexical or the syntactic complexity required for high-level writing through the direct transposition of our spoken language or the transposition of raw thought-matter. Nor do we usually think about truly complex things spontaneously and in one go. Although we can have moments of enlightenment and strokes of what might appear to us as a brilliant idea at the time, we tend to build our ideas by following other ideas, and by exploring, evaluating, and re-evaluating our thoughts and the way we phrase them. Is the difference between a first draft and a final piece of writing a matter of clarifying our language or of clarifying our thinking? Is clarity of language independent from clarity of thought? Is 'thinking language' independent from 'communicable language'? Surely, the process of re-writing, editing and polishing is one of refining our thinking as well as one of adjusting our expression to the linguistic nuances and the conventions that allow us to produce writing that others can understand and evaluate. None of this actually challenges Chomsky's theory of grammar, but what does it say for the idea of the 'autonomy of syntax'?

Colourless green ideas sleep furiously - poetics and clichés

Chomsky demonstrates the autonomous nature of syntax by way of the now famous grammatically perfect and nonsensical sentence *colourless green ideas sleep furiously*. But here is something interesting: the more I turn this sentence in my head and the less bizarre it becomes, I begin visualising a light feathery cloud; a transparency morphing towards green; and 'sleep furiously' begins to feel rather to the point. *Colourless green ideas sleep furiously* is now looking like a suitably poetic representation of the mental processes that have inspired this book; ideas filling with possibilities, boiling in the depth of the psyche, awaiting release. Indeed, others have conducted the same experiment, and concluded as I have done that the sentence has poetic value.[96] Not everyone is poetically inclined, of course, but we can also frame the problem in this way: Isn't this sentence, which is constructed to teach a truth beyond itself, a version of *the clapping of one hand*? Isn't Chomsky just playing with language? And surely, *colourless green ideas sleep furiously* has become as culturally meaningful to those acquainted with Chomskyan linguistics as *raining cats*

---

[96] See Manfred Jahn, 'Colourless green ideas sleep furiously: A linguistic case test and its appropriations.'
https://pdfs.semanticscholar.org/57e1/74196dd4e32098a09847a2eb3d1da1acef6e.pdf

and dogs is to the English people living under the English sky, and both are nonsense to the rest of the world. Discussing colourless green ideas with Howard Lasnik, Chomsky had this to say:

> Chomsky: Well, a small industry has been spawned by one linguistic example, namely, Colorless green ideas sleep furiously, which has been the source of poems and arguments and music and so on.
>
> Howard Lasnik: This is a very interesting sentence because it shows that syntax can be separated from semantics, that form can be separated from meaning. Colorless green ideas sleep furiously. Doesn't seem to mean anything coherent but sounds like an English sentence. If you read it back to front – furiously sleep ideas green colorless – that wouldn't sound like English at all.
>
> Chomsky: Well that tells us that there's more to what determines the structure of a sentence than whether it has meaning or not... [97]

But does it really tell us this? Should we not only utter the sentence backwards but as a jumbled up string of words – *sleep green furiously ideas colourless* – the utterance would also be entirely meaningless, and it would be truly and uncontestably meaningless because it would not be a grammatical sentence. Surely this tells us that what determines the structure of a sentence is precisely the connection between meaning and syntactic expectation. We speak grammatically for the sole reason that grammar makes language meaningful. Meaning and sense are not the same thing. A grammatically correct sentence will always produce *meaning* of sorts. If its underpinnings are sensible or its metaphors are culturally relevant or poetically congruent, we will say that the sentence or the idea makes sense, and if the words that have been strung together are incongruent, we will say that the sentence does not make sense. But if nonsense is the opposite of sense, it is not the absence of meaning. Nonsense does not demonstrate the autonomy of syntax so much as it proves that we have the capacity to say idiotic things. The only way we can truly empty a sentence of meaning is by messing with inflection or by juxtaposing words out of syntactic order. It may well be impossible to produce a grammatically correct sentence that would not mean *something* to someone somewhere, even if all it signified were the absurdity of what had been said.

Syntax may well be arbitrary. The fact that from one language to another, speakers can signify the same thing by following a different word order shows that word order *per se* is not as essential as the socio-cognitive conventions that decide on what constitutes meaningful word order. However, the fact that the difference between SVO and SOV arrangements is in some part dependent on whether

---

[97] Ibid.

speech is inflected or not, the fact that visual language (Sign) obeys a different grammar and the fact that languages do not change or evolve at random, all urge us to be cautious even on this point. At any rate, at the level of shared cognition and communication, which is to say, at the level of living languages rather than Chomsky's hypothetical ideals, word order and other aspects of syntax are all meaningful. Breaking the rules of syntax means breaking the rules of language.

Why syntax rules

The proposition that syntax is not autonomous from semantics is highly relevant to second-language acquisition. English speakers who are learning French will misconstrue what they hear, even when they understand all the words in a given French sentence, if they cannot make sense of the novel word order. Interestingly, they can also be confused when they understand all the words in a given sentence whose word order corresponds to something meaningful and familiar in English. And in both cases, confusion occurs because learners trust their English syntactic instincts over their capacity to deduce from the communicative context, which is truly remarkable and, indeed, highlights the limits of communicative language pedagogies. What follows is a real-life example.

John was having no problem conversing, switching from the *passé composé* to the *imparfait*, shifting auxiliaries and imitating my verbal patterns (imitating was the point of the exercise) until this happened:
- Tu t'es réveillé de bonne heure aujourd'hui?
- Oui, je me suis réveillé de bonne heure, mais je me suis levé tard parce que j'étais fatigué
- Tu t'es couché à quelle heure?
- Je me suis couché après minuit. J'ai regardé un film.
- Alors, tu as déjeuné à quelle heure ce matin?

A puzzled look appears on John's face, he hesitates and says:
- Normalement, je prends le petit déjeuner à sept heures.
- Oui, mais aujourd'hui, tu as déjeuné à quelle heure?

John grows even more confused
- Can't I say, *je prends*?
- Well, you could but why are you switching tenses? What am I asking you?
- When I have breakfast?

Now I am puzzled, and I reply:
'But that would mean that we switched the conversation to what you do on a regular basis, while we were speaking about what you were doing yesterday.'
'I know, that's why I don't understand why you are asking me this.'

And then, *I* understand. John has actually heard my question in English: *You have breakfast*. This is truly fascinating. He has learned that *prendre le déjeuner* means 'to have breakfast'. He is either unaware or has forgotten that the word *déjeuner* can be a verb. Furthermore, he does not usually say 'I breakfast' or 'I breakfasted' in English. Interestingly, he has just stalled because he is conscious of a disconnect between what *he has heard* me say and the gist of the conversation. He has possibly noticed that when I said *tu as déjeuné*, I did not include the article (we do say *le déjeuner*), which adds to his confusion. And yet he cannot compensate for the gap between what he has heard and what he knows he should have heard. What he heard were the words *tu, as,* and *déjeuner* which he knows as well in French as in English, and it is this natural ease with the vocabulary and word order that has allowed his English syntax to reclaim control of the situation and induced him to discount the *passé composé* in favour of a subject-verb-object construction. John has heard *tu as déjeuner* (you have breakfast) and not *tu as déjeuné* – 'you have breakfasted'. Word order analogy has outplayed the semantic field, his basic knowledge of French grammar (a noun is usually preceded by a determiner) *and* the communicative context. This demonstrates the power of native syntax and the connection between meaning, but it is also a manifestation of a psychological state experienced by quite a few learners. In the language class, students pass through the looking glass into a world where nothing is as it seems. Their powers of observation become neutralised. They can no longer trust their communicative sense, which is to say their common sense, because common sense does not apply in a world where tables are shes and eggs are hes and where people not of it think not more than that. I can now explain to John:

> 'Oh, I know what's happening! *Déjeuner* is a verb here not a noun. I was asking you about when you breakfasted!'
>
> 'Ah, now I get it. *Aujourd'hui, j'ai déjeuné à huit heures.*'

When students hear a familiar French structure with a different word order from English, they immediately translate and transpose what they have heard into English. This is a very interesting response, and I will return to it when discussing teaching techniques in later chapters. For now, it is enough to point out that if a learner can translate and re-order what he has heard, it is because he has understood what was said. Therefore, he is not translating to understand, he is translating to understand *better*, because the word order of his own language makes more sense and is *more real* than the word order in the language he is learning.

    The fact that syntax conveys meaning and is therefore not independent from semantics does not invalidate the proposition that syntax and the lexicon are differentiated entities. There is at least a procedural benefit in separating the lexicon from the syntactic system for the purpose of linguistic analysis as well as for the purpose of teaching second languages, just as there is a practical advantage to dividing form and content when analysing a text. But here is where things cease to be straightforward: English, a largely isolating language, lends itself to this segmenting better than French, a largely inflecting language. Setting aside the more obvious semantic implications of syntax in English (e.g. he is stupid, he is being stupid), it is possible to split the semantic field between lexical units and syntax because English syntax is in large part concerned with word order. However, this is not the case in French, where word order depends on syntactic categories, where a basic noun-adjective-phrase requires determiners and modifiers to agree with the noun in gender and number, and where modifiers, subjects and objects may precede as well as follow headwords and verbs.

The syntactic problems experienced by English-speaking learners of French

Unless we teach grammar explicitly, it is both unfair and unrealistic to expect our students' linguistic knowledge to extend beyond what they already know, which in most cases is what they learned in primary school and amounts to an understanding of the basic classes of words as 'naming words', 'describing words' and 'doing words'. Students may well have a very good command of standard and literary English, a good grasp of style, nuances and so forth, but they know how to speak 'correctly' because they know what Standard English sounds and feels like, and not because they understand what it is made of, not because they understand grammatical forms or syntactic relationships. Even the plural of English nouns may not elicit grammatical awareness. Students know, of course, that an *s* means plural, and that plural means the opposite of singular and that it has to do with grammar, but what exactly, that is another matter. Putting an *s* at the end of a word is just a normal thing to do when there is more than one of anything. In the same vein, putting an *s* on the third person verbal ending is what you do because that is what you say. What this has to do with grammar is really someone else's guess.

Students who think of an *s* as a natural outcome, students who have not been taught about verbal endings and other grammatical conventions are legitimately puzzled by the possessive case *'s*, the *s* ending of possessive pronouns, and the contracted *'s* of 'he has' and 'he is', all of which they tend to attribute, for lack of a better alternative, to the overall nonsense ruling English orthography. Hence the difficulties many people encounter when they are writing English, and the lack of conventional rigour in all sorts of texts produced for public consumption in Australia today.

The problems engendered by our students' lack of explicit grammatical knowledge can only multiply when they are learning French. To give an idea: some of my private students thought that the verbal ending of the first person plural *–ons* is written with an *s* because *nous* is plural, and they were quite naturally baffled by the *s* at the end of the second person singular, not to mention the silent *nt* at the end of the third person plural, which they so often omit. Quite a few students are under the impression that the second person plural *vous* means 'they'. And unless we explain this explicitly, students do not generally notice or understand that third person means 'anything or anyone I am speaking about' which is why they say things like: *le monsieur il porte un chapeau*. If we stop to consider that, except for a few nouns (*oeil, ciel, aieul*) and those ending in *–al* and *–ail* (*cheval, email*), French substantives have no audible plural but nonetheless require the addition of an *s* or *x* in writing, and that nouns are not only gendered but that gender is made apparent by the grammatical relationship between the noun, the determiner and associated modifiers, we can appreciate that even a simple Noun-Phrase in French is completely off our students' linguistic radar. The article-noun phrase, which is the easiest thing to do in English because you just have to order the thing in the right way, presents immediate and dumbfounding difficulties for grammatically unschooled or grammatically unprepared Anglophones learning French (more on articles in Chapter VI).

Schmidt's observation of how young children and adults differ in the learning of first and second languages bears on this discussion: 'we would predict incomplete acquisition of form by adults to the extent that they do not deliberately attend to form, especially for redundant and communicatively less important grammatical features. Because children have less control over the spotlight of attention, they may not be able to avoid noticing these communicatively less important grammatical features...' In fact, these differing powers of observation may have less to do with language learning than with how we learn generally. There are several reasons for not noticing the details that connect salient items of information: one is poor learning skills and lack of discrimination, which is to say, not being able to differentiate between the relative value of various data, but another is actually the result of efficient learning. The older we are, the more we come to rely on *sign-posting* to take in what is going on around us. In all fields of life, including language, the more we know, the less observant we need to be of the details which we can take for granted. Details become apparent by their absence, not their presence. Anglophone learners of French are not usually aware that the verb 'to wait' meaning *attendre* is actually 'to wait for' as distinct from 'to wait on' (meaning *servir*) but they will notice that something has gone astray when a French speaker says 'I wait you'.

    As Schmidt argues, powers of observation have implications for second-language learning. Our students, being competent speakers of English, have no need to notice the functional words in their own language, as for example, prepositions. Without explicit grammatical instruction, therefore, we can only expect second-language learners to use linking functional words as they do when speaking English. And this results in one of two things: either students use functional words unconsciously (*j'attends pour vous*) or they do not notice them at all and drop them out of their sentence constructions. Hence, even in Year 12, students come up with statements like *je suis la gare*.

>'Can you tell me what you just said? In English?'
>'Yes, I am at the station.'
>'But you said: *je suis la gare*...'
>'Yes, I am at the station.' [Puzzled look on the student's face.]
>'If you say, *je suis la gare*, you are saying: I am the station. You need to say, I am **at** the station, *je suis **à** la gare*.'
>'Woops! I do too!' [Big smile on the student's face because 'I am the station' does sound funny and perhaps also because she now knows how to solve her problem.]

If students have not learned to identify their grammatical purpose or the rule, they do not hear the preposition. If students have learned the grammatical principle and the rule [whenever you locate something in space you need a preposition, and when you locate something generally, you need the preposition ***à***] and if they have learned to consider the grammatical purpose of their speech [I am locating in space generally], they do not only hear the preposition when I repeat *je suis **à** la gare*, they are highly unlikely to omit it in the first place.

Pinker's mentalese – Is language not thought?

The blanks between thoughts, the blanks between lexicon and syntax are obvious to the speaker who finds herself at a loss for a word or searching for the best way to phrase what she is meaning to say. Such gaps are also obvious from the listener's point of view. The listener is taking in the context of the conversation and may guess or even pre-empt the speaker's intention. Should the speaker use a wrong word by accident, the listener may not actually notice, or he may notice and simply restore the correct word in his head. Alternatively, if he is intent on asserting a certain position or if the wrong word truly causes ambiguity, he might suggest a clarification: 'Do you mean *x*?' Such events, according to Pinker, tell us that thought is not the same thing as language. Pinker suggests that thoughts are couched in some silent and universal medium of the brain, which he calls Mentalese, and which becomes 'clothed in words' whenever we need to communicate what we are thinking.[98] In *The Language Instinct* Pinker delivers a blow to what he calls 'conventional absurdity' by demonstrating that reasoning

---
[98] Pinker, op. cit., p. 45.

and thought actually exist outside of language. And Pinker manages this coup with ample and magnanimous helpings of words, of course, because how else could he think up such things if he did not have the words to think them with?

In fact, it is true that we do not think *only* in words. We are able to understand a great deal by observing the world around us and without using words. When I am crossing a road and gauging the distance separating me from an approaching car, I am evaluating but I am not verbalising. When the driver of the car motions for me to cross the road, I process her meaning without the need for words on either of our parts. Here, auditory and visual perceptions are sufficient, and besides, there is no need to process something which I have learned *through language* when I was a child: that cars move fast and that I should be hit by one with serious consequences if I were to walk across the road unwarily. Then, of course, if we are doing maths, we are not doing language, and if we are doing music, we are also not doing language. The same can be said of dance and other activities which actually require us to free our consciousness from words, as for example meditation – a state of mind that must be learned and is difficult to achieve. We also experience certain mental activities as wordless images. Like Pinker, I know people who are adamant that they think in images rather than verbally and it is true that we process much of what we hear and read, especially stories, by producing sympathetic mental images. Finally, we understand better when certain types of information come with images and graphs, thus proving the cliché that a picture is worth a thousand words. In short, speech does not always hold centre-stage in our external and internal landscapes or in our consciousness.

And yet, language is persistent. We search for the right word perhaps because thought precedes language as Pinker says, *or* perhaps we search for the right word because the right word already exists in our mind, in our memory; and perhaps we search for the right word because certain thoughts can only exist in language and on account of language. Hence, if we can't find the right word, we will make one up or we will use a word that can do the job, all the while knowing that we are approximating rather than expressing our thoughts, trading our frustrated desire to think for a feeling of incompleteness. At the same time, it is also true that language pops up and rambles on quite independently of our intentions. We catch ourselves thinking about something or thinking about nothing, by which we mean that the words floating in our heads are of no obvious consequence. We can find it extremely difficult to stop the verbal rattling in our heads when we are awake and we talk when we are asleep. Thus, we can be wordlessly conscious as well as verbally conscious and unconscious. But do rambling thoughts and speaking in our dreams prove that thinking is independent from language or that language is independent from thinking? Indeed, not only language but also images, sensory perceptions and emotions surface independently of our volition in our waking states as well as in our dreams. That we experience non-verbal and verbal events in full awareness and sub-conscious states, and that we communicate with and beyond language does not demonstrate that language is not a particular expression of cognition, of information processing and communication. Rather all of this confirms that our thought processes occur in parallel, sub-conscious, unconscious, conscious and just as importantly plural modes. If this is the case, isn't Pinker's Mentalese, more broadly and perhaps more simply speaking 'consciousness'?

What is a mental landscape without language?

What would the world be like if we did not have language? What was the world like before we learned to speak? Helen Keller had the rare experience of not only being able to remember how she learned to speak but of learning to speak in full consciousness of the fact, and she wrote about it in *The Story of My Life*. When she was devoid of speech, Helen was conscious and she was able to communicate. She had developed about sixty signs with which to communicate her needs. She made a cutting motion to signify bread, she motioned the handle of the freezer and made a shivering movement to signify ice cream, she made a drinking motion to signify milk. She would bring an object to show she wanted something. She would know if her mother was preparing to go out thanks to various clues and by feeling and smelling the clothes she wore, and she signified her own intention of going out by dressing in her going out clothes. Helen could feel the vibration of doors closing and the air movement of doors opening, and she knew that people communicated with their mouths, which she could feel with her hands. She could also feel people approaching her from the vibrations of the floor, and she knew who was approaching by scent and feel. She was conscious of how her actions affected others: she locked her teacher Anne Sullivan into her room and hid the key of the door for weeks. But none of this, Helen Keller identified as *thinking*. Helen had troubles describing the wordless world she inhabited, which in the end, she described as a world of 'sensation'.[99] The connection Helen Keller made to language, as is well known, came to her through the word w-a-t-e-r which Anne Sullivan spelt into her hand and which she suddenly connected to the cool thing flowing over her hand from the well pump. She described this connection to language in remarkable words, 'a misty consciousness as of something forgotten, a thrill of returning thought, and somehow the mystery of language was revealed to me.'[100] Anne Sullivan also described the event in a letter written 5 April 1887. 'She dropped the mug and stood as transfixed. A new light came into her face. She

---

[99] In the language of psychology, we may call this 'embodied consciousness' or *le ressenti*.
[100] Keller, op. cit., p. 23. Note that after losing her sight and hearing, Helen had quickly forgotten all the language she had learned as a toddler but for the word water that she pronounced wa-wa. It is not insignificant that language was revealed to her by connecting the tactile sign with the only spoken word she remembered.

spelled 'water' several times. Then she dropped on the ground and asked for its name and pointed to the pump and the trellis, and suddenly turning around she asked for my name. I spelled teacher (...) all the way back to the house she was highly excited and learned the name of every object she touched so that in a few hours she had added thirty new words to her vocabulary.'[101]

There was no doubt in Helen Keller's mind that what language had restored in her was the faculty of *thought*. Being able to name the things around her meant something brand new and profound, which she had not been able to do. Language gave Helen Keller another type of consciousness. Language gave her the ability *to think the world*. In a deeply moving passage, she wrote that as she named the things around her, she grew a sense of 'kinship with the world'. She wrote: 'everything I touched seemed to quiver with life.'[102] How and why a world defined by direct sensory experience should be less alive, less knowable, than a world translated into 'arbitrary' signs is truly a wonderful and impenetrable mystery and yet, it is an undeniable fact of human existence and of the human condition. Helen Keller's pre-language world was not only a world of sensation, it was also a world of frustration and indeed despair. That we experience *consciousness* outside of language, that we have moments of enlightenment outside of language, that we speak without thinking and speak when we are dreaming, does not take away from the fact that language (speech, gesture or touch) is what we think *with and in*. Language is to thinking as walking is to ambulating: we may not have to walk to move since we can crawl on all fours or hop on one leg, but walking is not only our preferred and best means of natural ambulation, it has no other purpose than ambulation. In the same vein, language serves no other purpose than to provide us with thinking and the means of communicating our thoughts.

Does multilingualism imply a plurality of thought?

According to Pinker, we can translate a sentence from one language to another because there is something below words, because language is independent from thought. In conversation with Jeffrey Mishlove, Pinker said this: 'The fact that you can translate at all, when you think about it, shows that there's got to be something other than words, because what would it mean for two sentences in different languages to be translations of each other, if not for the fact that both of them have the same meaning, where the meaning isn't exactly the same as either string of words?'[103] That the same meaning can be expressed across different sounds

---

[101] Keller, op. cit., p. 316.
[102] Keller, op. cit., p. 422.
[103] See Pinker, op. cit., p. 47; and Pinker in *Thinking allowed, Conversations on the leading edge of knowledge and discovery*, with Dr Jeffrey Mishlove, 'Language and Consciousness, Part 1: Are our thoughts constrained by language?' with Steven Pinker, Ph.D.

and syntactic structures is cause for wonder but it does not really prove that language is undifferentiated from thought (more below). Just as importantly, Pinker makes the assumption that we can actually translate any thought from one language to another, but can we? Is everything translatable?

Perhaps we can say something in one language and then express the same thing in any other language that we can speak well enough, not because thoughts have an existence outside of language but rather because all languages engage our cognition. The same thought can be expressed in different languages *because* language *is* thought. Evidently, we can say *la mesa* in Spanish for *la table* in French because we know what a table is and because we can learn new words for old things as well as learn new words for new things, and we can repurpose words, and we can also invent new ways of putting words together in any and all languages. In practical terms, however, we are likely to be far more at ease expressing ideas in one language than in another: be it the ambient language, our native language, or our working language. Many bilingual and multilingual speakers cannot shift from one language to another to speak about certain things even when they are equally proficient in their languages unless they are practised at speaking about these things in this *and* that language. This is why multilingual speakers who share languages blend and switch languages when they are speaking with each other, because it is easier to think this thing in this language and that thing in that language than to retrofit a thought into an unpractised language pattern. And indeed, this is partly why native speakers as well as highly capable second-language learners experience difficulties speaking and writing about topics they have not previously explored and thought about.

Bilingual and multilingual speakers experience just how undifferentiated thought and language can be when they attempt to have a discussion about something they learned in a second language and suddenly find themselves speaking like second-language learners in their own native tongue. At one level, we can attribute these difficulties to the connection between language and culture, but the fact is that we actually think best, we remember and reason most effectively in the language(s) in which we routinely think and learn. Quite significantly, for expatriates, this simply turns out to be the language(s) they work and think in rather than their first language. Hence, a bilingual speaker may find it just as difficult to shift from a hybridized second-language back into his or her own native language as any speaker may find switching between clearly differentiated languages. And this is why, of course, it is crucial for bilingual as well as for second-language students to learn to think and solve problems in the language they are wishing to master.

But then again, there is more to language than language itself. We say that the word 'bed' means the object 'bed' because that is what a bed is called, but we could equally say the word 'chair' to mean the object 'bed' if a bed were called a

---

http://www.williamjames.com/transcripts/pinker1.htm

chair. Then again, we can say 'chair' by accident when we mean to say 'bed', and our interlocutors may not even bother correcting us. More strangely, we can say that something is hot or that something is cool or sweet to mean the same thing, because we don't actually have a real word to express what we mean when we say: 'it's cool', 'awesome', 'terrific', 'great' and so forth. We can say 'that's clever' while our tone means that it's stupid. We can say 'thing' or *truc* when we can't think of a word. And yet, as second-language learners, we can also find ourselves resisting a shift from weather to *temps*, or from time to *heure*, from *la mer* to *el mar* because our maternal language is infused with a meaningfulness that plumbs depths greater than our perception allows us to fathom; because our mother tongue operates a gravitational principle of sorts, a habit of heart and mind, a vital force that anchors our words in anything but arbitrariness and mechanical process.

In a similar vein to Pinker, Wei argues that multilinguals do not think 'in a specific named language separately', he writes: 'We do not think in Arabic, Chinese, English, Russian, or Spanish; we think beyond the artificial boundaries of named languages in the language-of-thought.'[104] Speaking from personal experience, I believe this needs nuancing. I as well as many of my friends and students think in French, and/or Spanish, and/or Arabic. Rather than mix our languages, we dedicate them to specific thinking purposes. For example, I think about my family in France in French, and of my family in Australia in English. For a long time, I was quite incapable of speaking about anthropology in French, although I read anthropology in French. Like many multilingual speakers, I revert to my native language when doing arithmetic, especially to multiply and divide numbers.

Multilingual speakers may code-switch because they are highly proficient in several languages *or* because their proficiency is limited and they are doing the best they can with what they know. It is true that language boundaries are not like fences around territories. Languages always share a degree of overlap at some level of phonology, syntax and stylistics, and they are differentiated on account of *some* features. We may think of these differences in ultimate terms and conclude, as Pinker and Wei do, that they are only minor in the grander scheme of Human Language. Or we may acknowledge that even small differences between languages are enough to result in incomprehension, and that surmounting linguistic differences is not an easy thing to do. When we learn a new language, however, we don't have to learn absolutely everything, since we know what language is and does, and since there are overlaps between languages. It stands to reason that we can best learn and remember the features of a language that most resemble those of our own, as well as the features which we practise the most, and those we hear the most frequently. By extension, we are likely to hybridize languages, just as we hybridize cultural modes, by adapting significant or similar features into our existing systems of signification. To borrow from Marshall Sahlins, we may

---

[104] Wei, op. cit.

perceive new linguistic knowledge as we perceive new cultural items, 'in the received order of structure'.[105] French speakers tend to use the present perfect in English because this is the closest thing to their *passé composé* while English speakers privilege *chaque jour* over the use of *tous les jours* because *chaque jour* resembles 'every day'.

When individual speakers hybridize, they can mix syntax, morphology, metaphors, as well as words. We can mix chunks of languages and we can also retrieve semantically from one language and syntactically from another. However, if language hybridizing can take different shapes for different individual speakers, it is unlikely to be entirely random, and it is even less likely to be independent from the languages one already speaks. A French speaker who has been speaking English for a very long time and an English speaker learning French may both come up with *j'ai trouvé une combination*. But a French speaker is unlikely to come up with *ma langage est oon mélanger de Français et Anglais* while the learner of French might say something along this line. In all evidence, the difficulty of learning a new language does not lie with hybridizing, which we will do naturally enough, but in differentiating enough of the new language from the language(s) we already know. And this is more difficult than it sounds because in order to speak differentiated languages, we need to know what the differences between our languages are, where they lie and how they fit in with the features that are not different from our existing language(s). Once we have acquired a language as a differentiated system, we may still be subject to what Interlanguage theorists call interference or we may mix very little or even not at all, so that whatever we do and however we go about it, we use language to think and to communicate the best way we know.

Indeed, there is habit in thinking and not least there is also context since thinking is the product of cumulative personal and social experiences. Aspects of our thinking, of our languages and our cultures, are partially submerged in the individual and the collective unconscious. And so, even though we can potentially think about, think of and think up anything in any language, we have to contend with *unconscious* and *contextual* forces, some cultural, some intellectual, some coincidental, some personal and psychological, and indeed some linguistic–insofar as our languages express all of the above. Pinker objects to the idea that language is thought, on the basis that it implies that language *determines* thought and therefore that specific languages would limit our intellectual prospects. But if language *is* thought rather than a vector for thought, then it is also a manifestation of intelligence and it is necessarily malleable and mutable.

The hybridized idiolects of multilingual speakers are not manifestations of Pinker's Mentalese insofar as they are not pre-verbal, but indeed, verbal events. Nor are they the manifestations of thinking beyond what Wei calls 'named languages'. They are certainly the manifestation of our capacity for making

---

[105] Marshall Sahlins, 'Other Times, Other Customs: The Anthropology of History', *American Anthropologist* (3) 1985; pp. 517-541; p. 528.

language, for 'languaging' as theorists may call it, but they are nonetheless manifestations of the languages we have learned. My French may interfere with my English on occasion, but I can be quite certain that my English will not be affected by Thai tonal patterns, Sandawe clicks or German auxiliary rules, because I have never learned these languages. When we hybridize, the form may be novel on the surface but its sources are retrievable. I am not making this point solely for the sake of debating the nature of language but for pedagogical reasons. When we are able to trace errors back to a departure point (as illustrated by John's breakfasting in the discussion above), we are in a position to help second-language learners and second-language speakers to *better differentiate* their languages and to *progress beyond unconscious hybridization*.

Do multilingual speakers have plural minds?

According to Li Wei, it is 'inconceivable from existing research evidence that the human mind can be divided into different languages. Some earlier experimental data did show that processing later acquired language might involve certain neural networks that are not central to first language processing. But that tells us more about the process of language learning than about the representation of different languages in the human mind.'[106] In fact, as we will see below, Patricia Kuhl's research in neuroscience very much supports the proposition that acquiring additional languages involves neural networks that are not central to first language processing. This is also suggested by a fascinating phenomenon associated with the sequential learning of languages. When learning a third or fourth language, multilingual students often retrieve reflexively from the *last* language they learned or from the language they control the least, rather than from their native language or from the language that would prove most helpful on account of linguistic relatedness. For example, one of my students was raised in Italian, learned English naturally as a young immigrant, then learned German at school and ended up fluent in all three languages. When learning French with me, he recalls German words and English syntax reflexively rather than Italian, even though Italian, when I ask him to think about it, makes French so much more accessible. Likewise, when I was learning Spanish, I tended to retrieve Chinese rather than French even though French makes a far more obvious model. In sum, the brain or the mind is bringing 'like-items learned in like-experience' to the surface. To use a metaphor suited to our times: the mind/brain is doing a 'foreign language' search rather than searching for the 'true' meaning of a word as happens when we learn a second language. Once a language is acquired (i.e. fluent), language interference may come from several sources including one's native language. From personal experience, I now fall back on French grammar rather than Chinese when I speak

---

[106] Wei, op. cit.

Spanish, although I will occasionally recall Chinese (syntax and words) if I have not spoken Spanish for a long time. On the other hand, I never recall Spanish when I am speaking Chinese. If I have not spoken Chinese for a while, I only have trouble speaking, and my tones become especially unreliable.

Does this mean that we store languages in different parts of our brains or our minds? It is generally known that what we learn last is forgotten first but in the case of languages, it is also a known fact that even a first language may be forgotten in a second-language environment. Looking at the brain, functional neuroimaging is not conclusive: some studies have shown different patterns of cortical activation associated with different languages in some multilingual individuals and other studies have not. On the other hand, clinical studies conducted with people suffering from Alzheimer's disease show that multilingual patients regress to a primary language. In fact, language regression is an important diagnostic tool for detecting early signs of cognitive impairment or oncoming dementia in bilingual and multilingual people.[107] While none of this tells us where different languages may be located in the mind, these studies support the proposition that languages can co-exist in our minds as differentiated systems.

Some things *are* untranslatable

Whatever the level of skills of individual multilingual speakers, it is undeniable that some things worded in one language cannot just be worded in another, as for example poetry, which engages the phonetics, the social, the affective, the rhythms, the aesthetic and the intra-referential and reciprocal dimensions of language and culture. As Octavio Paz wrote, translating a poem means creating a new poem. Consider the line *il a mis son manteau de pluie* from Prévert's 'Déjeuner du Matin', a poem often used to teach the past tenses of French. The aesthetic and emotional power of this line lies in the softness of its sounds, in the interwoven symmetry of the two *m*-initialled words *mis* and *manteau de pluie*, and in the internal rhyme produced by their respective endings. This is obviously untranslatable into English. To cite Octavio Paz again, the phonetics of a poem are like music, they are unique. But the meaning expressed in that ineffable word-play *manteau de pluie* is just as untranslatable even though from the perspective of word order and word signification, the transposition into English is child's play: 'he put on his raincoat'. But with this, pretty much everything that is said in French is not so much evaporated as smashed to smithereens in English translation. Some things cannot be translated without annotation and explanation and some things remain unsaid because they are untranslatable – hence, the very subtle and difficult art of literary

---

[107] Aaron McMurray MD, Erin Saito, MSC, and Beau Nakamoto, MD, 'Language Preference and Development of Dementia Among Bilingual Individuals', *Hawaii Medical Journal*, 2009 Oct, 68(9); pp. 223–226.

translation and the remarkable linguistic abilities required for simultaneous interpreting. In fact, even perfectly banal utterances can prove difficult if not impossible to translate from one language to another. *On s' f'ra un p'tit coucou demain* has no equivalent in English, just as 'G'day mate' exists only in Australian English. Hence, we will borrow not only words but also whole phrases from other languages when novel ways of knowing, thinking, feeling, and doing make their way into our (collective) heads. It is easier to extend our thoughts by adopting novel words and phrases than to try to match our newly acquired consciousness into ill-fitting language.

Perhaps, indeed, language and thought are not indivisible but language and thought are at the very least symbiotic and they are more than convergent, for thought inhabits language and language has no existence outside of our thoughts. Language means a great deal to us as individuals and as social beings. We may say, without exaggeration, that it means the world to us: because language powers knowledge, communication, learning and imagination. Language is a world contained in a novel; language is how we construct abstraction, how we store, and share centuries of wisdom and folly, stories, beliefs, technologies and science; the means by which we pass all of this knowledge on to the next generations and go on to create and share new knowledge and new things. It is also the means by which those who preceded us continue to live besides us, the means by which we can know the past and imagine the future, by which we can express what we must do, might do, could do, should do as well as what we did, we are doing and we will do. Our mother tongue is the repository of our intelligence, our creativity, our emotions, memories, and affections – the knife that wounds, the balm that heals the wound, the pun that makes us laugh, the word that spreads love, the word that spreads hatred, the word that liberates or enslaves, the word that speaks the truth and the word that lies. Our language is the language of our fathers and our mothers, the voice we heard from the womb. Hence, this remarkable faculty for producing meaning out of organised and ordered breath (because all speech is breathing) is at once the definition and the expression of our personhood, our social-hood, our culture-hood, and our humanity. To our ancestors, breath was 'soul substance'. Giving our word is a sacred contract because it is giving a part of our vital self. In the twenty-first century, we are still bound to others by our words, the words we speak to each other and the words we sign on the dotted line.

THE SYSTEMIC NATURE OF LANGUAGE EXPLAINS THE DIFFICULTIES INVOLVED IN LEARNING A SECOND LANGUAGE

The degree of difficulty we encounter when learning a second language must surely be measured against the power that our native language has over our conscious and unconscious being. Our first language translates the world for us and bonds us to it and to each other. Learning a second language confuses the world and isolates us from others. A language we cannot understand is simply noise, perhaps a pleasant noise, but noise nonetheless. We hear what other languages sound like because we cannot understand them, whereas we cannot hear the sounds of our own language because those are immediately meaningful to us. In this acoustic hall of mirrors, however, there is more than intellectual and affective estrangement, there is also a resistance that is inherent to the property of systems. Language is an integrated system of ordered sounds, imagery, analogy and syntactic relationships, and it is also a biological system because it resides in the brain. We necessarily perceive as noise what is extraneous to our mother tongue because, like all systems, our language rejects what does not belong to its own rules, much as the rest of our body rejects implants and foreign objects. To be effective, language cannot *randomly* assimilate what does not fit its rules. In other words, it is not anxiety that creates a screen and stops the new language reaching our Language Acquisition Device, as Krashen proposes, but the 'device' itself that proves impervious to alien intrusion.

Research in neuroscience supports this observation. Looking at why adults lack the facility of acquiring language like infants do, neuroscientists initially posited that 'the development of the corpus callosum in the brain affected language learning (Lenneberg, 1967; Newport et al, 2001)'[108] Then, Newport raised the 'less is more' hypothesis, according to which infants' cognitive abilities were enhanced by their limitations. Infants learned more because they knew less (Newport 1990). Then, in laboratory experiments, Patricia Kuhl and colleagues (Kuhl 2004; Zhang et al, 2005, 2009) developed the concept of 'neural commitment': once a neural architecture is able to detect phonetic and prosodic patterns of speech established early in infancy for one language or another, it is set for maximal efficacy and 'impedes the learning of new patterns that do not conform'.[109]

These observations have profound implications for second-language pedagogies. On the one hand, they partly explain why we are likely to retain a 'foreign accent' in a second language, but they also explain why generations of students were able to learn Latin as a dead language. When learning a language means learning *something new* rather than learning *to speak* anew, the new knowledge (say French) does not have to compete with our existing sense of reality and modes of thinking and communicating (say English). Generations of students were once able to learn additional languages on the basis of general principles of grammar and phonology, by knowing what languages are made of and what they do, which is to say according to the traditional grammatical method. Surely, they were able to do this because it is possible to learn a second language as we learn other things in other knowledge fields.

---

[108] Quoted from Kuhl, op. cit.
[109] Ibid.

THE SOCIAL NATURE OF LANGUAGE ALSO EXPLAINS THE DIFFICULTIES INVOLVED IN LEARNING A SECOND LANGUAGE

The observations which I have made so far throw light on the many layers of difficulties involved in learning additional languages: why it is time-consuming to acquire new languages; why we are more likely to blend languages than to speak differentiated languages; and why, even when we can perform all the correct mental operations in a second language, these may not feel quite as real as they do in our native language unless or until we have experienced this language in genuine cultural and social contexts. To get an idea of the importance of the socio-cultural context, it is helpful to look at how multilingual speakers learn and retain languages.

As we all know, young children can acquire several languages at the same time in a natural manner through social interaction alone, and their brain *for the most part* will sort out what belongs to which language. I emphasised 'for the most part' because although the languages of native multilingual children may be perfectly differentiated, this is not true for all children. In fact, the linguistic competency of children and adults who have acquired several languages in early childhood can vary greatly between individuals, even within the same family, between siblings, between parents, between spouses. Furthermore, maintaining multilingual competency may depend on a multitude of factors, such as, for example, the opportunities to hear and speak one's languages, the interest people have in speaking their languages, the degree of their emotional attachment to their languages, their capacity for observation, their memory, and not least the level of formal knowledge they have acquired about and in their languages. Native multilingual speakers who use their languages regularly and interchangeably in monolingual environments may speak differentiated languages. When speaking with other multilinguals who share their languages, they may use one language or they may code-switch to suit their cognitive, social, cultural and communicative purpose. Multilingual speakers living in monolingual communities where they have little opportunity to speak all of their languages are likely to start blending the languages they do not speak when they finally have the opportunity to speak them. And multilingual speakers living in multilingual communities who have the opportunity to draw from different languages with other speakers will develop blended languages. Indeed, this is how dialects and languages emerge and evolve. Moreover, children raised in one language and schooled in another may well end up speaking a little of the home language and all of the language they first encountered at school. A person might maintain the language she learned up to the age of five and develop little more competency in it: she will be able to communicate a range of needs, but she may not be able to discuss complex ideas or use her first language to process complex thoughts, or she may process complex ideas in a hybridised form of her maternal language. Hence, concerned parents may encourage their children to study the home language in a second-language class, or they may send their children to a community school on Saturday mornings to improve their skills and learn to read and write.

As anyone who works or lives with multilingual speakers knows, multilingual speakers do not usually maintain all their languages in watertight categories and in optimal speaking and writing order at all times and under all and any circumstances. This holds true for persons who acquired languages naturally when they were small children as well as for those who learned languages sequentially later in life. Furthermore, while multilingual speakers may engage in purposeful and creative mixing, they can also be entirely unconscious of the degree to which their languages blend with one another, how *faux amis* become reconciled and word endings are interchanged. The skills of the natural language speaker are not those of the professionally trained translator and interpreter. Over time, a language that remains unspoken and unheard will lose its affective and cultural powers and under such circumstances, not only speech but also comprehension may become significantly reduced.

The point I am making here is that, as every language teacher and every multilingual speaker knows, language proficiency is dependent *on practice*. However, this self-evidence should not be taken at face value, because in the context of what I have just discussed, practice is also another word for social dependence and social interaction, for shared cognition and shared affect, and not just another word for exposure or repetition.

How then should English speakers learn French?

Language and language competency are mysterious, fluid and slippery. Acquiring a new language goes against our preferred brain processes as well as against cherished notions of reality and habits. There is something about second-language learning that is both like and unlike other types of learning. The words we remember are the words we understand *and* the words we use. They are the words we are conscious of *and* the words we practise; the words we encounter frequently, *and* the words we are aware of because we know the part they play in a connected whole. Ultimately, a second-language teaching method must benefit from recognising that a new language can be learned as anything else is learned, but that to become real, a language needs to be used for real and needs to 'feel' real; it needs to be heard, it needs to be spoken with others and it needs to be inhabited by thought and affect. So, how should we proceed?

Learning a language requires first of all that we learn its sounds and rhythms. Some students may find this difficult and daunting and others take to it like ducks to water. Native language phonology is powerful. Indeed, none of the students to whom I taught English, French, Spanish or Chinese ever learned any of these languages with anything else than their own accents. My Thai-, Chinese-, Farsi- and Spanish-speaking students did not learn French-accented English. They learned Thai-, Chinese-, Farsi- and Spanish-accented English. Evidently, we learn to pronounce a new language with varying degrees of success because the brain architecture, which our native phonological system has constructed, is rejecting the alien noises.[110] This also means that our articulatory muscles have trouble executing the new exercise, and that our 'inner ear' is not a very reliable tool (see Chapter VI). Once the sounds of the new language have been sufficiently internalised, however, we are able to learn new words relatively easily. The good news is that there exists a general agreement among French language teachers that the acquisition of vocabulary is the least problematic aspect of learning French. This is in part because we are used to naming and renaming things in our own language and because we never cease to learn new words in it, often with little effort:

'What do you call this thing?'
'A gasket.'
'Oh, okay, a gasket.'

Abstract words are more difficult to acquire because we must learn the ideas and the principles they embody, but we mostly manage the task, and we may even excel at it. Evidently, acquiring vocabulary in a new language is also easier to do when we can relate new words to similar words in our own language, such as, for example *moteur* and motor. English speakers can learn French words with relative ease because a substantial amount of vocabulary is common to both English and French, so much so in fact that numerous educational websites profess that speakers of English are already halfway to speaking French by virtue of these lexical commonalities. Of course, this view of things oversimplifies the task at hand. In order to hear, read and pronounce French words, learners have to learn to alter their English pronunciation, they have to become acquainted with the phonological conventions of the French language and of French spelling, and they must beware of *faux amis*. All this requires work. More importantly, in order to internalise French words, learners also have to make the new words real, and this involves more than memorisation. When learners encounter new words in French, they may encounter a distortion of their own words or simply *noise*. Either way, the new words they are learning are empty of the affect that fills their English words. To inject life into their new words, learners need *to experience* them, which they can do through etymological connections, through translation back and forth between English and French; by using and re-using words in grammatical context for true

---

[110] Kuhl, op. cit.

communicative and cognitive purposes; and not least by using their words in a memorable social context. At some point, a French word is acquired for good, just as an English word is.

Still, for English speakers, the most difficult part of learning French appears to lie with French syntax and its academic conventions. And it is really interesting that syntax should prove so much more difficult to learn than vocabulary. It is interesting and it does not entirely make sense. In absolute terms, a language comprises a limited number of syntactic rules as opposed to tens of thousands of words. Why should it be more difficult to acquire a relatively small number of grammatical principles than to acquire thousands of words? The answer to this question, I have come to believe, may lie in part in the fact that native syntax is more resilient and more resistant than native vocabulary, but it also has to do with the way we go about teaching grammar.

As noted by Pinker and Bodmer among others, languages can borrow widely from other languages but they tend to resist the inclusion of alien functional words. Borrowed vocabulary tends to be integrated into existing syntactic as well as phonological, morphological and semantic references.[111] Under certain political, economic and cultural pressures, languages may change drastically and indeed die, but under politically, socially and economically stable circumstances, we are unlikely to alter the rules of our own phonology and syntax so drastically that we risk ending our natural lives speaking a language our parents and our children would not understand. In addition, education, as, for example the study of literature and historical sources, allows old-fashioned and archaic language to remain meaningful long after it has fallen out of common use. Over long periods of time, however, the cumulation of relatively minor linguistic variations operates substantial changes, which is why today's French is not quite the same French that people spoke in the 1950s, or at the turn of the twentieth century, let alone in the time of Louis XIV. But then again, since there is no law of nature that culture may not attempt to improve, language evolution can be slowed and re-directed by political and cultural will, through administrative and educational action, as George Orwell argued in 'Politics and the English Language'. It is because government policy mandated that generations of children be schooled in standard forms of French that, with relatively little learning, people can still read Molière today with no difficulties. It is also because syntax consists of a limited number of rules that the alteration of only a few rules such as, for example, the discarding of nominal and adjectival gender, may alter a language in a profound manner – which is how Old English came to be transform into the gender-less and mostly isolating language which we speak today and which our ancestors would no more understand than we understand Old English. And this, in a nutshell, is why

---

[111] Pinker, op. cit., p. 111. In addition, Pinker notes that functional words give the most reliable clues to the structure of a sentence and he provides very amusing examples to make the point, see p.112.

learning to speak any language without paying close attention to the rules of its grammar adds up to approximating rather than speaking the language.

Australian learners of French who have not been sufficiently schooled in formal grammar are naturally oblivious of the syntax of their own language and they will naturally approach French as they use English, which is to say semantically. Hence, they will surf unconsciously on their native syntax, forgetting to conjugate verbs, forgetting adjectival agreements, forgetting or misusing prepositions, using articles randomly, confusing pronouns and their placement (*lui* and *le*, *qui* and *que*), and so forth. From this point on, linguistic proficiency becomes a matter of degree: interlocutors can compensate for grammatical errors but their accumulation will inevitably result in a French that has limited communicative, cultural and cognitive reach.

It seems quite simple after all. Our students' biological, social, affective, and linguistic apparatus is working against their acquiring French for the good reason that they already speak English or indeed English and other languages. It is difficult to acquire the syntax of another language because we cannot acquire a new grammar as we acquire new vocabulary, by simply renaming things. To acquire syntax, we must not only build new scaffolding but also learn new rules of cognition and communication. To do this, we need to *take notice* of the rules, something we did not have to do when we learned our mother tongue as babies. It is entirely possible for English speakers to acquire French to the highest degree of grammatical proficiency but there is no reason to believe that to conceive of a table as a 'she' and of a stool as a 'he', to accept a meaningless word order, to leap from an isolating language to an inflecting language, and to pick up the silent complexities of alien academic conventions is easy. There is even less reason to believe that all of this can be made more entertaining or more accessible by sidelining our students' intellectual faculties, their consciousness and their curiosity. And if the successful language classroom must engage students' cognitive powers, then it must necessarily engage what the communicative methods attempt to circumvent: the students' mother tongue.

Book Two

FRENCH GRAMMAR

HOW TO ORGANISE IT

AND

HOW TO TEACH IT

V

Mapping the French Language and Essentials of French Grammar

La grammaire étant l'art de parler et d'écrire

… is at the heart of the comparative-narrative approach to language learning and teaching. But the comparative-narrative approach does not teach grammar by rote. The comparative-narrative method does not treat grammar as a thing to be remembered or operated, as a mechanism or a machine, but as meaningful dynamics to be understood and to be experienced. In this chapter, I provide an overview of the essential concepts which students need to learn in order to begin to understand French grammar, along with an overview of essential structural categories and a discussion of significant structural differences between French and English. All of this is consistent with the grammatical instruction required in the Victorian upper-school curriculum. As the reader will see, I have rationalised grammatical categories and conventions not by simplifying or limiting the number of syntactic structures but by identifying the fundamental structures which English-speaking students need to learn in order to speak French. The reader, however, should be aware that this chapter offers a relatively limited sample of how I have mapped the French language, and does not include how to sequence the teaching of these structures. Finally, this chapter is concerned with the organisation of the knowledge field only. I discuss methods of teaching in subsequent chapters.

Syntax turns words into thoughts and meaningful speech
The drill method failed to teach French in a motivating manner because it treated grammar as a set of dead operations to be memorised through the repetitive practice of model examples. It was boring because grammar is not a mechanism,

and students are not machines. The communicative methods are failing at teaching French because they treat grammar as the ghost in the attic. But grammar is no dead thing. And syntax is not simply 'form', it is truly what breathes life into the lexicon; it is what allows words to morph into thoughts and into meaningful communicable language – meaningful at all levels because grammar not only carries the 'natural' syntax of a language, it also expresses and reflects a whole range of socially constructed conventions, which is to say, culture and socio-political relations. Striving for syntactic accuracy in our mother tongue usually means striving to meet the academic expectations of the standard language but striving for syntactic accuracy in a second language means striving to speak and write as native speakers speak and write. English-speaking learners of French not only have to contend with remembering accented and silent letters, gender inflection and conjugations, they also have to learn that the articles, the prepositions, the word order, the verb tenses and the grammatical cases governing French may have no direct correspondence or even equivalence in English. When teaching French to English speakers, we must put at least as much effort into teaching grammar as we do teaching vocabulary but we must also put some effort into teaching students *about* grammar because syntax, unlike vocabulary, cannot be substituted or traded for: it is the part of language that must be understood and that can be explained. The table is *la table* and philosophy is *la philosophie* and there is a reason why this is so.

The value of teaching grammar also lies in how we speak about it

As a compromise between teaching no grammar at all and teaching grammar reluctantly, teachers have been encouraged to teach French grammar incidentally, which is to say at the point when 'it is needed'. This falls in line with thinking that we acquire other languages by speaking them rather than by speaking about them, but at the bottom of this idea lies another matter of confusion to do with thinking of grammar as an oppressive system dictating normative and therefore artificial and elitist ways of saying things. No doubt, learning grammar *is* about learning academic conventions but learning *about* grammar is also about becoming conscious of the underlying forms of which we are not normally conscious when we speak. In fact, second-language learners need to learn grammar according to linguistic and prescriptive principles, and we can teach both grammars intelligently and critically. At this point, I should clarify that the grammar I teach and which I outline in this book is intended specifically to teach French to native English speakers who have a purely formal knowledge of grammar, a limited knowledge of grammar or indeed no knowledge of grammar at all. There are some significant differences between this grammar and the grammars that might be found in past and contemporary textbooks, whether the latter are aimed at second-language learners of French or at native speakers.

To begin with, there are a few differences of terminology. Naming the things we learn is integral to any learning process and this is what we do in any other sphere of school and life. We expect students to acquire the metalanguage of biology, maths and literary analysis, and indeed the second-language classroom cannot be the only place where students must be kept from using relevant terminology. When naming grammar, however, the *choice* of terminology makes a difference.

In a sentence such as *The dog is playing in the park*, students are more likely to grasp the logical and relational principles at work if I speak of a subject, a verb, a preposition and a circumstantial complement of location, than if I describe the said sentence as a 'subject-verb-plus-predicative-prepositional-phrase predicate'. The linguistic descriptor may be academically appropriate but it is bereft of the slightest whiff of democratic spirit. The point is important. When students understand that a 'circumstantial complement' is nothing more than how we complement the meaning of a verb by giving the circumstances in which the verb does its thing, which is to say, the when, why, how, and where of it (not a difficult concept to grasp), they can easily reflect on the fact that in English, when they locate something or someone in space, for example, *in* the park, *at* school, *on* the train, they use a preposition of sorts.[112] From this, it is a small step to understanding and remembering that they need to use a preposition in French *every time* they are locating something or someone in space wherever and whatever that space happens to be. The object of teaching grammar to second-language students is to make language more intelligible and to enable learning autonomy. Therefore, I use traditional grammatical terms when those make more obvious sense than linguistic terms, and linguistic terms when those are more intuitive than conventional terms, and when neither quite does the job, I coin a valid term. Students may also come up with formally valid terminology. For example, Lauren proposed to rename the prepositional function as 'leading' rather than 'introducing' the complement of the verb.

To be effective, grammatical instruction must show students how to *reason* about language. It must have depth, range and order: specific points must relate to general principles as well as to what has already been learned, and it must anticipate what will be taught later. Grammatical instruction needs to be in English for two reasons: firstly, to ensure that students understand the layers and the web of principles that structure the rules of all and any language including

---

[112] In the same vein, it is easier for students to grasp why/when/where phrases as complements of circumstances rather than as adverbial phrases. For the sake of simplicity, I also name subordinate (or dependent) clauses by referring to their most obvious function: time, cause, and so forth, or I may refer to these more generally as circumstantial. What is important is for students to be able to differentiate circumstantial clauses from relative and object clauses.

their own, and secondly, to ensure that students know the difference between English and French. Students have to understand what they do in English and how they say things in English in order to understand and *experience* what they need to do and say in French. Therefore, if students don't know what they are doing in English, their French teacher needs to explain English grammar.

Teaching Year 7-12 French with the comparative-narrative approach

No one devises a pedagogy to set students up for failure. The problems of teaching second languages are genuinely complex because learning languages, even in immersion, is rarely easy and it is always time-consuming. As in so many other areas of life where we have a lot at stake and all intentions to do good and well, language education is dogmatic; we are for this and against that rather than being for this in this context and for that in that context. Hence, we are against repetition because we are for creativity, we are against grammar because we are for natural speech, we are against language accuracy because we are for communication, we are against toil because we are for fun, we are against objective standards because we are for self-esteem, and so forth. Why, however, could we not be for all of these things in just the right amount in the right places? Why should we think of hard work as the opposite of fun? Surely both have their rewards. And of course, why can we not strive to teach students to master the fundamentals of the French language *and* provide them with communicative skills?

Evidently, in order to teach languages effectively, or indeed to teach anything effectively, we need to have some idea of the goal, of what it is that we want students to have learned at the end of a given process. As in all disciplines, setting goals and developing curriculum for language learners relies in part on convention and in part on renewable theoretical outlooks. But language teaching raises its own particular questions. For if we cannot expect Year 12 students who have not spent time in exchange programs to speak French fluently at the end of several years of schooling, what should we expect students to achieve, and more to the point, to gain from learning French?

The approach I am proposing is not a quick or an easy way to learn French. Rather, it is a measured, intelligent, profound and fascinating way of approaching language learning and teaching. It is a method that makes acquiring French possible while learning much that is worthwhile along the way. And this is a method that is as appealing to teach as it is to learn by. The comparative-narrative method aims for students:

1. to learn to speak French authentically and fluidly within the limitations of a content-based curriculum;
2. to acquire objective language skills and knowledge to continue learning;

3. to acquire language-based analytical skills to improve their command of language generally;
4. to expand their cultural capital;
5. to expand their general knowledge and interest in the world;
6. to become ever more reflective individuals and to know themselves better as cultural persons;
7. to expand their knowledge of the English language and acquire an explicit knowledge of English grammar; and
8. to be wonderstruck, and to remember their French class as a place where they learned to speak French and a great deal more.

These goals, as the reader can see, are entirely in line with current pedagogical expectations – and a little more. Regarding point 7, students of languages past and present frequently report that they learned more about English grammar in their language classes than in their English classes. This, we tend to treat as a side effect of learning languages – *l'ironie du sort*. I am proposing to validate this reality, and to recognise and embrace the fact that the language class is the perfect place for students to learn about English grammar. Regarding point 8, is what I am proposing here possible? Indeed, it is. And isn't it worth a try?

A cognitive and structural approach to the development of course materials

Whatever we learn, complex tasks are always made easier by breaking down the whole into manageable and appropriate sequential steps. In language learning, a balance must also be struck between working on bits of language (words and grammar points) and using the language for communication and composition. Ideally, every unit of instruction should result in students understanding, speaking, reading and writing *some* French, and understanding, speaking, reading, and writing *more* and/or *better* French than they were able to do before the unit.

Cognitive and communicative purpose should guide course development because knowing and communicating are what language is about. What do we do with language? We ask questions, we answer, we affirm, we negate, and we narrate. We name things and ourselves, we describe things and ourselves, we locate and relocate things in space and time; we do things under certain circumstances, when, where, why; and we do things to, for, against, with, and without each other; we express moods, feelings and states of body and mind; we compare, we evaluate, we relativise, we connect things to other things, we argue for and against, we hypothesise, we command, we imagine and we count. The advantage of a cognitive-structural approach over a communicative-situational approach lies in the fact that if we can name and describe one thing, we can potentially name and describe anything: *c'est un chien de chasse, c'est une économie de marché*. If we can locate one thing in space, we can locate anything else in space: *mon oncle habite à Melbourne, le collège est à cinq kilomètres, j'ai mal à la tête*. If we can attribute one thing, we can attribute everything: *la plume de ma tante, le siège du gouvernement*. But we can only apply the rules so long as we know the rules *and* our grammatical purpose, which is to say, so long as we understand that the structures we are learning have a broader functional purpose than our immediate semantic intention.

Evidently, sensible course development must not do away with situational learning, for words also acquire meaning according to context, which is to say according to the situation. Hence, I am not arguing that there is no place for communicative language in the comparative-narrative classroom. Rather, I am saying that situational learning needs to be integrated into a structural approach. Unlike a communicative-situational syllabus, a cognitive-structural syllabus does not teach grammar as a 'topic' in language learning. Rather, it allows grammar to drive instruction. Hence, it identifies foundational structures by considering their semantic reach and their inter-connectivity. The syllabus also takes into account which particular unit of grammar must be taught when and how each unit contributes to the larger project. Finally, the syllabus considers the degree of difficulty – the latter being dependent on 1) the distance between French and English, 2) the distance between the French which students need to learn and the French which they already know, and 3) the problems which aspects of standard French may present even for native French speakers.

Developing a French language course based on these principles is a balancing act. For example, students find it more difficult to master articles than to master object pronouns because articles in French differ substantially from articles in English. Nevertheless, articles must be taught from the moment we introduce students to naming things because one cannot speak French without using nouns and articles, and because articles are the key to gender and plural. We can meet these challenges with careful sequencing and planning, and by taking a helical approach rather than a brick by brick approach. This is why, rather than building or scaffolding, I think of the French class as *growing* students' language.

A comparative-narrative language course is built on a helical approach rather than a brick by brick approach

The helical approach addresses three problems of second-language learning: that some aspects of grammar can only be assimilated in small bites, that aspects of grammar may be partially rather than wholly understood, and that students often forget what they have learned. The helical approach helps students acquire language by visiting and revisiting language units and grammatical concepts. These cycles allow students to experience, and then to re-experience, learn, re-learn and learn more on subsequent rounds. The helical approach also allows a teacher to decide on how much information and practice is just right for students at a given time and how to adapt to students' needs, knowing that a particular knowledge point and even a whole language unit will be revisited at a later date.

Illustrating the helical approach

In any complex area of knowledge, we do not usually realise the full implications of what we have learned until we have acquired more knowledge. To put it another way: we don't really know what we know until we learn something else about what we have learned. The helical approach takes this into account. For example, when I first introduce articles, students can accept that *le*, *la* and *les* are all aspects of 'the'. The difficulty lies in understanding gender and number rather than the fact of the article. Where the indefinite articles are concerned, the issue of gender aside, students learn easily enough that *un* and *une* are like 'a/an'. However, they do find it remarkable that there is a difference of meaning between 'the' and 'a/an' – because they have never thought about this before. They also find it difficult to comprehend that *des* is the plural of *un* and *une* because the plural article does not exist in English. They understand this better, and are therefore better able to use articles, when they are made aware that in French, it is the determiner that marks the plural of a noun whereas in English, it is the *s* at the end of the noun. Of course, French adds an *s* at the end of plural nouns in writing but this *s* is silent.

Students get the *idea* of gender and plural without a problem if this is taught explicitly, experientially and systematically, although retaining gender is another story (See Chapter VI). They are also able to differentiate between *les* and *des* if we explain what is meant by definite and indefinite articles, if we follow through with specific experiential exercises and we continue to treat articles as an important part of speech in all subsequent classes. Students will fully appreciate the concept of definite and indefinite when they have learned about other types of indefinites. We will revisit the indefinite articles and other indefinite determiners (*quelques, plusieurs, aucun, un peu de, beaucoup de*), when we learn about the indefinite direct object pronoun *en*, and the third-person indefinite pronoun *on*. Having learned the notion of definite and indefinite, students will be able to identify words like *quelqu'un, certains, personne* as indefinite pronouns. They will also able to understand the function of the indefinite relative pronouns *ce qui, ce que*, etc.

➢ Note: I have explained how to teach articles in Chapter VI.

THE KNOWLEDGE FIELD: IDENTIFYING THE CORE STRUCTURES OF FRENCH

While the way to learn a difficult skill is to break constituent elements into manageable steps, a good way to teach something difficult is to begin with what Bodmer called a bird's eye view of the whole. The map I have devised for the teaching and learning of French grammar is based on the identification of fundamental structural categories (for the purpose of teaching French to English speakers) and the subcategories each of these commands. Three groups of words command the fundamentals of French grammar; they are nouns, pronouns and verbs. The helical approach involves moving back and forth and weaving through these three structural categories.

A bird's eye view of the basic grammatical structures and functions in French

- ➢ Nouns and their attendants: articles and other determiners (possessive, demonstrative, indefinite and quantifying) and descriptive adjectives; common nouns almost always require the use of a determiner; nouns elicit relative clauses headed by relative pronouns; compound nouns are often expressed as prepositional noun-phrases as is the complement of possession; nouns inflect to show plural; their attendants inflect to agree in gender and plural.

- ➢ A very large number of pronouns: personal, possessive, demonstrative, indefinite, locative, directional and relative pronouns assume the functions of nouns; aside from some indefinite pronouns (e.g. *personne/rien*), pronouns inflect to show gender and plural; personal, locative/directional, relative, and interrogative pronouns are also case sensitive. Pronouns and verbs drive questioning. Pronominal word order differs from nominal word order.

- ➢ Eight types of verbs command the fundamental structures and substructures of French: 1) *être, avoir, aller* (stative, possessive, and locative functions; auxiliary function); 2) action verbs (intransitive and transitive commanding nominal and infinitive objects); 3) action verbs (double transitives commanding nominal and infinitive objects); 4) action verbs (transitive indirect followed by animate and inanimate indirect object and other prepositional complements; 5) stative-locative and directional verbs followed by locative and directional complements; 6) reflexive verbs and verbs used reflexively (direct and indirect transitive; action; locative); 7) modals and states of mind (transitive + noun and transitive + infinitive); 8) catenative verbs (*faire* + infinitive, *laisser* and verbs of perception +

infinitive). Impersonal verbs (third person only verbs) may be fitted in the eight categories aforementioned.

Verbs conjugate, marking person, mood, time, aspect and voice (active, passive and reflexive). Verbs obey and control the role players (subject, objects, instrumentals), and the modifiers or circumstantial complements (locative, directional, time, cause, etc.). Nominal indirect objects, instrumental and circumstantial complements are introduced by prepositions as are some infinitive object complements. Types of verbs command past participle agreements. Verbs elicit the subordinate clauses headed by conjunctions. Verbs drive negation and verbs and pronouns drive questioning.

Looking at this bird's eye view, we can confirm that our students are engaged in a serious learning venture but a venture with a beginning, a fair bit in the middle, and an end in sight, the latter should ideally correspond to the end of Year 11.

What students learn, when, and for which purpose
The grammar outlined in this chapter can be taught to students in Years 7-11, although the more complex sentence structures may be fully mastered in the first term of Year 12. If students have not learned grammar explicitly in the lower-school, teachers will not be wasting their time if they decide to focus on grammar in Year 11. Upper-school students learn grammar with great interest as they have the benefit of the partial knowledge of the language and have a lot of questions about it. Formal grammatical instruction puts into order what students have been taught implicitly and unsystematically and can thus dispel many areas of confusion.

Obviously, I cannot claim that mastering this core grammar will result in students speaking French like native speakers. However, mastering fundamental structures will enable students to speak with relative ease about a great deal. If they have mastered the greater part of the language map detailed in this chapter, students who decide to stop French at the end of Year 10 will have acquired the communicative skills to speak some French in many circumstances. They will also have acquired significant transferable skills for learning other languages, and for improving their knowledge of Standard English. Should students decide to pursue their French studies after Year 10, they will be well positioned to engage in more complex tasks, to absorb more complex and nuanced language, to deepen their understanding and their use of the language through literature and other media.

AN OVERVIEW OF ESSENTIAL GRAMMATICAL CONCEPTS

Students are about to embark on a journey of discovery. Grammar is the art of reflection, and as such, it is not a motor and not quite a computer program. In order to reason grammatically, however, learners will need to understand and know the following concepts.

General concepts and terminology
- Inflection (external and internal)
- Agreement
- Grammatical function
- Notion/function
- Person
- Gender
- Number (plural/singular)
- Headword
- Simple and compound (verbs, nouns)
- Antecedent
- Determiner
- Modifier and modified
- Phrase, clause, sentence
- Prefixes, suffixes
- Word classes (nouns, adjectives, articles, verbs, adverbs, prepositions, conjunctions, pronouns, and interjections and their adjectival references: nominal, adjectival, pronominal, prepositional).
- Students need to know how to identify word classes according to morphology and, very importantly in English, according to what a word does, which is to say according to grammatical function: e.g. a learner, to learn (I learn); education, an educator, to educate; a prison, a prisoner, to imprison; however: 'Love makes the world go round' (noun), and 'I love you' (verb).
- Stem and ending
- Auxiliary

Students learn about semantic units
Students need to learn that, in both English and French, a semantic unit may be phrasal, which is to say that it may use several words to mean one thing, as for example:
- Compound nouns: washing machine, swimming pool
- Prepositional phrases: in front of, next to, because of

- Phrasal verbs: to go up, to look after, etc.

Students also need to learn that some phrasal units in English correspond to single words in French – to go up: *monter*; to look for: *chercher*; in front of: *devant*; swimming pool: *piscine*, and the other way around – because: *à cause de;* to visit: *rendre visite à*…

Students need to learn to differentiate a simple conjugation from a compound conjugation, and a simple noun from a compound noun. They will also need to learn that compound nouns in French may require a preposition: *une salle de bain*, *une machine à laver*. I explore the latter below to provide an example of the method.

Compound nouns: general notions
The prepositional use of *à*, *de*, and *en* in the formation of French compound nouns is neither lexical nor random but syntactically dependent on the class of words used to complement the headword. The basic structure is noun + *de* + noun (*une salle de bain*) and noun + *à* + infinitive verb (*une salle à manger*). However, prepositional use is also dependent on the **deep grammar** ruling the compound construction. For example, *un verre de vin, une tasse de thé* can be understood as 'someting full of' or simply measurement which is just like English: *un litre de lait, une cuillerée de sucre, un mètre de soie, une tasse de thé, un verre de vin*. On the other hand, in the construction noun + *à* + noun (*un verre à vin*), the preposition *à* implies an underlying verb.

When *à* implies an underlying verb and...
 ...*the headword does something to the modifier*
- un couteau à pain; un couteau à poisson
- un couteau à (couper le) pain; un couteau à (couper le) poisson as opposed to un couteau de cuisine

 ...*the headword does something with the modifier*
- un bateau à voile, un stylo à encre
- un bateau (qui fonctionne avec) une voile, etc.

When the headword is *made of* the modifier, the compound is formed with *en*
- un pot en terre
- un bracelet en or
- un couteau en plastique
- une robe en soie

Note 1: Just as we can say a wooden table or a wood table in English, in French we can say *une table en bois, une table de bois, un robe en soie* or *une robe de soie* We can opt to link two nouns with *de* when there is no ambiguity, no risk of confusing what a thing is made from with what it might contain or what it might measure. There is no chance of filling up a table with wood or a dress with silk. On the other hand, there may be a risk of ambiguity if we say *un sac de coton* when we mean *un sac en coton*.

Note 2: There is also an idea that to use *de* instead of *en*, as for example, *une table de bois* or even *un pot de terre* (which is ambiguous) is more elegant than using *en, mais ça, c'est peut-être la faute à Gavroche.*

Compound nouns formed with a verb + noun
- The verb + noun compounds obey the order of V-O predicate: *un lave-vaisselle; un porte-clé; un portemanteau.*

Compound nouns formed with a modifying prefix + noun, adjective + noun, or adverb + noun
- *autoroute, grand-père, avant-garde*: the modifier comes before the noun.

  ➤ Note: more on compound nouns in Chapter VII (pp. 216-7).

Students learn about relational function

Object complements
Students need to be able to identify relational function, which is to say, to identify and name the role players: subject, direct object, the indirect object/dative case (also called the attribution object or the second object) and the other oblique complements (indirect object/ instrumental/ cause and so forth). These relationships establish the rules governing the agreements of the past participle, the rules governing prepositional use, and the choice of pronouns, i.e. *me/moi; toi/te; le/la/les//en; se; lui/leur/ lui/elle/ eux/ elles* as well as the placement of these pronouns in relation to the verb.

Circumstantial complements
Students need to identify the modifiers as complements of circumstances, things which complement the meaning of the verb by telling us the circumstances in which the action takes place – location, time, cause, intention – almost all of which are introduced by prepositions in French.

Clausal complements

Students need to learn to identify main clauses and subordinate clauses; to identify how subordinate object clauses and subordinate circumstantial clauses are introduced by conjunctions; they need to learn to identify relative clauses which complement a noun, noun-phrase or a clause and to identify the relevant relative pronouns. They also need to know that conjunctions and relative pronouns can never be omitted in French as they may be in English.

A STRUCTURAL-FUNCTIONAL MAP OF SIMPLE FRENCH SENTENCES

The lists given below represent the fundamental structures of French as they may be encountered in everyday speech and in our textbooks.

Five basic NP + V+ adjectives/ nouns/ noun phrases

1) NP + V +N
La dame est professeur.
2) NP + V + Adj
La dame est grande.
3) NP + V + NP
Le chien mange un os.
4) NP + V + NP + [*prep* + NP]
La dame donne un os au chien.
5) NP + V + [*prep* + NP] + [*prep* + NP] + [*prep* + NP]
La dame habite à Paris dans un studio, en hiver, à cause du froid, etc.

Three NP + V+ infinitive phrases

NP + V + à N-P + *prep* + infinitive V + NP
La dame demande au chien de faire le beau; la dame apprend au chien à faire le beau.
NP + V + NP + *prep* + infinitive V + NP
La dame aide le monsieur à monter l'escalier.
N+ V + infinitive V (+ NP)

La dame aime écouter la radio; elle fait rire les enfants; elle écoute chanter le monsieur; elle est partie travailler.

Six basic pronominal structures calling for many types of pronouns

1) Subj + Pr + V
Je le regarde, j'en achète; j'y vais; j'en viens; j'en parle; j'y pense; je me lève; ils se disputent.
2) Subj + Pr + Pr + V
Je lui en parle, il me l'a raconté.
3) Subj + Pr + V +*prep* + Pr
Je l'ai regardé avec lui; j'en parle avec eux.
4) Subj + V + Pr.
Il aime, déteste, adore ça.
5) Subj + V + *prep* + Pr.
Elle travaille pour ça, avec cela, pour rien.
6) Subj + Pr + V + infinitive V
Elle les laisse faire; elle les écoute chanter; elle leur fait apprendre les conjugaisons.

If we compare the first two groups of structures with the third group concerned with the pronominal constructions, it becomes obvious that the complexities of French grammar hinge not so much on the way we order and join different types of words (nouns, adjectives, verbs, prepositions, etc.) but on the way types of verbs call for different role players in nominal, pronominal and infinitive constructions. In fact, eight classes of verbs command the most fundamental structures and substructures of French. I have mapped these verbs and the structures they elicit in the following pages.

EIGHT CLASSES OF VERBS PRODUCE THE FOLLOWING FUNDAMENTAL STRUCTURES

1) STATIVE VERBS – ÊTRE, AVOIR, ALLER

Être
Subject + *être* + Attribute [adjective/noun]
The attribute, adjective or noun, agrees with the subject
- Elle est grande; elle est chanteuse.

The pronominal attributes are *moi/toi/lui/elle/nous/vous/eux/elles* and the word order remains SVA.
- C'est moi, c'est toi.

Subject + *être* + Attribute + *de* + infinitive V + complement
- Il est heureux *de* revoir ses parents.

Note: The verb *être* also expresses location (*je suis à la gare*), and substitutes for the verb *aller* in familiar speech: *j'ai été au marché* ('I've been to the market'). In the pronominal form, the order is S + Loc + V: *j'y suis*; *j'y ai été*.

Avoir
Subject + *avoir* + DO [noun]
This is a SVO structure.
- J'ai faim; soif; froid; chaud; peur; sommeil; honte; mal.

Avoir is transitive and makes use of the indefinite and definite direct object pronouns; in the pronominal form the word order is SOV.
- J'en ai deux.
- Je les ai.

Subject + *avoir* + DO + *prep* + infinitive V
- J'ai envie/besoin/peur/l'occasion/la chance *de* partir (stative).
- J'ai *à* lui parler; des choses *à* faire; du temps *à* perdre (modal/lexical)

Both *être* and *avoir* are conjugated with the auxiliary *avoir* in compound tenses. The past participle *été* is always *invariable* because *être* is not followed by a DO complement but by an attribute of the subject or a locative complement. The attribute agrees with the subject of the verb *être* and the past participle of the verb *être* plays no role in this arrangement:
- Elle a été très contente.
- Je reconnaissais la petite fille qu'elle avait été.

On the other hand, the verb *avoir* does take a direct object, and so the past participle of *avoir* (*eu*) agrees with the DO if the latter is placed before the verb:
- Je les ai eues à bon prix.

Aller

Subject + *aller* + Adverb
- Je vais bien.

In the past tense, the stative *aller* logically requires the *imparfait*, which is the stative aspect.

2) ACTION VERBS + TRANSITIVE SINGLE OBJECT

SINGLE DIRECT OBJECT

When the direct object is a noun
1) Subject + Action Verb + Definite Direct Object + *prep* + Complement of Circumstances. This is a SVO structure.
- Je garde les enfants à la maison tous les soirs pendant la semaine.

In the pronominal form the structure is SOV and the pronouns are *me/te/le/la/nous/vous/les*.
- Je les garde à la maison; je les ai gardés.

These verbs are conjugated with *avoir* in compound tenses. The past participle agrees with the direct object when the latter is in front of the verb.

2) Subject + Action Verb + Indefinite Direct Object + Complement of Circumstances. The structure is SVO.
- J'achète du chocolat tous les lundis.

In the pronominal form the structure is SOV and the pronoun used is *en*.
- J'en achète tous les lundis.

These verbs are conjugated with *avoir* in compound tenses. The past participle is *invariable* because *en* is indefinite and neutral.

When the Direct Object is an infinitive verb or an infinitive clause
Subject + Action Verb + *prep* + infinitive V
The structure is SVO.
- J'arrête **de** parler.
- Il a commencé **à** parler de ses problèmes.
- J'exige **de** partir.
- Je **l'**exige.

Unlike nominal direct objects, the infinitive object is linked by the prepositions *à* or *de*. Note the use of the direct object pronoun in the last example. In complex sentences where the object clause contains a conjugated verb, the subordinate clause is introduced by *que*: *j'exige qu'il vienne*.

SINGLE (Indirect) DATIVE OBJECT

Subject + Action/Transmission Verb + *à* + Dative (+ *prep* + Complement of Circumstances)
- J'ai parlé aux enfants (dans leur chambre).
[S +V + *prep* +Dat]

In the pronominal form the structure is SOV and the pronouns are *me, te, lui, nous, vous, leur*.
- Je leur ai parlé (dans leur chambre).
[S + Dat + V]

The verb is conjugated with *avoir* in compound tenses. The past participle is invariable because the dative complement is an indirect object.

3) ACTION/ TRANSMISSION VERBS - DOUBLE-TRANSITIVE

When the Direct Object is a noun
1) Subject + Action/Transmission V + Indefinite Nominal DO + *à* + Dative
[S + V + DO + *à* + Dat]
- La dame donne du chocolat aux enfants.

In the pronominal form, the structure is: S + Dat + DO + V. The dative pronouns are: *me, te, lui, nous, vous, leur* and the direct object pronoun is the indefinite pronoun *en*.
- La dame leur en donne.
- La dame leur en a donné.

The verb is conjugated with *avoir* in compound tenses. The past participle in the example above is invariable because the direct object *en* is indefinite.

2) Subject + Action/Transmission V + Do + à + Dative
[S + DO + V + à + Dat]
- La dame a donné les chocolats aux enfants.

In the pronominal form the structure is S + Dat + DO + V. The dative pronouns are: *me, te, lui, nous, vous, leur*. The direct object pronouns for this structure are *le, la, les* and *en*, but note that the word order excludes the use of two *l*-initialled pronouns.
- La dame t'en as donné.
- La dame lui en a donné.
- La dame leur en a parlé.
- Tu me les as donné(e)s.
- Elle nous les a présenté(e)s.
- Je vous les ai envoyé(e)s.

<u>With two *l*-initialled pronouns</u>
When the dative and the DO pronouns are both *l*-initialled, the shortest sounding pronoun comes first. Note that this is a phonetic and not a syntactic rule.
- La dame les leur a donnés.

The verb takes *avoir* in compound tenses. The past participle agrees with the DO if it is on front of the verb.

When linking an infinitive verb to a clause containing a dative construction
We link an infinitive to a verb + dative construction by *de* or (less frequently) *à*. The infinitive complement may also be replaced by the direct object pronoun *le*. We can consider the infinitive the DO of the first verb or the dative can be construed as the semantic subject of the infinitive. In speech, it is often omitted if two third-person pronouns are involved. It is also barely audible.

Subject + Action V + *à* + Dative + *de/à* + infinitive V
- J'ai demandé aux enfants de parler français.
- Il a appris aux enfants à parler français.

In the pronominal form, the structure is S O V and the pronoun is *le*.
- Je (le) leur ai demandé.
- Il (le) leur a appris.

These verbs are conjugated with *avoir* in compound tenses, and they follow the usual rules. Since in all the structures listed above the DO is an infinitive phrase, and therefore neutral and invariable, the past participle is invariable when the verb is used with the direct object pronoun.

4) ACTION VERBS – TRANSITIVE INDIRECT

When *à* and *de* mean 'about' or 'of'

1) In the pronominal form the structure may be SVO
- J'ai pensé à lui/à elle.
- Il a pensé à moi.
- Tu as parlé d'eux/d'elles.
- Vous avez parlé de lui.
- Tu as parlé de ça.

Using the pronouns y *and* en

2) When using *third-person* pronouns, the structure is dependent on whether the antecedent is animate or inanimate.

A - Subject + Action Verb + *à/de* +Indirect Object Animate [SVO] or [SOV]
- J'ai pensé à mon amie: j'ai pensé à elle or j' y ai pensé.
- J'ai parlé de mes amies: j'ai parlé d'elles or j' en ai parlé.

B - Subject + Action Verb + *à* + Indirect Objects Inanimate [SOV only]
- J'ai pensé à mon voyage: j' y ai pensé
- J'ai parlé de mon voyage: j' en ai parlé.

In other words, we can say *je pense à elle, j'y ai pensé,* and *j'ai parlé de lui, j'en ai parlé* when speaking about persons but we cannot use *à lui, à elle* or *de lui, d'elle* when referring to things and concepts.

NOTE: With the action/transmission verbs given in previous sections, the *nominal direct objet* was placed directly next to the verb while *the infinitives* introduced by the prepositions ***de*** or ***à*** were also direct object complements. In the above structures, the complements introduced by ***à*** or ***de*** are <u>indirect object complements</u> but they are not <u>datives</u>. In the pronominal form, therefore, the important thing is to identify whether the indirect object is inanimate or animate: the animate object pronoun follows the prepositional verb: *moi/toi/lui/elle/ etc.* or (if using a third-person) it may also appear before the verb as ***y*** or ***en***. Inanimate indirect object pronouns may be expressed with ***y*** or ***en*** and thus precede the verb or they may be expressed with *ceci/cela/ça* and follow the verb.

Subject + Verb + *de* + Indirect Object
- Je rêve de grands voyages; j'en rêve
    The nominal antecedent is inanimate → *en*
- Je rêve de voyager très loin; j'en rêve
    The antecedent is the infinitive verb and the antecedent is inanimate → *en*
- Je rêve de mon ami(e); je rêve de lui/elle
    The nominal antecedent is animate → *lui/elle* (or *j'en rêve*)

All the above are conjugated with *avoir* in compound tenses. The past participle is invariable since the object complement is indirect.

PHRASAL VERBS

It is helpful to encourage students to think of the verbs that must be followed by the prepositions ***à*** and ***de*** as phrasal, as for example: *jouer de, jouer à* as distinct from *jouer; servir à quelque chose* as distinct from *servir quelque chose à quelqu'un*. It is also important to identify the complements in *répondre à une question* and *répondre à quelqu'un* not as 1) a thing and 2) a person but as 1) phrasal verb + indirect object and 2) verb + dative. The former elicits the indirect object pronoun *y*, the latter elicits the dative pronouns *lui* and *leur* in the third persons.

NOTE: a few verbs such as *ressembler à, résister à* use the dative pronoun to reference persons: *Il ressemble à sa mère: il lui ressemble*; and the indirect object pronoun *y* to reference an inanimate object: *Cette robe ressemble à la mienne; elle y ressemble*.

OTHER COMPLEMENTS INTRODUCED BY PREPOSITIONS

Other indirect object complements introduced by prepositions (*avec, à cause de, pour, sans, etc.*) are always placed after the verb. They call for the *animate* oblique pronouns *moi, toi, lui, elle, nous, vous, eux, elles*, and the *inanimate* pronouns *ceci/cela*.

Subject + Action Verb + *prep* [*avec, sans, à cause de, etc.*] + Animate Complement
- Je suis allé au cinema avec (sans) mon amie.

In the pronominal form:
- Je suis allée au cinéma avec (sans) elle.

Subject + Action Verb + *prep* [*avec, sans, à cause de, etc.*] + Inanimate Complement
- J'ai écrit avec un stylo bleu.

In the pronominal form:
- J'ai écrit avec ceci/cela/ça.

5) LOCATIVE/DIRECTIONAL VERBS (VERBS OF MOTION)

A verb of motion or displacement (location/direction) elicits the questions where, where to, where from?

Subject + Verb + *prep* + Location/Direction
- Je suis à Paris
- Je vais à Paris.
- Je viens de Paris.
- Il est tombé dans l'eau.
- Elle est montée sur la chaise.

In the pronominal form, locative and directional complements elicit the structure is S + LOC/DIR + V.
- J'y suis; j'y vais; j' en viens; j'y suis allée; elle en sont revenues; j'y suis née; il y est mort.

With the exception of the locative *être*, verbs of location and direction are conjugated with *être* in compound tenses. The past participle agrees with the subject.

NOTE: When *monter, descendre, sortir, rentrer* are followed by a direct object, they are no longer verbs of motion but verbs of action. A verb of action elicits the question 'doing *what?*' Verbs of action are conjugated with *avoir* in the active voice and their past participle agrees with the DO if it is placed before the verb: *j'ai monté les valises; je les ai montées.*

When followed by an infinitive
When verbs of motion are followed by an infinitive, the infinitive is placed directly after the conjugated verb.

Subject + Verb + infinitive V
- Je pars travailler à dix heures.
- Je suis venue chercher les enfants.
- Je suis sortie faire des courses.

Note that the infinitive is here a complement of intention (*complément de but*) which, in English, is elicited by the preposition 'to' meaning 'in order to': I came (in order) to take the children home.

6) THE REFLEXIVE VOICE AND THE REFLEXIVE VERBS

All reflexive verbs and all verbs used in the reflexive voice are conjugated with *être* in compound tenses.

<u>1) When verbs are used in the reflexive voice</u>

Subject + Reflexive Verb + DO
- Je me suis lavée; je me suis lavé les mains; je me les suis lavées.

All verbs conjugated in the <u>reflexive voice</u> are conjugated with *être* in compound tenses and follow the general rules of agreement. The past participle of a verb of action used reflexively agrees with the DO if it is in front of the verb. In the first example, the reflexive pronoun is also the direct object of the verb. Phrased in this way, the agreement informs us that the antecedent is feminine. The verb *s'en aller* is intransitive and obeys the rules applying to verbs of motion (*aller*) and the past participle agrees with the subject of the verb: *Elle s'en est allée* or *elle s'est en allée.*

2) Verbs that exist *only* in the reflexive form

All purely reflexive verbs and verbs that acquire a distinct meaning in the reflexive form (*se douter de*) agree with the subject. Here, the reflexive pronoun can be considered a semantic formality, grammatically undifferentiated from the subject pronoun. These verbs are not complemented by direct objects (except for *s'arroger*). They may be followed by indirect objects (non dative) or circumstantial complements of location or direction. *S'arroger* is transitive direct and follows the rules of verbs of action. In the past participle form, it agrees with the direct object if it is placed in front of the verb.

- Elle s'est évanouie.
- Ils se sont réfugiés.
- Les pouvoirs qu'il s'est arrogés...

7) MODAL VERBS, VERBS OF PREFERENCE, AND STATES OF MIND

When they are followed by an infinitive object

These verbs do not require a preposition between the auxiliary verb and the infinitive:
Subject + Modal Verb + infinitive Verb + Direct Object
- Je préfère lire mais j'aime regarder des documentaires.
- Je dois/peux/veux faire mon lit.

In the nominal form, the DO is placed after the verb of which it is the object:
Subject + Modal Verb + DO/NP
- Je voudrais du café.

In the pronominal form, the DO is placed before the verb of which it is the object:
Subject + Modal Verb + DO pronoun + infinitive Verb
- Je dois/peux/veux *le* faire.

Subject + DO Pronoun + Modal Verb
- Je *le* veux (je veux faire quelque chose).

Subject + DO Pronoun + Modal Verb
- J'*en* voudrais (je voudrais du café).

8) CATENATIVE VERBS
(Verbal chains)

Catenative verbs, like modal verbs and verbs of preference, do not require a preposition to link the second infinitive verb to the conjugated auxiliary (first) verb. Catenative formations, however, differ from the <u>Verb + infinitive Verb</u> structures explained above insofar as the DO pronoun is placed before the first verb even if the direct object is, grammatically speaking, the direct object of the second verb.

FAIRE + INFINITIVE

S + ***faire + V infinitif*** + DO
- Je <u>fais cuire</u> les oeufs.
- Il <u>a fait rire</u> la petite fille.

S + *DO* + ***faire + V infinitif***
- Je *les* fais cuire.
- Il *l'*a fait rire.

The best way to understand this is to identify *faire + V infinitif* as a single unit (the verbal chain). However, the past participle of the catenative *faire* is invariable because the DO is always the DO of the second verb.

Note that the dative pronoun likewise precedes the verbal chain.
- Il *lui* a fait réciter le verbe être.

LAISSER + INFINITIVE

This construction is a pivotal sentence in English:
- He let the musicians play.

Here, 'the musicians' is at the same time the grammatical DO of the verb 'let' and the semantic subject of the infinitive verb 'play'. In French, the structure may be expressed either as:
- Il a laissé jouer les musiciens.
- Il a laissé les musiciens jouer.

However, if the second verb has a direct object, the semantic subject must precede the infinitive verb and the structure is here as in English.
- Il a laissé les musiciens jouer Mozart.

In the pronominal form, the direct object of the first verb (*laisser*) is placed before the verb chain:
1. Il **les** a laissé**s** jouer.
or
2. Ils **les** a laissé jouer.

There are two schools of thought regarding the past participle agreement of *laisser*. Accordingly, in sentence 1) *laissés* agrees with its direct object (the semantic subject of the infinitive verb) which is placed in front of it. The antecedent of the DO pronoun *les* being *les musiciens*, *laissés* is written with the plural *s*. In statement 2), *laisser + V infinitif* is treated as *faire + V infinitif* and the past participle remains invariable in all cases. The latter is in agreement with the recommendations of the Conseil supérieur de la langue française de 1990 (*nouvelle orthographe*).[113]

In the sentence below, *la musique* is the direct object of the second verb:
- Il a laissé jouer la musique.
- Subject + *laisser* + infinitive V + DO

In the pronominal form the structure is:
- Il l'a laissé jouer.
- Subject + DO + *laisser* + infinitive V

And in this case the past participle *laissé* is invariable since its antecedent *la musique* is the direct object of the infinitive verb *jouer* and not that of *laisser*. Here, the participle agreement follows the general rule.

---

[113] See the discussion in: *Le Nouvel Observateur*, 'La conjugaison; l'accord du participe passé devant un infinitif', at: http://laconjugaison.nouvelobs.com/regles/orthographe/l-accord-du-participe-passe-laisse-devant-un-infinitif-182.php
For other implications of this reform see Danielle Béchennec and Liliane Sprenger-Charolles, *Guide Pratique de l'orthographe rectifiée*, CNRS et Université Paris-Descartes.
http://www.cahiers-pedagogiques.com/IMG/pdf/GuidePratiqueOrthographeRectifi_e-2-09-2011.pdf

VERBS OF PERCEPTION + INFINITIVE
voir, regarder, entendre, écouter, sentir

Verbs of perception + infinitive Verb are analogous to *laisser* + infinitive Verb. The catenative construction is less a syntactic obligation than a matter of emphasis. Given that the infinitive verb has no object of its own, we can say:
- La dame a écouté les oiseaux chanter.
- La dame a écouté chanter les oiseaux.

AND:

If the subject of the infinitive verb is omitted, the structure is logically:
- La dame a entendu chanter.

If the subject of the infinitive verb is omitted and the second (infinitive) verb has a direct object, the DO follows the infinitive as in all other S V O constructions.
- La dame a entendu chanter la Marseillaise.

However, as with *laisser + infinitif*, in the pronominal form, the direct object of the infinitive verb comes before the whole chain and not before the verb of which it is the object:
- La dame l'a entendu chanter.

The past participle is invariable since the pronoun *l'* (which replaces la Marseillaise) is the direct object of the infinitive verb and not that of the conjugated verb.

And this is it for the particularities of these verbs, because:
If the second verb is followed by an object or a modifier, the word order is as per usual and similar to English.
- La dame a entendu les enfants parler à leur mère.
- La dame a entendu la maman leur répondre tout doucement.

Both the placement of pronouns and the agreement of the past participle obey the normal rules. In the pronominal form, the direct object of the first verb precedes the verb of which it is the object. The past participle of the conjugated verb agrees with its direct object. Therefore:
- La dame *les* a entendu*s* lui parler.

The direct objects precede the verbs of which they are the objects as per usual.
- Je regarde un monsieur acheter *des croissants*.
- Je le regarde *en* acheter.

The same goes for the dative pronoun, which is also placed in the normal order:
- J'ai vu la dame acheter *des croissants* **aux enfants**.
- Je l'ai vue **leur** *en* acheter.

In these sentences, the placement of pronominal objects and the past participle agreements follow the general rules. The semantic subject of the second (infinitive) verb being the direct object of the first (conjugated) verb, it appears before the verb of which it is the object. The past participle agrees with the direct object since it is placed before the verb. The direct object of the second (infinitive) verb also goes where it normally goes, which is to say, in front of the verb of which it is the object.

In sum, there are two funny things about catenative verbs
1) If the verbal chain is headed by *faire*, the two verbs act as one unit. The nominal complement is placed after the verbal chain and the pronominal complement is placed before the chain. The direct object complement is always the object of the whole chain and the past participle of *faire* is thus invariable.
- *Il a fait chanter les enfants.* [SVVO]
- *Il les a fait chanter.* [SOVV]

Note: We may treat *laisser* in the same manner: *il les a laissé chanter*.

2) If the verbal chain is headed by a verb of perception, things depend on whether the infinitive verb has an object complement or a modifier attached to it. If it doesn't, the *semantic* subject of the second verb is both the object of the verbal chain and the object of the first verb. Therefore:
- In the nominal form, we may place this grammatical object at the end of the chain *j'entends chanter* les oiseaux; *je regarde partir* les dames. [SVVO]
- And in the pronominal form, the direct object is placed before the verbal chain and the past participle agrees in gender and number with the antecedent of the object pronoun: je **les** ai entendu**s** chanter; je les ai vu**es** partir. [SOV$_{es}$V]

Other constructions follow the usual rules governing pronominal placement and past participle agreements.

UNIFYING THE RULES GOVERNING THE PAST PARTICIPLE AGREEMENT

We teach students about 'the house of Mrs Vandertramp', and we tell them that when they conjugate verbs with *être*, which includes the reflexive verbs, the past participle agrees with the subject; and when they conjugate verbs with *avoir*, the past participle agrees with the direct object if it is in front of the verb. And then, we teach that the reflexive verbs also agree with the direct object if they have one, and that other reflexive verbs agree with the subject, and some don't agree with anything; and then we sometimes teach that the verbs *monter, descendre, sortir, etc.* can also be conjugated with *avoir* when they mean 'to take' rather than 'to go'. French grammars intended for native speakers and advanced second-language learners teach that when *monter, sortir, etc.* are transitive direct, they are conjugated with *avoir*, and they refine the past participle agreement rules as follows: the past participle of verbs conjugated with *avoir* agrees with the DO if it is placed before the verb; the past participle of verbs conjugated with *être* agrees with the subject – except that 1) the past participle of reflexive verbs agrees with the reflexive pronoun if the reflexive pronoun is the direct object of the verb, and 2) the past participle of the reflexive verb is invariable if the verb does not have a direct object unless 3) we are using an essentially reflexive verb like *s'enfuir, s'évanouir, s'en aller, s'évader, se repentir, s'apercevoir etc.* in which case the past participle agrees with the subject with the exception of the verb *s'arroger* which agrees with the direct object.[114] Hence, whether we are teaching beginners, advanced students or native speakers, the whole thing adds up to a bit of a headache.

In fact, we can rationalise the rules and eliminate the exceptions if we teach the choice of auxiliary and the past participle agreement rule as two different issues, and if we teach the passive voice as a distinct category – which, incidentally, the above explanations leave out altogether. So, setting aside the passive voice for the moment, we may proceed as follows.

---

[114] For an overview of fifty years of teaching along these lines see among others: Cauffman-Crocker Mary E, *Schaum's Ouline of French Grammar*, Schaum, 2013; Jean Dubois and René Lagane, *La nouvelle grammaire du Français*, Larousse,1973; Horan and Wheeler, *A New French Course*, 1967; Maurice Rat, *Le Français facile pour tous*, Garnier,1964. On line: FrançaisFacile.com, 'L'accord du participe passé'; https://www. francaisfacile.com/ exercices/ exercice-francais 2/ exercice francais 34890.php; *L'OBS La conjugaison*, 'L'accord du participe passé'; http://la-conjugaison.nouvelobs.com /regles/ orthographe/l-accord-du-participe-passe-161.php; Cordial.com, 'L'accord du participe passé avec être et avoir'; https://www.cordial.fr/index.php.

The choice of the auxiliary depends on two things: 1) the class of verbs and 2) the presence of a reflexive (or reciprocal) pronoun. Simply speaking: All verbs of motion and all verbs conjugated with a reflexive pronoun are conjugated with *être*. All other verbs are conjugated with *avoir*.

The past participle agreement is ruled by the syntactic function attached to the class of verbs. There are two conditions:

1) The past participle agrees with the direct object *whenever* the verb has a direct object *so long as* the DO is placed before the verb, whether the verb is in the active or the reflexive voice and whether it is conjugated with *avoir* or *être*.

2) The past participles of verbs of motion and of purely reflexive verbs agree with the subject.

If the direct object follows the verb, if the verb is not a verb of motion, nor a purely reflexive verb, then the past participle remains invariable whether the verb is conjugated with *avoir* or *être*. The five examples given below show that if we consider the class of verbs and their syntactic function, there are no exceptions to these two general principles. [115]

TWO PRINCIPLES, FIVE FUNDAMENTAL CONSTRUCTIONS AND NO EXCEPTIONS

First principle: the past participle agrees with the direct object if the verb has a direct object and so long as the DO is placed before the verb.

1) The past participle of *any* verb that takes a direct object (including *monter, descendre, sortir, se regarder* and *s'arroger*) agrees with its direct object when it is placed in front of it, and only then, whether the auxiliary is *avoir* or *être*.

- Elle les a vus.
- Elle s'est vue faire une grimace.
- Elle les a montées.
- Elle s'est regardée dans la glace.
- Elle s'est lavé les mains [*se* is now indirect/dative].

---

[115] Where the agreement of *laissé* is concerned, the traditional DO rule is now optional but it is formally consistent with the DO object rule and it remains a legitimate option.

Second principle: the past participle agrees with the subject

2) The past participle of a verb of motion agrees with the subject of the verb. A verb of motion is by definition intransitive.

- Elle est allée en France.
- Elles sont venues à la maison.

NOTE: *Monter au deuxième étage* is a verb of motion that translates into English as 'to go up to the second floor' [verb + *prep* + location]; *monter les valises* is a verb of action that translates into English as 'to take up the suitcases' [verb + direct object].

3) The past participle of essentially reflexive verbs agrees with the subject. Essentially reflexive verbs are verbs that exist only in the reflexive form. These verbs are not too difficult to identify because they are straight verbs of action in English: *s'évanouir* is 'to faint', *se souvenir de* is 'to remember', *s'apercevoir de* is 'to notice', *s'arroger* is 'to arrogate'.[116] Essentially reflexive verbs include verbs that acquire a distinct meaning in the reflexive form (e.g.: *douter/se douter; tenir/se tenir*) It is also interesting to note the resultative feel these verbs acquire in the *passé composé*.
- Elle s'est évanouie – *she fainted*.
- Elle s'est souvenue de toi – *she remembered you*.
- Elle s'est enfuie de la maison – *she fled from the house*.

Note1: The verbs *s'enfuir* and *s'en aller* are also verbs of motion. Formally, the directional pronoun follows the reflexive pronoun: *elle s'y est réfugiée, elle s'en est allée* [academic standard] but in *la language parlée*, we say *elle s'est en allée*. Note how *s'enfuir* provides an analogical model for *s'en aller*, which spoken French transforms into *s'enaller*. Meanwhile, academic standards require that we omit the redundant directional pronoun *en* when using *s'enfuir*. Hence, *elle s'est enfuie* and not *elle s'en est enfuie*.

---

[116] With some of these verbs, as for example *se résigner* and *s'absenter*, we may have a faint perception of the reflexive pronoun as the direct object of the verb, but this is entirely absent from verbs like *s'apercevoir, se douter, se souvenir*. Interestingly, *s'évanouir* originates in the OF verb *esvanir, esvanire* in Latin, meaning to disappear, dissipate, dispel. Formally, we could at a pinch think of *elle s'est évanouie* as we might *elle s'est endormie* as 'she dispelled herself' but this would be stretching the point semantically as well as the Anglophone imagination since the verb *s'évanouir* translates as 'to faint'. Refer to Centre National de Ressources Textuelles et Lexicales (CNRTL) http://www.cnrtl.fr/definition/évanouir; and Jacqueline Picoche, *Dictionaire Etymologique, Les usuels du Robert*, Robert, Paris, 1979. 'Vain', I, 3, p. 678.

Note 2: The verb *s'arroger* is usually considered an anomaly among essentially reflexive verbs because it is transitive direct but it is not an exception to the past participle agreement rule (or the rule governing auxiliaries). The past participle agreement of the verb *s'arroger* with the Direct Object follows the pattern exampled above in construction 1.

If none of the above applies:

4) The past participle is invariable, whether the verb is used in the active or the reflexive voice, and whether the auxiliary is *avoir* or *être*.

- Elle a marché très vite.
- Elle a donné à manger aux enfants.
- Elle s'est dit qu'elle ne reviendrait pas [*s'* is an indirect object].

5) The past participle of the verb *être* is invariable and *être* never takes a direct object. It is followed by an *attribute*, which is a complement of the subject and not a complement of the verb. The attribute provides information about the subject; it tells us about the condition or the state that the subject is in. In the sentence below, the verb *être* serves as a link (copula) between the subject and the attribute.

- Elle a été *heureuse* de me voir.

AND NOW FOR THE PASSIVE VOICE

The past participle of a verb used in the passive voice agrees with the grammatical subject of the verb. The past participle has attributive value, as the adjective does in construction 5. The past participle informs us of the condition or state of the subject (nominative predicate). Formally speaking, in French, the subject of a verb in the passive voice is always the direct object of the verb in the active voice. Hence, in the passive voice, the past participle agreement obeys the principles as shown above in examples 5 (overt grammar) and 1 (inferred grammar).

- Le volcan a détruit la ville.
- La ville a été *détruite*.

TO FORM COMPLEX SENTENCES: take the models above, add a conjunction and repeat the patterns...

Je lui ai dit que j'irai à Paris cet été quand j'aurai le temps, quand il fera beau et quand les gens seront en vacances, parce que je déteste le froid et je n'aime pas la foule.

Remaining aware of ...

Modal verbs and verbs of emotion and states of mind
- ➤ *vouloir que...* requires the subjunctive (intention/desire)
- • Je veux/voudrais qu'elle vienne.
- ➤ *douter que...* requires the subjunctive (doubt)
- • Je doute qu'il vienne.
- ➤ *souhaiter que...* requires the subjunctive (desire, wishful thinking)
- • Je souhaite qu'il vienne.

- ➤ *savoir que, penser que, croire que* require the indicative and express a belief or an assumption of a true possibility.
- • Je sais/je pense/je crois qu'il viendra.
- ➤ *espérer que* requires the indicative. It expresses a true possibility (note that an older meaning of *espérer* is *attendre*).
- • J'espère (bien) qu'il viendra.

Note the semantic difference between: *j'ai peur de nager*, and *j'ai peur qu'il ne vienne*. The first expresses a true state of mind, the second a hunch about something.

Third-person verb of obligation **falloir** *and the modal verb* **vouloir**
- ➤ Il faut le faire [general statement].
- ➤ Il faut que je le fasse [personal statement].
- ➤ Je veux le faire [subject 1 = subject 2 ⇒ infinitive V].
- ➤ Je veux qu'il le fasse [subject 1 ≠ subject 2 ⇒ que + subjunctive].

Manquer à quelqu'un
- • Mes parents me manquent.
- • Mes promenades me manquent.

This is a Subject + Dative + Verb because *quelqu'un ou quelque chose manque à quelqu'un*.

❖ See Chapter VIII (p. 237) for suggestions on how to teach this structure.

Real condition, imaginable and impossible conditions and the **si** *constructions*

<u>Si + real condition</u> requires the mood to correspond in the subordinate and the main clause. This construction uses the present and the future of the indicative since the condition and the proposition are both realisable in real time.
- Si tu peux venir demain, ça me fera plaisir.
- S'il pouvait venir, il venait.

<u>Si + non-existent condition</u> and <u>si + imaginable condition</u> require the *imparfait de l'indicatif* in the subordinate clause and the *conditionnel* in the main clause; the condition is open-ended, since it is imagined, and the realisation is in the *conditionnel*, the mood of the imaginable. [117]
- Si j'avais un livre, je lirais.
- Si tu pouvais venir demain, je serais contente.

Relative clauses

A relative clause may complement a noun or another clause. The relative pronoun may replace a nominal antecedent (*who, whom, which, that*).
- L'homme *qui* m'a parlé était assis devant moi.

It may have a clausal antecedent (*, which*).
- Je me suis bien reposé ces derniers jours, *ce qui* m'a fait beaucoup de bien.

It may also be indefinite and have no antecedent (*what*).
- Il m'a dit *ce qu'* il pensait.
- Je ne comprends pas *de quoi* il parle.

Relative pronouns come in simple and compound forms. Simple forms inflect into the subject, object, possessive, and locative cases. Relative pronouns differentiate between animate and inanimate antecedents (see pp. 153; pp. 227-8).

---

[117] For more on the *conditionnel*, refer to the discussion in Ch. 1, pp. 17-18, and footnote 6.

THE IMPORTANCE OF THE ROLE PLAYERS

The most important functions for students to identify are the role players: subject, direct object, dative, other indirect objects, instrumentals, locative/directional and the antecedents. These role players determine almost every pronominal usage, including relative and interrogative pronominal use, and they determine the past participle agreements. All the complications involved in the structures I have described above pose difficulties for learners on account of pronominal use and of past participle agreements, and all are dependent on the correct identification of the role players and other complements. I call *me/te/lui/nous/vous/leur* 'dative pronouns' to differentiate them from the indirect object animate and the indirect object inanimate pronouns *y* and *en* anteceded by the phrases introduced by the prepositions *à* and *de*. The disjunctive pronouns serve several functions 1) indirect object (*je pense à toi/ je rêve de toi*), 2) circumstantial (*à cause de toi*), 3) directional (*vers moi*). These pronouns can also be placed in apposition or be used without a preposition when they serve an emphatic function (*j'ai fait ça, moi?*). To keep things simple, I use an umbrella term encompassing form and function and call these pronouns 'obliques pronouns'.

The pronouns that are the same in English and in French
The *animate* pronouns *moi, toi, lui/elle, nous, vous, eux/elles* create no real difficulties for English-speaking learners because they most resemble the English object pronouns me, you, him, her, us, you, them. The pronoun *soi* is more elusive – 'oneself'.

The *inanimate* pronominal complements introduced by prepositions: *avec, sans, pour etc.* are also like English: a*vec cela, avec ceci, pour ça, sans rien, pour rien*, are simply: 'with this', 'with that', 'for that', 'with anything', 'for nothing'…

The pronouns that are different in English and in French
English does not differentiate between direct, dative and other indirect object pronouns. In French, however, the direct object and the dative pronouns are distinct and they are also different from the oblique pronouns (the latter may serve several functions).
- me/te/le/la/en/nous/vous/les/en – Direct Object
- me/te/le/lui/nous/vous/leur – Dative Object (no preposition)
- moi/toi/lui/elle/soi/nous/vous/eux/elles – Indirect Object (introduced by *à* and *de*) and other complements (introduced by *avec, sans, à cause de, par, pour, vers*)

The *inanimate* indirect object complements when they are introduced by **à** (about) and **de** (about) are also not like English indirect object complements. In the pronominal form, this function may require the pronouns *y* and *en* which are placed before the verb.

Without differentiating the various complements: direct object, dative, indirect object, instrumental, directional, locative, and circumstantial (cause, intention, etc.), without differentiating: inanimate, animate, definite, indefinite, nominal, infinitive and clausal, teaching and learning the pronouns and structures above result in endless confusion. By contrast, when students have learned to differentiate and identify grammatical function, everything falls into place. Introduced sequentially, via a questioning method and by leveraging English usage, students can master French pronouns without too many problems.

❖ See Chapter VII for teaching the pronouns that precede the verbs.

TABLE 1 showing the pronouns that precede the verb

Subject	Reflexive *and* Reciprocal NB: These may also be DO and Dative	Direct Object replaces N-P.	Direct Object replaces an infinitive phrase linked by *à* or *de*	Dative	Indirect Object following *à* or *de* meaning about and postpositions in phrasal verbs.	Locative and Directional replaces an antecedent
Je	me	me		me		
Tu	te	te		te		
Il/elle	se	le/la [def.] en [indef.]		lui	y [à] en [de]	
On	se		le			
Nous	nous	nous		nous		
Vous	vous	vous		vous		
Ils/elles	se	les [def.] en [indef.]		leur	y [à] en [de]	
						y [location]
						y [direction]
						en [direction]

The pronouns that follow the verb

The *animate* disjunctive pronouns introduced by the prepositions *pour, avec, sur, à cause de, vers, par, au lieu de, à, de, etc.* follow the verb. They are: *moi, toi, lui/elle, nous, vous, eux/elles*. The *inanimate* pronouns introduced by all prepositions (note that *à* and *de* may also antecede the pronouns *y* and *en*) are expressed with *cela, ça, rien, tout, etc.*: *à cela, avec ça, pour tout, à cause de cela, pour rien, etc.*

- Je suis venue en retard à cause de lui.
- J'ai raté mon bus à cause de ça!
- J'ai travaillé pour rien.

<u>Note</u> that we say:
- *J'aime [ça]*.
- *Je l'aime* is reserved for persons.

TABLE 2 showing the pronouns that follow the verb

Oblique Pronouns *Animate only* following all prepositions	Other Pronouns *Indefinite and inanimate* following all prepositions
moi	
toi	
lui /elle	ceci, cela, ça, rien, tout...
nous	
vous	
eux/elles	

TABLE 3 : RELATIVE PRONOUNS

Function	A With animate nominal or pronominal antecedents (eg. la dame; moi, elle, lui; personne, quelqu'un).	B With animate or inanimate nominal antecedents (people, animals things)	C With a clausal antecedent (1)	D With no antecedent: (2) the indefinite relative pronouns
Subject *who/which/that*	qui	qui	, ce qui	**animate** qui *who* quiconque *whoever* **inanimate** ce qui *what*
Direct object *whom/which/that*	que	que	, ce que	**animate** qui *whom* **inanimate** ce que que/ quoi *what* quoi que *whatever*
Possessive *whose/of which*	dont	dont		
Locative/time Directional		où d'où/ par où etc.		où/quand d'où/par où
Relative pronouns following prepositions				
All complements following a preposition, e.g. dative, oblique, location, time, intention, direction, instrument, cause, etc.	à qui de qui *also* **dont** pour qui avec qui sans qui en qui, vers qui etc.	auquel/à laquelle auxquels/auxquelles duquel/de laquelle desquels/desquelles *also* **dont** pour, avec, sans, vers lequel/ laquelle /lesquels/ lesquelles etc.	, ce **dont** , de quoi , (ce) en quoi , (ce) à quoi , ce pour quoi , sans quoi etc.	**animate** de qui/à qui/ pour qui/en qui avec qui **inanimate** (ce) **dont** (ce) de quoi (ce) en quoi (ce) à quoi (ce) dans quoi (ce) pour quoi etc.

1) J'ai terminé mes devoirs, ce qui me rend heureux, ce que je voulais faire, ce dont je suis très fier, ce pour quoi je peux me reposer et sans quoi je n'aurais pu m'endormir.

2) Subject: Je ne sais pas ce qui lui ferait plaisir; qui(conque) me le dirait, je l'écouterais.
Direct Object: Je ne vois pas qui tu regardes; je ne comprends pas ce que tu dis; quoi que tu dises, il ne t'écoutera pas.
Location and time: Je ne sais pas où j'ai mis ce carnet, par où il est passé ou quand je le retrouverai.
Other complements: Je ne sais pas de qui il parle; je ne sais pas de quoi il parle; je danserai avec qui tu voudras; je ne crois pas à ce qu'il croit; elle ne t'a pas dit à qui j'avais pensé; il ne t'a pas dit (ce) à quoi j'avais pensé; nous avons acheté ce dont nous avons besoin; elle t'a dit dans quoi (où) elle l'avait lu.

NOTE: When the antecedent is the indefinite pronoun *quelque chose*, the relative pronoun follows column B in the subject and DO cases; and column D after the prepositions (*ce* omitted): Il a dit quelque chose qui m'a touché, que je désirais entendre, dont je me souviendrai toujours; en quoi je crois très fort, à quoi je pense souvent, et de quoi (dont) j'aimerais te parler.

PREPOSITIONAL USE

In French, the subject, the nominal direct object, the infinitive complement of modal verbs, verbs of preference, verbs of perception and verbs of motion, and certain time complements (*le lundi, le soir, toutes les semaines*) are used *without* prepositions. Every other role player and every other complement requires a preposition.

Identifying verbal postpositions and prepositions

French uses many prepositions (*sur, sous, dans, à cause de, pour, etc.*) that find direct equivalents in English and therefore are not problematic for students to learn so long as they can remember to differentiate the true prepositions which introduce various complements of the verbs from the *post*positions which complete phrasal verbs in English:

- I am staying ⇒ **at my friend's house**
- **I am looking at** ⇒ the computer screen (more below).

Identifying the syntactic functions of the prepositions *à*, *de*, and *en*.

When it comes to prepositions, the greatest difficulty for English learners of French lies with the fact that French uses three prepositions *à*, *de* and *en* for a great many purposes and these can be translated as 'in', 'at', 'to', 'towards', 'from', 'of', or indeed nothing at all. Adding to this, *en* can be a preposition, an indefinite direct object pronoun, a directional pronoun, or an indirect object pronoun other than a dative. I have found that students have no difficulties identifying the correct prepositions when they learn prepositional use in functional-structural context, which is to say when they are aware that when they are saying *x*, they are locating in space, when they are saying *y*, they are moving towards something, as opposed to learning that when they say *je suis à la gare*, *à* means 'at', and when they say *je vais à la gare*, *à* means 'to', and so forth.

    The prepositions *à*, *de*, and *en* are *logical* and *formal* rather than lexical. Their function is syntactic – to link complementary units: *une salle de bain, une salle à manger, le bureau de mon frère, une table en bois; je parle à mon frère, je me prépare à partir, je finis de parler, je suis à la gare; je vais à la gare; je viens de la gare; je suis en vacances, etc.*

    To appreciate the propensity to repeat simple prepositions in French, it is helpful to think of French as retaining aspects of case grammar. For example, while we will say *I spoke to John and Mary*, in French we can mark each referent in the dative semantic role with *à*: *j'ai parlé à Sandrine et à Michel*; mark each referent in the locative semantic role with *en*: *j'ai voyagé en voiture et en train*, etc..

Prepositional use is rich and complex,[118] but where *à, de* and *en* are used to introduce complements of verbs, we can simplify their usage:

TABLE 4: Basic function of *de, à* and *en* in verbal constructions

	de	**à**	**en**
COMPLEMENTS OF CIRCUMSTANCES			
Location in time generally	de 3 heures	à sept heures	
Location/during: the week, the year, the season, the month		au printemps	en semaine, en 2018, en hiver, en décembre
General location concrete space		à la gare, au marché, à Paris	
General location conceptual space.		à la retraite	en vacances, en guerre, en retraite
Transportation on it (à) in it (en)		à cheval, à pied	en voiture, en train
Loc/direction fem. countries			en France, en Australie
Loc/direction masc. countries		au Pérou, aux Etats-Unis	au Pérou
Direction towards		à la gare, au marché	en France
Direction from	de la gare, du marché, de France, de Paris		

---

[118] See the Canadian government's Bureau de la Traduction website at: https://www.btb.terminusplus.gc.ca/tpv2guides/guides/rdp/index-fra=html?lang=fra&lettr=&page=../preposition. For a comparison of English and French prepositional use and their acquisition in L2, see Abeer Naser Eddine. *Interlanguage prepositions: an analysis of French learners' productions in L2 English.* Linguistics. Université de Grenoble, 2012. English. NNT : 2012GRENL014 . tel-01057881

	de	**à**	**en**
OTHER COMPLEMENTS			
Dative [to whom]		à quelqu'un	
Infinitive Object	de	à	
Oblique [about/of] Phrasal verbs +	de	à	
Possession	à [moi]	de [ma mère]	
STATIVE (être +)			
Psychological			en colère
Physical			en sueur
WITH THE PRESENT PARTICIPLE			
'while doing'			en chantant…

NOTE 1: the prepositions *à* and *de* linking an infinitive verb or introducing dative and indirect object complements have a locative/directional feel: *à* suggests location and forward direction (into/to/ towards/about) while *de* suggests continuity and provenance (of and from).

NOTE 2: *en* is often used in a conceptual rather than in a concrete/pragmatic dimension, and nouns introduced by *en* do not need a determiner.

WHEN ADJECTIVES ARE FOLLOWED BY *à* AND *de*

Adjectives + à or de + infinitive Verb
> **C'**est triste **à** voir.
> **Il** est triste **à** voir
> **Il** est triste **d'**entendre quelqu'un parler comme ça.

Why do we say *c'est bon à manger, il est bon à manger,* and *il est bon de manger tôt*? Why *il* or *c'* and why *à* or *de*? These shifts are not entirely related. Firstly, the pronouns:
1) The pronoun *c'* replaces 'the thing' we are referring to, as for example, this book: *C'est facile à lire = ce livre est facile à lire* = <u>this</u> is easy to read.
2) The pronoun *il* is a third-person singular masculine pronoun and it replaces the book: *il [le livre] est facile à lire* = <u>it</u> is easy to read.
3) The pronoun *il* is an impersonal pronoun heading an <u>impersonal</u> cleft structure anticipating the infinitive subordinate clause:
   - Il est facile de lire des romans quand on aime les livres.
   - *It is easy to read novels when one likes books.*

- Lire des romans est facile quand on aime les livers.
- *Reading novels is easy when one likes books.*

The shift from of *c'* to *il* is semantic: *c'est facile à lire* (this, meaning this book); *il est facile* (it, meaning the book); and il est facile de lire (impersonal it, as in 'it is easy to do something'). The shift between *à* and *de* needs to be explained syntactically.

The preposition **à** links an adjective to its attribute to form a single semantic unit: a compound adjective.
- Ce lapin en chocolat est [beau] et [bon **à** manger] – *good to eat.*
- Il est [sympa] mais il est [difficile **à** supporter] – *hard to take.*

The preposition **de** links the complementary infinitive clause to the attributive clause.
- Il est important [**de** manger tôt] et [**de** se lever de bonne heure] si on veut avoir une vie saine.
- Il est très gentil [**de** venir] - elle est très gentille [**de** venir].

*Il est important **de** manger tôt* can be turned around: *manger tôt est important* showing *manger* as the subject.

NOTE: We say *il est facile de dire ça* rather than *c'est facile de dire ça* – which translates as: 'this is easy to say that'. However, in *la langue courante*, *c'* is often the preferred impersonal pronoun, in which case it has no demonstrative value. *Il* may be more naturally perceived as a personal pronoun and *c'est* may disambiguate (see also p. 255).
- C'est bien sympa de faire ça.
- Il (elle) est bien sympa de faire ça.

Adjectives + *à* or *de* + noun or pronoun
As for above, **à** links the adjective and its attribute in one semantic unit, forming a compound adjective. Question: What is he/it like?
- il est prêt à tout [ready for anything]
- il est bon à rien [good for nothing]

and **de** introduces a complement of the attributive predicate. Question: how is she and what is she happy, satisfied, tired of?
- elle est satisfaite de son travail [with]
- elle est contente de lui [about]
- elle est fatiguée de tout [of].

THE WORDS *POUR* AND FOR ALSO NEED ATTENTION

PROJECTING FORWARD: *POUR*

LIKE ENGLISH

1) The preposition *pour* can be used with the disjunctive pronouns *moi/toi/lui/elle/soi/ nous/vous/ils/elles*, in which case it follows the verb and it works just like 'for' in English.
- Tu as fait ça pour moi?
- *Did you do this for me?*

2) *Pour* can express a goal or a projected duration, and here too *pour* works like 'for' does in English
- J'ai acheté du pain pour le dîner.
- *I bought bread for dinner.*
- Nous allons partir pour une journée.
- *We'll be going for a day.*

3) *Pour* may express the idea of giving to or doing something to someone and thus introduce a dative. In this case, the complement introduced by *pour* can be replaced by the dative pronoun. And here again, *pour* works like 'for' in English.
- J'ai acheté ce live pour Alain; je lui ai acheté ce livre.
- *I bought a book for Alain (to give to Alain); I bought him a book.*

UNLIKE ENGLISH

4) *Pour* can express intention or a goal and introduce an infinitive phrase. This is expressed by 'in order to' or 'to' in English
- J'ai retiré de l'argent pour payer le restaurant.
- *I withdrew some money [in order] to pay for the restaurant.*
- Pour réussir un gâteau, il faut d'abord avoir le temps de faire la cuisine.
- *[in order] To make a cake successfully, one must first of all have the time to cook.*

CAUSAL: FOR

5) 'For' in English can be a conjunction introducing a causal relation or an explanation, which is not translated by *pour* in French but by the conjunctions *car* or *parce que*:
- He loved learning for he was very intelligent.
- *Il aimait apprendre car il était très intelligent.*

WHAT ELSE GOES WITH FRENCH VERBS AND WHERE

Adverbs of negation

The locutions
ne.. pas
ne… plus
ne… jamais
ne …pas encore
ne… toujours pas [*toujours* modifies *pas*]
ne… pas toujours [*toujours* modifies the negated verb predicate]

- *ne* is placed immediately *after the subject* and the second locution *after the conjugated verb* hence also after the *auxiliary* in compound tenses (as it is in English: I have *not* said it; I have *never* done this before).
- Il ne me l'a pas donné; il ne m'en a rien dit; il ne le lui a jamais dit; il ne lui en a pas encore parlé; il ne me l'a toujours pas donné; il ne me l'a pas toujours donné.

There are no exceptions to this principle in subject + verb constructions.

When students have internalised this word order, they can learn without much trouble that *ne* remains *in situ* when in the imperative mood: *Ne m'en parle pas!* where we need only delete the subject.

Teaching this formation also helps student negage verb + subject structures. We leave *ne* at the usual place and we move the subject pronoun after the veb: *N' a-t-elle pas fait ses devoirs?* Treating *n'a-t-elle* as a unit (thanks to the hyphens), *pas* remains *in situ* after the auxiliary/conjugated verb.

Conversely they can easily learn that we say: *ne pas faire* since the infinitive verb is not conjugated.

Other adverbs

1) When an adverb modifies an adjective or another adverb, it is placed before the word it modifies as in English.
   - Elle est trop intelligente.
   - Il est fort beau.
   - Il a parlé très rapidement.

2) When an adverb modifies a verb, it is placed after the verb.

The adverbs of frequency, quantity and quality: *souvent, encore, toujours, trop, beaucoup, un peu, mal, bien* are placed immediately after the verb which they modify, after the auxiliary in compound conjugations, and after the second negative particle *pas, jamais, etc. Toujours* is placed in front of *pas* when it modifies *pas*. Note that this statement is best understood as one semantic unit: *toujours pas*, which corresponds to the English 'not yet'.

- Il fait toujours attention.
- Je n'aime pas beaucoup marcher.
- Je n'ai jamais beaucoup aimé marcher.
- Je n'ai pas bien entendu.
- Il a mal dormi.
- Il parlait doucement aux enfants.
- Il a parlé longtemps de ses enfants.

4) When the adverb modifies the V-O predicate and is emphasised by another adverb, it can be placed after the V-O predicate.
- Il a dit ça bien joliment.

5) When the adverb modifies a clause, it may be placed either at the start or at the end of the clause it modifies.
- Malheureusement, je suis venu trop tard.
- Je suis venu trop tard, malheureusement.

ESSENTIAL ENGLISH TO FRENCH COMPARISONS

The place of the descriptive adjectives and other modifiers

In English, the modifier precedes the modified. In French, the modifier follows the modified; this *general rule* (not absolute) applies to descriptive adjectives, adverbs, compound nouns, and compound adjectives.

Whereas in English the descriptive adjective is placed before the noun it modifies, it is the other way around in French. In addition, three particularities apply to French adjectives: 1) a few adjectives are normally placed before the noun, as for example, *beau, jeune, nouveau* (but not *neuf*); 2) even fewer adjectives are placed before or after the noun to express a different meaning: *un homme grand, un grand homme*; and 3) some adjectives normally placed after the noun may be placed before it to produce an aesthetic or rhetorical enhancement (*une brillante artiste*). Students need to internalise the general rules – a few adjectives come before the noun (*petit, gros, beau, etc.*) but generally speaking adjectives come after the noun (*intelligent, charmant, nerveux, etc.*), before they are introduced to stylistic refinements. This is important because other modifiers (nouns, infinitives and adverbs) likewise usually follow the word they modify (noun or verb). Thus, in French, we can announce 'the thing' and then describe or modify it – the headword or the modified comes before the modifier.

- an intelligent woman: *une femme intelligen*te
- a handbag: *un sac à main*
- he did this often; he often did this: *il faisait souvent cela; il faisait cela souvent*

Learners of French have to learn this back to front word order if they are to use adjectives and other modifiers correctly. They also need to internalise this rule to develop a native feel for the difference between the pedestrian and the aesthetic use of modifiers. When, at a later date, we refine their knowledge about adjectival placement, we can remind learners of the plasticity of language and point out to them that, in English, we may place adjectives after a noun for effect.

Pronouns and their functions

In French, we need to be especially aware of the object, locative and directional complements because, unlike English, French dedicates different pronouns for these different functions, and French pronominal word order differs from nominal word order.

Verbs

We need to make students aware of the many differences between French and English verbs. English and French make use of different stative and impersonal verbs whilst French verbs of action, displacement, perception, and preference call for differentiated grammatical treatment (refer to the map above). In addition, students must learn about the differences between the reflexive voice in English and the reflexive voice in French, and of the singularity of essentially reflexive verbs in French since the latter do not exist in English. Finally, students need to be aware of phrasal verbs, of their frequency in English, and of their respective particularities in English and French.

Modal verbs in English and in French

English modal verbs come as truncated verbal forms and expressions. The verb 'must' does not inflect and only exists in the present tense. To express obligation in the past and future tenses, we will use 'to have to'. On the other hand, the modal verbs *vouloir, pouvoir, devoir* are complete verbs. Thus, students must learn to identify the modal function in expressions like: 'I will have to tell her to get here earlier', if they are to find their way to the French verbal equivalent. If not, they will naturally translate 'I have to' with the verb *avoir*.

In the past tenses, however, French modal verbs present specific difficulties. The sentence *j'ai dû lui dire de venir plus tôt* is just as likely to mean 'I must have told her to come earlier' as to mean 'I had to tell her to come earlier'. In other words, *j'ai dû* can express possibility or obligation. To express obligation unambiguously, we may prefer to say *il a fallu que je lui dise de venir plus tôt* or *j'ai été obligée de lui dire de venir plus tôt*. Both these constructions are grammatically elaborate: the former requires a subjunctive and the latter the passive voice.

The reflexive voice and the reflexive verbs

English has a reflexive voice, e.g. to tell oneself something, to do something to oneself or to address oneself to someone else. In English if I say: 'I am brushing myself' or 'I hurt myself', I am using the reflexive voice. French uses the reflexive voice more broadly than English since it may use it where English uses the passive or indeed the active voice, as well as for emphasis and affectionate speech (e.g.: *on se fait un petit café*). French also has purely or essentially reflexive verbs – verbs that exist only in the reflexive form or that acquire a different meaning in the reflexive form from what they mean in the active form. For example, *s'évanouir* has no other form in French than the reflexive form, and *elle s'est évanouie* is translated as 'she fainted'. The verbs *douter* and *se douter de* are almost opposites, *sentir* and *se sentir* also have different meanings as do *apercevoir* and *s'apercevoir*. It is important to bring students' attention to the fact that these verbs are *not* in the reflexive voice. This is why in the language map given above, I classed 'reflexive verbs' as a distinct category of verbs. Verbs in the reflexive voice and essentially reflexive verbs deserve special attention because their respective past participles are not ruled by the same syntactic considerations. The past participle of verbs used in the reflexive voice agrees with the direct object of the verb if it precedes the verb. The past participle of essentially reflexive verbs agrees with the subject of the verb.

Essential differences between English and French reflexive forms:

1) A French verb exists only in the reflexive form:
   - *Elle s'est évanouie.*
   - She fainted.
   - *Elle s'est enfuie.*
   - She fled.

2) Some French verbs mean one thing in the reflexive voice and another in the active voice:
   - *Je me lève.*
   - I get up.

- *Je lève mon verre.*
- I raise my glass.
- *Je m'appelle Christine.*
- My name is Christine.
- *J'appelle mon amie sur Skype.*
- I am calling my friend on Skype.

3) French uses the reflexive form of various verbs, including *faire*, where English may use the verb 'to get' or a verb followed by the postposition up:
- *Je me suis levée*: I got up.
- *Je me suis réveillée*: I woke up.
- *Je me suis habillée*: I got dressed.
- *Je me suis fait voler*: I got robbed.
- *Je me suis fait mal*: I got hurt.

4) French can use the reflexive voice where English uses the passive voice:
- *Comment se prononce ce mot?*
- How is this word pronounced?
- *Je m'appelle Jean-Pierre.*
- I am called Jean-Pierre.

5) In French, reflexive pronouns and reciprocal pronouns (each other/one another) have the same form:
- *Nous nous parlons souvent.*
- We talk often.
- *Elles s'entendent bien.*
- They get on well.

In the first three singular persons, we need to add a preposition + oblique pronoun to clarify that we are not using the verb in the reflexive voice, but using reciprocal pronouns.
- Je me dispute souvent *avec elle*.

6) In English, the reflexive pronouns and the emphatic pronouns have the same form:
- I did this to myself (reflexive); I did it myself (emphatic).

7) In French, the emphatic pronouns are *moi-même, toi-même, etc.*:
- Je l'ai fait moi-même.

English phrasal verbs

In English, some verbs must be followed by a postposition in order to acquire their full meaning (at, to, in, up, into, for, etc.). Although French has some phrasal verbs (followed by *à* or *de*, as for example: *jouer de* and *jouer à*) English phrasal verbs often find their French counterparts in prefixed verbs.
- to come and to come *back* – venir and *re*venir.

More often than not, French makes use of a single semantic unit where English uses a phrasal verb.
- to look at   regarder
- to look for   chercher
- to look into   rechercher
- to look after   garder
- to go in   entrer
- to go up   monter
- to go down   descendre
- to take up   monter /commencer
- to take down   descendre/démonter
- to take apart   démonter

It is essential to help students identify English phrasal verbs. We call the locutions that follow the verbs *post*positions when they are an integral part of the verb. We know they are integral to the verb because they decide on the meaning of the verb and the verb cannot be used without them: 'looking at a person' is not the same as 'looking after a person', and in either case we cannot say 'looking a person'. In contrast, prepositions introduce a dative, an indirect object, a directional complement or a complement of circumstances (location, cause, time, and so forth): she went <u>from</u> the station <u>to</u> the school; he was pacing <u>up</u> and <u>down</u> the hallway; he said this <u>to</u> me; she ate <u>at</u> five o'clock; he ate <u>after</u> I arrived; he was sitting <u>on</u> the chair.

    Differentiating prepositions and postpositions helps students identify the correct category of complements in French, and with this, the correct pronominal forms. When students know that 'to look at' forms one semantic unit and is *regarder* in French, they can easily identify the direct object complement; when we can explain that 'to wait for' is phrasal, students can accept and remember that there is no need to say *attendre <u>pour</u> quelqu'un*.

TO CONCLUDE

The structures outlined above do not account for all and every possible sentence formation in French. The descriptions and explanations I have provided do not account for everything that can be said about the grammar of these constructions. However, these structures are *foundational* and their aquisition takes students a long way in their acquisition of the French language. I explain a number of these structures in greater depth and discuss strategies for teaching them in the remaining chapters of this book.

VI

Phonology, Pronunciation and Grammatical Acquisition

With a focus on gender and number

A spoken language is above all else a working combination of a limited range of sounds and sound associations that exclude many other sounds which may be found in other languages. There are obvious and less obvious reasons why pronunciation is supremely important. The most obvious, of course, is that pronunciation *is* language. Pronunciation is what differentiates a French word from an English word even when both mean the same thing, have the same origin and are written in exactly the same way. Reasonably accurate pronunciation, as we all know, is needed for clarity of expression and for communication. However, pronunciation also expresses and affects syntax. I have found it helpful to explain to students that the phonological system is one of three language domains we engage with in language learning, the other two domains being the syntactic-lexical and the stylistics-metaphorical domains. Phonology exerts its power over the syntactic-lexical domain through the law of least effort, resulting in contracted forms and affecting word order. It also exerts its power through analogy, so that what sounds like something else ends up being used like it and/or meaning the same thing, and phonology is subject to history and culture because the way we say things changes over time and under certain circumstances.

Phonology and grammatical-orthographic exceptions
In French, many grammatical irregularities and some orthographic oddities derive from the phonological system. Exceptions may express euphony (*le lui*) or adjustments to the rules of writing (*mangeons*). Funny writing may also be a product of history (*monsieur*). Exceptions are the stuff of living and breathing languages. Teachers and learners should not fear them because exceptions almost always

provide us with interesting stories: Is this way of putting things completely odd or is there a competing language rule at work? Where does this word come from? Is this a survival from distant times or a more recent adaptation, or a borrowing from another language, or an attachment to academic tradition?

Importantly, we need to remember that there is a crucial difference between teaching rules and exceptions to French speakers and teaching those rules and exceptions to English-speaking learners. Teaching French grammar to native French speakers is in large part concerned with the teaching of academic conventions and writing. Unlike second-language learners, French speakers know what most of the words they are using at school actually mean. Hence, it makes sense to teach native French speakers that the plural of nouns is marked with a silent *s*, and that the words ending in *-al* and *-ail* inflect to the plural *-aux*, except for *festivals, carnavals, régals, éventails, etc.* Native speakers already know that the *au* ending is different from the usual word endings, and can thereby accept that this merits a plural *x* rather than an *s*, just as the contracted *au (à le)* becomes *aux*. They usually have noticed that not all words ending in *al* and *ail* inflect to the plural *aux*. Native speakers have an idea of the exceptional nature of the words we call exceptions, even when the rules of academic French do not coincide exactly with the rules of their own spoken French. The difficulty for native speakers lies in remembering the exceptions, not in remembering the rules. Learning prescriptive grammar either confirms what they already know or it extends their knowledge of the standard language

Second-language learners' experience of the French language is of an entirely different order. For second-language learners, there is nothing remarkable about the endings *al* or *ail*. *Eventail, carnaval, cheval, réveil, ville, bocal, chien, bouteille, chat, homme, garçon, fille, table, tapis* and so forth are all words that end differently. Second-language learners are learning to speak as they are learning to read and write, and they are therefore learning the rules of the language as well as the rules of the academic standard. Given this, students need to learn the exceptions in a way that will not confuse the general rules for them. Since second-language learners do not have the benefit of knowing a large number of words or syntactic expressions, the key to teaching a grammatical rule is to use examples and models that are representative and consistent, and the key to teaching grammatical exceptions is *to keep those for later*. Exceptions, however, are always intriguing and if students have understood and internalised a grammatical rule, exceptions become highly visible and memorable rather than confusing.

Pronunciation: communication, memory, and grammar
As we all know, the clearer our pronunciation and the better we are likely to be understood. Furthermore, the better our pronunciation and the more control we have over our speech, the more confident we feel. And of course, the more

confident we feel, the more eager we are to speak, and the more we speak and the better we learn. Beyond this, clear pronunciation also bears on how well learners *hear and remember* because, even in our own language, we will usually refrain from speaking words that sound fuzzy in our heads and which we cannot pronounce. All teachers, of course, know that pronunciation is crucial for clarity of communication. However, teachers are not always aware of where and how pronunciation and grammar intersect, and of the crucial role pronunciation plays in their students' acquisition of grammar.

Unless pronunciation impedes communication, teachers of French may prefer to avoid making a fuss of their students' approximations, and this is problematic because grammar is manifest in enunciation. In French, we *sound* the difference between masculine and feminine: *une petite chienne, un petit chien*. We identify a plural noun not by the way we sound the ending of the noun, as in English, but by the way we pronounce the determiner: *le chien*, **les** *chiens, mon chien,* **mes** *chiens, son chien,* **ses** *chiens*. We identify the difference between *elle parle* and *elles parlent* through context because we have announced the antecedent, not because of the way the pronoun and the verb are pronounced. We differentiate between *je mange, je mangeais* and *j'ai mangé* by differentiating the way the verbal endings sound, and not only by the way these sounds are expressed by the letters *e, é* and *ai*.

While we cannot expect students to speak perfectly accented French, we do need to identify when English-accented pronunciation is the best French our students can produce at a point in time, and when English-accented pronunciation is actually an indication that students are accommodating French into their natural English grammar. Some French sounds give our students trouble because they are outside of their native phonological system. However, students also have troubles with French pronunciation because their English syntax is all too happy to accommodate whatever their English ear is able to hear, not hear, or hear approximately. Hence, we need to differentiate between an approximate pronunciation that is about pronunciation, and an approximate pronunciation that is about grammar. Where the former is concerned, we can help students improve speech clarity through pronunciation exercises. As for the latter, we need to teach grammar – I will discuss the issue of grammar later in this chapter.

On the importance of prosody

Pronunciation involves the way words (phonemes and morphemes) are sounded, and not least the way words are phrased, as well as intonation, rhythm, stress, pitch, and volume. How we sound a sentence is as important as how we sound a word. To begin with, suprasegmental features help us identify semantic units within the unbroken strings of words that make up our speech between pausing for breath and thinking of what to say next. More evidently, prosody also helps us differentiate mood, intention and assertion. In casual spoken French, prosody, rather than syntax, usually makes the difference between a statement and a question:

- *Tu aimes le café.*
- *Tu aimes le café?*

Students are better able to hear and produce French rhythms, stress and pitch when they learn *about* prosody because they are not usually conscious of prosody in their own language and of how prosody helps them make meaning in speech and in writing. Of course, they are sensitive to the meaning of tone, speed, volume and pitch in English, but they are not aware of the linguistic specificity or the systemic dimension of English prosodic features, all of which they perceive as a natural expression of language. We can demonstrate prosody by speaking a few sentences in different languages or by playing audio segments of languages students cannot understand. Students can try to reproduce the prosodic patterns they are hearing in various languages (tata*ta*data*ta*da). They immediately notice how different languages create different rhythms and they are very intrigued by this.

In English, prosody may also be used to ask a casual question: 'So, you're coming?' However, because French has a different rhythm from English, our students tend to depend on word order and sign-posting (for example, they may expect to hear *est-ce que*), and not all students are able to differentiate a question from a statement on account of tone and pitch without being taught explicitly.

ON THE IMPORTANCE OF PRONUNCIATION FOR READING, WRITING AND GRAMMATICAL UNDERSTANDING

Fundamental differences between English and French phonology

The most distinctive phonemic differences between French and English are /r/ /gn/g/j/; the double consonant sound /ch/ which is always pronounced *sh* in French; and most vowel sounds. Some students may never be able to pronounce the letter *r* in some combinations as for example *arbitre* or *traitre*. Personally, I think this is of little importance. Pronouncing a soft English *r* does not impact on the clarity of French, and it is much better than making a horrible guttural sound. I tell students that a soft English accent sounds very nice in French, and indeed it does. To express themselves clearly, however, students need to produce vowels as closely as possible to the way French speakers produce them. That can be quite difficult. English makes use of long and short vowels and diphthongs whereas French vowels tend to be whole (monophthongs). French diphthongs, unlike English glides, are written as digraphs. French also has some vowel sounds that do not exist in English and which are marked by the letters *u, ou, é, è, on, en, un*.

Students find these difficult to hear and even more difficult to pronounce. Quite naturally, native English speakers tend to turn French vowels into diphthongs and to sound nasal consonants at the end of the nasalised vowels (*on, an, un*).

Teaching students how to read helps with pronunciation
Many students learn to read French as they learn new words rather than systematically. And yet, learning the conventions ruling the pronunciation of written French not only helps learners to read and write more accurately, it also helps them pronounce more accurately. Learning to read French at beginner-level encourages students to refrain from reading French words that look like English words as English words. The written word being a *visual* sign adds auxiliary sensory input, thus helping students differentiate sounds, and encouraging precision (*é/è; on/an/in etc.*). All this enables students to remember vocabulary. In addition, learning to read systematically by comparing English and French helps students develop an eye, ear and intuition for French-English cognates, which over time, enables them to deduce French words in conversational as well as written context. Indeed, awareness of cognates also helps students improvise French words – a double-edged blessing. Obviously, students should not make up words in place of learning vocabulary, but educated improvisation is a valid strategy. In conversation, word approximation can allow our interlocutors to make sense of what we are trying to say, and in turn, to supply us with the correct word.

This said, we need to exercise a degree of caution. Adult students in particular often ask to see words they do not understand by explaining: 'I am a visual person'. Indeed, we are visual when we cannot hear very well, and we are aural when we cannot see very well because we turn to other senses when one sense is not performing for us. In addition, students wish to see words they cannnot 'hear' because French words tend to turn into English words when they are written down. So we need to ensure that students do not become dependent on the written word at the expense of developing their aural skills. At beginner and intermediate levels, I *usually* teach new words and grammar orally to give students the opportunity to hear the words, hear the rules, experience and internalise the grammar as true speech. However, I emphasised *usually* because it can be more efficient to teach aspects of grammar by combining reading, writing and speaking. It is also better to write a word down and dispel students' confusion than to keep them guessing to no avail.

To speak or to write: where lies the value of written exercises for learning the language and learning the grammar?
Grammar needs to be learned on two levels: oral and written. The oral component of grammatical learning is *in large part* about acquiring French as a

natural language. The written component is *in larger part* about learning to read and write French according to academic conventions. As a general rule, we tend to learn what we have the opportunity to practise, therefore, to be able to speak, we must speak, and to be able to write, we must write. However, since speaking, writing, listening and reading are aspects of language rather than watertight compartments, reading and writing have a significant role to play in the acquisition of oral language. Furthermore, students need to learn to write because they are examined on their written proficiency rather than on their spoken language. Finally, reading and writing offer precious individual practice. If students are to learn French, and if they are to retain what they are learning, written grammatical exercises cannot be neglected. But then again, not all written exercises have equal pedagogical value.

To my mind, the type of exercise that requires students to re-write wrong sentences correctly is the most counterproductive of all, because students are just as likely to remember the erroneous constructions as the correct ones. Filling in blanks and writing out semantically random sentences can be fun and useful for students who understand and know the rule, but these exercises have no value for *teaching* the rule. For practice to be effective, students have to know what they are doing. We are unaware of this common-sense principle because we equate practice with repetition, but practising incomprehension means just this, practising incomprehension. In fact, written exercises can mask that students are not actually learning anything. Exercises that attempt to teach through conditioning and repetition do not usually require high-level problem solving since the idea is for students to learn by practising modelled language. Hence, students are able to complete exercises by paying attention to the examples provided to them, and to proceed from then on with minimal thinking. The same happens in repetitive oral drills when students switch to automatic gear. Unless targeted exercises involve students' focus, however, very little happens in the way of language consolidation. Students may get a perfect score in a 'grammar exercise', which is good for motivation in the short term, but they are not able to apply the rule they practised to conversation or free composition, which is discouraging. All of this confirms what practitioners of the communicative approach have to say about explicit grammatical learning. Learning grammar in this way is indeed futile.

Targeted grammatical exercises can highten students' awareness of syntax and consolidate their learning, but to do this, exercises must engage students in conscious and intelligent practice. Students need to be aware of their grammatical intent. They need to understand the functional purpose of the language they are using (naming, locating, directing, modifying, etc.), and they must know the formal grammar involved in this. Just as importantly, they need to know what the things they are writing in French actually mean in English. Translation is in fact far more useful than filling in blanks because it can fulfil all the above conditions. Short narrative writing and other meaningful, coherent, and purposeful writing can help students internalise language rules and develop both oral and written skills. Written composition can also extend students' knowledge insofar as students will learn new words at the point of needing them. However, at the beginner to intermediate levels, for the exercise to be worthwhile, we need to teach students the vital skill of phrasing and rephrasing their thoughts so as to contain their language within the grammar they know. Unless students control their grammar, composition inevitably extends beyond the language they have learned. The exercise results in hybridized language or, if they have their teacher's help, in incidental language production and incidental correction, all of which is just as quickly forgotten.

Correcting pronunciation to enhance grammatical accuracy

When correcting errors, whether in oral or written practice, I usually identify the grammatical issue directly rather than supply the correction – you need a verb… you needed an imperfect… can you tell me why? Or I may encourage students to think back over what they said or wrote: you said this correctly but can you explain why you used this verbal form? Or I will ask students to reflect on their linguistic purpose: you are directing yourself in space, are you moving from or moving forward? What preposition should you use in this case? The idea is to help students self-correct and self-direct. Correcting through questioning is also a diagnostic tool: If students cannot self-correct, it is because they have not learned, which means that I need to re-teach.

SUGGESTIONS FOR TEACHING FRENCH PHONETICS

We learned to pronounce the sounds of our first language by listening and mimicking. However, there is a rare agreement among linguists that we are unlikely to speak an additional language with the same degree of oral accuracy as we do in our mother tongue. Essentially, this means that listening and mimicking do not do for additional-language learning what they did for first-language acquisition. While brain functionality and processes of socialisation surely play a part in this, it is worth remembering that it takes children a few years to master the pronunciation of their mother tongue and that small children have a lot more opportunity to hear and speak their native language than our students have opportunity to hear and speak classroom French. There are many limitations placed on the oral performance of language students learning in the classroom. Some of these we can do little about, others we may have more power to act upon. We cannot help the fact that, in any language class, learners have at least as many opportunities to hear their peers as to hear their teacher's speech and therefore as many opportunities to model on the language that sounds most natural to them because it is closest to English. On the other hand, it is within our control to take the time to work on pronunciation when we introduce students to new words. It is also within our power to take the time to teach prosodic patterns and phrasing, something which is easily overlooked. It is also worth pointing students to web-based programs to give them pronunciation practice.

As for every other type of learning, students get better at pronouncing French when they understand what they are doing and what they need to do. Students enjoy discovering that vowels are produced by keeping airways open while consonants are produced by obstructing airways momentarily, and they can have fun experiencing this by sounding various vowels and consonants in both English and French. I also explain about English long and short vowels, diphthongs and various consonants so that students can become conscious of their native phonology. Try tab and tap, pig and sea, top and robe, then try /d/ and /t/: see how more air is pushed out when we sound a /t/. This is called aspiration. Feel where the sound resonates in your chest cavity or your throat when you say certain words.

In addition, we can help students become aware of how we use different facial muscles to produce different sounds. Language learners have difficulties with pronunciation in part because they have never used their facial muscles in the novel way they now need to use them. They also feel and fear that their faces are distorting. When making novel sounds, they sometimes feel like they are grunting because they are not used to hearing these sounds in their heads. It is worth showing students how to move their lips and mouths as well as reassuring them that the alien sounds they are producing are not as strange as they feel. To do this, I like to cite lines from a poem where words are immediately perceived as beautiful. I ask students to look at me and confirm that nothing too untoward is happening to my face. But it is also a lot of fun to help students develop a feel for their facial muscles by exaggerating sounds along with lip and mouth movements. Students can use a mirror to see how they are using their faces, and they can use recordings to hear the sounds they are producing. Once students see what they are doing with their mouths and compare this with what their teacher is doing, once they hear themselves on a recording, they are almost always able to redirect and better control their pronunciation.

Teaching the nasalised vowels
Many English speakers find it almost impossible to hear the difference between *en* and *on* especially when those follow the consonants *d*, *t* and *s* as in words like *dont* and *dent*, *son* and *sans*. To help students accept the idea that a similar sound does not equate to the same sound, we can point out to them that the distance between the vowel sounds in words like 'meal' and 'mill' and 'sew' and 'saw' is baffling to a

French speaker learning English. The following exercises help learners produce the nasalised vowels:

- on is produced by saying [o] and pushing the air back: there is no lip movement;
- en (an) is produced by saying [ə] and pushing the air back: there is no lip movement.
- un (ain, ein, in) is produced by saying [a] and pushing the air back: there is no lip movement.

It is a good idea to ensure that students are able to differentiate between these sounds aurally (if not orally) before showing them how to write them, because as soon as they see them on the page or on the board, they are tempted to sound the end consonants. When we write these vowels on the board, we need to stress that the consonant marks the pronunciation of a *vowel* sound, and that we do not hear [n]. It is important to write words featuring these vowels, and good practice to begin with words that exemplify the leading vowels we have been practising. Therefore, for /e/en/, we can choose *temps, lent, prend* rather than *quand, tant, grand*. For /a/ain/, we can write *pain, train, main, grain* rather than *pin, lin, un*. Once students have practised reading these initial combinations of vowels with real words, we can add more words to our lists to show that the same sounds can also be written in the following manner: *an* as in *dans, quand, tant, grand*; *in* as in *pin, vin, crin*; *ein* as in *frein, teint* and *un* as in *un, brun, etc*. It is very important to point out to students that *an, am, en, em; ain, un, in, im, ein; on, om* always sound *an, un, on*. Unlike in English, phonemes can be written differently in French, but the combinations of letters representing them are overall constant. There are few exceptions, as for example, *monsieur* and *femme*.

Tips for teaching u and ou
We are usually aware that students find it difficult to say /u/ [y] but, actually, quite a few students find it equally difficult to say /ou/ [u]. The sound [y] can be produced by first saying [i] and then by bringing the lips forward and rounding them into a tight circle. Most learners approximate *ou* well enough by sounding /oo/ as in 'shoe' or 'boot'. Hence, they will say 'root' for *route*, but some students really cannot do this at all, and they will say something like 'reute'. Students who find it virtually impossible to differentiate between *sur* and *sous* may have troubles hearing the letter *r* in *sur*. However, more often that not, the problem stems from their not being able to pronounce either or both *u* and *ou*. The sounds expressed by the letters *ou* and *u* are versions of each other and both are made by keeping everything in identical position but for the air. To put it into simple language, when sounding the letter *u* the air is pushed out of the mouth, and when sounding *ou*, it is held back, the throat is contracted. Some students can learn to produce the

phoneme /ou/ by sounding /oo/ in hoot and hood or even the /w/ is west. It helps too to inform learners that *w* is considered a semi-vowel rather than a consonant (hence the name double-u).

LEARNING TO LISTEN

Where do words begin and end? Students can hear that I am not leaving gaps when I speak French, but they are unaware that they do the same thing when they are speaking in English because they are making natural sense of English words, and because they are literate. They are under the impression that they are hearing each word separately and find it quite fascinating to learn that we can tell where words begin and end in English, not because we leave gaps between words as we do in writing, but because we detect stress and prosodic elements, long vowels, final consonants and so forth. Students find it equally fascinating to learn that in many writing systems, as for example, in classical Latin and Greek, words were not separated but followed one after the other in *scriptio continua* (continuous script) as when they are spoken, hence also the high value these traditions placed on oratory skills and rote learning.

In French, many words end in vowel sounds and all vowels are fully sounded, except for /e/, which may or may not be pronounced according to regional accents and register. Syllables are also relatively equally weighted. This makes it difficult for English-speaking learners to hear where French words begin and end. The problem is further complicated by contractions and liaisons, and I will say more about this in due course. The rhythms of French and English are especially evident in poetic mode where metre in English is accented whilst it is syllabic in French.

Accentuating the correct syllables in any language is important because it helps us identify the start and the end of words. When English words are disyllabic or polysyllabic, the first syllable is usually stressed. When a word is prefixed, however, the accent falls on the second syllable, as in, for example: 'unfold'. When it is suffixed, the accent will fall on the syllable before the suffix: 'education'. Like all other native speakers, English speakers are not conscious of how their language sounds unless they are hearing another English accent (national, regional or other), or they are meaning to produce a particular effect, or they are hearing or reading poetry. Native speakers cannot hear their own language because they are listening to what the language is saying, not to how it is sounding. On the other hand, English speakers are well able to hear how French or any other language sounds precisely because they do not understand the words. With a few comparative examples, students are able to hear that French stresses the last syllable of words and that it has a flatter intonation than English. Students of French also need to learn that French speakers may shift the stress from the last syllable of salient words when they are speaking emphatically.

Polysyllabic words in French and in English, and the schwa

It is important for students to know that languages do not only produce different individual sounds but specific sound combinations. Languages obey phonological rules and can be allergic to certain sound combinations. This explains contractions, liaisons and a number of apparent grammatical exceptions in French and English. English vowel sounds tend to shift with the consonant context. To make students aware of this, I will write the letter *a* on the board and ask for the sound of this letter. Students usually answer that this sounds [a] as in cat.

> 'So, now tell me how we sound the letter *a* in these words: impact, grape, rage, courage, adaptable, balloon...'
> 'Oh, I never realised this!'
> 'See how we tend to drop some vowels in these words: comfortable, adaptable, etc. the sound we make here is called a schwa.'
> 'A what?'
> 'A schwa. It is is a sort of no vowel sound, or if you prefer a vowel that is quasi-empty of sound. Now, compare what we say above with what happens in French: *grappe, rage, courage, adaptable, confortable, famille, ballon*, and see how stable vowels are in French, and how the final *e* is a schwa. Also note how rage becomes *rage*; cage becomes *cage*; age becomes *age*. How might you say the word garage in French? Page? See, you can learn lots of French words by just pronouncing the vowels in a French way.'

Teaching contractions

Because we do not leave gaps between words when we speak, we contract and liaise words. We need to teach students to hear and produce contractions straight away, just as we need to teach them to hear gender (*un/un – le/la*) and plural (*les/des*) with the first words they learn. It is not difficult for students to understand the principle of contraction since they use contractions in English with great frequency: don't, he's, etc. Hence, it is not hard to learn that we will say *l'éléphant* rather than *le éléphant*. Students can also understand easily enough that *à le, de le* and *à les, de les* are contracted to *au, aux, du, des*, and so forth. We only need to stress that these contractions, unlike 'can't' and 'don't', are mandatory. However, except where the partitive article is concerned (see below), it is important not to correct students when they say *de le* and *à le* by simply requiring that they say *du* or *au* because, in actual fact, they are using correct syntax. *Du* and *au* are best understood as euphonic arrangements rather than syntactic units. When students use *de le* and *à le*, I do not correct them by supplying the correct form but rather remind them that they need *to contract* the words, and I let them come up with the contraction on their own.

Teaching liaisons

Like contractions, liaisons are not especially hard to understand since they exist in English – 'my friends *z*are coming'. But we cannot really explain the French liaison by simple reference to English, because French liaisons are not so much extended from the preceding word (as in English) as they are carried onto the following word. Thus, we say *un néléphant*, not *oon éléphant*. Actually, this is something of an exaggeration because French speakers do extend their spoken words from written consonants when they are hesitating and marking space between words, and when reading poetry. However, because syllables are flattened rather than stressed in French, when language is flowing, the liaison is effectively carried over. If students are encouraged to liaise by extending final consonants, they will first of all sound English rather than French, and secondly, they will mistake second-liaised words for consonant-initialled words.

To explain liaisons, like all teachers, I show students a French word that ends with a vowel <u>sound</u> (not a letter) and another that starts with a vowel. Students can hear that if we have two vowel sounds in this position, we have a hiatus, a gap between the words. I explain that sometimes, as for example when we have an aspirated aitch, we are happy to leave the gap: hence, we say *les haricots*. However, more often than not, we need to close the gap to keep our speech fluid. To do this, we create a link by carrying a sound *suggested* by the written consonant at the end of the first word, and placing it onto the second word as though it actually belongs to that word: *un néléphant; un noiseau; des zéléphants; des zoiseaux; mon nami; mes zamis; elles sont tarrivées; un petit toiseau*. And I explain that in a few cases, where no silent consonant is available to guide the liaison a –*t*– is mandated to maintain language fluidity, as in '*Comment s'appelle-t-il?*'

It is well worth stressing the point that in French the liaised sound is conventional and that it is more closely allied to the written word than to the spoken word. If we say *les enfants*, we liaise with a [z] sound. We can see that there is an *s* at the end of *les* when we write the word but nevertheless *les* is pronounced [le] rather than [lez]. We say *lé zenfants* rather than *laiz enfants*. We say *petit* and *un petit tanimal*. We also say *un grand thomme* and not *un grand dhomme*. And the liaison is here more obviously independent, since not only is *t* the aspirated form of *d* but *grand* actually ends on the nasalised vowel sound -*an*. However, we do not say *un grand nhomme* anymore than we say *un grand dhomme*. Finally, I will teach students to say and recognise: *lwazo, nwazo, swazo, néléphant, léléphant, zéléfant, zamis, nami* and so forth. Indeed, learners of French are extremely unlikely to ever hear the words *oiseau* [wazo] or *éléphant* in an authentic French conversation.

Importantly, some of the problems our students encounter with the French liaisons are both phonological and syntactic. In English, nouns may or may not be determined and the stress falls on the noun rather than on the article (unless we are emphasising: 'This is *the* book you want to read!'). The stress will also fall on the main verb rather than on the auxiliary. In fact, the determiner and the auxiliary may be barely audible. Hence, Anglophone speakers who have had little formal grammatical schooling are just as likely to hear 'could of' as 'could've', and are quite unconscious that 'she's happy' and 'she's gone' may respectively involve the verbs 'to be' and 'to have'. In a French sentence, however, syllables have relatively equal weight and determiners (*les, mes, un, etc.*) and auxiliaries are enunciated. Thus, when we liaise a vowel-initialled word with a consonant, we effectively transform that word into a consonant-initialled word. The same goes for contractions, and so much so that French children commonly say *le néléphant, le nours, je sai fait mal, etc.* As regards to the degree of difficulty, liaisons are to phonology what pronominal inflection is to syntax. I have helped students to hear liaisons better by explaining some principles of phonology, drawing their attention to the written word, reading out loud, and encouraging them to learn vowel-initialled nouns by sounding the latter as consonant-initialled nouns with a range of appropriate determiners.

Liaising and identifying syllables for grammatical expression and comprehension

We must be careful not to encourage learners to say things like: dez, ellez, ilz... If students are free to pronounce the silent consonants, they will naturally drift back to their English reading habits and their natural pronunciation. This causes two problems. First it falsifies French prosody and the way liaisons tend to produce strings of consonant-vowel sounds (cvcvcv). Second, sounding silent letters and distorting syllabic unity places obstacles in students' acquisition of spoken and written grammar. Learners need to know that *il chante* and *ils chantent* are pronounced in exactly the same way, and they need to hear the difference between *ils zont* and *ils sont* so as to remember which word is *être* and which is *avoir*. None of this is simple.

Any anecdotal example will show that identifying where words begin and end in French requires English-speaking learners to make a significant aural shift. Students are better able to commit to this shift when they learn that these differences between English and French exist, and if they are given the opportunity to listen and explore these differences. By paying closer attention to stress, phrasing and vowel-consonant patterns, they learn to anticipate liaisons and contractions. The two tables provided below itemize the sentences: *Il est aussi utile de montrer aux élèves comment identifier les syllabes dans les mots français et comment la plupart de ces derniers commencent par des consonnes* and in English: 'It is also helpful to show students how to identify syllables in French words and how for the most part the latter begin with consonant sounds'. We can see at a glance that most of the French words listed below end on a vowel sound whereas most of the English words end on consonant sounds.

TABLE 5: The beginnings of French and English words

VOWEL-INITIALED WORDS		CONSONANT-INITIALED WORDS	
FRENCH	ENGLISH	FRENCH	ENGLISH
il	it	de	helpful
est *liaised*	is *liaised*	montrer	to
aussi *liaised*	also	comment	show
utile	identify	les	students
aux	in *liaised*	syllabes	how
élèves *liaised*	and	dans	to
identifier		les	syllables
et		mots	French
		français	words
		comment	how
		la	for
		plupart	the
		de	most
		ces	part
		derniers	the
		commencent	latter
		par	begin
		des	with
		consonnes	consonant
			sounds
5 unliaised 3 liaised	4 unliaised 2 liaised	19	20

TABLE 6: The endings of French and English words

WORDS ENDING ON A CONSONANT SOUND		WORDS ENDING ON A VOWEL SOUND	
FRENCH	ENGLISH	FRENCH	ENGLISH
il	it	est	also
utile	is	aussi	to
élève	helpful	de	show
syllabes	students	montrer	how
plupart	syllables	aux	to
commencent	in	comment	identify
par	French	identifier	the
consonnes	words	les	
	which	dans	
	for	les	
	most	mots	
	part	français	
	begin	comment	
	with	et	
	consonants	la	
	sounds	de	
		ces	
		derniers	
		des	
8	16	19	7

Also think of how dogs, ducks and birds generally communicate in English and French: woof-woof and *oua-oua*, quack-quack and *coincoin*, tweet-tweet and *cuicui*.

Differentiating and producing *é*, *è* and *un*, *une* is of fundamental importance to the acquisition of French syntax

Many Anglophone students of French have troubles producing and differentiating the sound marked by the letter *é* from that marked by *è* (also *ê*). Simply put, *é* proves particularly difficult whilst *è* is sounded as the diphthong [ei]. Still, I have never met a student who was not able to differentiate between *é* [e] and *è* [ɛ] after they were given explanations and aural exercises. Learners need to be able to *hear* the difference and see the change in lip movements, even if they are able to produce these different sounds some of the time in association with certain consonants and not with others. Although contemporary French speakers do not all differentiate *é* [e] and *è* [ɛ] when sounding *past participle* and *imparfait* forms, differentiating these sounds is crucial for Anglophones learners because it enables them to develop an ear for syntax, for not only do we sound the difference between the singular and the plural of nouns with *les, des, mes, ces* and so forth, but it is by differentiating between these phonemes that Anglophone learners can best learn - which is to say hear, produce and intuit the *présent*, the *passé composé* and the *imparfait* of the indicative: *je mange, j'ai mangé, je mangeais*.

Students have no physical difficulty hearing or sounding the letter *e* because [ə] is also produced in English as in 'the', although they may not differentiate between *e* [ə] and *eu* [œ] which they may also sound *u* [y]. Many learners have problems hearing the difference between *le* and *leur*. In part, this is due to the fact that the sound [ə] in English is accompanied by the letter [r] in words like girl, bird, thirst, third. Some learners automatically add an *r* to the sound [ə] when they are speaking and this also confuses their hearing. When they are reading, some students do not sound *é* and *è* for the reasons given above but also because they are confused by the accents. Without sustained coaching, and unless they are made aware of the role of accents and of the importance of differentiating between *e*, *é*, *è*, learners will read *le* as *ley* [lei] and *je* as *jey* [ʒei].

How *l*-whatever and oon restore the world as it should be (from the Anglophone perspective)

If they are left to their own devices, students will soon produce a sound between *le*, *la* and *les* which somehow blends the three inflections of the definite article into something which I call the *l*-whatever. In a similar vein, students pronounce *un* and *une* as 'oon'.

These intermediate sounds need to be addressed. If students do not differentiate between *le, la* and *les*, between *un* and *une*, and between *du, de* and *des*, they lose the most important tools for internalising the gender of nouns and for differentiating singular and plural forms. If they don't internalise that *es* in *les, mes, des, ces*, is the plural sound, they will naturally feel inclined to sound the plural *s* at the end of nouns. This will place even more obstacles in their learning of gender, of grammatical agreements, and of the formation of plurals.

Oon and the *l*-whatever are a problem of pronunciation that has deep roots in English grammar. It is true that *le*, *un* and *une* are alien sounds, but *la* is not while *les* can be approximated to [lei]. Hence, the issue is not only about pronunciation. In part, *l*-whatever and *oon* originate in English prosody: in English, 'the boy' is sounded *th*BOY, 'a boy' is sounded *a*BOY, and the article is only just audible because the stress falls on the word boy. Of course, French speakers also do this: *l'garçon*, but this is not what our students usually hear in their French classes from their teachers. English speakers do not tend to pay attention to the article in their own language and therefore, in French, second-language learners will produce the article as an incidental linkage when and if they produce it at all.

Beyond this and more importantly, *l*-whatever and *oon* are also syntactic solutions produced by the Anglophone grammar to restore the proper order of things, which is to say a gender-less world. These phonetically blended and unstressed articles have the advantage of aligning French articles with the English articles a/an/the, all of which are invariable. The *l*-whatever and *oon* thus eliminate gender and number – and not only from the article but also from the accompanying noun, because what determines the gender and number of a noun in spoken French (as opposed to the lemma listed in the dictionary) is none other than the gender and the number of the determiner. When students complement this process by sounding the silent plural *s* at the end of the plural noun and the silent final consonant on nouns and/or adjectives (*peti**t**, gran**d***) they are ready to absorb French vocabulary into their English syntax.

Evidently, it is important to teach students from the beginning to enunciate *le, la, les, un, une, des, du, de la* and to explain that because French is gendered and no *s* is sounded at the end of plural nouns, we must pronounce articles accurately and clearly in order to hear gender and number. We also need to explain and demonstrate that to hear singular and plural in French, English speakers need to shift their listening focus to what comes *before* the noun rather than what is at the end of the noun as in English: The book, the book**s**, *le livre*, **les** *livres*. Yes, there is a plural *s* in written French but it is an orthographic convention. As far as the contemporary language is concerned, *s* is not a requirement of the natural language. In speech, almost all French nouns are invariable.

How profoundly un-natural this grammatical fact is to our English speaking learners can be illustrated by a conversation I recently had with Lisa, who finished Year 12 last year. Discussing some aspects of grammar which we take for granted in English, I happened to mention that Chinese has demonstrative pronouns, measure words and numerals, but no articles and no plural inflection. In Chinese, we say one [measure word] dog, three [measure word] dog.

'Oh, that sounds so weird!' Lisa exclaimed. 'Three dog…'
'Does it? After all that's what we say in French: *un chien, trois chiens*.'
'OMG! Of course! I hadn't even realised this! How did I miss that?'

Actually, this is an easy thing to miss because our students learn to read French at the same time as they learn to speak, and the written language, when it happens to resemble English, compensates for the spoken forms that do not make English grammatical sense. Hence, students are far more conscious of the silent *s* at the end of the written plural noun than they are of its absence from the sounded word in speech.

Quite naturally, for our English-speaking students the real form of the word is the written form: *gran**d**, peti**t**, chien**s***, because this is the form that is either exactly like English or that most resembles English. It is interesting that students become far more receptive to the idea of not sounding certain letters when I point out to them that French school children have to learn *to add* letters which do not exist in their speech. Learners of French have to remember not to sound the silent letter but native speakers have to remember to write it in.

Pronunciation and gender

Gender is deeply ingrained in the French worldview. While for French speakers, gender begins with pronunciation, for our students, it begins with psychology. Students are far more likely to accept gender when they learn that English used to have gender. In fact, English used to have masculine, feminine and neutral genders, whereas French only has masculine and feminine. Students are fascinated to learn that in Old English, the word 'stone', for example, was masculine, while the word 'stone' can be either feminine or masculine in French (*pierre, caillou*). To help students make the psychological shift that entering a binary gendered universe demands, I will ask: 'In English, we have very few gendered words, can you think of any?' Students are likely to think of *she* and *he*. I will also explain that many languages do not have a different word for 'she' and 'he'. For example, in Chinese we say *ta* for everyone. In French 'everything' is gendered but we do not gender 'himself' and 'herself' (*se*), or 'to him' and 'to her' (*lui*). Like all teachers, I point out such things as *une personne* but *un individu, une giraffe male, une tortue, une gazelle, une souris, un cerisier, un pommier, un chemisier, une chemise, un tabouret, une chaise*. I make the point that although grammatical gender is somewhat connected to sexual differentiation, it is not about sexual differentiation; certainly gender is about the way that some word endings sound but not always so; and it is also about where a word has come from: whether it belonged to a gendered category in the original language or not, and what that gender was.

Grammatical gender means 'kind' or 'category' but what actually establishes this category, we do not really know. Basically, we know that a word is gendered because we must refer to it as 'he' or 'she'. Now, *un chien* may also be *une chienne*, *un professeur* can have a feminine aspect (*une professeure*) but *une table* can only be *une table*. A few words sound the same, are written in the same way and have a different gender, in which case, they usually mean different things (*le livre, la livre; le page, la page*) but as a rule, only the words referring to biologically sexed beings can have two genders. And thus, quite mysteriously, gender does not equate to sex in French. Simply put, *un tabouret* and *une chaise* cannot produce a baby-chair.

Still, rather than impressing on students that the gender of words is entirely arbitrary or just the way things are, I encourage a little wonder. Why would a language have masculine and feminine genders? Perhaps, a long time ago, our ancestors saw something that connected certain things with what they perceived as feminine or masculine characteristics, perhaps with the moon and the sun and the seasons. But what about neutral? In contemporary Standard English, he and she refer to people and pets, and in some sociolects cars, boats and countries. But in fact, 'he' and 'she' are as much about personhood as they are about sex, hence the use of 'they' as a neutral pronoun refering to persons rather than the neutral 'it'. Does a gendered language make it more difficult to express gender neutrality, or gender equality? Does a language filled with 'its' encourage us to think of the world as being filled with things rather than filled with living beings?

In French, speakers concerned with issues of social-sexual gender binarity have introduced neutral pronouns (*iel, lea, ille*) and other neutral word categories.[119] In standard French and in the common language, up to a point, gender neutrality is enabled by the indefinite *on*, somewhat like 'one', 'someone', 'anybody', 'they' and the generic 'you' work in English. Apart from the demonstrative pronouns *ceci/cela*, indefinite pronouns such as *on* and *personne*, and the relative *quoi*, standard French has no neutral gender. *Ceci* and *cela* and *quoi*, however, are not only neutral but also inanimate and therefore cannot refer to persons. Meanwhile, adjectives that modify neutral pronouns default to the 'masculine' (*c'est beau* and not *c'est belle*) because *grammatically* the masculine and neutral genders are conflated in French. Beyond this, in French as in English, the convention has been to express sexual-gender neutrality and sexual-gender inclusivity by the generic masculine – hence *l'homme* has included *la femme*... well, sort of. Indeed, French is keeping up with social change by coining feminine forms (*ingénieure, écrivaine, etc.*) and by merging stylistic adjustments with traditional etiquette (*celles et ceux*). These developments have not as yet received Academic approval, but they are already part of mainstream usage as evidenced in the

---

[119] See among many other websites: *Divergenres*, https://divergenres.org/regles-de-grammaire-neutre-et-inclusive/

'ecriture inclusive' found in some media, administrative and academic writing.[120] This and the fact that French opts for gender inclusivity rather than gender neutrality (an interesting contrast to English where 'actress' becomes 'actor') offers students plenty of food for thought and discussion.

What else can we say about gender?
Grammatical gender is something that French speakers cannot do without. French speakers need to ascribe gender to a noun. They do this spontaneously, or if in doubt, by asking someone or by looking the word up in the dictionary or on line. Gender is something that native French speakers hear and experience, although they are very unlikely to ponder the causes or the implications of the feminine nature of a chair and the masculine nature of a stool. Importantly, native speakers can make mistakes and ascribe the wrong gender to certain nouns, which is to say they can ascribe a gender that does not conform to dictionary standards. This occurs with words that begin with vowel sounds, words that are generally used in the plural and rarely used with adjectives, some scientific terms and other rare words, words that simply sound masculine or feminine because most words ending this way do, and other words which are given the gender of other nouns that mean more or less the same thing.

Examples of frequently used nouns which many native French speakers have trouble gendering correctly are *abysse, armistice, termite, apogée, tentacule, tubercule, aérogare, espèce, anagramme, octave, orque, mandibule, escarre, tique, autoroute*... Native speakers can get the gender of some words wrong because even though gender in French is nowhere near as connected to the sound of word endings as it is in Spanish or Italian, it is at least partially internalised on the basis of phonological patterns. To pursue the point a little, in poetry, feminine rhymes include all words that end with the vowel *e* and masculine rhymes the other endings. Simply speaking, to many French speakers, the consonants expressed in writing as *ette, enne, ise, ive, ote, ate, ite, ique* and so forth *sound* feminine whilst the vowel sounds expressed in writing as *ant, amp, ent, ain, in, ein, ot, au,* and so forth *sound* masculine.

And indeed, certain endings are 'always' feminine: *-tion, -sion, -euse, -ure, -aie, -ette, -elle* (except *violoncelle*, which is borrowed from *violoncello*); some are mostly feminine: *-eine, -aine;* some are 'always' masculine: *-at, -et, -ail, -euil, -eil* but not *-eille*, which sounds just like *-eil*; also masculine are the words that end in [o], except for *eau* and *peau*, which were respectively *aqua* and *pellis* and feminine in Latin, and words that have been abbreviated, e.g. *radio, moto, video*. Words that end in –*on* are generally masculine. Words ending in –*age* are masculine (*chauffage, garage*, etc.) with some exceptions: *image* and two syllable words like *cage, page, rage, plage, nage* which

---

[120] See Armaury Bucco, 'Pourquoi l'écriture inclusive a déjà gagné la bataille', *Le Figaro*, http://www.lefigaro.fr/vox/societe/2018/10/18/31003-20181018ARTFIG00104- pourquoi-l-ecriture-inclusive-a-deja-gagne-la-bataille.php

are feminine; –ing words and others borrowed from English, like *tweet*, are masculine...

Can gender be taught?
Recently, I asked a student what the subject pronouns *il* and *elle* meant, and she answered 'he', 'she' and 'it'.

'Are you sure?' She looked intrigued, expecting the unexpected, 'Yes...'

I continued, 'But there is no 'it' in standard French. Can't *il* and *elle* simply be he and she?'

'Yes, but not when we translate them.'

'That's correct. *Il* and *elle* can mean 'it' when we translate into English. But what if we are not translating, then what do *il* and *elle* mean?'

'He and she.'

'So, you see, when you're speaking French, everything in the world is a he or a she.'

'But it isn't really...'

'Yes, it is really, when you are in French.'

'Not in English.'

'No, not in English. But is English the measure of French reality?'

She laughed: 'So French people really think of the table as she?'

'Yes. We can try to see how it feels. Look at the table, she is very pretty, and what about my pen, what do you think of him?'

'You know, it sounds funny but it's not really that strange either. It makes everything sort of fairy tale like... like everything becomes little people...'

Where native French speakers are concerned, gender is constantly reinforced in speech and in writing through agreements with determiners and adjectives, and it is also consolidated in the formal study of French at school and through reading. Therefore, the nouns native speakers get wrong represent a very small proportion of French nouns. As mentioned above, native speakers usually ascribe the wrong gender because they associate certain word endings with one gender or the other. Indeed, gender has a sound. But gender is also not entirely without a *raison d'être*. Although I have heard French speakers refer to a noun that presents gender difficulties by shifting between the masculine and the feminine or even alternating between *un* and *elle*, this is rare. Gender reassignment certainly tests French speakers who are learning Spanish (*el mar* for *la mer*, *la leche* for *le lait*) because a masculine sea and a feminine milk simply don't feel right. In truth, this attachment to gender is a profound enigma because French speakers do not think of *la mer* as female or *le lait* as male, but they will and do ascribe gender to everything, and for the most part, once a word is associated with a particular gender, it sticks. Our students by contrast find it very difficult to ascribe gender to anything, and they will very quickly forget the gender of any noun that is not biologically sexed.

French speakers internalise gender by hearing and using nouns with determiners and adjectives, through phonetic association, and by refining and extending their vocabulary at school, at play and at work. Students of French can do something along the same lines. They can learn gender by always learning nouns with a gendered article *la* or *le*, and with *un* or *une* where nouns are vowel-initialled. They can pay attention to the endings of words wherever appropriate. It is also good learning practice to use nouns with a determiner and a descriptive adjective (*la petite maison, le petit parc*). When students hesitate to speak and they ask us for the gender of a word, it is a sign that they have internalised the *need* for gender when speaking French. If they are hesitating with words ending in *–tion, –ette, –teur, –ure, –age*, we may encourage them to make an *educated* guess but we can and should always supply the correct answer.

READING AND WRITING WHAT WE SAY: CODIFYING LANGUAGE

Reading, as Krashen recommends, is a wonderful way to engage with a second language and to learn language. Reading out loud is an excellent exercise to help develop pronunciation, phrasing and to practise correct grammar. However, for reading to be an effective learning exercise, students have to be able to pronounce what they are reading reasonably accurately. Evidently, reading French and English are two different enterprises, even though both languages make use of the Roman alphabet and share much of their vocabulary.

English-speaking students are not usually aware that the spelling of English is both visual and phonetic. Nor do they tend to be appreciative of the advantages of spelling homonyms with different combinations of letters. They are, however, well aware that English spelling is 'crazy' – because it is not always possible to match the same set of letters to the same pronunciation, as for example: lead and lead; read, deed and dead; ghost, enough, rough and bough, etc.

It fascinates and motivates students to learn about the respective histories of English and French and how both languages came to be written and codified. There are many wonderful documentaries available on the history of English on line, and students love to learn about runes and Latin, about Old English, Norse, Norman French, and so forth. Students can learn that in medieval times, the writing of French and English was more closely associated with how the languages were pronounced than written English and French are today, and how, depending on the dialects spoken by the writers, words could be spelt differently. Students should also learn about the influence of French on English; they can learn about the Great Vowel Shift and of the loss of declensions and gender. They can reflect on the problems and difficulties of devising a written language from a borrowed alphabet. When they understand that Latin letters were suited to Latin phonology, to Latin vowels and consonants, and that both English and French have many more vowels and several more consonants than Latin, they can accept that the current conventions guiding the writing of both languages are neither random nor entirely ridiculous.

We can show students how the writing of English and French is conventional rather than purely phonetic, how letters are *approximate* rendering of sound, signposts for the sounds that we are actually making. We can demonstrate the flexibility of vowel sounds in English orthography by writing out various words, as for example, rage and courage, and asking students to read these words out loud. We can point out how English speakers of various dialects will read a word differently even as they share a common understanding: water, wader, watta, wada; tomato, tomaito; li*bra*ry, lie-berry, libry, etc.

Finally, we need to explain that although grammar plays a relatively narrow role in English orthography, the spelling of English is at times guided by grammatical principles, and this is what causes problems for some spellers who do not understand the rationale governing the written conventions (whose, who's, they're, there, their, it's, its). Students can appreciate that their French class is the perfect place to learn about all this.

An overview of French orthography: silent letters and things like that
It is difficult to write in French, just as it is difficult to write in English. Although French orthography is in some respects more phonetically stable than English, it is complicated by silent letters and grammatical relationships. Some silent letters serve an aesthetic function, connecting French to Latin and Greek (through real and supposed etymologies), or to a former usage or a former pronunciation. Thus, silent letters are not just annoying, they are keepers of history and collective memory. In addition, as for English, French orthography can help us differentiate between homonyms: *quand, camp; temps, tant; tic, tique*; and announce morphological and inflected variations: *petit/petite; j'attends/attendon*s; and, like English spelling, French spelling has evolved over time as well as differently at different times under different cultural forces and circumstances. Taking everything into account, the most difficult aspect of French orthography lies with the fact that French makes grammatical relationships explicit in writing when those are not explicit in speech. And of course, this is also why writing is a privileged place in which to learn, experience and practise French grammar.

French uses diacritical marks called accents

Accents serve several purposes: they help differentiate homonyms (*à, a, ou, où, sur, sûr*); they are historical markers, indicating where a word might have lost a letter at some point in the past (which is fun because we often find the missing letter in the English version of the word – *hôtel*, hostel, *hôpital*, hospital); and finally, accents mark certain vowel sounds.

French uses accents to complement the spelling of its phonological repertoire. Hence, the letters *é* and *è* are not funny variants of *e* but sounds in their own right, and they are perfectly audible to the French ear, as audible as [i] and [o]. It is very important for students to know this, and, not least, to care about it. And very few students do, in part because the accent does not exist in English, but also because the phoneme /é/ is sometimes written *er* or *ez* or *–es* and the phoneme /è/ is also written *ei, ai, elle, ette, es, est* and *–et*, and there are no accents in any of these variants. Besides, learners have a natural tendency to pronounce the *e* in words like *le* and *je* as [ei], and this is not only wrong, it also means that they have no psychological need to differentiate between the sounds represented by the letters *e, é* and *è*. English-speaking learners will evaporate the sound of the letter *e* wherever their native English instincts find it expedient.

Accents are not easy to remember, and students have all my sympathy on this count; although I understand the importance of accents in French, I find accents in Spanish very inconvenient. But we do need to learn about accents, and in French the best place to start is when learners first learn to read and write. We should also encourage students to refer to accents correctly: acute, grave and circumflex, rather than the thingo above the letter, the apostrophe, and where do I put that little dot?

Leaving the acquisition of accents to learners' powers of observation results in accents being placed more or less over something or added to whatever just in case. Thus, we need to bring students' attention to the accents, and we need to teach them how to write accented letters, which is to say, to write those as we write all other letters, by placing the accent above the letter while moving our pen in a top down direction. Students need to practise writing words with accents, ensuring correct movement and placement, and completing the accented letter *before* they write subsequent letters: *les é-lè-ves*. Bringing the accent in line with the basic rules of handwriting means treating the accent as an integral part of a letter. And then, of course, it is also important to engage students in pronunciation exercises. I explain the sound of the letter *é* as being at some point between the sounds [i] and [y] or [i] and [ə]. We then practise the sequences [i],[e],[ə] and [i],[e],[y]. Then, we will practice [e] and [ɛ]. I will write *e, eu// é, er, ez, –es// è, ê, es, est, –et, ei, ai* on the board and we will practise reading and sounding these combinations of letters.

French combines letters differently from English but French vowels are sounded mostly as orthographic convention spells them out

Words like *pain* and *pin* may be written differently in French although they are sounded in exactly the same way (setting aside regional differences), just as homonyms are written differently in English ('sea' and 'see'). In French, however, the correspondence between sounding and spelling is overall stable. Unlike what happens in English when we write the letters *ou* in words like 'cough', 'court' and 'enough' or when we write the letter *a* in 'rage', 'cat' or 'courage', in French, letters such as *é, er, ez, –es* are 'always' pronounced the same way [e]; the same goes for *è, ê, ai, ei, -et, est* that are sounded [ɛ]; and *ain, ein, im, in* that are sounded [ɛ̃]; *on, om* sounded [ɔ̃] and so forth. In other words, French vowel sounds may be expressed with different letters, but these letters are normally sounded in a consistent manner – which is a relative advantage.

French spelling expresses syntactic relationships

Why bother with different letters to produce the same sound? What purpose can different letters serve besides identifying homonyms? The reason French spells *é, ée, ées, er, ez* is grammatical. It is about the function of the words and the relationship between the words: *é* marks the past participle masculine singular, *ée* marks the past participle feminine singular, *és* and *ées* the plural participle forms, *er* the infinitive, and *ez* the second person, formal, singular or plural, and all of these are sounded in exactly the same manner. To write French, therefore, even native speakers must be aware of the syntactic functions of certain words and of the syntactic connections between words. *Elle parle* and *elle**s** parle**nt*** are sounded in exactly the same way. The ending *–nt* identifies the third person plural in writing. In speech we can only differentiate between the third person singular and the third person plural of the verbs belonging to the first conjugation (ending in –ER) through context: because we have been notified of the antecedent or because the verb begins with a vowel and we liaise the third-person plural pronoun (*elles aiment*). Syntactic consideration does not only apply to verbs but also to quantifiers, nouns and adjectives. The plural of a noun is indicated by a silent *s*: *un garçon, des garçon**s***. The letter *e* may be a silent feminine marker (*poupée*) or an etymological convention (*musée*) or it may signify that a consonant must be sounded (*porte*).

When we first teach students to read French, we can explain why we need to add or subtract letters on account of grammar. We can make a point of calling silent letters 'silent', and of explaining how and why we need to write letters we do not pronounce. We can introduce students to a word's distant ancestors in Old French and in Latin, and connect it to its cousins in contemporary Italian and Spanish. We can explain that, although silent letters are not a necessity of speech, they are part of the language's memory and part of the grammar. Students can make friends with silent letters when they can appreciate that formal grammar is in many respects an art form, and when they understand that the language they are learning (and their own maternal language) is not the mechanical operation of dusty conventions but a living cultural entity, with a past and a present.

More about silent letters

Although one may be justified in thinking that it is trickier to write French than to write English on account of these grammatical conventions, *reading* French is not that difficult because the way letters are sounded in French is overall consistent. The final consonants that are almost always silent are: *t, d, p, z*. Also silent are *n* and *m* when they mark nasalised vowels. The plural *s* is silent, and so is the second person *s* and other letters in conjugated endings: *ons, ent, aient, etc*. The consonants *t, d* and *p* are sounded only when they are followed by the letter *e*. Thus, the letter *e* identifies what happens in speech, it identifies the sounding of the final consonant. In this way, the letter *e* marks the feminine form of adjectives. Therefore, if we sound silent consonants for no good reason, we can no longer identify gender. The orthographic convention, however, pre-empts the extended gendered form, as in *grand* and *petit*, which become *grande* and *petite* in the feminine, or reminds us of more ancient origins (real or supposed) as in *temps* and *camp* and/or differentiates homonyms as in *temps* and *tant, camp* and *quand, sang* and *sans*.

It is not difficult to reconcile students to *the idea* of silent letters, since those also occur in English (thought, knife, etc.), but that does not mean that they will feel appreciative. Indeed, reconciling learners to *the fact* of silent letters is another matter. From the students' perspectives, two wrongs don't make a right, and silent letters are just as 'stupid' in English as in French. Then, since sounding end consonants is part of the English reading experience, students are naturally inclined to sound every final consonant they read in any French word. Not least, they quickly perceive the advantages of sounding the end consonants of words like *grand, long, petit, excellent* because, as I explained above, doing this effectively turns them into real words (English), because it eliminates the problem of gender agreement, and because it also helps with remembering how to spell the words, which comes in handy in tests and examinations. In some cases, such as *ils* and *elles*, sounding the *s* helps Anglophone learners to remember that they are actually saying 'they', or as some students cleverly put it: 'shes' and 'hes'. In fact, it is very helpful for students to think of *ils* and *elles* as shes and hes, so long as they remember that we must not hear the *s* in French. Learning words orally before learning how to write them helps students keep silent letters silent. Bringing students' attention to the fact that the silent letters are *added* to the written word rather than *retracted* from the spoken word also encourages English-speaking learners not to sound silent letters.

Reading nasalised vowels and not nasal consonants

The letters *on, om, an, un, in* and so forth express nasalised vowels: the *n* (and *m)* do not act as consonants. When used in combination with a leading vowel, *n* (also *m*) expresses a whole vowel sound of a different kind. The letter *n*, however, is not used at random because *n* is a nasal consonant. Students can experiment saying *nnnn* and they will feel the air vibrating in their nose and their throat.[121]

Reading and writing vowels and diphthongs in French
- soft vowels: e i
- hard vowels: a o u ou
- diphthongs: oi ieu ui oui
- a i u ou oi ieu are always written and sounded the same way.

The letter *u* may be used for hardening a *g* as in *guide* or a *c* as in *cueillir*.
- e, eu, œ, œu may be sounded as a more open [ə] or closed [œ] depending on the regional or social version of French.

At the end of a word, the letter *e* is mostly used to sound the preceding consonant. It is also used to soften the letter *g* as in *nous mangeons*. In northern French pronounciation and familiar registers [ə] is often dropped: *j'suis, nous ach'tons*. Conversely, the letter *e* in *je, le* and other words is sounded in the more formal registers and in poetic modes.
- é, er, ez, et, -es (as in des/les/mes/ces)

When er is followed by t, d, l, etc. it is sounded *ère* (vert, couvert, merle) because the following consonant naturally opens the [e] sound.
- è is also ê, est, es, ai, ei, –et (poulet) and elle, ette
- i is also y
- when y is a semivowel, it is sounded [j] and [j] can also be written /–ill/
- o, au, eau
- on (written *om* before *b* and *p* as in English)
- en, an (written with an *m* before *b* and *p* as in English)
- un, in, ain, ein (written with and *m* before *b* and *p* as in English)

The spelling of consonant sounds requiring special attention
- –il and –ill are pronounced [j] or /y/– rail, bille, fille, bailler.
  - ➢ notable exception: la ville.
- gn which is pronounced [ɲ] as in o*n*ion – gagner.
- ch is pronounced [ʃ] or /sh/ – cheval.

---

[121] For an informative study on the development of nasalized vowels in French see Emily Dowd's masters' thesis, *Les voyelles nasales en Français, histoire, variation régionale et pédagogie*, http:/gets.libs.uga.edu/pdfs/dowd_emily_a_200508_ma_pdf.

- j and g before a soft vowel are pronounced [ʒ] in the same way – jaune, girafe (note that in English before a soft vowel, g is also soft: giraffe, congeal).
- hard g [g] before a hard vowel (as in English: gout, gut, goat) – gare; goûter.
  - ➢ u is used to harden the g before the soft vowel (as in guest and guide in English) – fatigué, guide.
  - ➢ e is used to soften the g before a hard vowel: geôle, mangeons.

As all teachers know, students find the following sounds confusing and difficult to remember.
- c is sounded [s] before a soft vowel (as in English: certificate, icy)
- c is pronounced [k] before hard vowels a, o, u, ou (as in English: cat, cut, coat)
- cu is sounded [k] before a soft vowel.
  - ➢ Note: cucillir is hard to read but easy to say [kəjir] /kcyir/.
  - ➢ Note: when *u* is not used to harden *c* or *g*, the letters *ui*, *oua* are diphthongs respectively pronounced [y.i] and [wa].
- ç is sounded [s] before a, o, u, ou – garçon, maçon.
- s between two vowels has the sound [z] – poison.
- ss between two vowels has the sound [s] – poisson.

It is worth spending time practising the above by providing lots of examples. I have noticed that even Year 12 students are confused by certain combinations of letters, as for example *vieillir, cueillir, oeil, yeux,* none of which is difficult to pronounce but all are indeed difficult to read if one has not mastered French orthographic conventions.

Also problematic: the silent and aspirated aitch
In French, aitches are of etymological interest, being of Latin and Germanic origins.
- The silent *h* is mute and is purely graphic: *l'héritage, l'herbe* (note also the American pronunciation of 'herb').
- The aspirated *h* is not truly aspirated. Rather, it marks a hiatus: *le haricot, les haricots*. The 'aspirated' *h* creates a hiatus, which is to say, an *audible* gap between words.

How to read and pronounce –ail and –eil, and ay–
These are confusing (also *oeil* and *euil*) and many students mispronounce the words *travailler* and *réveiller* well into Year 12 and beyond. They are especially confused as

to why the vowel is sounded [a] in the former and [e] in the latter, and they are confused by the respective use of the letters *y* and *-ill*. I explain that the letters *–ill* are sounded [j], hence *trava/iller* is [travaje], and indeed when we write 'travayé', students can pronounce *travailler* correctly. The letter *y* for its part is a semi-vowel. It is the equivalent of two *i* (i i). Hence, we will write and say:

- Crayon → crai   ion
- Rayon → rai   ion

The letters *ill* have the sound [j] and are worth one 'consonant' sound. In *réveiller*, the *i* of the *ei* sound and the *i* of the *ill* sound are absorbed into a single *i* (whereas in cueillir the *e* is differentiated from the following *i*):

- veiller → ve(i) iller
- réveil → réve(i) iller

By contrast, in travailler, the letter *a* is sounded [a].

- travail → trava   iller

In short:
The *e* in eil/eiller may be sounded [ə] or [e].
The *a* in ail/ailler is sounded [a].

THE NEGLECTED ARTICLES

I have included a discussion on the articles in this chapter because the best place to teach articles is in oral practice. Students need to hear the differences between *le, la, les, un, une, des, du, de la*, and the negative preposition *de*. They also need to *understand* and *experience* the range of articles by using those in real conversation in order to internalise what these locutions do for French speakers and for themselves when they speak French. Furthermore, students need to learn about articles from the very start because articles express the gender and number of nouns.

Understanding the difficulties involved in learning the articles in French

Frederick Bodmer genuinely believed that the most efficient way to learn any European language was to learn them all, because comparison explains everything. Bodmer was a philological genius, but even he found the articles of the Romance languages, and of French in particular, bewildering. In actual fact, it is far more difficult for English speakers to master the use of the French articles than to master the use of the French object pronouns. This might explain why articles are rarely taught in the classroom; although, looking at the place the article occupies in most textbooks, I am tempted to think that they simply go unnoticed. Why? Possibly because they are very small words, and so we expect that students will just acquire them, eventually and naturally, and perhaps also because we underestimate the extent of their syntactic resonance.

There is a reason why French articles are more difficult to acquire, to learn and to teach than object pronouns. Object pronominal use in French is more complicated than in English because English does not differentiate between direct object and indirect objects and because English obeys a SVO word order whether it uses pronouns or nouns. Nevertheless, both the accusative and the dative functions exist in English. To remember when to use *lui/leur*, it is almost enough for students to grasp that the dative case is *to* him/*to* her/*to* them, while *le/la/les* is simply him/her/them. Articles, however, are another story altogether because English can only approximate some of the articles used in French and it is entirely lacking others. The plural indefinite *des* and the indefinite partitive articles *du* and *de la* do not exist in English, and of course, neither do the contracted forms (prep + article): *au, aux, du, des*.

We often teach that *des* and *du/de la* are the equivalent of 'some'. This approximation is useful but it is not sufficient because 'some' can also express *quelques, certains, un* ('some guy told me this') and the indefinite direct object pronoun *en* ('I have some'/ *j'en ai*). In addition, equating *des, du* and *de la* with 'some' does not help students where French requires an article and not just any old article, and English draws a mandatory blank. None of the sentences listed below could accommodate 'some' or 'the' and retain their intended meaning.

- Philosophy is my sister's favourite subject.
- *La philosophie est la matière préférée de ma soeur.*
- Dogs are very intelligent animals.
- *Les chiens sont des animaux très intelligents.*
- I like coffee but I usually drink tea.
- *J'aime le café mais d'habitude je bois du thé.*

Among the most difficult things to acquire in another language are the *functional* words that do not exist in our own language and for which we have no cognitive or communicative use and no psychological need. Students cannot learn articles by being told that in French, people say 'the dogs are some very intelligent animals'. They cannot learn like this because this English sentence does not really make sense. We cannot learn or remember what is bereft of meaning. To acquire articles in French, students need to learn what makes articles necessary in French and English, and why English can dispense with them where French cannot. And the first thing, students need to know is what an article is and what it does. Students must therefore begin with learning about the determiners in English, and how to identify and name the definite and indefinite articles, possessive adjectives, demonstrative adjectives, and so forth.

The article determines the noun; it references it and sets it in context (tells us what we can infer about it at the time we are using it). Am I talking about something I have already mentioned ('the book I bought yesterday') or am I talking about something for the first time ('I bought a book yesterday')? That is what articles (simply speaking) do in English. We can also determine nouns with quantifying locutions: 'some books', 'a few books', 'lots of books', 'three books', and so forth, and by using demonstrative or possessive locutions: 'this book', 'that book', 'my book', 'your book'; in which case, the determiners are also adjectives since they modify the noun: 'this book' is not 'that book', and 'my book' is not 'your book' just as a round table is not a rectangular table. The article does not modify as other determiners do: if I say 'I bought a book today', and you say 'Could you show me the book you bought today?' we are still speaking about the same book. We can say that the article determines and references the noun while the possessive adjective determines and modifies the noun.

The types of articles and their functions
English has two articles: 'the' and 'a/an'. Broadly speaking, the use of English articles is as described in the paragraph above. In addition, we can say things like 'The tiger is king of the jungle'. French, like English, has two categories of articles: definite and indefinite, but there are also categories within these categories.

The definite article comes in two modes: as a specific reference (*le, la les*), and as a global/conceptual reference (*le, la, les*); the definite article is gendered in the singular and has a unique plural form.

The indefinite article comes in four modes. The indefinite article may express a countable reference (*un, une, des*) and is therefore gendered and plural. The indefinite article may also express a non-countable reference or partitive (*du/de la*) which is gendered but has no plural form for obvious reasons: if it cannot be counted, it can't be pluralised. [122] And the indefinite articles *un, une, des* as well

---

[122] Some French grammars intended for native French-speaking students consider *des* a partitive form as well as the plural of *un* and *une*, while French grammars intended for English-speaking learners sometimes ignore that *des* is the plural of *un* and *une* and thus frequently list the partitive forms as *du, de la, des* (possibly because all three may be approximated by 'some'). Not surprisingly, I have met teachers of French who were unaware that *des* is the plural of *un* and *une*. There is not a lot of advantage in thinking of *des* as a partitive form. *Du* and *de la* are indefinite quantities of something or other, which excludes both singularisation and pluralisation. If I say *j'ai acheté du thé*, I do not mean *j'ai acheté un thé* which would require more information, as for example, *j'ai acheté un thé vert délicieux;* the same goes if I were to say *j'ai acheté des thés*, which would also call for more information, as for example, *j'ai acheté des thés de tous les coins du monde*. The plural implies that I bought several kinds of tea, not an indefinite number of teas. *Des* is best understood as a certain number of something or other, and thus as the plural of 'a' and 'an'. Hence, if I say *j'ai cueilli des fleurs* and I put this in the singular, I end up with *j'ai cueilli une fleur* and not with *j'ai cueilli de la fleur*.

as *du* and *de la*, can each act as general references – *j'aime le café et je bois du café le matin et en général je bois du café (le café) sans sucre; les chiens sont des animaux de compagnie; un enfant est une petite personne.* How do we explain French articles to students? Articles need to be introduced sequentially, and in context of real language and real communication. Even then, it will take time for students to truly get on top of them. Students will forget aspects of the rules, and they will need to revisit the explanations along with more examples. The important thing is not to give up because they will eventually get there.

Teaching the definite and the indefinite articles
When asked to explain what they understand about the articles, students usually say that the definite article is 'specific' and the indefinite article is 'not specific'. This is not wrong, but I think it is the wrong way to go about it, because when I ask students: 'If I say, "there are three dogs in the yard", is this definite or indefinite?' They almost always answer: 'It's definite', and when I ask why, they answer 'because it's specific'.

I then agree that the number of dogs is specific... but what about the dogs? 'What's specific about the dogs?' Then I continue: 'Let's put this in the singular. What would we say if there were only one dog? There is the dog or a dog in the yard? So, if we say "there is a dog in the yard", which article are we using? That's right, the indefinite. By the way what else does "a/an" mean? 'One'. When we say "an apple a day", we also mean "one apple a day". Indeed, ān meant "one" in Old English.'

If I say 'the children are in the yard', we know the children about whom I am speaking. We have already mentioned the children, and therefore we have defined them; we are speaking about the children we know something about. If I say, 'there is a dog in the yard', we don't know who the dog is or whose dog it is, we have not *defined* it, and we could actually say 'an undefined dog' or 'one undefined dog has walked into the courtyard'.

Students think of the definite and indefinite articles as specific and not specific because this is what they have been taught, and because they are confusing 'specific' and 'specified', which evidently do not mean the same thing. Teaching students to understand definite as something we have defined and indefinite as something we have not previously defined has the advantage of explaining the concept and of sounding like 'definite' and 'indefinite'. It also frees the word 'specific' for another explanation, as we will see.

Students are able to understand the difference between the indefinite and definite articles easily enough when I take the line of questioning provided above.

As indicated in text, the partitive and indefinite articles can express an indefinite general condition (*je bois du café et je mange des fruits*) or a generalisation (*un enfant est une personne*), the difference between them lies in their determining a countable noun or a mass noun.

After this, they need to practise by naming the things around them or things shown in images, asking *Qu'est-ce que c'est? C'est un chien, une chienne, un chat, une chatte, un garçon, une fille, un stylo, une table*. At this point, we also need to keep students' attention on gender inflection. Therefore, we must keep the articles in the singular. We play a game whereby students substitute **le** *chien* for **un** *chien*, **la** *fille* for **une** *fille*, etc. And to ensure that students know that *le* and *un*, and *la* and *une* are not the same words, I will ask 'What does it mean?' to which they answer that *un chien* means **a** dog, *le chien* means **the** dog, and so forth.

The Rule: The article is always in agreement with the gender of the noun; a masculine noun calls for *le* or *un*; a feminine noun calls for *la* or *une*. Before a vowel, *le* and *la* are contracted to *l'*, and this does not change the gender of the noun.

Teaching the plural definite article
Once students have learned that whenever we say 'the' in English we will say *le* or *la* in French, they are ready to learn about the plural definite article. Here, I will use various examples, and say: *la chaise, les chaises, le livre, les livres*, etc. so that students identify that I am saying the book and the books. But quite a few students cannot actually hear the difference between *le/la* and *les* and most will not notice the difference, for the simple reason that this difference does not exist in their own language. Students know that I am saying 'books' and 'chairs' because they can tell the difference between a book and several books when I am pointing to them – *not* because they have actually *heard* me say *le, la*, and *les*.

Hence, I will need to make this explicit by saying 'the book', 'the books'... 'How do you know it's plural?' Students will answer that it is because of the *s* at the end of books. 'And when I say: *la chaise*, **les** *chaises, le livre,* **les** *livres, le stylo,* **les** *stylos*, can you hear what is happening in French? Listen, what tells you that something is plural?' At this point, students can hear *le/la/les*.

Once students are able to hear the difference between the singular and the plural in French, I will continue to practise with the real-life objects around us: *la chaise, les chaises, le livre, les livres*, and various objects in pictures which helps them practise the article and increase their vocabulary. I will ask students to make a show of finger(s) for singular or plural. Once we have done this for a while, students can take over and take turns in saying *la chaise, les chaises*...

Rule: In French, 'the' (*le* and *la*) must have a plural form because we do not mark the plural of nouns by adding an /s/ sound as we do with English nouns. Hence, to know whether we are speaking about the book or the book**s**, we need to say *le livre*, **les** *livres*; the chair or the chair**s**, *la chaise*, **les** *chaises*. *Les* is the plural of both *le* and *la*. Note that this does not affect the gender of the noun. The noun is still feminine or masculine even in the plural. Note also that we add an *s* when we write although we do not sound this letter when we speak.

Teaching the plural of the countable indefinite articles
I will pick up a book and ask students: 'What is this? A book. Good, now what is this? A pen. And this? A chair'. Then I pick up two books and I ask: 'What are these?' Students answer 'books'. Then, I will ask, 'what about these?' Students answer 'pens' and so forth. 'How do we show the difference between the singular and the plural in English? A book, books, right. Now listen to French, *une chaise, des chaises, un livre, des livres, un sac, des sacs…* We may also say *un livre, deux livres, trois livres*, and when we stop counting: *des livres*.'

<u>The Rule</u>: In English, a/an does not have a plural form. We can say 'some', 'a few', or 'several' chairs but we can also say 'chairs' because the *-s* suffices to tell us that we are speaking about more than one chair. In French, we rely on the article to give us the plural. Therefore, just as *les* is the plural of either *la* or *le*, *des* is the plural of *un* or *une*. And of course, even though *des* does not identify the gender of the noun, the noun is nevertheless gendered.

The contracted form de: Once students have internalised this rule thoroughly, we may teach at a later stage that before a plural adjective, *des* is usually contracted to *de*.
- J'ai de nouveaux amis.

Teaching the partitive indefinite articles
We say *une* or *des chaises* because we can count chairs. There are things, however, that we don't usually count like milk, water, butter, or bread. We can measure those things, and of course we can talk about 'butters' and 'milks', but only if we are referring to types of butter and milk, not the stuff that we keep in the fridge. In grammar, these words are called 'mass nouns' as opposed to 'count nouns'. And since 'mass' tends to suggest measurement or something solid, and thus leaves out liquids, I will make sure to use the words 'countable' and 'uncountable' to stress this difference. I then proceed in the following manner:

'In everyday conversation, we might say "milk" or "some milk", "butter" or "some butter" and you will notice that unlike when I say some chairs, the words milk and butter remain in the singular. Why don't we pluralise butter and milk?' Students will come up with the answer by themselves, and then I will continue. 'When we say "I bought milk" or "I bought some milk" at the shop, is this definite or indefinite? What would be definite? How about, I put *the* milk in the fridge? Is "some" milk a defined or an undefined quantity of milk? Okay, so "some milk" is undefined therefore it is…? Yes, indefinite. What if I want to specify a given quantity of milk, do I say "one milk", "two milks" or do I say "a bottle of milk", "a litre of milk?" Indeed, we measure milk rather than count it. Now, remember that in French we usually need to determine the noun. Since we do not count milk, we can't use *un* or *une*. Why not? Because *un* and *une* also mean "one". Furthermore, we can't say *des*, since *des* is the countable plural form. So, French has another indefinite article to reference uncountable nouns: **du** *lait*, **de la** *crème*. We say *du* and *de la* to refer to a certain quantity of something or other. This article often works like "some" in English, but unlike in English, we cannot omit it.'

After this, I will bring out real objects and flash cards in order to practise through visual association. To help students identify as well as experience and internalise the difference between partitive and definite. I will use many examples in this vein: 'If I want to say "there's milk in the fridge", in French, I will say: *il y a* **du** *lait sur la table, il y a* **du** *lait dans le frigo* but if I say, "**the** milk is in the fridge" I will say: **le** *lait est dans le frigo*.'

I will also bring students' attention to the fact that the feminine is in two parts but that it is one semantic unit. I never explain the partitive *du* as a contraction of *de le* because the <u>indefinite</u> articles *du, de la* and *des* must not be confused with the locution *de la* and the contracted prepositional forms du/des that involve <u>definite</u> articles. The former and the latter are as semantically and syntactically different as the English words 'her' in 'this is her' and in 'this is her father'. In the following phrases: *le stylo du boulanger, le chapeau de la boulangère, le père des enfants, je viens du stade, je viens de la plage, je viens des Halles, de la* and the contracted prepositional articles *du* and *des* express the complement of possession 'of the' and the directional complement 'from the'; in the sentences: *il joue de la guitare, du piano et des castagnettes, du* and *des* are contracted foms expressing the phrasal verb *jouer de* followed by the definite global article *le* and *les*, just as *elle joue au tennis et aux échecs* express the phrasal verb *jouer à* followed by the definite articles *le* and *les*.

Teaching the global definite article
Students need to learn another function of the definite article. The definite article is used in French to determine abstract nouns and concepts, or things in general, as, for example: *j'aime les chiens*, and *j'étudie la géographie*. I call this particular version of the definite article: the *global* definite, and I contrast it with the definite we have learned before and which is just like 'the' in English, with gender and plural added. This English equivalent, I call the definite-specific article.

Students can make sense of the global-definite article by reasoning in the following manner: If I say 'I am studying geography', I mean that I am studying the thing we call geography, geography globally speaking.

I also like to draw a circle with my arms, to associate a visual sign and a gesture with the idea of an all-encompassing abstraction. I continue: 'we mean *the whole thing*'. The same goes if I say 'I love geography', I love geography globally speaking (circle of the arms, signifying the whole thing). Likewise, if I say, 'geography is a great subject', I mean geography globally speaking (circle of the arms/the whole thing).

In fact, English also uses the global-definite article, albeit in relatively few expressions. For example, if I say: 'The rabbit is not a predatory animal', am I referring to a specific rabbit? No, I am speaking of rabbits globally. I am not speaking about *the* rabbit my friend keeps in her garden, but about the general idea which we have in our heads about rabbits globally speaking. And isn't it interesting that we can refer to the rabbit in the garden and the rabbit, king of the vegetable garden, in exactly the same way, and yet we know that the rabbit, king of the vegetable garden, is the idea of a rabbit while the rabbit in the garden is a real and specific rabbit?

French uses *le/la/les* to refer to concepts and abstract words, like philosophy, history, love, health and education, as well as general ideas about rabbits, tigers, dogs, strawberries and so forth. And the same principle extends to anything we need to reference globally or conceptually. For example, when we say *j'aime les livres*, 'I like books', I don't mean 'I like the books on my bookshelves' but 'I like books globally speaking'. I like the things that we call books, the idea of books. What if we like bread? *J'aime le pain*, globally speaking, what we call bread, the idea of bread.

In English, we do not normally use a determiner when we use concrete nouns abstractly. We say 'I like dogs, books, bread, chicken' just as we say 'I like philosophy'. But what is the difference between saying I like turkey and I like turkeys; I like lamb and I like lambs? What does the singular determine? What about the plural? Yes, the singular refers to meat and the plural to living animals (note that very few students are actually conscious of this feature of English). And English does not need an article, here, why not? Because English can differentiate between a singular and a plural noun by adding an *s* or otherwise inflecting the noun (goose/geese). But how can we differentiate between lamb and lambs in French? Indeed, we need to say *le* and *les* to do this.

We say, *j'aime le poisson, j'aime les poissons*. Can you tell me what that means? And what about: *j'aime le mouton, j'aime les moutons; j'aime le crabe, j'aime les crabes; j'aime le canard, j'aime les canards; j'aime la banane, j'aime les bananes; j'aime la fraise, j'aime les fraises*?

At this point, students can also learn to speak about the things they like and don't like (as distinct from naming things): *j'aime le poulet, j'aime les poules* (not difficult to understand since it is like 'I like pork' and 'I like pigs'); *j'aime les escargots* – what happens here? 'I like snails'. Do we usually keep them as pets or do we eat them? In Australia we may have them as pets but in France? Then, we talk about eating snails and how food relates to culture. We can also discuss language ambiguity and the importance of context. In English, we say 'I like fish' and 'I like fish', and yet we can usually tell if we are speaking about fish in our plate or fish in the aquarium thanks to the conversational context – and if not, we will ask for clarification, which we may phrase in this way: 'Do you mean that you like to eat fish or you like fishes?'

And then, should we use: *des/du/de la* or *le/la/les*?

Once students have learned about the articles above, things get more complicated. Why do we say: *j'aime **le** chocolat* and *je mange **du** chocolat* when, in both cases, we are speaking generally? Why do we say *j'aime **les** légumes* but *je mange **des** légumes*. Students respond well to the following explanation: *j'aime le chocolat* determines the idea of chocolate globally speaking, but *je mange du chocolat* determines the actual thing in a general manner rather than the idea of it – what actually ends up in our mouths or in our plates. In fact, both the definite and the indefinite articles are used to reference generally but when we use *du, de la* and *un, une, des*, we tend to be in the pragmatic or concrete realm, whilst when we use *le, la* and *les*, we are in the conceptual realm. Being in the concrete realm, if I said: *je mange le chocolat*, I would mean *I am eating the chocolate*. Another way of putting this is to point out that we don't eat the idea of something, we either eat 'the thing itself' or 'a quantity of that thing' or 'numbers of those things'.

- Je suis végétarienne, j'aime le tofu, je mange du tofu.
- I am vegetarian, I like tofu (globally speaking), I eat tofu [a quantity of tofu; tofu among other things].
- Je suis végétarienne, j'aime les légumes, je mange des légumes.
- I am vegetarian, I like vegetables (globally speaking), I eat vegetables [a number of vegetables].

The following sentence only appears tricky:
- Les chiens sont des animaux très intelligents.
- Dogs are very intelligent animals.

How can students understand the use of the articles in this French sentence or even better, produce the correct articles by themselves? In fact, if students understand the variations above, they are able to sense that we are meaning 'Dogs (globally speaking) are intelligent animals (among other animals)'. Importantly, by juxtaposing this English sentence in the plural and in the singular and then translating both forms into French, we can show students how French and English actually follow the same underlying syntax, and how the difference between French and English lies with the surface expression of the plural form.

In the singular, 'Dogs are very intelligent animals' may be expressed as:
→ The dog is a very intelligent animal.

We can see that in the expression above, we are using the definite article and then the indefinite. Translating the singular sentence into French, we get:
- → Le chien est un animal très intelligent.

And if we turn this sentence into the plural form, we get:
- Les chiens sont des animaux très intelligents.

More subtle usage of the article may not be so easily understood, as for example:
- Children are little people

If we wish to express this in the singular, what are we most likely to say in contemporary English?
- The child is a little person.
- A child is a little person.

Indeed, 'the child' is more likely to refer to the child we know about and we may possibly sound Dickensian if we intend with this sentence to refer to children globally. However, we do use 'the child' in expressions like 'the year of the child'. In the sentence above, however, as a general reference the definite article would sound inappropriate because it would objectify 'child'. By contrast, the universal statement 'a child' does not objectify because it individualises. In French, interestingly, *l'enfant* does not carry the same objectifying value as in English. Since this general statement applies to all children, *l'enfant* is not only the idea of a child (boy or girl) or the idea of a person in childhood but the idea that all children are small persons. Culturally, it is acceptable to say any of the three sentences below:
- Les enfants sont des petites personnes.
- L'enfant est une petite personne.
- Un enfant est une petite personne

By contrast, however, we would not say: *Globalement parlant, le garcon aime le foot, la fille aime le basket* because this would either refer to a specific boy and girl whom we have already referenced or be weirdly objectifying, just as it would be in English.

In Table 7, we can see just how different English and French articles are, and how gender can be the least of our students' problems. I have highlighted the places where French and English are alike in the table and in the examples that follow. We can see that where English uses *the*, French uses *le/la/les*; where English uses *a/an*, French uses *un/une*; and where English uses some + plural, French uses *des*, and where English uses some + singular, French uses *du* or *de la*. However, as shown in the examples, 'some' is optional in English while *des* and *du/de la* are mandatory in French (hence the lighter shading in the table). Furthermore, these correspondences are not automatic from French into English. We can see that French uses mandatory articles where English leaves a few mandatory blanks (marked as ...... in the table).

TABLE 7 showing articles in French and English

	DEFINITE ARTICLES		**INDEFINITE ARTICLES**			
			COUNTABLE		PARTITIVE [mass]	
	Value: A defined specific reference	Value: A global conceptual reference	Value: A certain number of	Value: A general undefined reference	Value: A certain quantity of	Value: A general uncountable reference
singular	le /la l' / l'	le/ la l' / l'	un/une	un /une	du/de la de l' de l'	du/de la de l' de l'
singular	the	the (1) ...... (2)	*a/an* (5)	*a/an* (8)	some (11) ...... (11)	...... (12)
plural	les	les	des de +adj.	des de +adj.		
plural	the	the (3) ...... (4)	some (6) ...... (7)	...... (9) ...... (10)		
	NEGATING the definite articles		**NEGATING the indefinite quantifiers**		**NEGATING plain indefinite articles**	
singular	le, la, l'		de	de	un/une	du/ de la
singular	the		*a/an* (13)	...... (15)	*a/ an* (16)	...... (17)
plural	les		de		des	
plural	the		*any* (14)		...... (18)	

1 The dog is man's best friend	*Le* chien est *l'*ami de *l'*homme.
2 Animals are sentient beings	*L'* animal est un être sensible
3 She works in *the* mines.	Elle travaille dans *les* mines.
4 Animals are sentient beings.	*Les* animaux sont des êtres sensibles.
5 There is *a* page missing	Il manque *une* page.
6 I bought (*some*) apples.	J'ai acheté *des* pommes.
7 She has children	Elle a des enfants.
8 *An* animal is *a* sentient being	*Un* animal est *un* être sensible.
9 Animals are sentient beings.	Les animaux sont *des* êtres sensibles
10 I eat apples.	Je mange *des* pommes.
11 I bought (*some*) milk.	J'ai acheté *du* lait
12 I drink coffee.	Je bois *du* café.
13 I don't have a pen.	Je n'ai pas *de* stylo.
14 I don't have (*any*) friends.	Je n'ai pas *d'* amis.
15 I don't drink coffee.	Je ne bois pas *de* café.
16 This is not *an* apple.	Ce n'est pas *une* pomme.
17 This is not milk.	Ce n'est pas *du* lait.
18 These are not apples.	Ce ne sont pas *des* pommes.

Negating the indefinite articles

Many students say things like: *j'ai de pain, je n'ai pas du pain, je n'ai pas des amis*, etc. To learn negation, students need to be aware of the quantifying dimension of the indefinite articles, the fact that the indefinite *un/une* can also mean 'one'. If they are aware of this, then they have no trouble at all learning and understanding the need to shift from the indefinite article to the preposition *de* in a negative sentence. Indeed, this rule is already in their English grammar ('I have some bread'; 'I don't have *any* bread'; 'he has (a few/several) children', and 'he doesn't have *any* children'). If we don't have 'any', we cannot say that we have 'some'. French works in the same way but extends the rule to 'a/an' when it implies a value of one ('she doesn't have a [one] brother'; *elle n'a pas de frère*). If we don't have one or more of a thing then we don't have any. Thus, *j'ai un, une, des, du* or *de la; il y a un, une, des, du, de la*, all become *je n'ai pas **de**, il n'y a pas **de***.

Note: We must ensure that students do not construe that *un, une, des, de la* and *du* are always negated by the preposition *de*. The rule concerns the indefinite articles that have a quantifying value, and indeed it also applies to other quantifiers such as *quelques, plusieurs, trois, quatre,* etc. We do say *ce n'est pas un stylo, ce ne sont pas des pois chiches, ce n'est pas du lait*. The nuance is relatively easy to understand since in English, we can distinguish between 'I have a pen', which we can convert to 'I have one pen', and 'this is a pen', which, unless we wish to count it, is evidently just 'a pen'.

A note on the gender of possessive adjectives

As all teachers know, students are naturally tempted to say *son/sa* to match his and her. However, learners' confusion over the gender of possessive adjectives reaches deeper than the agreement of third persons. Students who can use the possessive adjectives effectively and correctly have told me that they are confused about the gender of *mon, ma,* and *ton* and *ta,* as well as *son* and *sa,* and that even though they know the rule, they harbour nagging suspicions that the inflection must *somehow* relate to the gender of the possessor rather than the gender of the object possessed. Students' confusion stems from the collision of the French rule (which they know to be the correct choice) with two principles of English syntax: 1) possessive adjectives are the only adjectives that have gender inflection, and that is because they refer to gendered and therefore sexed persons, and 2) things are never gendered. In this struggle, French wins when and because students are *conscious of the rule* – because they know that *son/sa/ses* must agree with the thing(s) possessed and not the possessor or/and because they know that a possessive adjective, *like all other adjectives*, must agree with the noun that it modifies. But in the places where language really makes sense, in the places where things have no gender and human persons do, this choice does not feel quite right. Not yet. Hence, students feel that something is amiss even though they know that what they are saying is correct. And of course, this is why *ma livre, mon voiture, ma père* and *mon mère* will pop up on occasions even from the mouths of Year 12 students, not because the students have forgotten the gender attached to father and mother, but because gender is reclaiming the rightful place it occupies in their English syntax.

TO SUM UP

The use of articles and other determiners is not something students can learn in a few lessons. In fact, at the rate of a few lessons a week, it takes a couple of years for learners to fully internalise and acquire the capacity to intuit French articles correctly. To help students achieve this goal, we must ensure correct usage. We must begin by encouraging students to model *correctly* on our speech when they are first learning at primary school. At the point of teaching articles and other determiners explicitly, we need to explain the rules comparatively and sequentially, and we need to keep our examples and classroom language consistent and in line with these rules. We must also correct students systematically. Depending on the learning context, we may correct them directly by supplying the correct article, or we may remind them of the rules or ask them to elicit the rules. We can also provide students with simple charts, tables and examples, which we gradually complete with more nuanced language. Ensuring that students master articles and other determiners is worth our attention, our encouragements, our patience, and their efforts. Knowing *about* the articles, as well as knowing the articles, is especially useful as this enables students to acquire several foundational rules of the French language: rules about agreement, about gender and plural, about definite and indefinite categories, about countable and uncountable entities (incidentally, this also makes sense of 'an amount of sugar' and 'a number of people' in English), and about the conceptual and the concrete dimensions of the French language. With the determiners, students learn to pay attention to details. They understand that even a very small word can alter what we intend to say. They learn that English and French can express similar as well as different logical relations. They learn that they can master something difficult. They learn that they can learn.

VII

Teaching Techniques
The Comparative-cognitive Approach

With a focus on pronouns

Language is a gate to culture, to other ways of being, thinking, and doing. Conversely, culture is also a gate to language. Ideally, all language learners will, at some point, have the opportunity to experience speaking their additional languages *in cultura*. However, language and cultural immersion do not guarantee linguistic or cultural acquisition or competence. Language learning is dependent on several factors: first of all, of course, on exposure, but also on intellectual curiosity, on psychological flexibility, on the willingness to do things differently, on the desire to understand, on the ability to memorise, on the will to be understood, and on persistence. In this chapter and the next, I introduce teaching techniques that students have found useful for learning French grammar as well as techniques that help students be 'in French'. These techniques draw from a two-fold approach: a comparative-cognitive approach and a comparative-experiential approach. The comparative-cognitive approach fosters linguistic awareness; the comparative-experiential approach fosters language reflexivity. This chapter focuses on the comparative-cognitive approach. Chapter VIII discusses the comparative-experiential approach. Note that the material provided in this and in the following chapter is intended to be representative and that it is not exhaustive.

THE COMPARATIVE-COGNITIVE APPROACH AND ITS TECHNIQUES

Being able to identify parts of speech and the syntactic relationship between words and to use appropriate terminology allows us to learn a second language accurately. The grammatical and literary study of our mother tongue also deepens, strengthens and expands our native language skills and expressive capacities. Approaching French and English comparatively, as I have shown through the examples provided in previous chapters, facilitates students' learning of French grammar and language and improves their knowledge and skills in Standard English.

The comparative-cognitive approach is concerned primarily with the acquisition of grammar, which is learned by comparing English and French. Students find these comparative processes inherently fascinating. The study of comparative grammar takes language learners into the very heart of the mystery: Why does English do this, and French do that? How remarkable is it that we can actually say something in such a different way in a different language, and yet mean the same thing? And do we actually mean *exactly* the same thing?

The comparative-cognitive approach requires students to think and to reason about the workings of language, about the possible cultural implications, and the possible cultural values embedded in grammar. For example, English says 'every person' where French speakers will tend to use *tous les gens*: the former strikes an individualistic tone, the latter a collective one. Are French speakers less individualistic than English speakers? Perhaps they are in some respects but not in others? Whichever way students answer this question is much less important than the fact that they are asking the question. Why? Because it is an inherently interesting question to ponder, and because, having asked the question, they once again encounter grammar not as a life-less mechanical process but as an experience of life. And not least, because, having asked this question, they are very unlikely to forget that 'every' can be expressed with *tous* or *toutes* in French.

Translation

We make relatively limited use of translation in the contemporary French classroom: mostly we translate to elucidate a French text, to highlight differences between English and French, and we may occasionally produce short bilingual texts. The communicative methods that favour keeping students *in lingua* will naturally tend to shun translation. Of course, 'being in the language' is essential for building language reflexivity, but for 'being in the language' to be worthwhile, students must have the means to avoid hybridizing French into English. Importantly, valuing language fluency over grammatical accuracy actively promotes the direct transposition of English into French, whereas formal translation can play a crucial role in helping students differentiate French and English because nothing brings out the differences between the way things are said in different languages like formal translation.

Literal translation

When we learn a second language, we *need* literal translation to know what, in any given phrase or sentence, the words mean exactly and how they are ordered. Literal translation makes the grammatical and stylistic differences between French and English salient. Literal translation is a must if students are to avoid misconceptions and false equivalencies. I have come across students of French who were under the impression that *je m'appelle* literally means 'my name is' (same number of syllables) and students of Spanish who believed that the verb *es* means 'it' because they had learned that *es* means 'it is'. It is equally interesting that in the verbal phrase 'it is', the grammatically unconscious Anglophone drops *the verb to be* but not the impersonal pronoun 'it' – but more about this in Chapter IX, in the section titled *To be and ne pas être* (p. 248).

This said, literal translation has both *vital* and *limited* use. Many teachers actually attempt to teach grammar through literal translation rather than through explicit grammatical explanations. Hence, they will attempt to teach French pronominal placement by telling students that in French, we say: 'you me it give'. But literal translation is only useful to show students what each word means, and unless we explain the syntactic rationale driving the word order, literal translation can only confirm the nonsensical nature of the French syntax. Nonsense is not conducive to psychological acceptance or to memorisation.

The art of translation

Beyond literal translation, there is the art of translation. And this art of translation, which used to be at the core of language studies, is where the similarities and the differences between French and English are shown even more saliently. Translation is the magical art of authentic transposition. How do we do that? How come language is not just words strung together? How do we express the same affect, the same ideas, in such a different manner? Are there things we cannot translate? Or is everything translatable, somehow? Translation is an enchanting process. We should not deprive our students of this experience.

There are several ways to enjoy and benefit from textual translation: students can attempt their own translation of a poem or a text and then compare their translation with other published and on-line versions. This will make them aware of the experiential, aesthetic, stylistic and grammatical differences between French and English. They can also translate a text from French into English, and then translate the English text back into French. This exercise will test their knowledge of grammar and improve their memory. Both exercises are valuable. Interpreting games can also be a lot of fun for advanced students.

Syntactic analysis

Syntactic analysis is another worthwhile exercise that has disappeared from the contemporary language classroom. Syntactic analysis requires learners to identify the parts of speech and the syntactic relations in a given text. Syntactic analysis, evidently, goes together with translation, but it is also an excellent exercise in its own right. Syntactic analysis consolidates grammatical knowledge and helps learners notice and make sense of word order and inflection. It also helps learners develop a reflexive awareness of grammar. Language students who are well practised in syntactic analysis spontaneously hear subjects, objects, and verbal agreements. They can anticipate the need for the conditional and the subjunctive. Grammatical analysis is highly motivational. It requires thinking and reflecting, but it is not especially difficult, and it has the distinct advantage of being an objective exercise calling for right and wrong answers. Syntactic analysis achieves far more for grammatical retention than repetitive written exercises.

Dictation

The benefits of dictation are self-evident. Dictation promotes aural skills and grammatical skills. Dictation and translation are challenging, fun, and a decidedly objective measure of one's knowledge of the French language. Dictation also has cultural value: native French students learn through dictation and there are many *concours d'orthographe* organised in France outside of formal educational contexts.

Etymology

Learning French vocabulary can be greatly enhanced through etymological and philological inquiry. To see how English and French words connect in history, via Norman French, Latin, Greek, German and more recent exchanges is both fascinating and truly helpful for remembering vocabulary. Etymology injects life into new and hiterto meaningless sounds. For example, one of my students could never remember the word *voiture* until she discovered that the word originates in the Latin *vectura*, meaning transportation. She immediately connected the Latin word to 'vector' at which point she also learned the French word *vecteur*. In addition, etymology can explain and legitimise exceptions, as for example, why words like *musée* and *mausolée* end in *ée* and are not feminine.

Learning grammar by reasoning about language

In order to compare French and English and to analyse a text, students have to learn grammar. Learning grammar is an exercise in self-awareness. It is about naming the things that we do when we are speaking and seeing how these things work. Learning and 'doing' grammar involves identifying and organising into meaningful categories what allows us to turn words into meaningful speech. With the comparative-cognitive approach, learning grammar is about applying patterns and rules but it is also about *discovering* patterns and rules as well as *understanding* the functional dynamics and the semantic reach of patterns and rules.

What is grammar and where do we find it?

We find grammar in notion and function

To enable students to understand what grammar is, I do the following exercise. We read a short narrative in English, then I take away the texts, and I give students the same text with only functional words and pronouns left in it (and, to, at, they, she, etc.). I then ask if we can make sense of this new text, which we obviously can't and ask students why not. Students can see that this text has no meaningful words and therefore means nothing. After this, I will give students another text where all the functional words have been redacted and ask them if they can make sense of it. I will ask them to rewrite the text so it makes sense. Once this is done, I will ask students to compare their respective texts, and then to compare the texts they wrote with my own original text. With this exercise, students learn that small words make big words meaningful.

After we have completed this exercise, I am able to explain that the words in the last text include notions, our common ideas of what a word represents. We can literally *see* notional words in our heads – think of a dog and see what happens in your mind's eye. I will call out a few words, and we will see what happens in our heads, then I will repeat the process with the prepositions, conjunctions, etc. Students can now tell that functional words do not really create images in the way that notional words do, and they can understand that functional words do the following:

- Functional words connect notional words together.
- Functional words allow us to express the full meaning of the notional words.
- Functional words situate things in place and time and so forth.

In large part, grammar consists of being aware of how functional words connect the other words together. Functional words are called prepositions and conjunctions.

Other intriguing words are pronouns. Pronouns belong to both function and notion. Some pronouns mean something in their own right – I, you, someone, but some pronouns replace nouns, and so they only have a meaning if we have provided prior information. For example, if I say 'she's looking at me', what does this mean? Unless I have already named who 'she' is, you might just say that *she* is the cat's mother. Once they have understood the above, students are ready to expand on the knowledge of word classes which they acquired at primary school and to learn to identify: types of nouns, types of adjectives, types of verbs, types of adverbs, types of pronouns, prepositions, and conjunctions.

We find grammar in inflection

I explain inflection in the following manner. 'See how we say 'child' and 'children', 'boy' and 'boys', 'I am' but not 'I is', 'you are' and not 'you am'; we also say 'I' and 'me', 'he' and 'him', 'she' and …? Can you give me more examples? Do we say 'two child' or 'two children'? Do we say 'a mice' or 'a mouse'? Grammar requires us to change the form of a word in certain circumstances: plural or singular, who is doing what and when. This aspect of grammar is called <u>inflection</u>.

In English, we inflect verbs (I am, you were), pronouns (he, she, him, I, me, this, these), nouns (singular/plural), and the demonstrative adjectives (this, these, etc.). Inflection can be external (girls) or internal (mice).

Inflection does not exist in all languages, but in French many more words inflect than in English. You might think it is very complicated, but millions of people can speak French and they are not all geniuses. Also, once upon a time English had many more inflected forms than it has today. Latin, whence much of French originates, is very complicated on account of inflection and yet millions of children have learned Latin through the ages.'

To illustrate inflection, I will also show examples of declensions in both Latin and Old English.

We find grammar in word order

Grammar is about how we order words. To demonstrate word order, we can take a text, mix up a few words and show how our jumbled up sentences mean something else or nothing at all. I will show that saying 'Mary listens to Paul' is not saying the same thing as 'Paul listens to Mary'. Then, I will show that 'listens to Peter Mary' does not mean anything at all. Hence, the way we order words creates meaning.

To demonstrate that meaningful word order is not dependent on nature, I will write on the board:

1) Maxine is reading a book.
2) Maxine a book is reading.

Sentence 1) is how we say things today. Sentence 2) is the order we once used in Old English and in Latin. Students find this strange but they are already used to the idea that they are traveling in wonderlands, and they are curious about what might come next. I then take a book and open it as though to read it. What do you think? What comes first, the book or my reading it? Is the second sentence *that* strange?

Indeed, in English, as part of the marriage vows, we might still say today: 'I thee wed'. In the Australian Western Desert languages, one will say *minga gudjarra* 'ants two', whereas in both English and French we say 'two ants'. Such examples help students to be psychologically and intellectually open to the idea that English word order is meaningful because it is meaningful to English speakers whilst other word orders are equally meaningful to the speakers of other languages. Not only does this encourage students not to think of the word order they encounter in the new language as 'stupid', it also makes the point that learning a new word order is an integral part of learning a new language. In English, if we upset the word order, we do not make a lot of sense, and so, what might happen if we upset the word order in French? Word order is not set in universal laws, it is set in the laws and rules of specific languages. When we learn another language, we find not only new and different sounds but also a different word order, and just as we try our best to produce the sounds of the new language, we will try our best to observe and learn the new word order so as to make sense in that language. Word order is one of the most difficult aspect of learning a language. To adapt to a new word order is somewhat like trying to write with your left hand when you are used to writing with your right hand or the opposite.

When using nouns, French observes the same word order as Modern English. But when using pronouns, French uses the same word order as Old English and Latin.

- John loves Mary.
- John loves *her*.

- Jean aime Marie.
- Jean *l'*aime.

- John is speaking to Mary,
- John is speaking *to her*.

- Jean parle à Marie.
- Jean *lui* parle.

We find grammar in phrasing and prosody

Grammar is how we group words according to the hierarchical relationship between words. Sentences are made up of phrases and clauses. Let's look at the following sentence:
- The little white dog is eating a big fat bone under the tree in the middle of the day while I am having a nap because I am tired.

1) We can parse the sentence by finding all the verbs. Then, we order the most significant phrasing elements: the main clause, and the subordinate clauses. Then, we look at how the words (called conjunctions) that introduce the subordinate clauses give us information about the main clause, how these subordinate clauses in other words *complement* the main clause.

2) We look at the noun-phrase: 'the little white dog'. Are all words equal? What's the most important word: dog. This is called the 'headword'. What is the second most important word? The word you need to go with dog? Students will almost always select 'little', so I will rephrase my question. What is the word the phrase needs most to be complete? Would we say 'little dog is eating' or 'white dog is eating' or 'the dog is eating'? Put this way, students select 'the'.

3) What are the next most important elements?

4) Listen to how we put these words together when we speak, and now compare and contrast with how we say the same phrase in French: *le petit chien blanc*. What is the order observed in the French phrase?

5) Let's translate the entire sentence into French so that we can compare and contrast the different elements:
   - The little white dog is eating a big bone under the tree in the middle of the day while I am having a nap because I am tired.
   - Le petit chien blanc mange un gros os sous l'arbre au milieu de la journée pendant que je me repose parce que je suis fatiguée.

6) Now listen to how I say these two sentences. Students learn that phrasing organises word order, and they also notice how phrasing is expressed through prosody.

7) Now, look at the two sentences written below – what do they mean?
   - The lady hit the man with a cane.
   - The man saw a dog run next to the house.

The way we phrase these sentences through prosody makes the grammar of the sentences explicit. Grammar gives us meaning beyond individual words.

To sum up
The exercises above give students an understanding of what grammar is and what grammar does. Function, notion, inflection, agreement, word order and phrasing all work together to make language meaningful. Learning a new language is not

simply about learning new words by making new sounds, it is also about the way we put new words together and how we shape and reshape words.

TEACHING WORD CLASS, FUNCTION AND WORD ORDER

Teaching the grammar of modifiers: adjectives, adverbs, and compound nouns.

I explain the modifying function with this story: 'Think of a table and I will also think of a table. Do you think we have the same table in our respective heads? What is the table in your head like? Can you tell me what it is like?' Students come up with adjectives or other modifiers to describe the table in their heads. 'See, without these words, we would not know what we were speaking about because we would not have enough information. The words you used are ... adjectives, that's right, and they describe the noun.'

   Now, we could just tell students that an adjective is called a modifier, and that a modifier is so called because it describes, qualifies, quantifies, or otherwise limits a noun. But students will more than likely find this sort of 'explanation' incomprehensible. I explain adjectives and the modifying function in the following manner: 'Adjectives describe nouns; that's true, but perhaps it is a little more accurate to think of adjectives as modifying nouns. You see, a round table is not a rectangular table; a small dog is not a big dog. Is a red pen, a blue pen? Can you see why we say that the adjective modifies the noun? The adjective modifies because it alters the word it is describing, it changes the noun a little. Descriptive adjectives help us get a better idea of what a particular thing is by telling us what it is like.'

Types of adjectives

Some adjectives may modify a noun without describing it; for example, 'my pen' – *my* pen is not *your* pen. We call this a possessive adjective – can you tell me why? Then, there are demonstrative adjectives: this pen, that pen; and quantifying adjectives: a lot of people, a few people. And, yes these types of adjectives are also determiners as we saw earlier.

<u>Rule of English</u>: Adjectives function as modifiers. The headword (the noun) is the modified. The modifier of a noun always comes before the noun it is modifying.

Later, I will explain that nouns can also modify nouns (field notes), and even verbs can modify nouns (sewing machine). And we will also learn that adverbs modify clauses, verbs, other adverbs and adjectives.

The place of modifiers in French and in English

Broadly speaking, in English the modifier of a noun comes before the noun it modifies. In French as in English, determining adjectives (possessive, demonstrative, quantifiers, numbers) come before the noun, as do ordinal numbers (*premier, deuxième,* etc.), indefinite adjectives like *autre, même, certain* and a certain number of descriptive or qualifying adjectives pertaining to physical or moral qualities: *petit, gros, beau, grand, haut, nouveau, vieux, jeune, beau, vilain, mauvais, méchant,* and so forth. Other describing adjectives, such as colours and personal qualities, come after the noun. In other words, in French we may announce the thing first, then give information about what it is like.

- An intelligent, charming, wonderful, erudite, pleasant … what are we speaking about? Man, woman, dog, cat?

- In French, we can announce what we are speaking about and then complement it, describe it or modify it: *une femme, un homme, un chien, un chat* –*charmant(e), intelligent(e), intéressant(e),* etc.

Note 1: The indefinite article *des* is usually contracted to *de* when the plural adjective precedes the noun: *j'ai de bons amis*, and thus becomes *d'* before an adjective that begins with a vowel: *j'ai d'autres amis*. Students may learn this when they learn to place the adjectives, if they already have a good understanding of the articles. If not, it is best to leave this refinement of French grammar to a later date because the key to teaching *de* in these constructions is to teach it as a contracted article, and not as a preposition.

Note 2: Students can also learn that shifting the place of the adjective may create a different meaning (*un grand homme, un homme grand*) and, at a later date, that shifting the place of the adjective creates different aesthetic nuances. When introducing new grammatical concepts, it is important to keep things simple and consistent.

When a noun, an adjective, a preposition, or a verb modifies a noun permanently to form a compound

Adjectives were placed on Planet Earth to modify nouns, but nouns, prepositions and verbs can also modify nouns to form brand new words. Really? Yes, look!

- a blueprint
- an afterthought
- a kitchen knife
- a sewing needle

In English, we can form compound nouns by joining a modifier and a noun in a permanent relationship. This is done either by joining both words into a single word, joining them by a hyphen or by simply placing the words next to each other.

- a bathroom
- an air-vent
- a dining table

Sometimes, all three ways of writing a compound may be permissible, or there is a preferred form in American, British and Australian English.

In French, compound nouns are also formed by joining two words together: *télévision, aéroport*, and by placing two words next to each other: *jeu vidéo* or by using a hyphen between two words: *lave-vaisselle, station-service, chou-fleur*. However, many compound nouns in French require a preposition to act as a link between the headword and the modifying word, and these prepositions may be *de, à, en,* and *pour*. These locutions work as a hyphen might, and they take into consideration the class of words and the underlying syntax that links the two parts of the compound together (see also Chapter V, p. 127).

Students enjoy learning about compound nouns and they like to come up with their own valid compounds. Evidently, we need to point out that sometimes French has a single word where English has a compound, as in *piscine* and swimming pool; English might use a verb to form a compound where French might use a noun or vice versa (waiting room, *salle d'attente*; *lave-vaisselle*, dishwasher) and French might also use an adjective where English uses a noun (*crème solaire*, sun cream).

Something fun to notice:
- *une table en bois*
- a wooden table
- *une robe en laine*
- a woollen dress

Lucinda who noticed that French and English word orders tend to work in opposite direction came up with this: Look if you read 'wooden table' from right to left, you get 'table en wood'... 'dress en wool'... That's so neat! And it sure is.

NOTE: The plural agreement of compound nouns is dependent on the grammar usually attributed to specific classes of words:
- <u>verb + noun</u> (*lave-vaisselle**s***), the noun is inflected, not the verb,
- noun + noun (*chou**x**-fleur**s***) both nouns inflect in the plural form,
- noun + à/de+ noun (*des couteaux de cuisine/à pain*) the headword inflects,
- <u>noun + adjective</u> (*belles-mères; coffres-forts*): both words inflect since the adjective agrees with the noun,

BUT: *nouveau-nés*: *nouveau* is considered an adverb and is invariable; *grands-pères* follows the rule <u>adjective + noun</u> but *grand-mères* doesn't. The latter *grand is* invariable – note that it is also not *grande-mère*. Then, there is *demi-frères. Demi* is an adjective but it is always invariable when it is hyphenated to a noun. When *demi* follows the noun, it agrees with the noun it modifies – hence we say *une demi-heure* and *une heure et demie*.

Why teach the grammar of compound-noun formation as opposed to teaching compound-nouns as we do other nouns?

Teachers have asked: What is the point of teaching the grammar of compound nouns formed with prepositions? Are we not complicating students' lives for nothing? We can just as easily ask students to memorise compound nouns, and to learn those as they learn other nouns. Evidently, students have to memorise the compound nouns that are formed with hyphens (*chou-fleur, libre-service, abat-jour, auteur-compositeur*) but there are real benefits to teaching the grammar of compound nouns that are linked with prepositions.

1) First, once students start to accumulate a few compound nouns, they start confusing *à* and *de*. Do we say *un couteau à pain* or *un couteau de pain*? Furthermore, they get annoyed at French because they have to remember these little words that apparently mean nothing: Why, oh why is it *un couteau à pain* and un *couteau de cuisine*? Learning about the structure helps them remember the compound and also reconstruct it when their memories fail them. Is it *à* or *de*? Well, it has to be *à* because the knife is used for cutting the bread, and *de* because the knife is not used for cutting the kitchen...

2) Learning about these structures helps students make up valid compounds when they are short of vocabulary (*un truc à/pour faire quelque chose; un truc en plastique*).

3) Learning about compound nouns introduces students to aspects of the formal logic governing the prepositions *à, de* and *en*, all of which serve many other constructions in French.
4) Learning about compound nouns makes students think about grammar beyond word order and inflection.
5) Learning about compound nouns is motivating because it is fun to figure all this out, to see the formal logic at work, and to be able to produce new words that are grammatically and lexically valid. Learning about compound nouns is one of the game aspects of grammatical learning.

TEACHING FRENCH PRONOUNS

Pronominal use in French is more complicated than in English. Firstly, there are more pronominal forms in French than in English, then the French pronominal word order differs from English, and it also differs from the French nominal word order, and that is only part of the business.

To teach pronouns successfully, we need to observe a hierarchical sequence and ensure that, at each level, students have mastered the correct usage and know what they are doing. Logically, we begin with the subject pronouns, which means that we need to explain [again] what a subject is and does. Having learned the grammar of the personal subject pronouns, students can acquire the relative subject pronoun *qui* semantically – all we need to point out is that French makes no difference between animate and inanimate in the subject case: whether we refer to persons or things, we use *qui*, just as we use *il* and *elle* when speaking about people or things. Where object pronouns are concerned, the oblique pronouns *moi/ toi/ lui/elle, etc* can also be learned semantically and incidentally, but only up to a point and with circumspection. Being so alike English object pronouns and presenting a common feature with the subject pronoun *elle*, these pronouns should be used sparingly until students have studied and mastered the direct object, dative and reflexive pronouns. Students who have free access to the pronouns *moi/ toi/ lui/ elle, etc* naturally use the latter as they would English object pronouns and confuse the subject and the indirect object *elle(s)*, and consequently find it very difficult to internalise the French pronouns that precede the verb.

This said, I do introduce students to the *basic* function of the reflexive pronoun ahead of teaching the object pronouns because all beginners must learn *je m'appelle*. *S'appeler* is not a purely reflexive verb as for example *s'évanouir* or *se souvenir de* but *s'appeler* cannot be understood in the same way as *je me lave* or *je me réveille*. *Je m'appelle* means 'I am called' in English and not 'I call myself'. In other words *s'appeler* is a case of French using the reflexive voice where English uses the passive. Accordingly, I begin by explaining that the verb *s'appeler* translates literally in

English as 'I call myself'. I show the word order 'I myself call' (students are already conscious of word order). I then explain that verbs can be used in different 'voices'. The reflexive voice is the 'voice' we use when we are doing something to ourselves, as distinct to the active voice, which is when we are doing something, and the passive voice, which is when something is being done to us. I ensure that students truly understand all this by providing and requesting a lot of examples in English: 'I brush myself', 'I am looking at myself', 'I am speaking to myself', 'I am eating the cake', 'the cake was eaten by the mice', 'this student wrote the letter', 'the letter was written by this student', 'the student wrote to herself', etc. Once students are able to identify the active, the passive and the reflexive voices in English, I explain that the reflexive pronoun is thus named because it *reflects* the subject, I and myself. This is a mirror relationship, and we can see how neatly this relationship is expressed in the position of the pronouns in French: *je me, tu te, il se, nous nous, vous vous, ils se*. Once this is understood, we return to the verb *s'appeler*, and I inform students that there is more to the reflexive voice in French than 'doing something to oneself' in English. In English, 'I call myself' implies that I call myself by one name and other people call me by another. In French, *je m'appelle* actually means 'I am called'. In other words, French can use the reflexive voice where English uses … which voice? The passive voice, that's correct! You are brilliant! So what does *je m'appelle* mean? 'I am called!' Yes! And what form does it come in in French? The reflexive! Excellent! And which of these two pronouns is the reflexive pronoun:

'*Je* or *me*?'
'*Me!*'
'*Ah vous êtes fantastiques!!!*'

And we will leave it at this for the moment. Students will return to the reflexive voice, learn about *se lever* and *se réveiller*, and about essentially reflexive verbs in due course – after they have mastered the French direct object and dative pronouns.

Students need to learn French pronominal use sequentially. The following order seems optimal: we begin with the definite direct object pronouns *me, te, le/la, nous, vous, les*, follow with the indefinite direct object *en*, then the dative pronouns *me, te, lui, nous, vous, leur*, then the reflexive pronouns *me, te, se, nous, vous, se* which double up as reciprocal pronouns. Having mastered the direct and dative object pronouns, students are able to understand that French reflexive pronouns serve two primary functions: mirroring whilst also being direct object or dative complements. Having internalised the placement of the direct object, dative and reflexive pronouns, students can easily acquire the locative and directional pronouns *y* and *en* which precede the verb. After this, they can learn the oblique pronouns *moi, toi, elle, lui, etc* which they have encountered incidentally and which, being like English pronouns, present no difficulty. From this, it is also a small step to learn the demonstrative pronouns *celui-ci, celle-là etc*. The indirect object pronouns *y* and *en* are next and more complicated. Here, French differentiates between persons and things, and *y/en* replace nouns and infinitives acting as indirect object introduced by *à* and *de* meaning 'about' as well as following phrasal verbs such as *jouer à, se souvenir de* – but they do not replace infinitives joined by *à* or *de* to verbs like *apprendre, finir, etc* (refer to pp.133-134). Finally, students have everything in their tool kit to learn the relative pronouns and make sense of the most difficult grammar: *ce que, ce dont, de quoi,* and so forth.

Importantly, the difficulties which students experience learning French pronouns have little to do with memorisation. There are very few words to remember. This is all about comprehension, about understanding the role that the different pronouns play in relation to the verb. There is, however, plenty of potential for confusion and therefore the best way to teach is grammatically (comprehension), sequentially (observing a hierarchy of knowledge) and slowly (ensuring that students have the opportunity to consolidate and master one element at a time).

Identifying role players and modifiers through intuitive questioning

We must first explain that French is a verb-driven language: the verb is at the core of the sentence. Somebody does, feels, thinks, wants something, and goes somewhere, when, where, because, with, and so forth. The verb is like the sun in our solar system, the nouns are the planets, the determiners and the adjectives are the moons. Then, we can teach the subject and the direct object functions.

Identifying the subject of a verb

We could explain that the subject of a verb is the thing or the person that the sentence is about, as the Oxford Dictionary explains it, and thoroughly confuse students.[123] Or we can teach what a subject is the way I was taught as a French-speaking Year 3 pupil in France: The subject does the action, we find the subject by asking the question: _who or what_ is doing it?

- John is reading a book… *Who* is reading? John. John is the subject. John is happy. He is smiling. *Who* is smiling? He is the subject. The novel won a prize. *What* won the prize? The novel is the subject.

Identifying the direct object complement

The object is the thing or person affected by the verb.[124] In other words, the object expresses the objective, the aim of the verb, I am doing *what*? I am watching *what*? I am eating *what*? We find the object of the verb by asking the question: doing, watching, eating *what*? To make this clearer, I will show students how some verbs cannot be used without an object. 'Can I simply say "I like"?' To which students

---

[123] https://en.oxforddictionaries.com/grammar/subjects-and-objects
[124] Ibid.

answer that I must say what it is that I like. In other words, I like *what*? I like apples. 'Apples' is the direct object of like.

Subject	Verb	Direct object
who	*is doing/does*	*what ?*
Nabil	is watching	a movie
Marie	is reading	a book
I	am drinking	chocolate
John	likes	tea
You	drink	milk
She	loves	John

The doing *what* complement is called the *direct* object complement (DO) because it is the straightforward objective of the verb and it comes directly next to the verb in both English and French. Once students have understood this, they can practise identifying subjects and direct objects in French

- *Je mange du chocolat; il regarde un film; je regarde Amy, etc.*

NOTE 1: When teaching syntax, it is important to use English first, and then to use the French vocabulary students are most familiar with so that they can focus on the structure. New vocabulary can be introduced after students have internalised the structure.

NOTE 2: Students who can identify a subject and a direct object complement can easily learn to refer to the subject and the direct object pronouns by the correct grammatical terms. Students who are able to do this will have no problem at all learning that where pronouns are concerned, French abides by a SOV word order.

❖ Refer to Chapter V for Tables and pronominal usage.

TEACHING THE OBJECT PRONOUNS

The definite direct object pronouns: *me, te, le, la, nous, vous, les*
The definite object pronouns *me, te, le, la, nous, vous, les* replace a noun-phrase determined by a definite determiner. If students have learned about *word order*, they have no problem at all accepting that when a direct object pronoun is involved, the French word order is S DO V. We can remind them that they have already seen this principle with *je **m'**appelle*.
- Tu me regardes.

- Je te regarde.
- Je la regarde.
- Il nous regarde.
- Vous les regardez.

It is important to impress on students that *le/la/les* are not articles although they look exactly the same as the articles. To remind students that word class depends on what a word does and not only on what a word sounds or looks like, we can point out to the word 'her' in 'this is her' and in 'this is her book'. These two 'her' are not the same, and this is very obvious when we substitute the masculine forms 'this is him' and 'this is his book'.

The indefinite direct object pronoun *en*

Students learn that *en* is the indefinite DO pronoun and that it replaces a noun phrase determined by an indefinite determiner, an article or a quantifier: *un/un, deux/trois/quatre/des, du/de la/beaucoup de*. The order is also S DO V. Students learn that when there is a quantifier, we retain it because *the pronoun* only replaces *the noun*, not the quantifier. If students have mastered the rules of the articles, they can easily recognise *en* as an indefinite pronoun.

- J'ai deux *livres*.
- J'*en* ai deux.
- J'ai un *chien*.
- J'*en* ai un.
- J'ai beaucoup d'*amis*.
- J'*en* ai beaucoup.

When the quantifier has not been defined, we use *en* to replace *the noun*, and do not worry about anything else since there is nothing more to specify.

- J'ai de la *chance*.
- J'*en* ai.
- J'ai du *pain*.
- J'*en* ai.
- J'ai des *chocolats*.
- J'*en* ai.

If we examine these structures in the light of English grammar, we can see that *en* stands for of them/of that/some of it or some.

- *J'en ai deux.*
- I have two (of them).
- *J'en ai un.*
- I have one (of them).

- *J'en ai beaucoup.*
- I have a lot (of them).
- *J'en ai.*
- I have (some of it).
- *J'en ai.*
- I have (some).

Teaching the dative function and the dative pronouns: *me, te, lui, nous, vous, leur.*

I call 'dative' the function of the indirect object, also called the second object or the transmission object in some French grammars. I prefer to call this object 'dative' because the word 'transmission' tends to suggest agency to students, and the dative is *the recipient* of the transmission and not its agent. I do not use the term 'second object' because it does not identify the function of this particular object with any precision, and more importantly because in English, the dative is not always the second object. In English, the dative can precede the direct object: 'I gave him chocolate'. The word 'dative' is relatively user-friendly. It is a single word that resembles no other terms. The word dative thus clearly differentiates this particular object function from the direct object function as well as from the other indirect object functions which may call for the pronouns *y* and *en* when *à* or *de* mean 'about' or 'of' (*je pense à toi; je rêve de voyager*) and the other complements introduced by other prepositions (*sans, avec, pour, à cause de, etc.*) The dative case is so named because it comes from the verb Latin verb *dare/datus* meaning to give/given. The dative is the recipient of what the verb is transmitting/giving/doing.

The logical structure of a dative construction can be summed up as: somebody is doing/giving/ saying/ teaching/singing (something) *to someone*.
- The lady is giving a bone to her dog.
- The lady is giving her dog a bone.
- The teacher taught grammar to her students.
- The teacher taught her students grammar.
- *La dame donne un os à son chien.*
- *Le professeur a appris la grammaire à ses élèves.*

To identify the dative complement, students need to understand and become familiar with the concept of transmission. A dative implies that something is transmitted: given, passed on, told, written, phoned, sold, or done to someone. Therefore, we can identify the dative by asking the question: Doing (whatever) **to whom?** In French, the nominal dative is introduced by *à* and in *some cases* by ***pour***. Likewise, in English, the dative is introduced by 'to' and sometimes by 'for' when for implies 'to give to'. If students use the question *'Doing whatever to whom?'* they have no trouble at all identifying the dative in the following sentence: 'The lady is giving the dog a bone.'

In the examples given above and in examples given in the next paragraphs, the underlying structure always infers doing, giving, saying, transmitting something to someone: *faire/donner/dire/transmettre quelque chose à quelqu'un*. It is really helpful to leverage students' English here because 'doing something **to whom?**' identifies the dative case unequivocally. This question *only* identifies the dative case, whilst in French, the preposition **à** can identify another indirect object function which is expressed in English by 'about' or 'of'. *Je pense à lui* means 'I am thinking **about (of)** him'. *Lui* is also an indirect object but it is not a dative, hence we say, *je pense à elle* and not *je lui pense*. Students learn very easily that the dative pronouns in French are *me, te, lui, nous, vous, leur*. They learn just as easily that the word order is S + Dat + V.

Teaching the less obvious uses of the dative pronoun

In a sentence such as *Le garçon a volé le chapeau du monsieur,* **du** indicates possession and supplants **à**. The deep structure is here: *on vole quelque chose* **à** *quelqu'un* and evidently, stealing from someone is doing something to them. In other similar constructions, the preposition **de** is used instead of **à** because in the process of doing something (good or bad) to someone or for someone, something is taken away from somebody. The nominal construction is identical in French and English, but the pronominal construction is not.

- The boy pulled the thorn from the lion's paw.
- *Le garçon retira l'écharde de la patte du lion.*
- *Il **lui** retira l'écharde de la patte.*

A similar logic underpins the sentence below:

- The dentist pulled his tooth out.
- *Le dentiste lui a arraché une dent.*

From the perspective of the English-speaking learner, the French pronominal construction is far from evident but the formal logic that underpins it can be made salient. The dentist did something to him and for him: the dentist pulled out a tooth for him. Other seemingly idiosyncratic uses of the dative from the perspective of English grammar include *manquer à*, *ressembler à*, and *résister à quelqu'un*.

Teaching pronominal word order in double-transitive constructions

Once students have mastered the DO and dative pronouns, they can learn that the pronominal word order in the double-transitive construction is:

S + Dat + DO + Verb.

Note too that the DO is not only placed before the verb but also immediately next to it, just as it is in the nominal structure. The pronominal structure is a mirror image of the nominal structure. At this point students can use all the dative object pronouns in combination with the direct object pronouns, but *we must avoid* constructions that make use of two pronouns beginning with *l-*, *which we must keep for later*. We may use *tu me le donnes, je t'en donne, il nous les envoie*, but we must avoid *le/lui, les/lui*, and so forth. All students need to do is to memorise the word order: Subject Dative Direct Object Verb. They do not need to memorise or copy model sentences. Once they have memorised S Dat DO Verb, they can apply the S Dat DO Verb order orally to the construction of their own sentences until their language comes easily and fluidly, which, depending on the capacities of individual learners, may take between five minutes and two or three classes.

Once students can identify and produce Subject Dative Direct Object Verb constructions fluidly, they are ready to learn the *only* exception to the rule, and which results of the *phonological* system. Simply put, French does not like the sounds: *lui-la, leur-les*. I ask students to try and say the following:

'Try to say this: *leur-les*, now try *les-leur*, which rolls off the tongue?'

'*Les-leur.*'

'Therefore, when we are using two pronouns that begin with *l*, the shorter sounding pronoun comes first: *le lui, les lui, la leur*, etc.'

NOTE: It is crucial NOT to present this structure as a grammatical exception or to get students to say things like: 'in the third person singular, we place the indirect object before the direct object'. This will confuse the rule for them. Importantly, this is not only a pedagogical issue, it is also a grammatical misconception: the *lx-lxx* structure is *not* a syntactic exception, it is nothing less and nothing more than a *euphonic* adjustment to do with the two pronouns beginning with *l*. Indeed, Spanish phonological rules, like French phonological rules, resist sequencing two *l-*initialled object pronouns. Although Spanish does not alter the pronominal word order in such constructions, it nevertheless requires a phonetic adjustment, and thus converts the dative pronoun *le* into *se* which is normally the form of the reflexive pronoun.

- *usted **lo** ha dicho*,   you said it (direct object)
- *usted **le** ha dicho*   you said to him (dative)
- *usted **se lo** ha dicho*   you said it to him (dative + direct object)

RULE: In double-transitive clauses the word order is S + Dat + DO + V except when both object pronouns begin with *l* [short cut: when there are two *l*] in which case, the shorter sounding pronoun comes first.

Teaching the locative and directional pronouns *y* and *en*.

Students will easily learn the locative and directional pronouns *y* and *en* (refer to Chapter V, p.151) through the same process and with the same questioning technique. A locative is identified by the question: where? A directional by the question: where to, where from? *Y* can be approximated in English by 'here/there' and 'to there' and *en* by 'from there' but unlike *ici* and *là*, *y* and *en* replace an antecedent.

- *y* replaces *à* + NP ⇒ Je suis *à la gare*, je vais *à la gare*;
- *en* replaces *de* + NP ⇒ Je viens *de la gare*.

Teaching how to negate a pronominal clause

To negate a pronominal-verbal construction, just place *ne* after the subject and *pas* after the conjugated verb as usual. The order is therefore S + *ne* + DO + V + *pas*. Since there are no exceptions to this rule of negation,[125] it is strange that we have been teaching forever that *ne* goes before the verb. This is highly confusing because a lot of things can go before the verb in French:

- Tu ne les lui as pas données.
-

❖ Refer to Chapter V for the placement of adverbs of negation (pp. 158-159).

TEACHING THE RELATIVE PRONOUNS

The relative pronouns with nominal or pronominal antecedents

The relative pronouns that replace nominal antecedents do not prove especially difficult for students who have mastered the following concepts: subject and object functions, animate and inanimate, and especially the **antecedent**. The real difficulty arises when students need to adjust their thinking to learn that *qui* applies to all subjects, that *que* applies to all direct objects and that French begins to differentiate between inanimate and animate pronouns with the cases involving prepositions, whereas English differentiates persons and things from the subject case onwards: who/which. A direct benefit of learning relative pronouns in French is that students at last get to understand the difference between 'who' and 'whom' in English and why their spell-checker suggests putting a comma before 'which'.

---

[125] Note that [*toujours pas*] is a semantic unit meaning 'still... not' or 'not ... yet' and where *toujours* modifies *pas*: *Je n'ai toujours pas mangé* ('I still haven't eaten', 'I have not eaten yet'). On the other hand, when t*oujours* means 'always': *Je ne mange pas toujours à la même heure* ('I do not always eat at the same time)', it modifies the negated verbal statement and therefore comes after it.

Unlike in English, simple French relative pronouns do *not* differentiate between animate and inanimate subjects and direct objects.

- Le livre **qui** est sur la table est le mien.
- L'homme **qui** me parle est mon prof.
- C'est lui **qui** a fait cla.
- Le livre ***que*** j'ai acheté est sur la table.
- L'homme ***que*** je regarde est mon professeur.
- C'est ça ***que*** j'ai regardé.

   ❖ Refer to Chapter V (p. 153) for the table showing relative pronouns.

The relative pronouns with clausal antecedents
When students know what the antecedent is and what it does for the pronoun, it is not difficult for them to identify how, in English, when the relative pronoun has a clause rather than a noun or a pronoun for antecedent, it is preceded by a comma [, which]. In French, we may consider *ce que, ce qui, etc.* as compounds. Students, however, respond well to the explanation that the demonstrative pronoun *ce* replaces a clause aforementioned. Thus, where English leaves a blank space, the neutral demonstrative pronoun *ce* supplies the antecedent for *qui, que, dont, etc.*

- My teacher spent a lot of time explaining this to me, [ ] *which* really helped me in the exam even though I did not fully understand.
- Mon professeur a passé du temps à m'expliquer ça, [**ce**] *qui* m'a bien aidé pendant l'examen même si je n'ai pas tout compris.

The relative pronouns with no stated antecedent
Let's face it, the indefinite relative pronouns, which is to say the relative pronouns with no antecedents, are a bit of a headache. Their acquisition is dependent on students understanding the following concepts: antecedent, inanimate, animate, definite and indefinite. As in English, the antecedent-less relative pronouns are different for persons and things. In the subject case: *Je regarde qui arrive*; *je regarde ce qui se passe*; in the DO case: *Je regarde qui tu regardes, j'écoute ce que tu écoutes*. Students may find this complicated because *qui* is now used for both the animate subject and the object cases while *ce qui* is used for the inanimate subject case and *ce que* for the inanimate object case. However, things are easier with the prep + pronouns, since the latter function as they do in English. Here, the animate pronoun is *qui* and the inanimate pronoun is *quoi*, corresponding to 'who' and 'what'. We can help students by stating that with the antecedent-less (indefinite) pronouns, qui is used for people in all cases. *Ce qui* and *ce que* are used for inanimates and [prep] *quoi* with all prepositions.

- I know <u>who(m)</u> I am talking about: *je sais de qui je parle*
- I know <u>what</u> I am talking about: *je sais de quoi je parle.*

To sum up on relative pronouns

Students need to have a fluent understanding of the grammatical principles at work (role players, antecedent, animate, inanimate), and they need to learn sequentially. Comparing and translating from English into French and from French into English is essential. Students also need to compare casual and formal English word order to understand what relative pronouns are in English and to access the word order in French.

- the man I was speaking *with*
- the man *with* <u>whom</u> I was speaking
- l' homme *avec* <u>lequel</u> (qui) je parlais

In English, we have a fair bit of flexibility with relative clauses. We can reduce the relative pronoun 'whom' to 'who', we can omit the pronoun altogether, and we can place the introductory preposition after the verb rather than at the beginning of the relative clause. We cannot do this in spoken or standard French. However, we can see from the examples provided above that the French construction corresponds to the formal Standard English construction. Therefore, if students practise shifting from casual English to formal English and they become at ease with the latter, they can learn the French construction without too much trouble. To shift to formal English, students need to *notice* the preposition in the casual word order. Finally, it is helpful to draw a table where students can add the new pronouns as they learn them (again refer to Table 3, p. 153 and to the examples provided on the same page).

VIII

Teaching Techniques

The Comparative-experiential Approach

The comparative-experiential approach is about helping students resolve the cognitive and ontological differences between French and English. It is about helping students be 'in French' and thus to by-pass unconscious transposition and verbalisation from English into French. The experiential approach, like the comparative-cognitive approach, is a gateway to intercultural understanding and competency. Its purpose is to build *genuine* language reflexivity. In the following paragraphs, I describe and explain five techniques I have found especially useful for experiential learning: 1) the Bridging Grammar, 2) Mental Imaging and Sensory Reflection, 3) Creative Imitation, 4) Conscious Repetition and Drills, and 5) Listening, and Listening and Reading. In this scheme, Immersion is an end-stage. It is the goal, the point of it all, and the reward of students' efforts. I provide examples of how to integrate some of these techniques in real-life teaching in the section entitled *Combining experiential and cognitive techniques*.

1) The Bridging Grammar

This technique leverages learners' English to make French grammar meaningful, to help transcend the strangeness of unusual word order, grammatical usage, and apparently odd lexical expressions. The Bridging Grammar is a counterpart to the techniques described in the previous chapter detailing the comparative-cognitive approach. I first developed this technique not as a teacher, but as a student of Chinese. In order to grasp and then to internalise the *semantic* dimension of Chinese syntax, I made extensive, purposeful and systematic use of a type of paraphrasing which I called a Bridging Grammar. This technique allowed Chinese syntax to feel natural a long time before I was able to speak Chinese fluently. I have found the Bridging Grammar equally effective for helping students make sense of difficult (which is to say alien) French syntax. This technique may be considered a 'translanguaging' technique.

We can bridge English and French grammars in the following manner:

1) By using English and French grammar in tandem, for example, using a question in English and requiring an answer in French, or using part of the sentence in English and part of it in French. This is particularly useful for helping students internalise French verbal usage and conjugations.

2) By transposing a literal translation of a seemingly odd French grammatical structure into the closest possible English word order that *begins to make sense*. I have stressed *begins to make sense*, because here lies the difference between a literal translation and a bridging translation: the bridging structure may not be entirely correct or real English, but it must amount to something *comprehensible* in English. As I mentioned in the previous chapter, literal translation is a necessary process. However, the usefulness of literal translation is limited by the fact that it actually reinforces the apparently nonsensical structure of the target language. Literal translation is of limited use for memorisation because it is difficult to memorise nonsense. The Bridging Grammar is effective because it makes sense, because it allows students to *experience* the French structure in English, and therefore to experience it in a meaningful way.

2) Mental Imaging and Sensory Reflection

Mental imaging and sensory reflection consists in asking students to pay attention to the way words and verbal expressions resonate in their internal universe, how words produce mental images and/or emotions and/or physical sensations. In other words, it is about being aware of the effects words produce upon us. Can English and French produce different images, emotions and sensations? This technique helps students understand the difference between verbs of action, stative verbs and modal verbs, as well as to internalise some stylistic differences between French and English, as for example: why French speakers 'have' years, when English speakers 'are' years old.

3) Creative Imitation

Creative imitation is about listening to our interlocutors' native language and taking from it what we need in order to shape our own responses with confidence and accuracy. Creative imitation facilitates communication, accelerates automaticity, and helps learners stay in French and avoid verbalising into English.

Unlike small children, language students are not natural imitators. Imitating is a skill that must be learned or indeed re-learned. Unless I actively encourage students and, not least, *show* them how to model their speech on mine, they are not usually able to retrieve and copy the useful parts of my speech to keep the conversation going. In part, high school and university students are reluctant to imitate because they have acquired good learning habits that discourage plagiarism and encourage individual creativity. Certainly, some students are reluctant to imitate because they feel that they are faking if they simply copy what I am saying. However, there is more to this. As discussed in Chapter IV, we find it difficult to imitate and repeat what people say in our own language because we are receiving meaning rather than words. Second-language learners are not very good at making use of what they hear because they are too busy listening for meaning, and more often than not because they are also too busy translating what they are hearing, to pay attention to how things are being said.

In conversation, outside well-rehearsed speech and canned dialogue, students almost always verbalise a translation of the French they are hearing (refer to the discussion in Part Two of Chapter IV). They may do this to re-assure themselves that they have understood correctly before they risk a response, but they will also do this reflexively. At this stage of language learning, translation is a reflex. However, once students have either translated or rephrased what they heard in French into English, they are even less able to remember what they actually heard in French. They are back in their English-mind-brain space and they must now respond by translating their thoughts from English into French, at which point, they are far more likely to rely on their English grammar than on what they have learned of French grammar.

In actual fact, purposeful listening requires more than technique, it also requires a certain psychological attitude as well as a certain type of confidence. I try to build this confidence by explaining to my students that if they are able to translate what they heard, it is because they have understood what was said and therefore, they don't need to translate. In fact, what I am really trying to do is to convince students *not to verbalise* from French into English. Until we are fluent in a language, there is always a degree of translation taking place in the depths of our mind, because our mental universe is fully occupied by our own language. Hence, until we gain true fluency, we will continue to 'hear' things in our own language.

Let me show you what I mean. A few months ago, I interviewed Adrian, a new student (Year 12), and asked: *Il y a longtemps que tu apprends le français au collège?* To which he answered: '*C'est six ans mon francais*'. Evidently, Adrian understood the question, but he could not provide an answer in grammatically correct French because he did not know the correct French structure, because it did not occur to him to copy my language, *and* because he did not hear the French structure. When I asked if he could repeat what I had said, he answered by giving me a translation.

'Yes, that's what I meant, but what did you hear me say in French. Can you repeat in French what I said in French?'
'Oh, can you say it again?'
'Sure: *Il y a longtemps que tu apprends le français au collège?*'
'Mmm… *tu apprendre longtemps français(e) au collège* … '

Recently, I was practising the present of ER verbs with a very dedicated student. Isabel was sailing through *chanter, payer, acheter, jouer, étudier* (often a tricky one), *copier, laver, marcher... parler* and then she said, *je parler, tu parler, elle...* and I corrected her. Then, I said *aimer*, and she said: *j'aimer, tu aimer...* and I corrected her again, and she stopped, feeling frustrated:

'Oh, why am I doing this?'
'When I said *aimer*, did you say "to like" in your head?'
'Yes.'
'That's why. You see, when you thought "to like", you returned to your English grammar, and so you continued in your English grammar: to like, I like, you like... like, like, *aimer, aimer,* you see?' (See Chapter IX for how English productive rules govern students' performance of French conjugations).
'Oh, that's so interesting. Can we do it again?'
So we did. On two other occasions, she just caught herself on the verge of reverting to the infinitive but she held the correct form.

To teach students to hear French and to listen actively, I first explain that understanding, hearing and listening are different things. To demonstrate what I mean, I will read a complex English sentence from a book and ask students to tell me what I said. They will tell me by rephrasing what they heard. When I read the sentence again and I ask them to attempt a word for word rendition, students will attempt to repeat, but they will leave words out as well as some of the information. I will then explain that we do not really listen to *how* people say things in our own language because we *understand* what they say. Thus, even though we hear and understand the words that provide us with meaning, we do not usually remember what we are told word for word. In some circumstances, we may be able to repeat a couple of lines, especially if those struck us emotionally or intellectually, but we are rarely able to repeat several lines *verbatim*. How difficult is it to tell a joke we heard someone else make? 'Well, the way he said it was better'. Repeating what someone says or writes word for word is an art, the art of the actor, not the accomplishment of the average speaker.

Creative imitation needs to be learned. It does not come automatically because, even in our own native language, past early childhood, we listen to *what* is being said, we listen to and for *meaning* not to phonology, not to grammar, and not always to the words we are hearing. Hence, if, in the middle of a lively conversation I ask my interlocutor 'Could you please pass me the bread' while pointing to the butter, she is likely to do as I meant to say rather than to respond to what I actually said, whether or not she bothers to clarify my meaning: 'You mean the butter?' Hence, also lies the difference between how younger children and adults hear and use language (as cited in Schmidt in Chapter IV). Faced with passing the thing to which I am pointing or that which I am voicing, a little child is more likely to ask me to clarify my meaning than an adult listener.

Students lose their grammatical faculties when they try to answer what I am saying in French because 1) they are making sense of what I said rather than listening to how I said it; 2) when they are recalling my meaning, they are recalling in English; and 3) when they try to put something into French by remembering what I actually said, they try to recall the noises I made rather than the words they heard and rather than using what they know of French grammar.

We can teach students to avoid 'translating' unconsciously from English. We can also explain why they need to recover their capacity for imitation. We can build their confidence by reminding adolescent and younger adult students that, not so long ago, they were still experts at pretending and imitating. We can show students how to pay attention to the patterns they are hearing in French; to note how these patterns match the patterns they already know and have learned; and how to piggy-back on the speech they are hearing. It is very helpful to teach students that if they hear: [Tu habites] *en Australie*, they can simply repeat the sentence and slot in their answer: [J'habite] *en Australie*. [Tu vas] *au collège en bus? Oui*, [je vais] *au collège en bus*. When someone is speaking in the third person, and we happen to agree with them, we can answer by repeating without any substitution: *Il va à l'école en bus? Oui, il va à l'école en bus*.

Students, however, are better able to imitate grammatical patterns when they know what they are actually listening to and listening for, in other words, when they know the grammar they are hearing. And once they realise that to construct accurate sentences they can retrieve what they need from their interlocutor's speech, they become so very good at imitating that we must then ensure that they do not simply parrot our speech. Students must learn to imitate but they should not become dependent on imitation. They also must be able to replace nouns with pronouns appropriately, and not least, they must have the knowledge and confidence to initiate new lines of thought and conversation

Rote learning inhibits creative imitation
Students cannot imitate when they learn by rote, for the simple reason that they don't know that the grammar they are using can generate brand new meanings: they have only learned to copy formulaic language, which is to say, sequences of words which they understand at the semantic level and in a specific situational context, and more often than not, in a very general manner. When I ask students who have been learning by rote to repeat something that I have just said, they

abandon all attempts at understanding or at drawing on their knowledge of French: they do their absolute best to regurgitate the sounds I have just made and they inevitably get lost in the process. Students are perfectly aware of this too. Virtually all my private students have confirmed that in oral drills in class, they focus on copying the noises they hear without giving any thought at all to the meaning of the words they are repeating. Rote learning can teach learners to respond reflexively to a limited range of canned language with an equally limited range of canned language and is of no use at all for teaching students to imitate creatively in a real conversation.

4) Conscious Repetition and Drills

Repetition is necessary to consolidate articulation, to promote memory and to build automaticity, but for repetition to be useful, it must be conscious, and it must be meaningful. Repetition with awareness combines conditioning with experience, and it is effective. Repetition with awareness requires that students understand what they are saying; this means understanding the words they are using, the word order and their own grammatical and communicative purpose. I do not use a lot of repetitive drilling to teach grammar, but I do use repetition to help students with pronunciation and with prosody. On the other hand, I use substitution phrasing to demonstrate and reinforce the semantic reach of a grammatical pattern, but here I mix working from translation with working in French and with visual association. I will ask, for example, 'How would you say "I am going to the station" (*Je vais à la gare*)? What if you are going to school? (*Je vais à l' école*) what about the office?' And so forth. I work from translation to ensure that students do not slide into automatic sound reproduction, where they no longer notice what they are saying. In order for drills to promote memory, students need to be conscious. I use question-response drills to help students make appropriate grammatical shifts, as for example with the verbs *aller*, *avoir*, and *être*, teaching students to answer with the first person when hearing a question in the second person. I drill other verbs in the first two persons to build pronoun reflexivity, not verb conjugation, because other verbs have much simpler patterns: *Tu veux? Je veux; Tu aimes? J'aime; Tu regardes? Je regarde*, etc. Question-response drilling of *être*, *avoir* and *aller* helps students master the conjugation of these verbs and it helps them build reflexivity in the *passé composé* and in the immediate future.

- *Tu es?*
- *Je suis*
- *Tu vas?*
- *Je vais*
- *Vous avez?*
- *Nous avons.*
- *Vous allez?*

- *Nous allons*

I also use drills to help students build reflexivity to express negation: *Tu es? Je ne suis pas; Tu veux? Je ne veux pas, etc.* If students are challenged to think on their feet in order to respond to a drill, they do not find the exercise boring, but rather treat it as a challenge and a game. The important thing to remember is that drills are useful only when and if students can actually produce the correct language. Students are not learning the pattern with the drill, they are practising what they have learned in order to internalise the language through experience.

5) Listening, and Reading and Listening

Listening, of course, is vital. However, as with everything else, listening must be conscious. Students need to listen attentively and for meaning. The best listening exercise consists in listening attentively to a spoken text several times over until we can hear all the words and understand without effort. For this to be possible, however, a text needs to be comprehended in the first place, or it needs to include mostly familiar vocabulary and syntax, so that students can hear the words they do not know and either deduce them or look them up. Reading while listening to a recording of the same text builds immersive comprehension, as well as grammar and vocabulary. Reading and listening to the texts we have studied in class provides ideal homework at beginner and intermediate level, because it allows students to work independently while minimising the potential for learning errors.

6) Immersion

Immersion is the goal – the point at which language really becomes real. Once students have understood what the new structures and words mean, once they have practised the new language in various activities, informed by English whenever needed, they are ready to just 'speak French'. At this point, it is important to keep to the structures students know, although a few items of vocabulary can be introduced *in lingua* through Comprehensible Input. More importantly, immersive activities should include some problem-solving and play so that students are given the opportunity to think in French and to experience the language communicatively. This can be as simple as asking students what they do when, where and with whom; to reflect on why a character in a story did or did not do something; or why they like this character rather than that other. And here, indeed, the longer students remain in French, the better, and of course, the more fun. Immersion is the ultimate reward. This is when students discover and confirm that they can speak better and a bit more French than they could the week before.

Teaching the catenative structure: *faire + V infinitif*

This structure can be baffling whether students are using a nominal or a pronominal form. *Il fait rire le bébé* is a pivotal sentence in English: 'He makes the baby laugh', which is entirely consistent with the English SVO rule: he makes [the baby laugh]; he makes the baby [laugh]. The baby is at once the grammatical DO of the first verb (hence we will also say, he makes *him* laugh) and the semantic subject of the following infinitive: the baby is the one laughing. In other words, in English, [something or someone] causes [something or someone] to do something. In French, the baby is actually the DO of the second verb and in the pronominal form, we must say: *Il **le** fait rire* which evidently differs from what students have learned in constructions like: *je dois faire mes devoirs, je dois **les** faire*. And the key here is to call this construction by its name. This is a *catenative* verbal phrase. Indeed, the word catenative makes an impression students do not forget. A catenative verbal phrase is a verbal *chain* (*catena* means 'chain' in Latin, and *un cadenas* is 'a padlock' in French). The direct object pronoun precedes the chain.

We can help students understand the structure of *faire + V infinitif* by choosing a sentence where word order and semantics are more obviously connected, as for example, *je fais bouillir de l'eau*. Students respond very well to the following explanation: if you think about it, we don't actually boil or cook anything since we can't sit on it and cook it directly. When we boil water, *we actually do something that boils* the water. Hence, in French we say: I cause/make boiling something:

- Je fais bouillir *what?* de l'eau.
- Je fais cuire *what?* des pâtes.

And since the verb-chain is unbreakable, in the pronominal form, we will write: *je **la** fais bouillir, je **les** fais cuire*.

To say that we make the baby laugh or we make the children work, we use *faire + V infinitif*, just as in the examples above:

- Je fais rire *what?* le bébé.
- Je **le** fais rire.

The verb *faire* is a semi-auxiliary and the verb chain is not breakable. The direct object pronoun precedes the *verb chain*, just as the direct object pronoun precedes the auxiliary of compound tenses. However, the catenative form differs from a compound conjugation in one significant way. Formally speaking the direct object of *faire + V infinitif* is always the object of the second infinitive verb and therefore when *faire* is conjugated in a compound form, the past participle is invariable.

- Je ne les ai pas fait cuire.

After this, we can switch to immersion, and make use of visual aids: *Voici Auguste Escoffier, il est cuisinier. Que fait-il? Il fait cuire quoi? Des pâtes ou des oeufs? Voici Charlie Chaplin, il est très drôle, il fait rire qui? Les adultes ou les enfants? Il vous fait rire? Il me fait rire aussi;* and so forth.

- ❖ Refer to Chapter V (pp. 140-143) for the structure of catenative constructions (including *laisser* and verbs of perception) and their past participle agreements.

Teaching *manquer à quelqu'un*

The verbs 'to miss' and *manquer* speak about an anomalous and regrettable absence or how we feel about it. Something is missing that should be here, or we are missing something or someone who we wish were here. In English, we can say, 'Three pens are missing from my desk' and 'I am missing three pens'. In French, since the pens happen not to be where I expected to find them and they did not remove themselves, we will tend to favour an impersonal form and therefore to use *il* (as in *il faut* and *il pleut*): **il** manque trois stylos, and if the pens happen to be missing from my desk and therefore 'from me': **il** me manque trois stylos and in the third person: *il lui manque trois stylos*. The construction requires a dative and it may be understood semantically in the following manner: It (i.e. fate, the universe or whatever causes pens and socks to disappear) is depriving someone of three pens – in other words, doing something not so nice to someone.

We can also say that we miss somebody or something when we *feel* for the absence of something or someone, and this is where English and French part ways in a more obvious manner. In English, we feel for something or someone that is missing, in French the thing or the person that is missing acts upon us: *Quelque chose ou quelqu'un nous manque*.

Compare
- I miss my parents.
- Subject + verb + direct object
- Mes parents me manquent.
- Subject + dative + verb

Teachers sometimes try to teach a construction like *mes amis me manquent* by turning to the passive voice: 'my friends are missed by me'. This approach, however, is not very helpful – because the passive statement is too artificial to fully compensate for the French word order and because it doesn't solve the syntactic differences between 'I miss you' and *tu me manques* which involves not only word order but also different object complements. The French construction is not just back to front to

English, it also requires a dative complement. Hence, to express 'he is missing her', we must say *elle **lui** manque* and not *elle **le*** manque.

Formally, *manquer* works like *parler*. *Parler* elicits the dative, not the direct object, because we speak or transmit [words] **to** someone – 'words' being implied in the verb to speak. Speaking is the action of conveying words. *Manquer* is the action of conveying longing for someone or something missing. Hence, just as we say *mes parents me parlent*, we will say *mes parents me manquent*. However, it makes a lot of sense to understand *manquer à quelqu'un* in the following manner:

- *Ils me manquent* – they are missing from me (from my life).

Actually, students learn this structure very easily when they learn that rather than saying 'I miss the person (or the thing) that is missing' as we do in English, we simply say that 'the person (or the thing) is missing from me'. These syntactic differences between the French and the English constructions are interesting to explore. In English, 'I miss you' states agency. The subject of the verb is doing the missing for the person or thing missing, so that when I say 'I am missing you', my longing and your absence are conflated. By contrast, when we say *tu me manques*, the person missing is absent from me and their absence is inflicted on me. When I say *tu me manques*, your absence *implicates* my longing for you. And so, although by a remarkable alchemy 'I miss you' and *tu me manques* speak for the same emotion, their respective syntax resonates slightly differently in our internal landscapes. 'I miss you' is pure longing since your absence and my suffering are merged. By contrast, *tu me manques* is an end point. Students tell me that *tu me manques* (you are missing from me) expresses deeper longing than 'I miss you'. As a bilingual speaker, I do not feel this difference of degree, but I can appreciate that, in this particular case, something has been gained in translation.

Teaching the complement of possession

The following is a conversation transcribed from a class with Sophie who was thirteen years old and who had been learning French for twelve weeks at the rate of one hour a week.

- *Comment est ta maison? Elle est grande?*
- *Non, elle n'est pas grande et elle n'est pas petite.*
- *Ah, elle est moyenne?*
- *Oui, elle est moyenne.*
- *C'est un rectangle ou un carré?*

Sophie has never heard these words before, but she understands through context and what I am drawing on the board, that *un rectangle* must be what it sounds like (a rectangle), and she answers:

- *C'est un rectangle.*
- *Il y combien de chambres?*
- *Il y a quatre chambres.*

I encourage students to answer in full sentences, and Sophie has learned to listen and to imitate. She is using my question to formulate her answer. I then draw a house on the board, and as she has not learned *à gauche* or *à droite*, I use gestures and refer to the drawing on the board, very much as a teacher using Krashen's method would do.

- *Les chambres sont à droite ou à gauche?*
- *À droite.*
- *Il y a une chambre ici?*
- *Oui, il y a une chambre.*
- *C'est ta chambre ou c'est la chambre de ton frère?*

Sophie has not learned the complement of possession. She answers:
- *C'est mon frère… mon chambre.*
- *Ok, c'est la chambre de ton frère. Et ici, c'est la chambre de ton frère ou c'est ta chambre?*
- *C'est ma chambre,*
- *Et là? Qu'est-ce que c'est?*
- *C'est la salle de bain.*
- *Il y a combien de salles de bain?*
- *Il y a trois salles de bain… oh non, il y a deux salles de bain.*

We keep going in this fashion, until we get to the last bedroom and I ask:
- *C'est la chambre de tes parents?*

She answers:
- *Mon parents chambre… non, mes parents mon chambre.*

Sophie's response shows the difference between deducing meaning and reproducing language. Her answer makes plain that she has understood that I was speaking about her parents' room, just as she understood that I was asking about her brother's room earlier on. And this was very clever because she had never heard this question before, and she had not been introduced to the *complement du nom* formally. She deduced my meaning from the context, as Krashen would explain, because we were speaking about her house, but also because she already knew what *ta chambre* and *ma chambre* mean. In other words, what I had asked was just above her current linguistic competence. I successfully introduced three vocabulary items: *moyenne, à gauche* and *à droite* through Comprehensible Input (1+1). However, Comprehensible Input did not work when I tried to elicit the possessive structure in French. Sophie understood my meaning through deduction but she could not *hear* the word order in French and she produced an answer based on her English grammar. She did this even after I repeated the sentence several times over. At some point, she was able to repeat after me but it took several attempts for her to get all of the words in order to say *C'est la chambre de mes parents* and then, she could not think of transposing this same structure to say: *C'est la chambre de mon frère*. I asked her:

'Do you understand what I am saying?'
'Not really'.
'I was saying your brother's and your parents' room.'
'Oh, yes, I thought you were, but I can't understand.'

And again, this is a very interesting response. Evidently, since Sophie made sense of what I was saying, what she meant by 'I can't understand' is 'I am confused by this word order that does not make any sense to me'. It is on account of the confusion caused by this novel and nonsensical word order that she deduced that she could not understand what she had actually grasped by context. So, I wrote on the board, in English: 'my brother's bedroom'.

'Now, are we speaking about your brother or the room?'
'The room.'
'Okay, so what's the headword?'
'The room.'
'That's right. So, in French, which will come first: the room or your brother?'
'The room.'
'Why?'
'Because the headword comes before the modifier.'
'How do we say the bedroom?'
'*La chambre*.'
'Great.' I write *la chambre* on the board.
'You see, the way we show possession in French is not with the *'s* like we do in English but with the preposition *de*. Here we are, *la chambre **de***, and how do you say my brother? *Mon frère*, good (I write: *mon frère*). So here you have it: *La chambre **de** mon frère*. See the way we say this in French: the bedroom of my brother…'
'It's a bit weird.'
'Yes, it's back to front or maybe English is back to front … What do you think?' (she laughs)… See if we go from right to left: my brother's room. How would we say my parents' bedroom?'
'*La chambre de mon… mes parents*?'
'Exactly! Excellent. Let's practise this for a bit.'

So we repeated the phrases a couple of times, and then, I pointed to a handbag on a chair and I asked:

- *C'est le sac de ta mère ou c'est ton sac?*
- *C'est le sac de ma mère.*

[Note that Sophie had never heard or said this before, this was unrehearsed. I continued in this vein}

- *C'est ton stylo ou c'est le stylo de ton père?*
- *C'est le stylo de mon père.*
- Do you think you know how to do this now?
- Yes!
- *Tu aimes les chiens?*
- *Oui j'aime les chiens.*
- *Tu as un chien?*
- *Oui.*
- *C'est un chien ou une chienne?*
- *Une chienne.*
- *Elle s'appelle comment?*
- *Elle s'appelle Sala.*
- *C'est ta chienne ou c'est la chienne de ton papa?*
- *C'est la chienne de ma famille, mais elle préfère mon père.*

Once the complement of possession was explained and experienced in the context of what Sophie had already learned about French grammar and sentence formation, she was able to apply the new structure to speaking creatively. Thus, she was able to utter a brand new grammatically correct sentence that she had never heard before. This involved the conscious use of an article, two gender agreements and a novel word order, none of which exists in her native English grammar. The following week, when we returned to the complement of possession in conversation, she experienced some difficulty. Again, I wrote the structure on the board. At this point she said: 'It's like saying the room of my brother, isn't it?' Yes, I replied. Then, I asked her: *C'est le collier de ton chien?* And then I continued in this vein, using *C'est à qui?* Pointing to things around the room and using pictures, I asked her to attribute several more objects to persons. She was able to answer without a problem and without making a mistake. At the end of the class, she commented, 'It's really easy now'. The structure was acquired for good.

IX

Verbs and their Conjugations

Learning and acquiring verbal usage is not easy in English or in French and the proof lies in that even native speakers require schooling to master the subtleties of all the voices, moods, tenses and aspects of their own languages. The conjugations discussed in this chapter do not account for all French conjugations, all the usage made of all tenses and all the difficulties involved in conjugating French verbs. In the following pages, I discuss some of the more salient problems English-speaking students encounter when they are attempting to express time in French. I also explain how and why verbal conjugations must be understood and memorised, and how we can provide students with meaningful and informative general principles that will enable them to learn more subtle and complex verbal expressions when they pursue more advanced studies.

To begin with: what are conjugations and how complicated are they?
Organising French conjugations is no simple matter. To give an idea: French school children are taught that the first conjugation contains the verbs ending in ER, the second conjugation contains the verbs ending in IR to which we add *ss* in the three plural persons, and then there is a third conjugation which contains all the other verbs. In the 1930s, however, the third conjugation was named and headed by verbs ending in OIR and RE. In the nineteenth century, French verbs were classed into four categories, ER, IR, OIR and RE (in this order).[126] And in the 1980s, French language teachers in Australia taught that there were four groups of verbs: ER, RE, IR and OIR. Based on my experience of teaching French verbs and of learning and teaching Spanish verbs, I have come to the conclusion that it is more helpful to increase the number of conjugations by

---

[83] See Larive et Fleury, *La Classe de Français*, Armand Colin, 2015, a reproduction of Larive et Fleury, *La première année de grammaire*, 1936.

paying attention to four infinitive endings and to particular stem patterns than to simplify categories at the cost of multiplying the irregularities and the exceptions.

French verbs are not so terribly complicated insofar as most belong to the first conjugation, and aside from *aller*, these verbs are virtually all regular. The phonetic-spelling adjustments required to enunciate and to write the conjugation of verbs like *acheter* and *jeter* need to be explained, but there is no real reason to teach these verbs as irregular verbs. The same applies to *manger*, which is entirely regular since the letter *e* is inserted where there is a need to maintain the soft *g*. Nevertheless, French conjugations are complicated. Although most verbs do not possess truly unique patterns, there are many variations on a few themes. Four infinitive endings RE, IR, RE, and OIR/OIRE command three types of conjugated endings in the indicative present: *e/es/e/ons/ez/ent*, and *s/s/t-d/ons/ez/ent* or [*x/x/t/ons/ez/ent ons/ez/ent*, but what precedes these infinitive endings also contributes to the many patterns that do not fit the basic rules.

A bird's eye view of French conjugation (general principles)
The conjugations of the indicative present are the most difficult since they are the most diverse and those which students must learn first. These conjugations, however, are more regular in speech than they are in writing. With the exceptions of *avoir*, *être* and *aller*, the first three persons of all verbs repeat the pattern set by the first person (*je chante/tu chantes/il chante//je veux/tu veux/il veut*). The first-person and the second-person plural of almost all French verbs are regular: infinitive stem + ons, and infinitive stem + ez. With the exception of *avoir*, *être*, *aller*, *faire*, and *dire* from *nous* onwards, verbs ending in IR and RE conjugate like *chanter*. Therefore, when they are speaking, students are able to conjugate most verbs in the present tense by knowing the first-person singular and the first-person plural. Writing out verbs requires a different sort of attention as well as knowledge of the subject-verb agreement rules. However, spelling the ending of French verbs correctly, remembering that *s* goes with *tu* and *ent* with *ils* and *elles*, is the least problematic aspect of this grammar.

We conjugate verbs that end in ER (except for *aller*) by dropping the infinitive ending and by sounding the stem, with either a final consonant (*je chan**t**e*) or a final vowel sound (*je j**ou**e, j'étud**i**e*). We conjugate the first-person plural and the second-person plural by adding *–ons*, *–ez* onto the stem. We add the silent *–ent* on the third-person plural, with the result that the third-person plural and the third-person singular sound exactly the same.

When conjugating verbs in IR, we remove half of the infinitive ending; we take away the *r* and we keep the *i*. From *nous* onwards, we add *ss* to the stem (*finiss*) onto which we attach the *ons*, *ez*, *ent* endings. Therefore, the first three persons sound exactly like each other, and exactly like the stem (*je finis, tu finis, il finit*); and the three plural persons sound just like the verbs ending in ER (*nous finissons, vous finissez, ils finissent*). If the stem ends in *vr, fr*, as in *ouvrir* and *offrir*, the conjugation follows the ER pattern with all persons. In the present tense, *cueillir* and *assaillir* also conjugate like ER verbs, but not so *bouillir* or *vieillir*. *Sentir, partir, sortir, servir, dormir, courir, vêtir, etc.* are conjugated like the verbs ending in RE (in speech); and *tenir, venir* and *mourir* follow a similar pattern to OIR/OIRE verbs. *Acquérir, requérir,* and *conquérir* do their own thing.

We conjugate verbs ending in RE by reducing the stem to either the final vowel sound (*je bats*) or to the final vowel + r if there is an *r* in the stem (*je perds*). In both cases, the end consonant attached to the stem is not sounded in the first three persons. From *nous* onwards, the consonant is restored (*nous battons, nous perdons*) and the verb follows the same pattern as ER and IR verbs. *Prendre* and its derivatives follow another pattern since the *d* of the infinitive stem is not restored in the first person plural, but the *d* is more of a feature of the infinitive than its absence is a feature of its conjugations. With the verbs ending in IRE and UIRE (also *coudre*) from *nous* onward, we must add a consonant (*s*) to the stem in order to attach the endings *ons, ez, ent*. With verbs ending in EINDRE and OINDRE we convert *n* into *gn* in the plural persons. Verbs ending in URE are regular in the first three persons: we remove RE and add *s/s/t* to the stem, and from *nous* onwards, we simply attach *ons, ez, ent*. In speech, therefore, these verbs conjugate just like *jouer*. The verbs *connaître* and *paraître* require the same treatment but the addition of *ss* means that in the last three persons, they are conjugated like IR ending verbs. Verbs ending in SOUDRE have their own patterns.

Verbs ending in OIR and OIRE as well as *tenir, venir* and their derivatives form sub-patterns within yet another pattern.

- vouloir → veux/voulons/veulent
- devoir → dois/devons/doivent
- pouvoir → peux/pouvons/peuvent
- tenir → tiens/tenons/tiennent
- venir → viens/venons/viennent
- savoir → sais/savons/savent
- valoir → vaux/valons/valent
- boire → bois/buvons/boivent
- croire → crois/croyons/croient
- voir → vois/voyons/voient

How can we facilitate the learning of French verbs?
The bird's eye view of things confirms that learning French conjugations is no picnic. There is no argument that acquiring conjugations is a memory game, and that teachers and students need to devote a sizable amount of time to this mission. French conjugations are not so diverse that they should be learned purely by rote, but they are too diverse to be learned incidentally or on the basis of a few general

principles. Interestingly, students who learn with the comparative-narrative method and who therefore spend relatively little time engaging in rote activities very much enjoy reciting conjugations. This may seem odd but it makes anthropological (if not pedagogical) sense, for the world over and from time immemorial, people have learned to memorise through rhythmic chanting. We can also help students learn conjugations by grouping verbs that follow the same pattern. We can teach *partir, sortir, sentir, dormir, etc.* together with other verbs ending in RE. We can teach verbs ending in IRE and UIRE (*lire, conduire, produire*) as one conjugation. We can ensure that students know that verbs may have derivatives which follow the pattern established by the primary verb: *apprendre, comprendre, surprendre, reprendre, se reprendre* are conjugated like *prendre*. The verbs derived from *dire*, like *contredire* and *médire*, are an exception to this rule, but they have the merit of observing the regular pattern on the second-person plural. Grouping *vous êtes, vous dites, vous faites* forms a mnemonic pattern with semantic resonance. We can also explain to students that these second-person plural are not so much irregular as reminiscent of the original Latin (*estis, dicitis, facitis*).

    Students are usually able to memorise the conjugation of French verbs if they are given enough time and practice. Knowing conjugations, however, will not translate into using verbs accurately – not because memorising the forms is useless but because we must not only teach the forms but also teach *how and when to use them*. It goes without saying that before the recitation of conjugations can be of any use at all, students must first of all understand why we conjugate French verbs according to a six-person pattern, and what each person represents and implicates. But even this is not enough for students to be able to apply the conjugations in creative speech and composition. Claude Germain explains the problem in light of neurolinguistic research and the functional differentiation of declarative and procedural memory: '*le savoir ne peut pas se transformer en habileté.*'[127] Verbal conjugations are stored in our declarative memory but the construction of a sentence is dependent on our procedural memory and this, as Germain explains it, equates to a difference between conscious and unconscious processes. What is conscious cannot become unconscious, and there can be no *direct* connection between declarative and procedural memory, hence the futility of teaching verbal conjugations explicitly.[128]

    In Chapter III, I argued that, from my teaching and learning experience, correction without explicit grammatical awareness has very limited impact on second-language performance. I shall now disagree with Germain's take on the opposition of *savoir* and *habilité*. My typing of these few words is not only proof that I once learned to spell English words but that I mastered the English language keyboard. And this began with locating each key representing each letter. Next, I had to make the effort of *remembering* where each letter was stored on the keyboard

---

[127] Germain, op. cit., p. 151.
[128] Ibid.

(declarative memory/*savoir*). From the start, I was able to put letters onto the screen by striking at the keys intentionally, thus connecting the facts of the keyboard to my writing purpose. With practice and experience, I began moving from key to key faster, until one day my fingers found the keys automatically and I could type sentences without thinking about the keys (procedural memory/*habileté*). In the same vein, when we learn to ride a bicycle, we first learn what a bicycle is: wheels, pedals, seat and handlebars; we then learn to place our feet, hands and body on the bike; and then we adapt what we can already do, which is to balance ourselves and walk on our own two feet, to pedalling and balancing ourselves on the seat of the bike. In other words, procedural behaviour is the unconscious production of learned sequences linking facts stored in our declarative memory. Perhaps, automaticity is less about the unconscious production of behaviour than the unselfconscious rapid production of sequenced actions. But whatever it actually is, we can be sure that automacity is not entirely unconscious because we are able to break down, analyse, refine and enhance automatic behaviours through reflection and conscious application. Indeed, in all arts and sports, automaticity is the basis on which better things and more skilful performances are built. Second-language fluency can be the reward of the purposeful, painstaking and conscious application of organised language. It is also the beginning of greater things.

Our students cannot transfer the conjugations they have memorised to creative conversation, not because we cannot apply factual knowledge to automatic performance, but because applying conjugated forms to speech and producing conjugations intuitively is dependent on a multilevel, complex process of acquisition. Simply speaking, acquisition is a three-stage process: 1) knowing the forms, 2) retrieving the forms, 3) applying the correct forms in a real language exchange. Learning to recite conjugations fulfils a basic condition: knowing the forms (1). This, of course, is quite useless if students do not understand what conjugating means. If they do, however, the conjugations provide a filing system from which learners can retrieve verbal forms (2). Following from this, learners are able to produce correct verbal forms consciously and with practice to integrate the forms and eventually to produce those spontaneously (3). Evidently, I agree with Germain that students cannot transition directly from the formal study of conjugations to the production of correct conjugations spontaneously. In fact, students cannot transition directly from stage 2 to stage 3. This transition, as I will attempt to demonstrate in the remainder of this chapter, depends on a yet other processes involving layered knowledge and consciousness, and *types of practices*.

Before we can take students from the objective knowledge of the forms to a formal and eventually intuitive application of the forms, there are several issues to consider. To start with: why do students who have learned French in immersion, and who have become fluent speakers of French have no trouble with many verbal forms, including the subjunctive forms *il faut que j'aille, que je fasse, qu' il vienne*, etc.

and yet continue to default to the infinitive or other interesting alternatives when using a great many verbs in the indicative tenses? In particular, why do some fluent speakers mix the *imparfait* and the *passé composé* of verbs in ER? Why are some of our Year 12 students inclined to say *je suis faire* or even *je suis faisant* or *je venir* or *je venu*, when they have never heard this from their teachers or come across anything of the sort in the authentic language materials provided to them in their classes? Conversely, given the overall simplicity of English verbal formation, why do French-speaking learners of English experience just as many difficulties using English conjugations as English-speaking learners of French do using French verbs?

Indeed, if verbal inflection were truly the problem, we could expect time constructions to present no difficulty for Anglophone and Francophone learners of Chinese, since Chinese has no verbal inflection and uses only a few aspectual locutions. And yet, these language students commonly produce erroneous time constructions in Mandarin. But if inflection is not the (only) problem, what is? In large part, of course, the problem is pedagogical: many of our students do not really understand what verbs do and what conjugations are. But the problem is also in part ontological because verbal usage is deeply etched into our experience of time. Simply put, French conjugations are difficult for English speakers (and vice-versa) because they require learners to verbalise and thus experience aspects of time in a new way. And time is at least as tricky as gender because time rules how we experience everything we do and feel. The passage of time is the passage of our existence.

As it turns out, not all French, English or Chinese time constructions are difficult to acquire; the difficult ones concern those aspects of time that may not exist or may not be easily identified in our own language(s). For our Anglophone students, the difficulties of learning French verbs do lie with the inflected forms, but they also lie with what English verbs do that French verbs don't do as much as with what French verbs do that English verbs don't do. And then, the difficulty *also* lies in the fact that there are different types of verbs in French and English which are not only distinct on account of being French and English, but on account of eliciting distinct syntactic treatments within French and English – as for example, verbs of location and direction in French, and modal verbs in English. Learning what a verb is and identifying the classes of verbs is therefore a first step in learning verbal conjugations and developing procedural memory.

IDENTIFYING THE CLASSES OF VERBS

In primary school, students learned that verbs are 'doing words'. And of course, they are, but not all verbs are doing words. Verbs can also express who and what we are, where we are and where we are at; how we feel; what we want; what we need; what we must do; what we love and what we love to do; where we are going and coming from; and none of these things are about *doing* anything. Indeed, when I say 'I am eating', I am doing something, but what about when I say 'I am happy'? And what if I say, 'I want to read'? 'To be' and 'to want' are verbs, but they are not actions: they are states we find ourselves in, states of being and states of mind. Hence, some verbs are called verbs of action or activity verbs, and others are called stative verbs (I am happy, I am at the station). There are also modal verbs, which embody a mood (I must go out: obligation; I want to go out: intention; I may go out: possibility). There are locational and directional verbs, called verbs of motion or verbs of movement, which express our 'movements' in space (I am going to school).

Identifying classes of verbs through mental imaging and sensory reflection
Students enjoy the following exercise. I will call out a statement such as 'I am sleeping', and ask the following question: 'What happened in your mind's eye, did you get an image?' to which students will answer that they did. I will then keep going and call out: 'I speak', 'I am riding', 'I write', and so forth. Students will confirm that all these produce mental images. But what about: 'I love'? Do you have an image or a sensation? Where do you feel it? Love is invariably felt in the chest, around the heart. What about: 'I want'? Some students feel this in their heads, others in their chests or in their stomachs. How about 'I want a croissant'? This is usually felt in the stomach. What about: 'I want to learn French'? This may be felt in the head, chest or stomach. And what about: 'I have'? 'I have' usually draws a blank and students may say: 'I need more information' or 'What do you mean?' Students will produce the same response when I say 'I am'. The utterance produces no internal impression unless it is uttered in a certain tone or it is accompanied by an attribute. Conducting the same exercise with French speakers produces the same responses with verbs of action, verbs of emotion and modal verbs. However, *je suis* produces a strikingly different reaction. All the French speakers with whom I have conducted this experiment have reported that *je suis* produces a whole-body response. In French, *je suis* elicits a physical awareness of being. And this goes a long way to explain why the verb 'to be' has far more uses than the verb *être*.

Once students understand that English verbs express different categories of being, feeling, thinking, locating-relocating as well as doing, they are ready to be introduced to the different classes of verb in French as I have detailed in Chapter V, and to which the reader should now refer: see pp.131-144. The discussion below is concerned specifically with issues pertaining to the verbs *être* and *avoir*. I address the teaching of conjugations pp. 256-276.

To be and *ne pas être*

The verb 'to be' is more flexible and lighter than the verb *être*. In fact, the verb 'to be' is so light that almost all my native English-speaking students have serious difficulties identifying it as a verb. When they are learning formal grammar and they are asked to identify the verb in a statement like: 'He is happy', students invariably select 'happy', not 'is'. In addition, students have troubles relating the inflected forms (am, are, is, was, were) to the infinitive 'to be'. The idea that 'am' and 'were' are expressions of the same verb is very abstract to learners who have not grown up with formal grammar. Again, it helps to alert students that there were *two* verbs 'to be' in Old English, *beon* and *wesan*, as well as showing their conjugated forms (*beo, beom, waes, waere, etc.*). We also need to explain that the difficulty in identifying the verb 'to be' in the statement 'he's happy' is legitimate – here, the verb 'to be' is empty. It is a linking verb (copula); it is not an action, not a mood, not an intention, and not a state of mind. The state of mind is contained in the adjective, not in the verb, which is precisely why students feel that 'happy' is the verb. At any rate, we should not be surprised that our students frequently forget to use *être* in French sentence constructions.

For its part, the verb *être* has more existential weight than the verb 'to be'. The verb *être*, like the verb 'to be', expresses who we are, how we are feeling, and where we are, but the verb *être* is always at least in part inhabited, and this is why it is not used to express the types of temporary states that are dependent on environment rather than essence – hence, the use of *avoir* and *aller*. To understand when to use *être* and *avoir* in stative constructions, we need to differentiate between psychological/soul states and what we owe to the cosmic realm, and physical states and what we owe to the physical world and society. In the first instance we use *être*; in the second, we use the verb *avoir* and, in a more limited manner, *aller*.

Être [+ adj] [+ noun]
- Existential and essential states, and personality: *elle est grande, intelligente, depressive, joyeuse, australienne, riche, pauvre, aisée, professeur(e), médecin, ingénieur(e), serveuse*. Note: we use no articles with professions; professions are attributes of the subject like adjectives.
- Psychological or soul states: *il est triste, malheureux, heureux* and *il est malade*.

Avoir [+ noun]
- Passing physical, social, age, and psychological states: *j'ai faim, j'ai soif, j'ai froid, j'ai dix ans, j'ai peur, j'ai honte*.

Aller [+ adv.]
- Polite formulas; passing psychological and physical states: *je vais bien, je vais mal*.

We can help students understand this meaning of *aller* by reminding them that in English, we use 'to go' in a similar way when we say: 'How are you going?' We also say: 'he is doing well', 'he's faring well', 'they are not traveling too well'. Note that the etymology of 'fare' lies in the Old English word *faran* meaning 'to travel', hence also the expression 'farewell'. There is beauty in these expressions, for they conflate lived experience with traveling and the passing of time.

This three-part classification provides students with a *general* guide and a *degree* of rational differentiation, and much more. Evidently, some conditions pertaining to the use of *être* and *avoir* do not quite fit. In the lists given above, students will contest the following: having a profession is surely a temporary state; being sick is a physical state and more often than not it is also a temporary state; and being afraid or ashamed are psychological state (and indeed we can also say: *je suis honteux*). These objections should be encouraged, as they provide an opportunity to explore the historical, cultural and philosophical implications of French and English stative grammars. Until recently, a profession was a permanent state: people chose a life career, and for much of French history, boys were obligated to have the same trade or profession as their fathers. In fact, professions and trades were so permanent that they gave rise to family names like Boulanger, Pottier, Dujardin (Baker, Potter, Gardiner). Women's lives were defined by their families, the house, the convent, and social rank which explains why the names of many professions existed only in the masculine form although most are now feminised (*ingénieure, écrivaine*, but note also the history inherent in *actrice, nonne, directrice, sage-femme, maîtresse, duchesse, princesse, poétesse*, etc.). Before the advent of medical science, people conceived of illness as an imbalance of the humours and the manifestation of sin, all of which are internal states; fear is usually the result of an external rather than an internal cause and the word *honte* originally meant dishonour, a social state *par excellence*. Discussions along these lines provide an opportunity to explore important things about life and to contribute to students' general culture. Not least, they help students remember the particularities of French stative verbs.

Il fait chaud when it is hot
For similar reasons, in French, we speak about what 'the weather' does, not what 'the weather' is, perhaps because the weather changes too often, but also because we do not know what is actually causing the weather, we can only observe weather conditions: *Il fait chaud*.

To have and not to have
The verb *avoir* does not entirely correspond to the verb 'to have'. Just as the verb *être* does not correspond entirely to the verb 'to be'. One function of *avoir* (*j'ai chaud, j'ai peur*), as we saw above, is expressed by the verb 'to be' in English. But in

French, we also say things like *prendre un café*, as in English we say 'to have a coffee' and we say that we *have* an age, rather than we *are* so many years old. But even in English, the verb 'to have', like the verb *avoir*, has other functions besides marking possession. What do we mean when we say that we are having a coffee, and why do Americans take a shower (as French speakers do) when Australians have a shower?

Why *prendre* and not have?

When I say 'I have a dog', I am expressing possession, but if I say 'I had a coffee this morning', 'I am having breakfast', 'I had a shower', I am referring to something that I am doing or did, and not to something I own. In French, we say *j'ai pris une douche* and *j'ai pris un café*: I took a shower and I took a coffee. Notice, however, that in English, we rarely say 'I drank a coffee' or 'I ate dinner with friends', but rather we say that we had coffee or dinner. Indeed, to drink and eat are physical actions, the type of thing that we, along with all other animals, need to do to survive. On the other hand, to have dinner and to have tea or a coffee, *prendre le dîner, prendre le thé et prendre un café* are socio-cultural and ritual behaviours; 'civilised things' we do for pleasure and to share with others; things, in other words, which exceed biological necessity. Still, why should the French and the Americans *take* a shower rather than *have* a shower as Australians and British people do? Are the verbs 'to take' and 'to have' so different from one another, or is there a connection between taking and having? After all, we take something because we want to have it, and we cannot have a thing if we do not take it.

Anthropology sheds an interesting light on this question. We may begin by reflecting on a profoundly anchored principle of human relations that opposes taking and having to giving and reciprocating. In all societies, there exists a rule that all that is given (be it spiritual or material) must be given back. Marriage partners, sacred knowledge and material goods are exchanged and circulated between individuals or groups of people, and they are always reciprocated with other gifts of appropriately established social value. This universal rule which anthropologists call 'reciprocity' creates interdependence and cements social relations in all traditional societies.[129] In our modern, commercially driven world, we think of gifts as being free because we do not pay for them, but we are no less ruled by the moral imperative to give back when we have been given to. A gift is never free of obligation, hence also the restrictions applying to giving to politicians, judges, policemen, teachers and so forth. Furthermore, we call takers those who fail to reciprocate, those who keep for themselves what should be given back. Expectations of reciprocity, in short, differentiate barter from theft, trade

---

[129] See the classic anthropological works on gift, debt and reciprocity by Marcel Mauss, *The Gift, the form and reason of exchange in archaic societies*, Routledge, 1990 (first English edition 1924), and Bronislaw Malinowski, *Argonauts of the Western Pacific*, Routledge, 1922, among many other and more recent editions.

from piracy, and diplomacy from territorial conquest, which is to say that people everywhere in the world differentiate between taking and giving back, and between taking and keeping – taking and having.

The connection between 'to have', 'to possess', 'to own' and 'to take' is very much alive in the English verb 'to get', which means all of the above as well as a lot of other things. In Modern English, the verb 'to get' is a skeleton key that opens many doors. It can mean to have something ('I have got money'); to obtain something ('I got some money'); to catch something ('I got the flu'; 'I got a fish') as well as to arrive somewhere ('I got home late'); to rise from bed ('I got up early'); to make a start ('I'll get going'); and to understand ('I got it'). Etymological enquiry further enlightens us on the connection between the verbs 'to get', 'to have' and 'to take', as well as on old ideas about ownership and possession. The *Online Etymology Dictionary* gives the origins of the verb 'to get' in the Old Norse *geta* meaning 'to obtain', 'to reach', 'to be empowered', 'to be pleased' and the noun 'get' meaning 'booty'. The Proto-Indo-European (PIE) ancestor of 'get' is *ghend meaning 'to seize'.[130] The origins of the verb *avoir* lie in the Latin *habere* meaning 'to have', 'to hold', and 'to possess', while those of the verb 'to have' are found in the Old English *habban*. *Habere* and *habban*, for their part, share a distant ancestor in the PIE gʰehıbʰ meaning 'to grab' and 'to take'.[131] Meanwhile, the original meaning of the English verb 'to own' is 'to master' and 'to possess', while the verb 'to possess' enters English from French in the fourteenth century meaning 'to hold' and 'to occupy'.[132] According to the *Littré*, the origins of the French verb *posséder* lie with the Latin verb *possidere* and the French verb *pouvoir*. *Posséder quelque chose* in other words means 'to hold something within one's power'.[133] Hence, 'to have', 'to take', 'to grab', and 'to possess' are kindred terms, and we can confirm without more ado that we may just as well take as have a shower and grab as have a cup of tea – or as we say in French: *prendre une douche et prendre un thé*.

Avoir un âge

In French, as in a few other languages, we don't say that we are twelve or forty or sixty-years-old but that we have twelve years, and so forth. If it sounds strange, think of it as: I have twelve years of living under my belt, and next year, I will have thirteen! From the French perspective, we cannot really *be* thirteen, since next year we will not be thirteen but fourteen, and the year after, we will be fifteen, and so forth. The following exchange makes the point effectively: 'Oh, you're Thirteen!

---

[130] *Online Etymology Dictionary* at https://www.etymonline.com/search?q=get
[131] See PIE entry on 'habeo' in Michiel De Vaan, in *Etymological Dictionary of Latin and the other Italic Languages* (Leiden Indo-European Etymological Dictionary Series; 7), Leiden, Boston, Brill (2008), p. 277.
[132] See the entries 'to get' and 'to possess' in the *Online Etymology Dictionary*.
[133] See *Littré* on line: https://www.littre.org/definition/posséder

Nice to meet you Thirteen, I am Christine!' This also makes students laugh, which is a very good thing.

Thinking about 'to have' and 'to be'

Do you think that saying that we have x number of years as opposed to saying that we are x number of years old, possibly influences how we feel about age? Could this influence how we experience the passage of time, our passage through life, and our sense of identity? A perfunctory Internet search typing the words 'ageing' together with the word 'French' brings forth no shortage of clichés: Ageing like French women; French women and the secret of ageing gracefully; ageing the French way; French women and the art of ageing. Typing the words 'ageing' and 'English' on the other hand brings up several websites discussing the relative value of spelling 'ageing' as 'aging'.

More interestingly, let's reflect on the fact that *être* and *avoir*, 'to be' and 'to have', express the fundamentals of our existence: who we are, where we are, what we feel, what we possess... Isn't it interesting that these verbs are also preferred auxiliary verbs, the verbs we use to form the conjugations of other verbs? Isn't it interesting that the fundamentals of our biological and cultural existence should provide us with the fundamentals of our grammar?

To use *c'est* or *il est*?

This is one of the most vexing aspects of French usage for English-speaking students because *c'est* and *il est* can both mean 'it is'. And often, in casual registers, French speakers may well have the option of using either *c'est* or *il est*. We saw in Chapter V (pp. 156-157) that we need to shift from *c'est facile à faire* to *il est facile de faire ça* when the infinitive verb is not only the attribute of the adjective but is itself followed by a complement. In this construction, the demonstrative value of *ce* is brought to the fore and therefore makes nonsense of *c'est facile*. As I pointed out, however, French speakers are just as happy, if not happier, to say *c'est facile de dire ça* as they are to say *il est facile de dire ça*. In other words, usage turns the neutral pronoun *ce* into an impersonal pronoun, emptying it of its demonstrative value. French speakers may also say: *c'est* or *il est mon meilleur ami*. Indeed, it is in the nature of the demonstrative pronoun to evolve into other types of locutions. The third-person subject pronouns (*il, elle*), the object pronouns *(le, la, les)* and the definite articles *(le, la, les)* have evolved from the Latin demonstratives *ille, illa*. The definite article *the* in English has also evolved from the Old English demonstrative pronouns *þe* (masculine), *þa* (feminine), and *þaet* (neutral).

Furthermore, French speakers gravitate towards the neutral demonstrative *c'* in preference to the impersonal *il* on account of both the phonology and the nature of the verb *être*. The impersonal *il* has no antecedent. It is a non-existent subject, an empty word that allows us to use an impersonal verb as, for example, when we say *il pleut, il fait chaud, il faut, il y a*. Indeed, unlike the other Romance languages, French has lost sufficient verbal endings to require all verbs to show a grammatical subject. In the absence of a *semantic* subject, the impersonal *il* allows subject-less verbs to conform to this rule. Nevertheless, French speakers commonly say *Faut le faire, Faut y aller, Y a* and so forth, which shows that la *langue parlée* can easily dispense with *il* in impersonal verbal constructions – although speakers will say *est facile de dire ça* in jest only (unlike *faut, ya, yaka, yapadquoi* which are used as a matter of course).

To recapitulate, French speakers use *c'est* rather than *il est* for three main reasons. Firstly, they use *c'est* because saying *c'est* requires less effort than saying *il est* and because *est* on its own does not have the phonological weight of *faut* or *ya*. Secondly, *c'* is a neutral pronoun and is therefore naturally suited to the impersonal form, while *il* is more often than not a masculine personal pronoun. And thirdly, French speakers are somewhat reluctant to pair the verb *être* with a non-existent *il*, on account of the existential weight of the verb *être* which implies that something *is* – that *it exists*. Thus, *il est* is likely to suggest that *il* is replacing a something or someone that happens to be something or someone, or happens to be somewhere, or a someone that happens to be feeling something.

Students respond well to the following explanations and guidelines. When French speakers use or hear *il est*, they are usually thinking of a masculine someone or a masculine something referencing an antecedent. *Il est heureux, il est ici, il est gentil, il est professeur de Français, il est sur la table* imply that *il* replaces someone or something that has been named. When French speakers use *c'est*, on the other hand, they are usually identifying, indicating, announcing or pointing to something or somebody that has not been named. Pointing to is also the rightful function of demonstrative locutions. The word 'demonstrative' implies 'to show' or 'to point to'. Hence, we will say: *C'est mon stylo et il est rouge; c'est un chien et il est très gentil.*

French speakers use *c'est* when they are saying something along the line of: 'he's a man' (this person I am going to tell you about is a man); 'she's my teacher' (this person I am speaking about is my teacher); 'it was great' (this thing I did was great); 'it's a nice day' (this is a nice day); 'it's expensive' (this thing is expensive); 'it's easy to say' (this is easy to say).

French speakers mostly use the dummy *il* with *être* for truly impersonal constructions, which are relatively few and are also found in English: *il est huit heures, il est tard*. They will say things like *il est important de parler correctement* exactly as we phrase the same sentence in English, when they feel inclined to conform to the formal requirements of the standard language. We can see how the demonstrative value of the neutral pronoun *c'* gets in the way of formal logic when we translate *c'est important de parler correctement* into English since the sentence literally means 'this is important to speak correctly'.

> Also refer to pp. 156-157.

<u>Identifying, pointing to: *c'est*</u>
- *C'est un homme* – this/he is a man, this [person I am indicating] is a man.
- *C'est la professeure de Français* – this/she is the French teacher, this [person I am indicating] is the French teacher.
- *C'est mon père* – this/he is my father, this [person I am indicating] is my father.
- *C'est moi qui ai fait ce meuble* – it is I who made this piece of furniture. This is called a cleft sentence, a structure used to create emphasis. Cleft sentences are also very common in English. *C'est* is here mandatory on account of the relative clause. If we were to say *il est moi qui ai fait ce meuble*, we would hear: 'He is me who made this piece of furniture'.
- *C'est intéressant* – it is interesting, this [thing] is interesting.
- *C'est bon* – this/it is good.
- *C'est un livre* – this/it is a book.
- *Ce livre est le mien! Ah, c'est le tien* – this book is mine! Oh this one is yours.
- *C'est à moi* – this / it's mine'.
- *C'est à moi de le dire* – this/ it is up to me to say.

<u>And also</u>
- C'est l'hiver, c'est l'été, c'est le printemps
- It is winter, summer, spring.

<u>Describing, referencing the antecedent: *il est, elle est, c'est*</u>
- *Voici Madame Legrand, elle est professeur de Français.*
- Here is Madame Legrand, she (Mme Legrand) is a French teacher.
- *Il faut que j'appelle Madame Legrand... oui, elle est ma prof de Français.*
- I must call Madame Legrand... yes she (Mme Legrand) is my French teacher.
- *Cette robe est très jolie mais elle est plutôt démodée.*
- This dress is pretty but it (she-the dress) is rather old-fashion.
- *J'ai acheté ce livre hier, il est formidable.*
- I bought this book yesterday, it (he-the book) is fantastic!
- *J'aimerais acheter ce livre, mais il est trop cher.*
- I would like to buy this book, but it (he-the book) is too expensive.

- *J'ai acheté un livre magnifique hier, c'est formidable!*
- Yesterday I bought a beautiful book, and this or it (the fact that I bought the book) is great!

The impersonal *il est*
- Il est important de comprendre la grammaire.
- Il est bon/bien de se reposer.

These examples are cleft sentences in French and in English. In *la langue parlée*, we are likely to say: *C'est important d'apprendre la grammaire* and *c'est bien de se reposer*.

And also
- Il est onze heures de l'après-midi.
- Il est midi.

Short rule: We use *c'est* where *c'* can substitute for 'this thing', 'this person'. We use *il est* or *elle est* when the pronoun is referencing its antecedent. We use *il est* to speak about time and we use *c'est* to speak about the seasons.

TEACHING CONJUGATIONS

How different are French and English verbs?

There are profound differences between French and English verbal conjugations to do with inflection and issues of mood and tense correspondences between the two languages. First indeed, there is the fact that English verbs have few inflected forms, and while English conjugations may appear simple, this absence of inflection when combined with our students' lack of formal grammatical knowledge or awareness adds up to something really confusing. In English, the lack of verbal inflection makes conjugation appear so natural that native English-speaking students have no means of knowing that they are actually doing anything at all with the verb when they say I do, I will do, I would do. To our students, that's just 'do', like, you know… do.

The infinitive stem is the form English speakers use to conjugate the present tense and which they inflect on occasions and combine with auxiliaries to form a number of tenses. It is also the form which English speakers who have no formal knowledge of grammar in general and of English grammar in particular are most conscious of, because it is the *semantic* aspect of the verb. Students who know no principles of formal grammar do not and cannot understand that what linguists and grammarians call 'language' is anything other than the communication of information. They cannot differentiate between linguistic output and meaning output, and they cannot know by instinct that there is a syntactic difference between the word speak in 'I speak' and the word speak in 'to speak'. For native English speakers, verbs have overt lexical value not overt syntactic value.

Evidently, English grammar also has at its disposal several aspects (including the progressive aspect) that do not exist in French. So what about 'doing'? I am doing, I was doing, I will be doing – but that too is just, you know…doing. And while students are naturally aware of the progressive present, they have little idea that when they say 'I play guitar', they are likewise using the present tense. Why is this a present tense when they are not playing guitar at the present time? And how come there are two present tenses anyhow?

To return to the question of learning verbal conjugations and, with this, the original issue, it should now be obvious that students are going to find it very difficult to learn French verbs if they do not understand what verbs are, and how verbs are used in English. To learn French verbs, students need to know about conjugations in a general grammatical sense. They need to know what mood, tense, aspect, auxiliary, simple and compound tenses mean generally speaking, and they also need to know what these mean in the context of English and French. Conjugations are difficult to explain because of the lack of inflection in English, but we can teach principles of conjugation successfully with the comparative method by aligning Modern English, Old English, Spanish and Latin forms with French forms; we can discuss conjugations and their names in English and in French; we can reflect on how English and French conjugations correspond and don't, and where conjugations require second-language learners to acquire a new awareness of time.

Understanding the principles at work in French conjugations
English-speaking students face obvious difficulties when they must remember to say and write *parle, parles, parlent* and *parlé, parlée, parlez* and *parlais, parlait, parlaient*. Without phonological and grammatical knowledge, producing these forms correctly is near impossible. These forms are difficult to hear, to say and to write. Conjugations involve many facets of grammar: grammatical persons, the connection between person and verb ending, which is to say, the subject-verb agreement; the morphology of the verb: stems and endings; the differences between a conjugated verb, a verb in the infinitive and a verb in the participle form; the way the infinitive of a verb along with certain stems determine the conjugated endings; the forming of tense and aspect through final and internal inflection; and more. I explain below how to help students learn the present tense of the indicative with the comparative-narrative method.

Firstly, I teach students to use the three singular persons, and the third-person plural of ER verbs in speech only: *J'aime le chocolat. Le chien regarde le chat. Tu aimes le chocolat? Tu aimes les chiens? Les chiens aiment les chats?* I teach verbs in this manner for obvious reasons: all these persons sound exactly the same – almost like verbs sound in English. I will also introduce other verbs, *je veux, tu bois, tu sais*, and so forth, since they too sound the same in the first three persons. In this way, students can use a few verbs orally early in their learning. Within a few lessons, however, I will introduce students to the full form of the verbs in ER, show them how to write the conjugation, and explain the principle of conjugation, persons, subjects and verb endings. I will also introduce the full conjugation of several irregular verbs over several weeks: *être, aller, avoir, faire, dire, prendre, savoir* before introducing the formal conjugation of verbs ending in IR, RE and OIR/OIRE.

Understanding verbal inflection: endings and the verb-subject agreement
Once students have begun using *être, avoir, aller* and a few ER verbs in conversation, we can write the conjugations on the board. At this point, I usually explain verbal inflection in this way: 'French conjugations have Latin origins and what we are looking at on the board, as you can see, is not really what the verb sounds like in speech. In fact, these added letters retain a memory of their Latin origins and of a former pronunciation.' I will then write the conjugation of this same verb in Latin. 'Look at the conjugations of the verbs on the board. Latin speakers did not use I, you, we… can you see why?' Students immediately get the idea that there was no need for personal pronouns because the endings provided the necessary information. Once students have understood the principle at work in verb endings, I explain the how and why of the conventional six-person arrangements. Conjugations are to grammar what multiplication tables are to maths: the six-person conjugation represents all the things a verb can do in French in a particular time aspect. We will see many more patterns like these as we progress in our learning. Memorising conjugations allows us to remember which form of the verb goes with which person. It also helps us retrieve the correct form of the verb when we can't produce it automatically because we can run the conjugation in our heads and select the form we need. I do not expect students to remember everything or to understand everything perfectly (especially the six-person concept) when I first introduce this grammar.

We will revisit all of this when learning about the infinitive, a week or two later. Indeed, we will need to revisit these concepts many times over. Students, however, are now ready to memorise the present of the verb *être* and of verbs ending in ER. We will discuss the endings, explore the particularities of the verb *être*, look at its Latin ancestor, as well as how and why the ER conjugations follow a model that is repeated across many verbs. Once they have understood the principle of the subject-verb agreement (we don't say 'I is', but 'I am'), and the idea that the written forms include silent letters, students are ready not only to learn the verbs by heart (which they need to do) but also to use these verbs for real.

When learning conjugations, students must be given the opportunity to speak meaningfully. They need to make use of the verbs they are learning in a true communicative and cognitive context, to speak for real about real things: who they are, how they feel, where they are, who and what they like, who likes what, who is who, etc. I will reserve the whole of the following lesson to explain and practise the infinitive. Up until then, silent verbal inflection and subject-verb agreements are enough of a challenge. When teaching conjugations, it is also important to encourage students to substitute third-person pronouns for noun-phrases (*la dame parle français; elle parle français; les messieurs sont gentils, ils sont gentils, etc.*). We must take the time to explain how grammatical persons (nouns and personal pronouns) work because very few students know that when we say *le monsieur regarde le chien*, we are using the third-person, even when they know that we can replace *le monsieur* by *il*. Very few students actually understand that in English 'he/she/it/they' and the lady, the gentleman, the boy, the girls, the dogs, *and* the books are all third persons, even though they have learned about first and third-person narrative in their English classes.

Since students find gender unnatural, they have a difficult time recognising that 'it' must necessarily morph into an *il* or an *elle*. When they hear *il* and *elle*, they think of a human person or a pet, and if they have not internalised the gender of nouns or made the psychological shift to understand that they are now in a gendered world, where everything that surrounds them is a he or a she, they will be confused by third-person pronouns and they will find it difficult to understand what we say in French, even if what we are saying is very simple. Another level of difficulty students experience with the third-person is actually an outcome of the communicative approach, which tends to focus on dialogue and therefore on first and second persons. It is really worth taking the time to explain that the third-person is anyone or anything we are talking about, either in the singular or in the plural. When I write the conjugation on the board, I write the name of a thing or a person on the third-person lines, and then I show how we replace the thing(s) and the person(s) by he or she (or they). I follow this with various exercises that allow students to substitute nouns for pronouns and pronouns for nouns.

The fact that students produce *le monsieur il s'appelle...* results from their having learned the conjugations by heart without further procedural learning. Of course, native French speakers frequently double the subject of a verb in this manner but English speakers don't. Hence, students' use of *le Monsieur il...* shows that they are not fully conscious of the role of the pronoun, and that they do not entirely understand the third-person function.

Understanding the infinitive
It is impossible for students who have had little or no tuition in formal grammar and who have no understanding of syntactic principles to understand what an

infinitive is, and, in particular, what the infinitive is in English. Simply put, English verbs come in very few inflected forms: do, doing, does, did, done; and listen, listening, listens, listened. On this basis, it is very difficult to understand how 'to do' and 'to listen' can be equated to *faire* and *écouter*.

I introduce the infinitive form of both English and French verbs after I have taught the full present tense conjugation of the verbs ending in ER. This allows me to explain that *aimer* is the name of the verb, and that it means 'to like' and 'to love'. In the same way, *je chante, tu chantes, etc.* has a name, *chanter*, which means 'to sing'. The infinitive is the name of the verb. In fact, it can work just like a noun because we can say 'to sing makes you happy' just as we can say 'music makes you happy'. In English, the locution 'to' is part of the infinitive form but we can also use the infinitive without it, as when we say 'I must sing'. And this is when the Old English verbal forms can be invoked to perform the miracle.

'A long time ago, English also had infinitive *endings*, and when English speakers conjugated their verbs, they did things like speakers of Latin did and French speakers still do today.' I then write a short list of English verbs in their Old English present form, which I choose on account of their being easily recognisable: rid**an** (to ride); I/ic rid**e**, thou/þu rid**est**, etc. (I ride, you ride, etc.) find**an** (to find); I/ic find**e**, þu find**est,** etc. (I find, you find)… And I explain that Old English had two infinitive forms, sing**an** and **to** sing**enne**. And so now, we can see the full transformation of the inflected Old English verbs into the barely inflected Modern English forms, and we can understand why Modern English has two infinitive forms, 'to sing' and 'sing', which we can match to 'to sing~~enne~~' and 'sing~~an~~'.

For obvious reasons, it is not a good idea to include the past infinitive in this introduction. The point of showing students the Old English infinitives and conjugations is to help them understand a grammatical principle, to help them make sense of 'to sing' and 'sing', and to make them see that 'sing' in 'I sing' is not the same as 'sing' in 'to sing' or 'sing'. And of course, it is to help them make sense of the infinitive and conjugated endings in French. The value of using Old English lies in that even in its older forms, English makes sense to English-speaking students in a way that French doesn't. Besides, students love learning anything about Old English – at least in small doses. The Old English verbs clearly show stems and endings, as well as the distinct character of the infinitive, all of which throws light on the principle at work in French verbs. Students can now see how the infinitive *–an* worked just like *–er* in French, and how the conjugated endings differed from the infinitive endings. They can see how the *s* of the third person singular is what is left of the OE conjugation, which finally explains why the third person *s* in 'she sings' is not a plural.

After this, when we compare the Old and Modern English verbs with Latin verbs, for example, *cantare* and *amare* which students can easily recognise in *chanter* and *aimer,* and which they saw when they learned the present tense, they can understand that French has dropped most of the Latin endings, and that it keeps only a distant memory of those in writing.

Students will revisit the infinitive and learn more about the infinitive forms of English and French when they learn the past tenses. I will then introduce the concepts of finite and non-finite forms. At yet a later point in the future, they will learn that in English, the gerund can be used instead of the infinitive (I love *to sing* and I love *singing*) but never in French where it is always *j'aime chanter*.

TENSE AND ASPECT IN THE PRESENT OF THE INDICATIVE

Using comparative-cognitive techniques

Once students have been introduced to the conjugated forms and the infinitive, they are ready to learn and acquire the present tense in French, in speech and in writing. I now write the conjugation of *parler* on the left hand-side of the board, asking students to recite and to translate the conjugation for me. They will say, *je parle, tu parles, etc.*, and they will also provide me with 'I speak', 'you speak', etc. or 'I am speaking', 'you are speaking'. Both present forms, of course, are correct. Hence, I will write these English forms next to the French forms. I then ask students to try and explain why we use two aspects in English, and why we use only one aspect in French. If they can't come up with a valid answer, I will explain: in English we differentiate between what we are doing now, 'I am speaking to you' and what we do normally, habitually, as for example, 'I read to my little brother before he goes to bed'. We can also use the present tense to show that we can actually do something, as a statement of general fact, as for example, when we say 'I play guitar' or 'I speak French'. By contrast, whether something is happening right now or now in general, French uses a unique present tense – which simplifies life a bit.

'I speak' and 'I am speaking' are aspects of the present tense in English. The word tense comes from Latin *tempus* and old French *tens*, which we now write *temps*. You can see that if an English speaker read this word, she or he would more than likely say something like tem*ps*. So, tense is simply present, past and future, but since we may have something different to say about certain aspects of the present, the past, and the future, languages can have a number of conjugations in the present, past and future. For example, we say 'I did my homework last night', we don't say 'I have done my homework last night' or 'I used to play football last Saturday'. We say 'I have done my homework' and 'I played football last Saturday. We call these different ways of speaking about time, *aspects of time*. Hence, tense is *when* in time, and aspect is *how* in time. Once we have covered this foundational knowledge, we return to the present tense, and we examine each aspect of the English present in turn and learn to identify and name English conjugations.

The fact that English has more than one present tense and more than one past tense comes as a great surprise to many students. French has only one present tense,[134] but English can express the present in four different conjugations: present progressive, simple present, present perfect progressive and present perfect. Students have few problems identifying the present value of the present progressive. The present progressive shows that we are doing something in the present – 'I am learning French at school' ('I am in the process of learning'); 'right now you are listening to me' ('you are in the process of listening'). By contrast, they do not immediately recognise the simple present as a present tense, since we do not use this conjugation to refer to what we are doing right now. We use the simple present to speak about what we do habitually, normally, or what we are able to do, as for example: 'he speaks English', 'he talks a lot', 'he teaches at the local school every Thursday afternoon'. To understand that we are in the present, think how we don't say 'I speak English last month' or 'I sing in a choir last year every Saturday', but 'I speak English and that is what I am able to do in my present life, and not what I was able to do in the past'. The present perfect progressive can be introduced in a similar manner. And here, I name the form for students but I promise them that I will explain what it means later when we study the past tenses. For now, it is enough to point out that the name has progressive in it because of the –ing form. To enable students to experience the how and why of the present perfect progressive, I ask:

'If I say, "I have been living in Melbourne since 2014", what time frame am I in? Am I still living in Melbourne now? Yes. Therefore, I am in the present time.'

'Yes, but it's in the past too.'

'Excellent observation, you are absolutely right, there is an aspect of the past in this too because I am still doing something that I started in the past. This English conjugation has one foot in the past and one in the present. In French, however, this verbal form doesn't exist. So, if you're still doing something, then you are doing it, and so it doesn't matter if you started some time ago, you are in the present tense. Nevertheless, when I say, *J' habite à Melbourne depuis 2014*, I do indicate that it started in the past. Can you show me which part of the sentence tells us that I started living in Melbourne in the past?'

'*Depuis?*'

'Yes, that's right. Excellent and fantastic! Here, let me show you something interesting about this preposition. The word *depuis* is made up of two words: *de* and *puis* which respectively mean "from" and "then" as in "from then until now". We can better understand the French structure by thinking of it in this way: "from this date 2014 until now" or "from a certain number of years ago until now"".'

---

[134] I introduce *en train de* after students have mastered all indicative tenses in French. I explain it as 'being in the middle of doing something' so that students are not tempted to substitute it for the English progressive present.

I will also bring to the students' notice, or they will come up with this by themselves, that in order to hear or express 'I have been doing whatever since 2012' or 'I have been doing whatever for six years', in French, they need to shift their listening focus from the verb to the preposition. Of course, students know what *shifting our listening focus* means if they have learned to hear and express the plural of nouns by shifting their attention to what comes before the noun (the determiner) rather than by paying attention to the ending of the noun as they do in English.

Using comparative-experiential techniques: leveraging students' English and Bridging their Grammar
To help students internalise the unique French present, I will ask them to translate from French into English and from English into French. At this point (and again from time to time over the following weeks and months) I will ask students to tell me how many presents we have in English, and how many in French. 'Look at the little boy in this picture: *Il parle avec sa maman* [he is speaking to his mother]; *il joue avec le chien* [he is playing with the dog]; *il parle français?* [he speaks French]. *Il habite à Melbourne* [he lives in Melbourne]; *moi, j' habite à Melbourne depuis trois ans* [I've been living in Melbourne for three years].'

The Bridging technique also helps students internalise the French present as well as develop language reflexivity. I will ask a question in English:

'What are you doing now, are you speaking in French?'
'Oui, je parle français.'
'Do you normally speak in French?'
'Non, je parle anglais.'
'Do you live in Paris?'
'Non, j'habite à Melbourne.'

Since the question is asked in English, students understand and have no need to translate. With this technique, they are able to transcend the grammatical differences between English and French. They can reflect on what they are hearing in English, and how they answer in French. We're speaking about something that we are doing now; something we do usually; and something we've been doing for some time, and in all cases French uses the same verbal expression. Once they have understood the principles at work, students can learn a few adverbial complements, and we can now practise asking and responding in French: *en ce moment, je ...; normalement, je ..; je .... tous les jours; je ... depuis...* At a later date, we will learn *il y a trois ans que ...* and *ça fait trois ans que ...*

With this approach, students can learn to shift their centre of reference from the verbal formulation in English to the verbal, adverbial and prepositional formulations in French. They do this consciously, by knowing and understanding the patterns and by modelling on their teacher's speech and their readings.

Keeping the language real (about real things), they begin to sense what they are saying. They are able to experience that they are actually saying the *same thing* in French as in English, all the while knowing that they are doing this *by different means*. And this, when we stop to think about it, is rather strange and wonderful.

And then, of course, we must stop and ponder the implications of this grammar for translating important ideas. Descartes famously said *Cogito ergo sum – je pense donc je suis*... Did he mean: I think therefore I am or I am thinking therefore I am? Is the difference important?

The present perfect as a present tense and the issue of tense correspondence
Tenses confuse not only students but also teachers of French who are not fully aware that there may be no direct correspondence between English and French conjugations. More precisely, there is no direct or straightforward one-to-one correspondence between French and English present and past tenses *across every single class of verbs*. Furthermore, in English as in French, a conjugation may imply a range of temporal modalities. To find *la correspondance des temps*, we need to think about where and how we situate ourselves in relation to the past, the present and the future *and* what class of verb we are using in English and in French. Indeed, with certain verbs, the present perfect may elicit the present tense in French, just as the present perfect progressive does. When we say 'I have known about this for years', we still know it; the same goes for 'I've loved him for a long time', we are still loving; and in French, we will use the present tense: *je sais cela depuis longtemps, je l'aime depuis des années*. On the other hand, when we say 'I have always done/wanted/liked something or other' we are expressing a different time value. We are speaking about something we have experienced *up until* the present, and here we will use the *passé composé*: *j'ai toujours voulu jouer de la musique*. We can help students feel whether they are expressing the past or the present by using adverbs of time: I have done this *in the past*; I have done this *in the past and up until now*; I have lived here a long time *now*.

The present tense in other contexts
In English as in French, the present tense can express the historical or narrative present (used very frequently in French). The present tense can also express the future: I am leaving next month, I leave next month, *je pars dans un mois*. When students learn this dimension of the present tense, they need to revisit the concept of circumstantial reference. When we say 'I am leaving in a month' or *je pars dans un mois*, what informs us that we are speaking of a future event? Indeed, not the verb but the time complement. And how do 'I am leaving in a month, 'I leave in a month', and 'I will leave in a month' differ? How does *Je pars dans un mois* differ from *Je partirai dans un mois*?

The indicative present is crucial for learning all conjugations

The *présent de l'indicatif* is the tense we teach first and which students need to learn first. Its conjugations are also among the most diversified. Consequently, the present tense is the most difficult conjugation to acquire. All the other conjugations, including the dreaded subjunctives, are more regular and will prove easier to remember. Knowing the present tense is especially important because its plural first and third persons provide the starting points for other conjugations – specifically, the stem of the first-person plural provides the stem of the *imparfait de l'indicatif*, and the stem of the third-person plural provides the stem of the *présent du subjontif*.

THE PAST TENSES IN THE INDICATIVE MOOD

Students have encountered simple and compound conjugations when learning the present tense, when they compared English and French. Acquiring French past tenses requires them to revisit these notions as well as to learn a whole new set of grammatical concepts and forms. When we speak about the past in French, we use the *passé composé*, the *imparfait*, the *plus-que-parfait* and the *passé immédiat* of the indicative; we also use the present and past tenses of the conditional, the subjunctive and the infinitive: *il m'a dit qu'il viendrait'*, *'il m'avait dit qu'il aurait fini avant que j'arrive'* [ref. pp. 17-18]; *j'ai fait cela avant qu'il vienne, j'ai fait cela avant de venir*. In addition, there are the literary and narrative tenses: the *passé simple* and the *passé antérieur* of the indicative and the *imparfait* and *plus-que-parfait* of the subjunctive. Lower-school students learning at intermediate level need to acquire the indicative past tenses used in spoken French.

Learning the *passé composé*, the *imparfait*, the *plus-que-parfait* and the *passé immédiat* means learning how to form new conjugations as well as how to use them. Balancing these two poles is tricky because we cannot simply teach form then procedure, or the other way around. Rather, we need to move back and forth between form and procedure. To form the *passé composé*, students must be able to conjugate *être* and *avoir* in the indicative present; they must know about past participle forms; and they must know that, in French, the class of verbs rather than aspect determines the choice of the auxiliary. Before they can learn how to form the *imparfait* of all verbs including *être* and *avoir* (the latter gives them not only the *imparfait* but also the *plus-que-parfait*), they first need to know how to conjugate regular and irregular verbs, as explained above. At some point, students will also need to learn about past participle agreements – and to do this, they will need to have a thorough understanding of the function of role players along with a fluent knowledge of the classes of verbs (ref to Chapter V). Finally, students need to know the present tense of the verb *venir* in order to learn the *passé immédiat*.

Procedural learning: why are past tenses confusing?

We usually explain to students that the *passé composé* expresses a completed action, while the *imparfait* is for on-going actions. Supposing that we do not forget to mention that we are speaking of on-going actions *in the past*, this formal explanation provides a reasonable road map. However, students are confused by what we mean by 'completed action', because from their perspective, anything that has happened in the past, was happening, had been happening, or used to happen is by definition over and is therefore finished and completed. As a Year 12 student recently put it: 'Why is "I ate at this restaurant yesterday" completed but not "I used to eat at this restaurant" since in both cases, I don't do it anymore?'

In fact, students are onto something here, because the modulations of the *passé composé* and the *imparfait* express aspects of experience that are not entirely contained nor sufficiently explained by the words 'completed' and 'on-going'. The *passé composé* does not solely voice a completed action, which in English is expressed specifically by the present perfect (I have done something), it can also mark an action that took place at a certain point in time as well as an action that occurred in an undetermined period: *j'ai installé la wifi au deuxième étage, j'ai téléphoné à mon frère hier soir, j'ai vu des gens faire ça, j'ai appris la musique*, all of which call for the simple past in English. Hence, the *passé composé* may function as an aorist as well as an experiential, episodic, resumptive, or resultative past tense,[135] and this is *not* how English speakers give voice to their experience of time. Meanwhile, the *imparfait* can express an incomplete action, a concurrent action, a habitual or recurring action, which are also ascribed discrete conjugations in English. Furthermore, the *imparfait*, like the *passé simple*, is a narrative tense: *Il était une fois, un petit renard qui vivait dans les bois. Comme il courait très vite, il faisait souvent...* which we would translate into English in the simple past: 'Once upon a time, there was a little fox who lived in the woods. As he could run very fast, he often did...' And then, the *imparfait* can express a supposition in the present: *si j'avais le temps*, in which case it is not a past tense and, in English, this calls for the subjunctive present. To further complicate matters, in English as in French, we voice the past differently according to what it is that we are actually experiencing: actions, thoughts, possession, emotions, displacement, states of being or states of mind. For example, the auxiliary 'used to' does not express the same aspect of time when we say 'I used to leave the house early', and when we say 'I used to know this person'. By the same token, *j'ai su* is less the perfect aspect of *savoir* than the preterit of *apprendre*.

---

[135] For a fascinating and thoroughly informative historical analysis of the evolution and function of the *passé composé*, see Apothéloz, op. cit.

Simply put, however, verbal expression in *spoken* French is concerned with three things: 1) the modulations of the perfect aspect, which corresponds to the *passé composé*, 2) the modulations of the imperfect aspect, which corresponds to the *imparfait* and 3) <u>when</u> in the past. The past before the past calls for the *plus-que-parfait*; the present in the past requires the *imparfait*; and the future in the past may be expressed with the *conditionnel* or with the infinitive or, after certain conjunctions, with the subjunctive (*e.g.: il m'avait dit qu'il viendrait, il m'avait dit qu'il le ferait avant de partir/avant que je parte*). To use the *passé composé* and the *imparfait* meaningfully and accurately, students need to translate their experience of time from English into French rather than transpose their conjugations. This may not only necessitate adjusting to different verbal modes but also require a lexical shift and the addition of adverbial complements. *French and English past tenses do not correspond to one another but they share common elements* and it is in these commonalities that we find a way of translating our experience of English time into an experience of French time. Where verbs of action and motion are concerned, these commonalities are found in two umbrella categories: the perfect and the imperfect. Where states of body, mind and heart are concerned, different values are at work.

Teaching the perfect and imperfect aspects of verbs of action and verbs of motion

Learning past tenses should begin with the verbs of action and motion as this is where the common elements between English and French are most accessible. The first thing Anglophone students need to do, is to reflect on what they say in their own language, so as to be able to recognise, identify, feel, experience and name the past conjugations in English. The simple past is an aorist: I did this. The simple past also expresses the punctual-perfect aspect: I did this yesterday (at a point in time). The present perfect expresses the resolved aspect of an action projecting towards the present: I have done it (and I don't need to do it anymore) *or* I have done this up to the present (and I may or may not keep doing it); or indeed, it expresses an unresolved action that is continuing in the present: I have done this for some time now and I am still doing it, in which case, French uses the *présent*. Once students are at ease with this grammar, they can move onto the progressive imperfect forms (I was doing/I had been doing) and the habitual imperfect (I used to do). To understand how an action may have been on-going, concurrent, habitual, punctual, or completed, it is also essential to allow students to compare what we don't say with what we do say. For example, we don't say: 'I have done it yesterday', we say: 'I did it yesterday'; we don't say: 'I used to do this last Monday' but 'I did this last Monday'. We don't say: 'I had eaten at six this morning' but we might say: 'They came to get me for dinner at 6:30, but I had already eaten and so I did not go with them'. We must also bring students' attention to the range and flexibility of the simple past ('I did this yesterday', 'I did it already', 'I did this everyday', 'I did this before they did that').

Once they are fully aware of how they express time in English, students do not find it difficult to differentiate and identify the perfect and imperfect aspects running through the various English conjugations. The simple past and the present perfect share a perfective value: if we did something, we have done it, and if we have done it, it is because we did it. When we say 'I ate breakfast at 10:00 am', are we in the perfect or the imperfect? What about when we say 'I used to eat breakfast at this café when I lived there?' Is this perfect or imperfect? When students can identify perfect and imperfect without hesitation, they are ready to learn the past tenses in French. They can understand and *feel* that when they say 'I did it and I've done it', whatever they did was and is done for. When they say 'I was doing' and 'I used to do', whatever they were doing was neither resolved, nor contained, nor a one-off event but on-going, concurrent, or habitual. They can also identify the difference between an event (perfect) and a state of affairs or a state of being (imperfect). The next step is relatively simple. The perfect aspect of English conjugations translates into the *passé composé*, and the imperfect aspect into the *imparfait*.

Thus, when we are using verbs of action and motion, we can usually exchange the simple past and the present perfect for the *passé composé*, and the progressive and the habitual imperfects for the *imparfait* as shown in Table 8 (p. 271). Importantly, this table is *not* a substitute for the experiential and reflective exercises I have described above. The table will help students sum up what they have learned but it is not a short-cut for teaching or learning the past tenses in French. It is essential that students become aware of their conjugations in English before they attempt to learn how to use the *passé composé* and the *imparfait*. If not, they will be tempted to transpose their English conjugations onto French according to the recipe: I did and I have done = PC, and although this may work in most instances, it will not work in all instances. Compare: 'I ran every Saturday for a year' (PC) and 'I ran every Saturday when I lived in Paris' (*Imparfait* and *Imparfait*). Furthermore, this will not work for other classes of verbs: *j'ai été, j'étais, j'ai su, je savais, etc.* Students need to learn to translate their *experience* of English conjugations because they cannot transpose English *forms* directly onto French. Beyond the perfect and the imperfect, aspectual nuances (preterit, resultative, progressive, etc.) are elicited by context and expressed verbally in English, whereas in French, they are expressed by the context and by what accompanies the verb (*hier, toujours, déjà, etc.*). If students proceed from their *experience* of form rather than from the *externality* of form, they will be eventually be able to use French past tenses intuitively; they will also learn the past tenses of other verb classes with remarkable ease. As we shall see below, however, there are still a few challenges ahead.

To use *être* or *avoir* in the *passé composé*?
Students tend to resist using the auxiliary *être* when they have learned that *avoir* is the norm, since it applies to most verbs and they learned its usage first. Introduced as a modification of the rule, the auxiliary *être* is perceived as a complication. Complications are complicated and most of us have a desire to avoid them, if not always the good sense to do so.

In fact, it is not difficult to learn from the start that compound tenses in French require the use of either *avoir* or *être* depending on the category of verb we are using. So long as students know *être* and *avoir* very well (which they should and can do) and so long as they have understood the structural and semantic differences between the verbs of action, the verbs of displacement and the reflexive verbs (refer to Chapter V), they can accept that *avoir* and *être* have a legitimate place in the *passé composé*. With the comparative-narrative method, students have already learned to differentiate verbs of actions and verbs of motion. They have learned that verbs of action elicit direct object complements, and verbs of motion are followed by a preposition because they elicit complements of location and direction. If students have not learned this grammar before learning the past tenses, now is the time to teach it. If they have already learned the grammar, now is the time to revisit it, to consolidate and extend their knowledge.

What are verbs of movement? Why do we say *je suis montée au premier étage* but *j'ai monté les valises*?
The term 'verbs of movement' or 'verbs of motion', it turns out, confuses students. Isn't flapping your arms a movement? What is the difference between 'I drove to school' and 'I went to school?' Why is 'to go' a verb of movement but not 'to drive', 'to fly' or 'to run'? It is useful to explain verbs like *rester, aller, venir*, etc. as verbs of location and relocation or verbs of displacement (in French: *verbes de déplacement*).

Students can experience the difference between a verb of displacement and a verb of action through reflection, critical reasoning and mental imaging. Verbs of displacement elicit the questions 'where, where to, where from?' They never elicit the question 'doing/feeling *what*?' If I say, 'I drove to school', I can ask, 'drove what?' And I can answer, 'I drove a car', but when I say 'I went to school', I can only ask, 'went where?' Now, let's think about what kind of mental image 'I drove to school' produces. Indeed, you can see what I actually did. And if I say, 'I went to school', what happens in your mind? Students often reply that they can see themselves arriving at school. We then discuss how 'I drove to school' shows what I did to get there (an action), but 'I went to school' simply shows that I relocated myself in space (displacement). When I say, 'I went to school', we know that I *was* somewhere (perhaps at home) and then I ended up *being* somewhere else (at school). Thus, we use the verb *être* (to be) to express this displacement in the *passé composé: je suis allée à l'école*. We can test this explanation with other verbs: *venir, sortir*, *etc*. But what about *naître* and *mourir*? Well, are not *naître* and *mourir* about coming into the world and leaving it?"

Students also appreciate learning that only a few hundred years ago, English followed a similar usage to modern French. Shakespeare wrote things like 'the actors are come hither, my lord' and people commonly said 'he is gone to London'. In fact, 'he is gone to London' does not feel very strange because 'he is gone' is a resultative construction in Modern English, while 'he has gone' and 'he is gone' are both enunciated as 'he's gone'. In addition, English verbs of motion are infused with a resultative nuance in the present perfect. Compare: 'He went to the station to fetch his mother' and 'he has gone to the station to fetch his mother'. The present perfect is likely to provide an explanation for someone not being where we expect him to be. The simple past may also do this or simply provide a statement of fact.

On this basis, we can easily teach the use of *être* and *avoir* with *sortir, rentrer, monter* and *descendre*. If students are conversant with the functions of role players and the concept of verbal class, they have no difficulty understanding that *sortir* in *je suis sortie du garage* is an intransitive verb of displacement which we express in English as 'I went out' (of the garage), and *sortir* in *j'ai sorti la voiture du garage* is a transitive verb of action which we express in English as 'I took out' (the car).

In time, students will learn that we keep the auxiliary in the figurative form (*je suis arrivée à la gare; je suis arrivée à le voir*). They will learn that a few verbs become directional and conjugate with *être* when they are prefixed with *a*, as for example, *accourir* and *apparaître*. And at some point, we will likely have to answer more questions about verbs like *sortir, partir, mourir, divorcer, vieillir, changer, etc.* which can be conjugated with *être* or *avoir* depending on whether we are speaking about what happened (*elle a divorcé*) or about a condition (*elle est/était divorcée*). This adjectival use of the past participle exists in English: 'she is/was divorced'. Nevertheless, students may understand *elle est divorcée* as 'she got divorced'. And, indeed, when we say: *il est mort, il est décédé*, we must rely on context to differentiate the *passé composé* from the resultative or the adjectival construction: *il est mort en 1867* (he died in 1867); *il est mort* (he is dead). The same goes for *il est sorti/ il est parti*, which, depending on context, can mean either 'he went out/he left' or 'he is gone'; likewise, *il est rentré* can mean 'he went in', 'he came back' or 'he is back'.

Rule: Verbs of displacement elicit complements of location and direction; they are conjugated with *être* in compound tenses. The complement of a verb of displacement is always introduced by a preposition. In English, we can enter and leave the house, but in French *on entre* **dans** *la maison* and *on sort* **de** *la maison*. When verbs like *sortir* and *entrer* have a direct object, they are verbs of action and require the auxiliary *avoir* in compound tenses. Therefore, we say *elle* **est** *sortie de la maison et elle* **a** *sorti la voiture*.

TABLE 8: showing the perfect and imperfect correspondences of English and French verbs of action and motion

PERFECT aspect	IMPERFECT aspect
simple past (preterit) present perfect **passé composé**	simple past progressive past perfect progressive **imparfait**
I spoke I have spoken **J' ai parlé** *I went I have gone* **Je suis allé(e)** *I woke up I have woken up* **Je me suis réveillé(e)**	*I was speaking I had been speaking* **Je parlais** *I was going I had been going* **J'allais** *I was waking up I had been waking up* **Je me réveillais**
past perfect (plus-perfect) **plus-que-parfait**	past habitual **imparfait**
I had spoken **J'avais parlé** *I had gone* **J'étais allé(e)** *I had woken up* **Je m'étais réveillé(e)**	*I used to speak I used to go* *I spoke ⁎ I went* *I would speak⁎ I would go* **Je parlais J'allais** *I used to wake up* *I woke up* *I would wake up* **Je me réveillais**

⁎ To identify the imperfect aspect when using 'I did' and to differentiate the imperfect when using 'would', try substituting 'I used to'. If it fits, the verb is in the *imparfait* in French.

Using the *imparfait* and the *passé composé* with the verb *être*

The next issue is this: 'When I say 'I was sick', do I use *j'étais* or *j'ai été* in French?' Generally speaking, if you can I say 'I have been sick', then use *j'ai été*, and otherwise, use the *imparfait*. You can feel the *imparfait* when you substitute the verb 'to feel' for the verb 'to be': 'I was feeling sick', rather than 'I felt sick'. In the same vein, if you want to say 'I was at the station', and you mean to say 'I was (waiting/standing) at the station', then use *j'étais à la gare*.

And what about...
1. *J'étais heureuse de la voir:* I was happy to see her.
2. *J'ai été heureuse de la voir:* I was happy to have seen her.
3. *J'ai été heureuse de l'avoir vue*: I was happy to have seen her.
4. *J'étais heureuse de l'avoir vue*: I was happy to have seen her.

Here again, we encounter the strange alchemy of grammar in translation. These sentences express similar affects but the French sentences also express slightly different temporalities which may or may not be felt in English. In sentence 1), the feeling (*j'étais heureuse*/I was happy) and the action (*de la voir*/to see her) are concurrent. In French, the *imparfait* expresses concurrence; in English, the simple past is here aoristic – and both aspects are logical applications of the respective rules of French and English. In French and in English, the second verb is in the infinitive present (the neutral form of the verb) and as such it is simply naming the condition of my happiness. We may conclude that these French and English sentences express the same experience.

In sentence 2), however, the feeling (I was happy) is voiced in the simple past in English but since this state of mind occured after the fact of seeing her, the second verb is quite logically in the past infinitive (to have seen her/perfective aspect). In French, by contrast, the after-the-fact statement is voiced by the main verb conjugated in the *passé composé* – the resultative-perfective aspect of the verb *être*. We say *j'ai été heureuse* because my condition is the result of the event. The event itself is expressed in the infinitive. Again, it is simply naming the condition of my happiness. Here too, we may consider that the French and English sentences express the same affect by different means. However, in sentences 3 and 4, we can see that the event may be expressed in the past infinitive in French as it is in English. In this case, the focus of my French sentences shifts, ever so slightly, from a simple statement of fact (*de la voir*) to the experience of having spent time with her (*de l'avoir vue*). Sentences 2, 3 and 4 are identical in English and they are virtually interchangeable in French. There is nonetheless a difference. In sentence 3, the *passé composé* expresses a statement of fact while in sentence 4, the *imparfait* expresses a statement of state. In English, we can perceive this difference when we substitute the verb 'to feel' for the verb 'to be'.

The *imparfait* and the *passé composé* of modal verbs

Students can experience the difference between the perfect and imperfect when using modal verbs by thinking: was this an event or a state/condition? However, with modal verbs things are also more complicated. Depending on context and tone, *il a dû venir plus tôt* can mean 'he must have come earlier' rather than 'he had to come earlier'. To express 'I had to do something' unambiguously, we may prefer to use *falloir* or *être obligé de*. In the same vein, *j'ai pu lui dire ça* can mean: 'I could have told her that' or 'I may have told her that' as well as 'I was able to tell her that'. To express 'I was able to tell her', students may prefer to say *j'ai réussi à lui dire*. As for the *imparfait*, *je devais le faire* can mean 'I was supposed to do it' as well as 'I was obliged to do it'; and *je pouvais le faire*: 'I could do it', and therefore, 'I used to be able to do it' or 'I was once able to do it'. The *passé composé* and the *imparfait* of the verb *savoir* call for a lexical shift in English – *je l'ai su* means 'I learned about it'; *je le savais* means 'I knew it' or 'I used to know it'.

The *imparfait* and the *passé composé* of verbs expressing states of mind and heart

The present perfect of verbs expressing states of mind and feelings may call for the present tense in French. To express 'I've known him for five years', we will say *Je le connais depuis cinq ans*, or *Il y a cinq ans que je le connais*. As noted above, we can easily identify the present by adding an adverb: 'I have known him for five years *now*'. With verbs such as *rêver, penser, aimer*, past aspects in French have equivalents in English, but the aspectual reasoning in both French and English is different from what it is for verbs of action and motion. For example, 'I did love him', 'I loved him', 'I used to love him' are interchangeable in English, and a matter of emphasis. We may also express a different degree of feeling through tone and context rather than through the choice of the grammatical form. And all these forms may be translated into French as *je l'aimais* or *je l'ai aimé*. However, there is a difference of nuance between *je l'aimais* and *je l'ai aimé*. With the verb *aimer*, the *passé composé* does not so much highlight completion since we can express 'I loved him' or 'I used to love him' (and I no longer do) by saying either *je l'ai aimé* or *je l'aimais*. Rather, the difference between the *passé composé* and the *imparfait* is here again the difference between a statement of fact and a statement of state. In English, this nuance is best rendered as: 'I used to love him/I loved him/I did love him' (*je l'ai aimé*) and 'I was in love with him' (*je l'aimais*).

On the other hand, if we watched a movie and we say 'I loved it', we will say *j'ai aimé, j'ai adoré*. And this is a statement of fact as well as a perfective/resultative expression, and it is easily contrasted with *j'aimais ça (quand j'étais petite)*, which expresses 'I used to like this when I was little'. Note, however, that the aspectual value of 'used to' is here duration and contemporaneity rather than habit, and in English we may say 'I loved this when I was a child' rather than

'I used to love this when I was a child'. Nevertheless, there is a constant running through these verbal forms – whether or not the verb is actually expressing duration, habit, projection or completion, we can identify the need for the *imparfait* in the circumstances where we can say 'used to', or we can substitute 'used to' for the simple past and retain our intended meaning.

Using the *passé composé* with *pendant*
When we say: *j'ai appris la guitare pendant trois ans*, the preposition *pendant* expresses duration but the *passé composé* expresses completion, we are no longer learning, we are *done* with it (it happened). Time is contained. This is expressed in English in the simple past 'I learned guitar for three years'.

Using the *imparfait* with *pendant* and *pendant que*
We will say: *je jouais de la guitare pendant la journée* to mean 'I used to play guitare during the day'. *Je jouais de la guitare pendant qu'il lisait* to mean 'I was playing guitar while he was reading'. In both cases, the *imparfait* is evident and similarly expressed in French and English. Note that *pendant que* is a conjunction and not a preposition.

Understanding the *plus-que-parfait*: the past before the past
The *plus-que-parfait* expresses the past before the past, and more precisely, the perfect before the perfect – hence its name. Of all the past tenses, the *plus-que-parfait* presents the least difficulty for English-speaking learners, so long as they are able to conjugate the verbs *avoir* and *être* in the *imparfait*, and so long as they understand that the choice of auxiliaries applies to all compound tenses and not only to the *passé composé*. The *plus-que-parfait* corresponds to the past perfect or plus-perfect as the conjugation was called traditionally. In fact, we can assume that, unless we are using a preposition calling for the subjunctive (i.e. *avant que*), wherever English uses the form 'had done' or 'had gone', French uses *j'avais fait*, *j'étais allé*, *je m'étais levé*. This applies even when English is actually using the past subjunctive rather than the plus-perfect of the indicative. The following sentence: 'If I had known, I would not have come' translates into French as *si j'avais su, je ne serais pas venu*.

Teaching the *passé immédiat*
Students can learn the *passé immédiat* as a matter of course if they know the *futur immédiat*. Firstly, however, they need to understand that adding 'just' to the present perfect in English amounts to a conjugation called the immediate past, which corresponds to something called *le passé immédiat* in French. All we need to do after this, is to bring students' attention to the symmetry between *aller* and *venir* and they are very quickly able to transfer 'to go to' and 'to come from' from the familiar spatial construction to the temporal construction.

- I am going to learn my verbs → Je *vais* apprendre mes verbes.
- I have *just* learned the present tense → Je *viens d'* apprendre le présent.

Fascinating problems: why students say things like *je venu and j'avais allais* and what to do about it

Many students have a tendency to forget conjugations and to default to the infinitive in creative conversation and written composition. However, while beginners often default to the infinitive in the present tense, advanced students are more inclined to say *je suis manger* or even *je suis mangeant* rather than *je manger*. In the past tense, errors can be fudged and are often overlooked thanks to fuzzy pronunciation. Where ER verbs are concerned, saying *jay manger* can effectively substitute for either *je mangeais* or *j'ai mangé*, while *jey venu* may be mistaken for an erroneous auxiliary (*j'ai venu*). The true construction appears when students write *je venu, je mangé, je manger* or *je mange* meaning to write *je mangé* and forgetting the accent. Note that in order to contain the discussion, I will ignore other possibilities such as *j'ai mange*, and *j'ai venir, ils rendre*, and so forth.

Where is the difficulty in forming the *passé composé*, when one knows the verbs *avoir* and *être*? In fact, there is more than one difficulty. Firstly, there is the problem of understanding what a conjugation is. With verbs ending in ER, especially, if students do not understand the difference between an infinitive and a conjugated verb, they cannot understand the difference between *j'ai manger*, *j'ai mangé* and *je (jei) manger*. It is therefore crucial to ensure that students understand what conjugating means. Assuming students know this basic grammar, there can be a problem with phonology. If students cannot hear and pronounce the difference between *e*, *ais/ai* and *é*, they will find past tense conjugations confusing if not impossible (*j'ai été* and *j'étais*). Thus, we must ensure that students differentiate between *je* and *j'ai* from the moment they are introduced to these words. Aside from these issues, learners are also confused by the fact that the *imparfait* is the simple form, while the perfect form, the *passé composé*, is the compound form, because, in English, all imperfect tenses are compounds and the preterit (the dominant past tense) is a simple tense. Therefore, when we teach students past tenses, we must ensure that students notice where English uses a simple form and French uses a compound; and where English uses compounds and French uses a simple form.

Mispronunciation and the crossovers between French and English simple and compound tenses, however, are only the most obvious of several reasons driving English-speaking learners to mark French past tenses with a single word. This tendency is also facilitated by the flexible use of the simple past and the limited reach of the present perfect in contemporary spoken English. It is very important to draw students' attention to the fact that although the present perfect and the *passé composé* have the same form (*j'ai fait*/I have done), they are not identical. We should not encourage students to understand or remember the *passé compose* by equating it to the English present perfect. The *passé composé* may encompass the present perfect but it is not equivalent to it. The present perfect voices a past experience, an action that has been accomplished with consequences for the present and with certain verbs it may also express an action that is continuing into the present. The present perfect is used less frequently as well as more specifically than the simple past. Indeed, the simple past is flexible enough to substitute for the present perfect (as well as for the plus-perfect and the imperfect 'used to') but we cannot use the present perfect in place of the simple past. We commonly say 'I did it yesterday' and 'I did it already' but we do not usually say: 'I have done my homework yesterday.' For obvious reasons, students are naturally inclined to think of *j'ai mangé* as meaning 'I have eaten'. If they learn this, they will reach, just as naturally, for a simple conjugation in French to translate the dominant past tense of their native English: I ate = *je mangé*. And this is not all.

The conflation of the *participe passé* and the *passé composé* is made all the more likely on account of two other features of English syntax. The first is the lack of differentiation between the simple past and the past participle forms of regular verbs and many others: I listened, I have listened; I bought, I have bought; I read, I have read – which, indeed, drives not a few native English-speakers to say: 'I been there', 'I done that', 'I should of went'. And the second is that this feature is a characteristic of English productive rules. Hence, all newly coined verbs in English are conjugated with the regular -ed ending (e.g. I facebooked you), and all regular -ed ending verbs have identical forms in the simple past and in the past participle.

From the perspective of English syntax, which is to say, in the submerged storeys of the English-thinking-speaking-mind, French verbs are newly coined verbs, a process that is greatly facilitated by the natural internalisation of the French ending *-é* into the English ending -ed. Without conscious learning and attention, students are well and truly driven to say *jey écouté*, as well as to write things like *j'écouté* and *je écoutais*. In all cases, they are transposing: 'I listened'. Evidently, students find it just as difficult to comprehend the difference between the word 'listened' in 'I listened' and the word 'listened' in 'I have listened' as they do understanding the difference between the word 'speak' in 'I speak' and the word 'speak' in 'to speak'. Hence, also, the importance of showcasing English irregular and regular verbs next to each other, when we explain what a past participle is, and when we want to show why and how *mangé* is not *manger*, and *je mangé* is not *j'ai mangé*.

Regular verbs	Irregular verbs
I listen	I write
I listened	I wrote
I have listened	I have written

CONCLUSION

A French speaker would never mistake a past participle for the *passé composé* ('I done it'), but she will come up with *j'ai allé, j'ai tombé, j'm'ai lavé les mains*. Our students might also say *j'ai allé* rather than *je suis allé* but not on account of French syntax. Rather, they will say *j'ai allé* because they forget to switch the auxiliary, and (or) because the auxiliary 'to have' is used to form perfect tenses in English while the auxiliary 'to be' is used to form the progressive tenses, including the *present* progressive – which, incidentally, also helps students confuse the present and past tenses of French verbs of motion as well as prompts them to say *je suis faisant*. The present progressive and the simple past are the tenses our students are most conscious of, and, in many cases, they are the only tenses students are conscious of. Students are absolutely stumped when they discover the number of conjugations they use in English, not least, because it takes learning French for them to discover this.

Repetition without knowledge and without awareness provides poor training at the best of times. In second-language learning, nowhere is this more obvious than in the acquisition of the conjugations of a verb-driven language. In French as in English, conjugations are a repertoire of flexible patterns deeply embedded in linguistic-cognitive processes and our experience of being. Aspects of these processes can only elude pedagogies invested in mechanical solutions. There are several reasons why students who can recite conjugations and score a perfect grade in structured exercises forget all about verbal endings in conversation and written composition. The difficulties Anglophone learners experience learning French verbs are much less a problem of failing memory than a lack of formal understanding and the manifestation of the hold that English syntax exerts on learners' experience of time. Hence, we may expose students to years of authentic classroom French, and subject them to hours and hours of repetitive exercises with equally marginal effect. But we can make students' learning effective as well as interesting by teaching form, by explaining how the form works, how language works and how their own language habits and life experience get in the way of their learning French conjugations. Students are fascinated when they discover their own grammar, when they are shown how and why their English syntax misinforms their acquisition of the *passé composé* and the *imparfait*, and not least when they are shown how and where to find in their English syntax the key to unlock the mysteries of French past tenses. Once students are aware of the processes at work on both sides of their linguistic experience, they are able to follow the path we set out for them, to flag the difficulties they occasionally encounter on the way, and thus to secure, on the basis of their knowledge, the proper grammatical form in French. At this point, practice has a chance to make perfect.

CONCLUSION

In order to acquire French, learners cannot simply replace English words with French words and keep their English syntax. They need to acquire a new grammar and create new 'scaffolding'. But how do we create new scaffolding when our 'mind-space' is fully occupied by our native language and our native language is fully occupied making sense of the world?

One way of acquiring a new grammar, of course, is to understand formal grammar in a general manner, and then to learn about new grammatical principles, and to apply them. This is how generations of school students once learned French: by understanding sentence construction, by learning about rules and exceptions, by differentiating syntax and vocabulary, by doing a lot of exercises and by applying their knowledge and their memory of the rules to reading, writing, listening and, if and when they had the opportunity, speaking.

Another way of learning a new grammar consists in turning off our native language so as to create 'a blank slate' and to absorb the new language, just as we learned to speak our mother tongue when we were toddlers. This is what we expect students to do when we teach them with the communicative and natural methods. Evidently, advocates of this approach are not wrong – we can learn to speak a new language without learning about formal grammatical principles or learning about rules and exceptions. We can learn by hearing the language, by copying and 'giving it a go' and, at some point, something will happen in our minds and we will be able to speak the new language fluently, even if not entirely accurately by native-speaker standards. We can certainly do this when we are in language immersion, when we have a vital need to speak, as well as sufficient exposure to the language over sufficient time. For the reasons discussed in Chapter III, however, the second-language classroom cannot replicate the conditions needed for the natural acquisition of language. Nor should it try to. Even in immersion, learning a new language from a base of zero is not always a lot of fun as many immigrants may attest. In the second-language classroom, turning off our students' own language is a sure way of turning students away, for the simple reason that few people find it pleasant to sit for hours not understanding what is going on. Not surprisingly, numerous studies have concluded that monolingual teaching in the language classroom increases students' stress levels.[136]

In fact, beyond the demotivating factor, turning off students' first language is highly impractical and, when all is said, quite impossible. In practical terms, it means expecting learners to leap from a perfect state of naturalised knowledge (speaking English) to an imperfect state of artificiality (classroom French) via an incomprehensible mode of progression (language that is not understood and goes wholly unexplained). This, of course, defies common sense. Thus, research has also shown that there is a lot more 'own language' spoken in the second-language classroom than teachers may be conscious of, or happy to admit. Whether in a monolingual or an openly bilingual classroom, the mother tongue is commonly used to relieve students' anxiety, to clarify points of grammar, build rapport and help with classroom management. It is also used to explore culture and cultural issues.[137] In short, even in the self-professed monolingual classroom, teachers make substantial use of the language that students can actually understand. So much so, that according to Graham Hall and Guy Cook, the difference between the target-language-only classroom and the other, is that in the first case, teachers often feel guilty about using their students' mother tongue, while in the latter, they feel justified doing so.[138]

Advocates of mother tongue in second-language instruction argue that students' own language is not only used far more widely than teachers are prepared to acknowledge, but that it is also under-utilised as well as over-utilised and randomly utilised, and therefore frequently misused.[139] What these scholars have in mind, indeed, goes well beyond using the mother tongue as a regrettable necessity, a last resort means of explaining a point of language, clarifying classroom instructions or speaking about culture. They advocate for 'contrastive-form-focussed instruction', translation and code-switching, and argue that the use of mother tongue ought to be fully acknowledged, researched, optimised, and systematised.[140] In their 2012 state of the art article, Hall and Cook wrote that second-language teaching was then at a turning point: 'the "long silence" about bilingual teaching has been broken (...) and the way is open for a "major paradigm

---

[136] Hall and Cook, op. cit.
[137] Hall and Cook, op. cit.; A Edstrom, 'L1 use in the L2 classroom: One teacher's self-evaluation', *Canadian Modern Language Review* 63 (2), 2006; pp. 275-290; also cited p. 187, in Hall and Cook; Alaadin Inan, 'The Role of Mother Tongue in Second-language Teaching', Mersin University, Education Faculty, ELT department, 2008 – among many others on this topic. Https://www.academia.edu/28111770/THE_ROLE _OF_MOTHER_TONGUE_ IN_SECOND_ LANGUAGE_LEARNING
[138] Hall and Cook, op. cit.
[139] Hall and Cook, op. cit. and Wolfgang Butzkamm's, 'We only learn language once. The role of the mother tongue in FL classrooms: death of a dogma,' *Language Learning Journal*, Winter 2003, No 28, 29-39.
[140] Hall and Cook, op. cit., p. 289; and Butzkamm, op. cit.

shift" in language teaching and learning.'[141] In 2019, however, researchers are still debating the role of own language and, not least, the relative value of explicit grammatical instruction in second-language teaching.[142]

How and where does the comparative-narrative method fit in current educational perspectives? From a broad pedagogical perspective, the comparative-method is about making learning tangible for students by keeping knowledge objectives concrete, measurable and achievable; and it is about teaching students how to learn to learn. From the perspective of language teaching pedagogies, the comparative-narrative method is a cross-linguistic method with at its core 'contrastive form-focused instruction', translation and code-switching. In this respect, it belongs with the theories advocating mother tongue in second-language teaching.[143] The comparative-narrative method, being a grammatical method, is also at home with the theories supporting explicit grammatical instruction. In fact, the comparative-narrative method is a bilingual method because it is a comparative grammatical method. And then again, given the importance it places on 'real language' and 'authentic communication', the comparative-narrative method is in part a communicative method. But the comparative-narrative method is also more than the sum of all these parts. As I explained in Book One, the comparative-narrative method originates in the remedial, practically oriented techniques I once devised to teach French grammar to students who were lost in the grammar-less communicative classroom. These techniques had no ambitions beyond complementing students' instruction, but they did foster observation and thus gave rise to an irresistible inclination to explain *why* students do what they do by explaining *how* French is not English.

If the comparative-narrative method is more than a syncretic approach to language learning, what are the theoretical implications? I should like to think that this question has been largely answered in the preceding chapters, but a book needs a conclusion and a reader deserves no less, and so I will attempt to sum up and hopefully clarify issues of theory a little further in closing this ultimate chapter.

---

[141] Hall and Cook citing (Maley 2011), op. cit., p. 299.

[142] See the many scholarly articles and researches conducted by applied linguists and educators, available at Research Gate, Google Scholar, Academia.edu., and so forth.

[143] See in particular Wolfgang Butzkamm's article cited above. There are significant differences between the comparative-narrative approach and Butzkamm's theory, mostly to do with the role of consciousness in second-language acquisition. Butzkamm is also more of a nativist than I happen to be. Hence, Butzkamm argues that the use of mother tongue in translation can help do away with grammatical sequencing and progression and can therefore promote a more spontaneous approach to language learning, whereas the comparative-narrative method places very high value on grammatical sequencing, grammatical accuracy and metalinguistic awareness; Butzkamm also advocates grammatical explanation by imitation (word for word translation) rather than analysis, whereas the comparative-narrative method insists on both. Nevertheless, there definitely is kindred understanding between Butzkamm's theoretical propositions and the comparative-narrative method.

We learned our first language because we were born to speak. We learn additional languages because we know the value of language, and what language can do for us. Indeed, in spite of the 'cultural dominance of the monolingual ideology', I don't think I know a single monolingual person who does not wish that they could speak another language. Learning a new language, however, is time-consuming and it is not easy. It is difficult because it challenges our memory and our sense of reality in a radical manner. Language and thought are, if not indivisible, at least symbiotic. Language informs much of what we know, much of what we are not conscious of knowing, as well as much of what we are not conscious of not knowing. Thus, as I see it, the biggest hurdle for English speakers learning French is that their mind is made in English and for English. But then again, knowing English is also to their advantage, because learning an additional language does not require learning to speak from nothing as a first language does.

One of my dearest anthropology teachers, Eric Ten Raa, was a linguist and a hyper-polyglot. Raised in four mother tongues and a speaker, writer and reader of a dozen more languages learned at school and as an adult, Eric was convinced that the more languages we learn (say after the fifth or so), the easier the learning becomes. As I wrote earlier, Frederick Bodmer believed that the best way to learn a European language was to learn them all. Very few of us are in these scholars' league, but we can take from their extraordinary experience that, short of living in different countries for significant periods of time, we are best able to learn new languages when we can compare new words and new forms with words and forms that we already know. Hence, multilingual students have a relative advantage over unilingual learners. While they can experience interference from all their languages, they are psychologically equipped to accept linguistic differences as well as able to make a range of connections to new linguistic knowledge. In the same vein, students who are thoroughly schooled in the grammar of their own language have an advantage over students who have limited or no explicit knowledge of their mother tongue.

The comparative-narrative method is effective *because* it is comparative. Comparison allows learners to make connections between French and English, and it allows them to encounter the mystery of language – to discover words, word order, overt and contextual meaning where previously only intuition and spontaneity existed. To be clear, I am not claiming that spontaneity has no place in language learning, or that intuition, parallel and sub-conscious processes play no role in second-language acquisition, or for that matter in any sort of learning. We experience going to sleep on a problem to find the solution when we wake up. We experience knowing things we did not know we learned. We experience the miracle of moving from painstaking focus to 'sudden' automaticity in the process of learning all sorts of things, including languages. But solutions come in dreams or in light-bulb moments to the seekers and the open-minded, and we are as unlikely to wake up speaking a language which we have never learned as we are to discover the laws of the universe without some interest in falling apples. What I am saying, therefore, is that students who are conscious that meaning comes out of their minds and mouths by way of organised sounds and ordered words, are much better placed to apply themselves to 'making language' and therefore to learning French on its own terms than students who are under the impression that speaking a second language is about stringing together weird sounding words in the best way one can manage.

In fact, and interestingly so, students who learn with the comparative-narrative method do not only monitor their language or control their grammar, they can also produce grammatically accurate language that I have not taught them. At all levels, students can speak creatively (within limits, evidently) because grammatical instruction provides them with the means to extend what they know, and the desire to do so – because knowing how to proceed is highly motivating and encourages students to speak. Intermediate and advanced level students, however, produce accurate novel language not only through conscious deduction, but also at times quite unconsciously. For lack of a better metaphor, I am happy to explain the latter as 'their brain gets it and does it for them'. Learning language systematically, it appears, allows students to produce language systemically, a phenomenon which I am tempted to ascribe, not to the activation of a Language Acquisition Device (although I have no doubt that brain processes are at work) but to the convergence of symbiotic processes that have to do with the nature of learning and the nature of systems – the fact that learning systematically is procedural learning and that syntax is the procedural aspect of language.

And then, the comparative-narrative method is effective because it takes into account that the acquisition of a language is not only dependent on knowing how language works but also on the authenticity of the language we use. This involves two things: true communicative exchange and language that makes sense. This is where the comparative-narrative method and the communicative method find common ground. We learn to speak when we connect the noises that we hear to what they *mean*. Krashen argues that such moments happen when learners are truly motivated to speak, and I think that he is absolutely right. However, our communicative pedagogies overlook a couple of things. Firstly, we must distinguish what 'motivation to speak' means in a classroom from what it means in a natural language environment. Unlike learner-speakers in immersion, language students are motivated by the desire to speak a language in the long-term (and passing their tests in the short-term), rather than they are motivated to speak about interesting or vitally important things in the immediate term. Secondly, the communicative perspective is missing something about language cognizance. Communication is a necessary condition of language cognizance: if no one speaks to us, we will never know what words are, but language cognizance is more than communication. It is the spark that fused w-a-t-e-r with the cool thing flowing over Helen Keller's hand. Language cognizance is intelligence in the most mysterious and inexplicable sense of the word. A first language initiates cognition. A second language initiates recognition. As Wolfgang Butzkamm puts it (and so perfectly): 'We only learn language once'. When we learn our first language, we begin to speak when we are able to *know* a string of sounds as 'a thing in the world'. In a second language, we begin to communicate when we are able to equate a string of sounds to *words* that we already know.

Nevertheless, the communicative method is also partially correct on another crucial point – in order to acquire a new language, we must get beyond equating our new words with the words of our native language. We must inhabit the new language. We need to move beyond knowing that *pomme* means 'apple', to knowing what *une pomme* looks like, smells like, tastes like. Words become real when they resonate with experience. But in the second-language classroom, experience cannot grow out of consequential communication as things happen in a natural language setting. Experience must grow out of the power of the imagination through narratives, visual, aural and textual studies along with every opportunity teachers and students have to create socially meaningful language. This of course involves the exchange of personal and real information – and more, for the classroom is a social unit where collective work, competition and solidarity, the discussions, the laughs, the frustrations and the successes can all contribute to students living with, and eventually living in, their new language.

The communicative approach is founded on the experience of learning an alien language in a real-life context. Thus, it takes for granted that living with ambiguity, incomprehension and discomfort is part of language learning because this is the normal state of things in natural language acquisition. I do not dispute that this is the case. Learning to transcend incomprehension is an essential aspect of language learning but incomprehension cannot become a pedagogy. Learning languages, as learning anything else, must foster understanding and curiosity. Learning is about making sense of what we do not understand and about discovering what we did not know existed. Incomprehension is the antithesis of learning. It is also the antithesis of language because language is, above anything else, intelligence. What I have outlined in Book Two: the sequencing and mapping of the French language, the identification of cognitive and communicative needs, the comparative and philological connections, the philosophical and anthropological musings, and the range of cross-linguistic techniques, all establish *a continuity of understanding and significance* between English and French. And the key here *is* continuity of understanding and significance. The comparative-narrative method is much less about adhering to the strategies and the explanations I have discussed in this book than it is about working from the principle that we need to know and understand where students are coming from, where they need to go, and what gets in their way before we attempt getting them to destination. I would not use this book in reverse to teach English to French-speaking students anymore than I would use it wholesale to teach French to Anglophone students thoroughly schooled in formal English grammar. The challenges and opportunities which all language students encounter depend on their own native grammar and phonology, their own state of formal and intuitive knowledge, as well as what the new language is made of and made from. Learning a new language is about establishing a continuity of understanding and significance between the language(s) that we already know and the language we are learning because all learning is built on existing knowledge, because there cannot be learning without understanding and consciousness, and because language can only be language when it is meaningful. In fact, this may even sound better in French: *la langue n'est langage que si elle est porteuse de sens*.

There is no doubt that teaching and learning with the comparative-narrative approach is no quick fix. Students will make mistakes, and teaching and learning with the comparative-narrative method requires effort and means work, but it is work that draws on the intelligence and nourishes the intelligence. It is work that gives persistence a real chance of turning into accomplishment. Not least, it is work that takes students and teachers to all sorts of fascinating places along the way. Illuminated by the language(s) we already know, by inquiry, explanation, comparison, cross-disciplinary references, cultural reflection, and critical thinking, learning a new language in the classroom may not only be to speech what walking on two legs is to human ambulation, but what knowing to walk brings to learning to dance.

In creative conversation, when they are immersed in French, students who learn with the comparative-narrative method do not regurgitate formulaic language or replace English words with French words, transposing from their English syntax unconsciously. They know that French is not English, and they are listening, imitating, copying as well as looking for the French means of saying what they mean to say. In other words, the comparative-narrative method achieves by way of bilingualism what a target-language-only approach cannot: it allows learners to set aside English and be in French. No doubt, students are still some way from being able to produce truly fluent and idiomatic speech, but in the meantime 'speaking French for real', because they can understand, read, hear or express themselves directly in grammatically accurate and therefore authentic French, is so gratifying and 'it feels so weird' as some of my students say when they feel so pleasantly *dépaysés*, that they are just as excited speaking about the chairs we happen to be sitting on, as about anything else that is real to them at that moment. They are excited, not because they are speaking about something exciting, but because they know that they are experiencing the wonder of speech.

Works cited

L' Académie française at http://www.academie-francaise.fr

Ackerman Farrell and Robert Malouf, 'Beyond Caricatures, Commentary on Evans 2014', *Language*, Vol. 92, No 1, 2016.

Apothéloz Denis, 'Sémantique du passé composé en français moderne et exploration des rapports passé composé / passé simple dans un corpus de moyen français', in Cahiers Chrono, *Aoristes et parfaits*, Vol. 28, 2016; pp.199-246. https://apps.atilf.fr/homepages/apotheloz/wpcontent/uploads/sites/59/2015/06/Cahiers_Chron_28.pdf

Bagarić Vesna and Jelena Mihaljević Djigunović, 'Defining Communicative Competence' in *Metodika*, Vol. 8, br. 1, 2007; pp. 94-103.

Bateson G. and M. Mead, *Balinese Character: A photographic Analysis*, New York Academy of Science, 1942 and 1962.

Béchennec Danielle and Liliane Sprenger-Charolles, *Guide Pratique de l'orthographe rectifiée*, CNRS et Université Paris-Descartes. http://www.cahierspedagogiques.com/IMG/pdf/GuidePratiqueOrthographeRectifie_e-2-09-2011.pdf

Bettelheim Bruno, 'Feral Children and Autistic Children', *The American Journal of Sociology*, Vol. 64, No 5, March 1959; pp. 455-467.

Bilash Olenka, 'Krashen's 6 hypotheses', *Best of Bilash*, May 2009.

https://sites.educ.ualberta.ca/staff/olenka.bilash/Best%20of%20Bilash/krashen.html

Bodmer Frederick, *The Loom of Language*, Tingling and Co, Liverpool, London and Prescot, 1968.

Borelli Giulia, 'Second-Language Acquisition, A Theoretical Overview', 2018. https://www.academia.edu

Bourcier Edouard et J. Bourcier , *Phonétique française, étude historique*, Editions Klincksieck, Paris, 1974.

Bucco Armaury, 'Pourquoi l'écriture inclusive a déjà gagné la bataille', *Le Figaro*, 18 October 2018. http://www.lefigaro.fr/ vox/societe/2018/10/18/31003-20181018ARTFIG00104-pourquoi-l-ecriture-inclusive-a-deja-gagne-la-bataille.php

Butzkamm Wolfgang 'We only learn language once. The role of the mother tongue in FL classrooms: death of a dogma,' *Language Learning Journal*, Winter 2003, No 28, 29-39.

Canadian government's Bureau de la Traduction, 'La préposition'. https://www.btb.termiumplus.gc.ca/tpv2guides/guides/rdp/index-fra.html?lang=fra&lettr=&page=../preposition

Cauffman-Crocker Mary E, *Schaum's Ouline of French Grammar*, Schaum, 2013.

Centre National de Ressources Textuelles et Lexicales (CNRTL), 'Etymologie: s'évanouir'. http://www.cnrtl.fr/definition/évanouir

Chomsky Noam, *On Language*, The New Press, New York, 2007.

Chomsky Noam: *1. Lecture*. https://www.youtube.com/watch?v=2v6XFkSwVys

Clay Zanna and Claude Tennier, 'Is over-imitation a uniquely human trait: insights from human children as opposed to bonobos', *Child Development*, September-October 2018.

Cordial.com, 'L'accord du participe passé avec être et avoir'. https://www.cordial.fr/index.php

De Francis John with Yung Teng Chia-yee, *Beginning Chinese*, Yale University Press, New Haven and London, 1963.

De Vaan Michiel, in *Etymological Dictionary of Latin and the other Italic Languages* (Leiden Indo-European Etymological Dictionary Series 7), Brill, Leiden, Boston, 2008.

Divergenres at https://divergenres.org/regles-de-grammaire-neutre-et-inclusive/

Domaradzki Mikolaj, 'Cognitive Critique of Generative Grammar'. http://lingua.amu.edu.pl/Lingua_17/lin-4.pdf.

Dowd Emily, *Les voyelles nasales en Français, histoire, variation régionale et pédagogie* (Masters' Thesis). http:/gets.libs.uga.edu/pdfs/dowd_emily_a_200508_ma_pdf.

Dubois Jean and René Lagane, *La nouvelle grammaire du Français*, Larousse,1973.

Edstrom Anne, 'L1 use in the L2 classroom: One teacher's self-evaluation' *Canadian Modern Language Review*, Vol. 63, No 2; pp. 275-290, 2006.

Edwards Michael, *Dialogues singuliers sur la langue française,* Presses universitaires de France, 2016.

English Language and Usage, 'When was "it" first used in weather sentences?' at: https://english.stackexchange.com/questions/286789/when-was-it-first-used-in-weather-sentences

Evans Vyvyan, *The Language Myth: Why Language is not an Instinct*, Cambridge University Press, Cambridge UK, New York, 2014.

Evans Vyvyan, 'Real Talk', *Eon*, 4 December 2014. https://aeon.co/essays/the-evidence-is-in-there-is-no-language-instinct.

Evans Vyvyan, 'Is Language an instinct?' *Psychology Today*, 19 December 2014. https://www.psychologytoday.com/au/blog/language-in-the-mind/201412/is-language-instinct

Français facile.com, 'L'accord du participe passé'. https://www.francaisfacile.com/exercices/exercice-francais-2/exercice-francais-34890.php

Fromkin Victoria and Robert Rodman, *An Introduction to Language*, Holt, Rinehart and Winston, 1974.

García Ophelia and and Li Wei, *Translanguaging, Language, Bilingualism and Education*, Palgrave Macmillan, Basingstokem, 2014.

García O. and A. Lin, 'Translanguaging and bilingual education' in García, O., Lin, A., May, S. (Eds.), *Bilingual and Multilingual Education*. Springer, Dordrecht, 2016.

Germain Claude, 'Acquisition ou apprentissage de la grammaire' in Melba Libia Cárdenas y Nora M. Basurto Santos (eds), *Investigación-Research-Recherche En Lenguas Extranjeras y Linguisticas Aplicada*, primera edición, Bogóta: Universidad National de Colombia; Faculdad de Ciencias Humanas, Departamento de Lenguas Extranjeras, 2017.

Hall Edward T., *Beyond Culture*, Anchor, 1976.

Hall Edward T., *The Hidden Dimension*, Anchor, 1990.

Hall Edward T., *The Silent Language*, Anchor, 1973

Hall Graham and Guy Cook, 'Own language use in language teaching and learning, state of the art', *Language Teaching*, Vol. 45, No 3, 2012.

Horan R.S. and J.R. Wheeler, *A New French Course*, Science Press, Sydney.

Hu Jane C., 'What do talking apes really tell us?', *Slate Magazine*, August 20, 2017. https://slate.com/technology/2014/08/koko-kanzi-and-ape-language-research-criticism-of-working-conditions-and-animal-care.html

Hymes Dell, 'On communicative competence', in J. B. Pride & J. Holmes (Eds.), *Sociolinguistics: Selected readings*, Penguin, Baltimore, 1972.

Inan Alaadin, 'The Role of Mother Tongue in Second-language Teaching', Mersin University, Education Faculty, ELT deparment, 2008. https://www.academia.edu/28111770/THE_ROLE_OF_MOTHER_TONGUE_IN_SECOND_LANGUAGE_TEACHING

Itard Jean-Marc-Gaspard, *The Wild Boy of Aveyron*, Appleton-Century-Crofts, Meridith Corporation, New York, 1962.

Jaspers Jürgen, 'The transformative limits of translanguaging', *Language and Communication*, (58), 2018; pp. 1-10.

Keller Helen, *The Story of My Life*, Hodder and Stoughton, 1904.

Krashen Stephen *Principles and Practices in Second-language Acquisition*, University of California, 1983.

Krashen Stephen, 'Why not give Immersion a try?' http://www.sdkrashen.com/content/articles/1995_immersion_try_fvr.pdf

Kuhl Patricia K., 'Brain Mechanisms in Early Language Acquisition', *Neuron*, Volume 67, Issue 5, 9 September 2010; pp. 713-727.
https://www.sciencedirect.com/science/article/pii/S0896627310006811

Lakoff George, *Women, Fire and Dangerous Things: what categories reveal about the mind*. Chicago University Press, 1987.

Langacker Robert, *Concept, Image, and Symbol: the cognitive basis of grammar*, Berlin, New York, Mouton de Gruyten, 2002.

Lankiewicz Hadrian, 'From the Concept of Languaging to L2 Pedagogy' in Hadrian Lankiewicz and Emilia Wasikiewics-Firlej, *Languaging Experiences, Learning and Teaching Revisited*, Cambridge Scholars Publishing, 2014.

Larive et Fleury, *La Classe de Français*, Armand Colin, 2015, a reproduction of Larive et Fleury, *La première année de grammaire*, 1936.

Laurent Samuel, 'Non, l'accent circonflexe ne va pas disparaître', *Le Monde*, 4 février 2016.
http://www.lemonde.fr/les-decodeurs/article/2016/02/04/non-l-accent-circonflexe-ne-va-pas-disparaitre_4859439_4355770.html

Le Nouvel Observateur, *La conjugaison*, 'L'accord du participe passé'.
http://la-conjugaison.nouvelobs.com/regles/orthographe/l-accord-du-participe-passe-161.php

Le Nouvel Observateur, *La conjugaison*, 'L'accord du participe passé devant un infinitif' at: http://la-conjugaison.nouvelobs.com/regles/orthographe/l-accord-du-participe-passe-laisse-devant-un-infinitif-182.php

Lévi-Strauss Claude, *La Pensée Sauvage*, Plon, 1962.

Littré Emile, Roland Eluerd, *Littré Grammaire, toutes les règles essentielles pour un usage quotidien*, Librarie Eyrolles, Paris.

Littré en ligne.
https://www.littre.org

Loyer Bertrand and Keebe Kennedy, 'Animal Language', *Animals like us*, 2004-2006.

Malinowski Bronislaw, *Argonauts of the Western Pacific*, Routledge, 1922.

Manfred Jahn, 'Colourless green ideas sleep furiously: A linguistic case test and its appropriations'.
https://pdfs.semanticscholar.org/57e1/74196dd4e32098a09847a2eb3d1da1aeef6e.pdf

Matacic Catherine, 'Ape "language ace" gets tripped by simple grammar', in *Science Magazine*, March 25 2016.
http://www.sciencemag.org/news/2016/03/ape-language-ace-gets-tripped-simple-grammar

Mauss Marcel, *The Gift: the form and reason of exchange in archaic societies*, Routledge, 1990.

Mayberry Rachel I, 'The critical period for language acquisition and the deaf child's language comprehension: a psycholinguistic approach,' University of McGill (undated report).
http://www.acfos.org/pubication/ourarticles/pdf/acfos1/mayberry.pdf

McMurray Aaron MD, Erin Saito, MSC and Beau Nakamoto, MD, 'Language preference and Development of Dementia Among Bilingual Individuals', *Hawaii Med Journal*, Vol 68, No 9, Oct 2009; pp. 223–226.

Merle Jean-Marie, 'Les origines du conditionnel français et de ses traductions en anglais', *Linguistique contrastive et traduction*, Ophrys, 2001; pp. 24-29.

Mishlove Jeffrey, with Stephen Pinker, 'Language and Consciousness, Part 1: Are our thoughts constrained by language?' *Thinking allowed, Conversations on the leading edge of knowledge and discovery*.
http://www.williamjames.com/transcripts/pinker1.htm

Online Dictionary of Etymology,
https://www.etymonline.com

Oxford dictionary
https://en.oxforddictionaries.com/grammar/subjects-and-objects

Paz Octavio, *Claude Lévi-Strauss: An Introduction*, Cape Editions, London, 1971,

Picoche Jacqueline, *Dictionaire Etymologique*, Les usuels du Robert, Le Robert, Paris, 1979.

Pinker Steven, *The Language Instinct*, Harper, Modern Classic editions, 2007.

Poirier Agnes, 'The Circumflex: A battle over an accent mark', BBC.com, 16 February 2016.
http://www.bbc.com/culture/story/20160215-the-circumflex-a-battle-over-an-accent-mark.

Raffaele Paul, 'Speaking Bonobo', *Smithsonian Magazine*, November 2006.
https://www.smithsonianmag.com/science-nature/speaking-bonobo-134931541/

Rat Maurice, *Le Français facile pour tous*, Garnier,1964.

Ray Alain, 'Le Français, une langue à l'épreuve des siècles'.
https://www.youtube.com/watch?v=qrza2HMjsSw

Sacks Oliver, *Seeing Voices*, Vintage, 2000.

Saffran Jenny R., Ann Senghas, and John C. Treswell, 'The acquisition of language by children', *Proceedings of the National Academy of Sciences of the United States of America*, Vol. 98, No 23, November 6 2001; pp. 12874-12875.

Sahlins Marshall, 'Other Times, Other Customs: The Anthropology of History', *American Anthropologist*, Vol. 3, 1985; pp. 517-541.

Sampson Geoffrey, *The Language Instinct Debate*, Continuum, London, New York, 2005.

Sheets-Johnstone Maxine, 'Kinetic Tactile-Kinesthetic Bodies: Ontogenetical Foundations of Apprenticeship Learning.' *Human Studies*, 2000.

Schmidt Richard W., 'The Role of Consciousness in Second-language Learning' *Applied Linguistics*, Vol. 11, No 2, 1990.

Schmidt R. and S. Frota, 'Developing basic conversational ability in a second language: a case study of an adult learner of Portuguese' in R. Day, *Talking to Learn: Conversation in Second language Acquisition*, Newbury House, Rowley, 1986.

Shurkin Joel, 'Colourless green ideas sleep furiously. Or maybe not.' *Inside Science*, December 10, 2015.

Smith Madorah E., 'Grammatical errors in the speech of pre-school children', *Child Development*, Vol. 4 No 2, June 1933; pp. 183-190.

Truswell Robert, 'Dentrophobia in bonobo comprehension of spoken English', Edinburgh University, linguistics and English language, paper given at the *Evolution of Language Conference*, Louisiana, 2016.
http://evolang.org/neworleans/pdf/EVOLANG_11_paper_87.pdf

Ullman Michael T., 'The Declarative/Procedural Model of Lexicon and Grammar', *Journal of Psycholinguistics*, Vol. 30. No 1, 2001.

Victorian Curriculum and Assessment Authority.
http://victoriancurriculum.vcaa.vic.edu.au/languages/french/introduction/rationale-and-aims

Vinay J.P. and J. Darbelnet, *Stylistique comparé du français et de l'anglais*, Didier, Paris, 1958.

Wei Li, 'Translanguaging as a Practical Theory of Language', *Applied Linguistics*, Vol. 39, No 1, 2018; pp. 9–30.

Wohlleben Peter (Jane Billinghurst transl.), *The Hidden Life of Trees*, Greystone Books, 2016.

Wong Kate 'Crawling May Not Be Necessary For Normal Child Development; in some tribes, babies skip the crawl', *Scientific American*, July 1 2009.

DETAILED

TABLE OF CONTENTS

BOOK ONE

SPEAKING OF LANGUAGE TEACHING AND LANGUAGE ACQUISITION

Chapter I

Introduction

Introduction p. 11

Boredom and the art of language learning p. 12

English, and reflection, in the task-based learning classroom p. 14

Grammar is not simply speaking 'form' p. 16

The comparative-narrative approach is a multi-modal approach p. 18

Anthropology and language teaching p. 20

Chapter II

The backstory

The Wonderlands of French Language Instruction

Introduction p. 22

Developing a grammatically-based, comparative pedagogy p. 23

Teaching French grammar with the comparative-narrative approach p. 25

To illustrate the comparative-narrative approach: teaching the weather p. 26

>*The impersonal* il p. 28
>*Bridging the impersonal 'it' and* il p. 29
>*Grammar points to do with the weather* p. 31

A magical mystery tour of our common and uncommon humanity   p. 33

Chapter III

A Discussion of the Communicative Approach
And Other Ideas about Second-Language Teaching

Introduction   p. 35

Unconscious Language Acquisition or Conscious Language Learning? p. 36
    Immersion, language learning, and language retention   p. 36
    Thinking of the Natural Method   p. 38
    Acquiring is learning   p. 40
    The Monitoring Hypothesis and the teaching of grammar   p. 41
    Are there multiple paths to learning a second or additional language? p. 43

Can the classroom simulate a natural language environment?   p. 47
    Motivation, authentic language and language resources p. 49
    Whose French are we teaching?   p. 51

On valuing 'fluency over accuracy' and why it is not an entirely good idea   p. 53
    Translanguaging: hybridization, communication and cognition   p. 54
    To correct errors or not, and how?   p. 58
    On the difficulties of correcting grammatically inaccurate language   p. 60
    Does grammatical accuracy matter, ever?   p. 62

Why the acquisition of standard French grammar cannot be entrusted to nature p. 63
    Written French and its many complications   p. 65

Conclusion: Why learning grammar can be more fun than talking about *la fête et les copains*   p. 66

Chapter IV

Thinking about Language and Second-language Acquisition
Part One: The Mystery of Language

Introduction   p. 68

The Nativist-Cognitivist debate p. 68
    The language children speak and the language children invent   p. 74
    Neuroscience and the nativist-cognitivist debate   p. 76

Language acquisition and social interaction   p. 78
    The wolf child, Victor de l'Aveyron p. 79

Is language an instinct? p. 81
    Does language make us human? p. 84
    How the language instinct partially explains the limitations of the communicative language classroom p. 86

***
Part Two: Language, Thought and Why Syntax Rules.

Language and the mind   p. 89
    Is syntax truly autonomous from semantics? p. 89
    Colourless green ideas sleep furiously - poetics and clichés p. 91
    Why syntax rules p. 93
    The syntactic problems experienced by English-speaking learners of French p. 95

Pinker's Mentalese: is language not thought?   p. 97
    What is a mental landscape without language? p. 99
    Does multilingualism imply a plurality of thought? p. 100
    Do multilingual speakers have plural minds? p. 104
    Some things are untranslatable p. 105

The systemic nature of language explains the difficulties involved in learning a second language p. 107

The social nature of language also explains the difficulties involved in learning a second language p. 108

How then should English speakers learn French?   p. 109

BOOK TWO

FRENCH GRAMMAR: HOW TO ORGANISE IT
AND
HOW TO TEACH IT

Chapter V

Mapping the French Language and Essentials of French grammar
La grammaire étant l'art de parler et d'écrire

Syntax turns words into thoughts and meaningful speech   p. 117

The value of teaching grammar also lies in how we speak about it   p. 118

Teaching Year 7-10 French with the comparative-narrative approach   p. 120

A cognitive and structural approach to the development of course materials   p. 121

A comparative-narrative language course is built on a helical approach rather than a brick by brick approach   p. 122
      Illustrating the helical approach   p. 123

The knowledge field: identifying the core structures of French   p. 124
      A bird's eye view of the <u>basic</u> grammatical structures and functions in French   p. 124

What students learn, when, and for which purpose   p. 125

An overview of essential grammatical concepts   p. 126
      General concepts and terminology   p. 126

Students learn about semantic units   p. 126
      Compound nouns: general notions   p. 127
      When **à** *implies an underlying verb*   p. 127
      Using **en** *when the headword is 'made from' the modifier*   p. 127
      Compound nouns formed with a verb + noun   p. 128
      Compound nouns formed with prefix + noun; adjective + noun; adverb + noun   p. 128

Students learn about relational function   p. 128
      Object complements   p. 128
      Circumstantial complements   p. 128
      Clausal complements   p. 129

A STRUCTURAL-FUNCTIONAL MAP OF SIMPLE FRENCH SENTENCES   p. 129
  Five basic groupings NP + V + adjectives/ Nouns/ Noun phrases   p. 129
  Three NP + V + infinitive phrases   p. 129
  Six basic pronominal structures calling for many types of pronouns   p. 130

EIGHT CLASSES OF VERBS PRODUCE THE FOLLOWING FUNDAMENTAL STRUCTURES   p. 131
  1) STATIVE VERBS – ÊTRE, AVOIR, ALLER   p. 131
  2) ACTION VERBS + TRANSITIVE SINGLE OBJECT   p. 132
    When the direct object is a noun
    When the Direct Object is a verb in the infinitive
    The single (indirect) DATIVE object
  3) ACTION-TRANSMISSION VERBS – DOUBLE-TRANSITIVE   p. 133
    When the Direct Object is a noun
    With there are two l-initialled pronouns
    When the Dative is followed by a verb in the infinitive
  4) ACTION VERBS –TRANSITIVE INDIRECT   p. 135
    When **à** *and* **de** *mean 'about'*
    Using the indiret object pronouns **y** *and* **en**
    When the verbs take other complements
  5) LOCATIVE/DIRECTIONAL VERBS (VERBS OF MOTION)   p. 137
    When followed by an infinitive complement of intention
  6) THE REFLEXIVE VOICE AND THE REFLEXIVE VERBS   p. 138
    When verbs are used in the reflexive voice
    Verbs that exist only in the reflexive form
  7) MODAL VERBS, PREFERENCE, AND STATES OF MIND   p. 139
  8) CATENATIVE VERBS (Verbal chains)   p. 140
    Faire + Infinitive
    Laisser + Infinitive
    Verbs of perception + Infinitive
  In sum, there are two funny things about catenative verbs   p. 143

UNIFYING THE RULES GOVERNING PAST PARTICIPLE AGREEMENTS   p. 144
  Two principles, five fundamental constructions and no exceptions   p. 145
    The past participle agrees with the direct object   p. 145
    The past participle agrees with the subject   p.146
  The agreement of the past participle in the passive voice   p. 147

FORMING COMPLEX SENTENCES   p. 148
  With modal verbs and verbs of emotion and states of mind   p. 148
  Third-person verb of obligation: falloir *and the modal verb* vouloir   p. 148
  Manquer à quelqu'un   p. 148

Real condition vs imaginable and non-existent condition: the si *constructions*   p. 149
Relative clauses p. 149

THE IMPORTANCE OF THE ROLE PLAYERS   p. 150
The pronouns that are the same in English and in French   p. 150
The pronouns that are different in English and in French   p. 150
The pronouns that precede the verb (Table 1) p. 151
The pronouns that follow the verb (Table 2) p. 152
The relative pronouns (Table 3) p. 153

PREPOSITIONAL USE   p. 154
Identifying verbal post-positions and prepositions   p. 154
Identifying the syntactic functions of the prepositions à, de, *and* en   p. 154
When adjectives are followed by + à or de + infinitive   p. 156
When adjectives are followed by + à or de + noun or pronoun   p. 157
The words POUR and FOR also need attention p. 158

WHAT ELSE GOES WITH FRENCH VERBS AND WHERE   p. 159
Negation   p. 159
Other adverbs   p. 159

ESSENTIAL ENGLISH TO FRENCH COMPARISONS   p. 160
The place of the descriptive adjective and other modifiers   p. 160
Pronouns and their functions   p. 161
Verbs p.161
  Modal verbs in English and in French   p. 161
  The reflexive voice and the reflexive verbs p. 161
  English phrasal verbs   p. 163

TO CONCLUDE   p. 164

Chapter VI

Phonology, Pronunciation and the Acquisition of Grammar
With a focus on Gender and Number

Introduction   p. 165

Phonology and grammatical-orthographic exceptions   p. 165

Pronunciation: communication, memory, and grammar   p. 166

On the importance of prosody   p. 167

ON THE IMPORTANCE OF PRONUNCIATION FOR READING, WRITING AND

GRAMMATICAL UNDERSTANDING   p. 168
    Fundamental differences between English and French phonology   p. 168
    Teaching students how to read helps their pronunciation   p. 169
    To speak or to write: where lies the value of written exercises for learning the language and learning the grammar?   p. 169
    Correcting pronunciation to enhance grammatical accuracy   p. 171

Suggestions for teaching French phonetics   p. 171
    Teaching the nasalised vowels   p. 172
    Tips for teaching u and ou   p. 173

LEARNING TO LISTEN   p. 174
    Polysyllabic words in French and in English, and the schwa   p. 175
    Teaching contractions   p. 175
    Teaching liaisons   p. 176
    Liaising and identifying syllables for grammatical expression and comprehension   p. 177
    Differentiating and producing é, è and un, une is of fundamental importance to the acquisition of French syntax   p. 180
    How l-whatever and oon restore the world to the Anglophone perspective   p. 180
    Pronunciation and gender   p. 182
        What else can we say about gender?   p. 184
        Can gender be taught?   p. 185

READING AND WRITING WHAT WE SAY: CODIFYING LANGUAGE   p. 186
An overview of French orthography: silent letters and things like that   p. 187
    French uses diacritical marks called accents   p. 188
    French combines letters differently to English but French vowels are sounded mostly as orthographic convention spells them out   p. 188
    French spelling expresses syntactic relationships   p. 189
    More about silent letters   p. 189
    Reading nasalised vowels and not nasal consonants   p. 191
    Reading and writing vowels and diphthongs in French   p. 191
    The spelling of consonant sounds requiring special attention   p. 191
    Also problematic: the silent and aspirated h   p. 192
    How to read and pronounce –ail and –eil and ay–   p. 192

THE NEGLECTED ARTICLES   p. 193
    Understanding the difficulties involved in learning the articles in French   p. 193
    The types of articles and their function   p. 195
    Teaching the definite and the indefinite articles   p. 196
    Teaching the plural definite article   p. 197
    Teaching the plural of the countable indefinite articles   p. 197
    Teaching the partitive articles   p. 198

Teaching the global definite articles p. 199
And then, should we use: des/du/de la or le/la/les? p. 201
Negating the indefinite articles p. 204

A note on the gender of possessive adjectives p. 204

TO SUM UP p. 205

Chapter VII

Teaching Techniques
The Comparative-cognitive Approach
With a focus on pronouns

Introduction p. 206

THE COMPARATIVE-COGNITIVE APPROACH AND ITS TECHNIQUES p. 206
Translation p. 207
    Literal translation p. 208
    The art of translation p. 208
Syntactic analysis p. 209

Dictation p. 209

Etymology p. 209

Learning grammar by reasoning about language p. 209
    What is grammar and where do we find it? p. 210
        We find grammar in notion and function p. 210
        We find grammar in inflection p. 211
        We find grammar in word order p. 211
        We find grammar in phrasing and prosody p. 212

TEACHING WORD CLASS, FUNCTION AND WORD ORDER P. 214
Teaching the grammar of modifiers (adj., adv., and compound nouns) p. 214
    Types of adjectives p. 214
    The place of modifiers in French and in English p. 215
    When a noun, an adjective or a verb modifies a noun to form a compound p. 216
Why teach the grammar of compound-noun formations as opposed to teaching compound-nouns as 'nouns'? p. 217

TEACHING FRENCH PRONOUNS p. 218
Identifying role players and modifiers through intuitive questioning p. 220
    Identifying the subject of a verb p. 220
    Identifying the direct object complement p. 220

TEACHING THE OBJECT PRONOUNS   p. 221
    Teaching the definite direct object pronouns me, te, le, la, nous, vous, les p. 221
    Teaching the indefinite direct object pronoun en p. 222
    Teaching the dative and the pronouns me, te, lui, nous, vous, leur p. 223
    Teaching the less obvious uses of the dative pronoun p. 224
    Teaching pronominal order in double-transitive constructions p. 224

Teaching the locative and directional pronouns *y* and *en* p. 226
Teaching how to negate a pronominal clause   p. 226

TEACHING THE RELATIVE PRONOUNS p. 226
    The relative pronouns with nominal antecedents p. 226
    The relative pronouns with clausal antecedents p. 227
    The relative pronouns with no stated antecedent p. 227

Chapter VIII

Teaching Techniques
The Comparative-experiential Approach

Introduction   p. 229

The Bridging Grammar   p. 229

Mental Imaging and Sensory Reflection   p. 230

Creative Imitation   p. 230
    Rote learning inhibits creative imitation   p. 233
Conscious Repetition and Drills   p. 234

Listening, and Reading and Listening   p. 235

Immersion   p. 235

COMBINING THE COGNITIVE AND EXPERIENTIAL TECHNIQUES   p. 236

    Teaching the catenative structure: *faire+ infinitif*   p. 236
    Teaching *manquer à quelqu'un*   p. 237
    Teaching the complement of possession   p. 238

Chapter IX

Verbs and their Conjugations

Introduction   p. 242

What are conjugations and how complicated are they?   p. 242

A bird's eye view of French conjugations   p. 243

How what can we facilitate the learning of French verbs? p. 244

Identifying the classes of verbs   p. 247
    Identifying classes of verbs through mental imaging and sensory reflection   p. 248
    To be and ne pas être   p. 249
        être
        avoir
        aller
    To have and not to have   p. 250
        Why prendre *and not have?*   p. 251
        Avoir un âge   p. 252
    Thinking about 'to have' and 'to be'   p. 253
    To use c'est or il est?   p. 253
        Identifying, pointing to: c'est   p. 255
        Describing, referencing the antecedent: il, elle, c'est   p. 255
        The impersonal il est   p. 256
        Short rule   p. 256

TEACHING CONJUGATIONS   p. 256

How different are English and French verbs?   p. 256

Understanding the principles at work in French verbal conjugations   p. 257

Understanding verbal inflection: endings and subject agreement   p. 258

Understanding the infinitive   p. 259

Tense and aspect in the present of the indicative   p. 261
    Using comparative-cognitive techniques   p. 261
    Using comparative-experiential techniques   p. 263
    The present perfect as a present tense and the issue of tense correspondence   p. 264
    The present tense in other contexts   p. 264
    The indicative present is crucial for learning other conjugations p. 265

Understanding the past tenses in the indicative mood p. 265
    Procedural learning: why are past tenses so confusing? p. 266.
    Teaching the perfect and imperfect aspects of verbs of actions and verbs of motion p. 267
    To use être *or* avoir *in the passé composé?* p. 269
    What are verbs of motion? Why do we say je suis monté au deuxième étage, *but* J'ai monté les valises? p. 269
    Using the imparfait and the passé composé of the verb être p. 272
    The imparfait and the passé composé of modal verbs p. 273
    The imparfait and the passé composé of verbs expressing states of mind and heart p. 273
    Using the passé composé with pendant p. 274
    Using the imparfait with pendant p. 274

Understanding the plus-que-parfait: the past before the past p. 274

Teaching the *passé immédiat* p. 274

Fascinating problems: why students say things like *je venu* and *j'ai allais*, and what to do about it p. 275

Conclusion p. 277

CONCLUSION
p. 278

The comparative-narrative method is motivating and effective because it takes into account that language is communication and cognition, that language and thought may not be differentiated, that all learning depends on understanding, and that speech is only language when it is making meaning.

Works cited p. 285
This Table of Content p. 293
Index p. 304
Acknowledgements p. 308
Other works by the author p. 309

EIGHT TABLES
TABLE 1: showing the pronouns that precede the verb p. 151
TABLE 2: showing the pronouns that follow the verb p. 152
TABLE 3: showing the relative pronouns p. 153
TABLE 4: showing the basic use of **de**, **à** and **en** p. 155-156
TABLE 5: showing the beginnings of French and English words p. 178
TABLE 6: showing the endings of French and English words p. 179
TABLE 7: showing the articles in French and English p. 203
TABLE 8: showing the perfect and imperfect correspondences of English and French verbs of action and motion p. 271

INDEX

A

Académie française, 51, 285
acquiring vocabulary, 110
Acquisition-Learning Hypothesis, 39, 42
Adults
   also invent words, 75
Affective Filter Hypothesis, 39
animal
   animal cognition and communication, 84
Anthropology and language teaching, 20, 293
anxiety, 39, 66, 107, 279
aphasia, 76
Apothéloz, D, 19
Audio-Lingual method, 12
Austen, J, 36
Australian Aboriginal
   southwestern languages, 21
Australian students graduating with a second language, 12
autism, 80

B

Bateson, G, 83, 285
Bilash, O, 40
bilingual education, 57, 288
bilingualism, 54
Bodmer, F, 79, 111, 124, 193, 281, 286
Boredom, 12, 293
Bridging Grammar, 26, 29, 229, 230, 301
Broca, P, 68
Broca's area, 76

C

catenative verbs, 124, 297
Chaucer, 75
Chicago Manual of Style, 65
children
   grammatical mistakes, 74
   invent words, 75
children copy their parents, 70
Chimpanzees, 85
Chomsky, N, 39, 68, 69, 70, 71, 72, 74, 76, 77, 78, 79, 89, 91, 92, 93, 286
cognitive linguists, 69, 77, 78
cognitive-structural approach
   vs commnicative-situational approach, 121
Colourless green ideas, 77, 91, 290, 292, 295
communicative skills
   importance of, 59
comparative-experiential approach, 7, 26, 206, 229, 301
comparative-narrative method, 1, 20, 26, 57, 58, 117, 257, 282, 303
Compound nouns, 126, 127, 128, 296
Comprehensible Input, 39, 40, 47, 239
conditioning, 14, 26, 77
conditionnel
   and the imparfait, 18
CORE STRUCTURES OF FRENCH see Chapter IV, see CHAPTER IV
correct errors, 58, 59, 171, 294

creative imitation, 26

D

Darbelney, J, 25
Dative, 133, 134, 135, 148, 150, 151, 156
De Francis, J, 79
Descartes, 84
dialects, 37, 44, 45, 56, 109, 186, 187
DiNapoli, R, 24
drill methods, 22

E

Early childhood
    critical language learning period, 78
Edwards, M, 25
erratic spelling, 65
    Seemingly erratic spelling of English, 65
ESL, 20, 48
ESL classroom, 48
Evans, V, 69, 71, 72, 74, 78, 285, 287
explicit grammatical instruction
    counter-productive, 60
external rules of language, 72

F

failed, 63, 74
fluency over accuracy, 52, 294
FOXP2, 85
futur simple, 16
future in the past, 17

G

García, O, 54, 55, 56, 57, 288
gardens
    French and English, 65
gender
    unnatural, 259
Germain, C, 60, 61, 77, 245, 288
grammar

is no dead thing, 118
grammatical accuracy, 23, 36, 48, 53, 58, 61, 62, 79, 294
granary
    language as granary, 55
Greek, 23, 187, 209

H

Hall and Cook, 279
Hall, E .T, 83
helical, 122, 123, 124, 296
homo sapiens symbolicus, 34
hybridization, 52, 54, 104, 294
hybridize, 103, 104

I

idiolects, 51, 104
Ildefonso, 80
impersonal *il*, 28, 33, 157, 253, 293, 302
Individual tuition, 23
Infants
    language acquisition, 107
Interactionist theory, 82
Interlanguage, 53, 54, 103
Itard, J-M-G, 79, 80

J

Jaspers, J, 55, 57, 289

K

Kanzi, 85, 86
Keller, H, 80, 82, 99, 100, 282, 289
kinship terminology, 76
Koko, 85
Krashen, S, 38, 39, 40, 41, 60, 107, 186, 239, 282, 289
Kuhl, P, 79, 82, 104, 107, 110, 289

L

Lakoff, G, 69, 289
Lamu Gatusa, 46
Langacker, R, 69, 289
Language Acquisition Device, 39, 78, 107
language gene, 85
language immersion
    adult acquisition, 87
language inclusivity
    politics of, 56
language instinct, 69, 81, 86, 87, 295, *See* social instinct
language interference, 281
language of thought, 75
language purity, 54
languaging, 58, 75, 104
    theorists, 75, 289
langue, 12, 25, 63, 64, 141, 157, 284, 287, 291
Latin, 24, 32, 80, 146, 184, 186, 187, 189, 209, 211, 212, 223, 252, 253, 257, 258, 260, 261
Learning Acquisition Device, 39
learning errors, 53
Lévi-Strauss, C, 76, 289
light-bulb moments, 281
Lin, A, 54, 56, 57, 288

M

Mead, M, 83, 285
mental imaging and sensory
    reflection, 26, 248, 302
Mentalese, 98, 99, 295
modelling, 70, 91
Monitoring Hypothesis, 41, 294
monolingual, 56, 57, 108, 279, 281
monolingualism, 55, 56
motivation, 39, 42, 47, 49, 88, 89

multilingualism, 13, 54, 55, 56, 100, 295

N

Nativist-Cognitive debate, 295
natural fluency, 37
NATURAL LANGUAGE ENVIRONMENT, 47, 294
Natural Order Hypothesis, 39, 43
Neuroscience, 76, 295
noise
    language as noise, 87, 107
nonsense
    as the opposite of sense not meanginglessness, 92

O

Old English, 16, 24, 112, 182, 186, 196, 211, 212, 253, 257, 260
    demonstrative articles, 72
Orwell, G, 111

P

pairing of opposite elements, 76
parole, 25
PAST PARTICIPLE AGREEMENT
    UNIFYING THE RULE OF, 144
Patterson, P, 85
Paz, O, 76, 105
Pilley, J, 86
Pinker, S, 37, 69, 70, 74, 76, 80, 81, 82, 83, 84, 90, 97, 98, 101, 102, 103, 104, 111, 290, 291
**plurality of thought
and multilingualism**, 100
politically named languages, 55
Prévert, J, 105
proficiency, 56, 78, 102, 112, 170
Proust, M, 36, 75
psychological disorientation, 47

R

Ray, A, 64
recognition
    in second language acquisition, 43, 283
relational function, 128, 296
relative pronouns, 153, 226
    table of relative pronoouns, 153
    teaching the relative pronouns, 226
repetition, 26, 40, 60, 61, 120, 234, 266, 301
Ronat, M, 78, 79

S

Sampson, G, 69, 76, 291
Saussure, F, 25
Savage-Rumbaugh, S, 85
Schmidt, R, 41, 73, 74, 96, 233, 292
Shakespeare, 75
situational learning, 122
social instinct, 82
sociolects, 51
spontaneous speech, 81
student retention, 13, 49
subjunctive, 18, 148, 161, 209, 247, 265, 274
Sullivan, A, 82, 99, 100
sympathetic mental images, 98
syntax
    is syntax autonomous?, 89
    turns words into thoughts, 117

T

terminology
    naming grammar, 119
The
    acquiring the definite article, 72
the drive to speak,, 87
the passing of time, 17
the verb to fall, 71
third person
    explaining the third person, 259
Thirdspace, 54
Tintin, 48
translanguaging, 20, 26, 53, 56, 58, 230, 289
Trustwell, R, 86

U

Ullman, M T, 77
Universal Grammar, 39, 69, 71, 72, 89

V

Victor de l'Aveyron, 79, 295
Victorian Curriculum and Assessment Authority, 14, 15, 51, 63, 292
Vinay, J-P, 25, 292
Vytgotsky, L, 82

W

Wei, L, 54, 55, 56, 57, 102, 104, 288, 292
Wernicke's area, 76
why questions, 22
wild children, 80
word order
    rules, 90

Acknowledgements

TO ALL MY STUDENTS for giving me a full and rewarding life, for teaching me so much and for sharing so many wonderful hours spent in all kinds of learning; to all my teachers and all those who have allowed me to learn languages, to speak languages and to teach languages; to John Marsden and Sarita Ryan for trusting me with the French program at Alice Miller School; to my friends – Bron Sibree for reading the manuscript and for her enthusiastic response; to Andy Green and John MacGregor for listening to readings, for their encouragements, comments and suggestions along with tea and Qi Gong; to Priscilla Alderton for lending her musicianship to her appreciation of French grammar; to Louise for helping me find the most attractive French grammar book when we were in Paris; to Arya Nick Bakht, Robyn Charlwood, Almay Jordan, Karen Halloran, Cam Gilmour, Stephen Philips and Edwina Wren who set me on the path of the comparative-narrative method; to Meg Somers who has shown unconditional enthusiasm for the method and for this book; to my friend and colleague Zoltan Klein who pointed out to me that the as-yet-unnamed comparative-narrative method was 'anthropology in language'; to Janine Oldfield who spent time discussing applied linguistics and other important subjects relating to bilingual education; to Lamu Gatusa, Robert DiNapoli, Barrie Machin, Alexis Michaud, Marjorie Strickland, Jacqueline Spurling, and my regretted friend and teacher Eric Ten Raa–who have taught me so much about language studies and anthropology and who have allowed me to benefit so generously from their erudition and from their life experience (of course, I take responsibility for any misconstrued ideas that might appear in this book); to my friend Dona Mannolini who is an accomplished and experienced teacher, for trialling teaching techniques when the comparative-narrative method was still in its infancy and, not least, for reading and offering warm and precious comments on a less than perfect earlier manuscript; to Hartley Mitchell who is also my colleague at Alice Miller School for reading the manuscript and for his comments and editorial suggestions; to Bob DiNapoli, my friend and editor at Littlefox, for the discussions, editorial advice and for his careful editing (all errors are now my responsibility); to my family, Euro, Sacha, Cassis, Holly, Felix, Freya, and Hester for their love and support always; to Cassis for designing a beautiful cover; to my husband Ari in Australia; to my sister Annie and my brother Thierry in France for letting me share all sorts of thoughts about French grammar and how to teach it, over breakfast and a long way past it –

THANK YOU

PREVIOUS WORKS BY CHRISTINE MATHIEU

Christine Mathieu is a professional anthropologist and a teacher at Alice Miller School in Victoria, Australia. She is a founding editor of the publishing imprint Littlefox Press, and a member of the Editorial Collective of *Matrix*, online journal of matricultural studies. Her work has appeared in the *French Australian Review* (2018), the online academic journal, *Intersections* (2004), the Melbourne-based literary magazine *Bread Wine and Thou* (2015-2016) and includes the books and articles listed below.

A History and Anthropological Study of the Ancient Kingdoms of Southwest China, Mellen Press, 2003.

Leaving Mother Lake, co-authored with Yang Erche Namu, Little, Brown, and Company, New York and London, 2003.

Adieu au lac Mère, co-authored with Yang Erche Namu, translated by Christine Mathieu, Calman-Lévy, Paris, 2005.

Quentin Roosevelt's China: Ancestral Realms of the Naxi, co-edited with Cindy Ho, Rubin Museum of Arts, New York and Arnoldsche Verlagsanstalt, Stuttgart, 2011.

'Mosuo *Ddaba* Religious Specialists', in *Naxi and Moso Ethnography*, Michael Oppitz and Elizabeth Hsü (eds.), University of Zurich Press, Zurich, 1998.

'History and other metaphors in Chinese-Mosuo relations since 1956', in *Dress, Sex and Text in Chinese Culture*, A. Finane and A. McLaren (eds), Monash University Press, Melbourne, 1999.

'Myths of Matriarchy: the Mosuo and the Kingdom of Women', in *Researching the Fragments: Histories of Women in the Asian Context*, Carolyn Brewer and Anne-Marie Medcalf (eds), Newday, Manilla, 2000.

'The Bon in Naxi History', *Asian Horizons: Giuseppe Tucci's Buddhist, Indian, Himalayan and Central Asian Studies*, in Andrea Di Castro and David Templeman (eds), Monash University, Melbourne and IIAO, Rome, 2015.

www.ingramcontent.com/pod-product-compliance
Lightning Source LLC
Chambersburg PA
CBHW080634230426
43663CB00016B/2859